BABY BLUES· 19 SCRAPBOOK

PLAYDATE: CATEGORY 5

Other *Baby Blues®* Books from Andrews McMeel Publishing

Guess Who Didn't Take a Nap?
I Thought Labor Ended When the Baby Was Born
We Are Experiencing Parental Difficulties . . . Please Stand By
Night of the Living Dad
I Saw Elvis in My Ultrasound
One More and We're Outnumbered!
Check, Please . . .
threats, bribes & videotape
If I'm a Stay-At-Home Mom, Why Am I Always in the Car?
Lift and Separate
I Shouldn't Have to Scream More Than Once!
Motherhood Is Not for Wimps
Baby Blues®: Unplugged
Dad to the Bone
Never a Dry Moment
Two Plus One Is Enough

Treasuries

The Super-Absorbent Biodegradable Family-Size Baby Blues®
Baby Blues®: Ten Years and Still in Diapers
Butt-Naked Baby Blues®
Wall-to-Wall Baby Blues®

BABY BLUES 19 SCRAPBOOK

PLAYDATE: CATEGORY 5

BY RICK KIRKMAN & JERRY SCOTT

**Andrews McMeel
Publishing**

Kansas City

Baby Blues® is syndicated internationally by King Features Syndicate, Inc. For information, write King Features Syndicate, Inc., 888 Seventh Avenue, New York, New York 10019.

04 05 06 07 08 BBG 10 9 8 7 6 5 4 3 2 1

ISBN: 0-7407-4665-0

Library of Congress Control Number: 2004105603

Find *Baby Blues*® on the Web at
www.babyblues.com.

To Gary Hardeman, for your knowledge, your patience, your kindness, and your willingness to crawl around on the living room floor
—J.S.

To Mrs. Van, Delores, and all the rest at Palo Alto Preschool—many thanks.
—R.K.

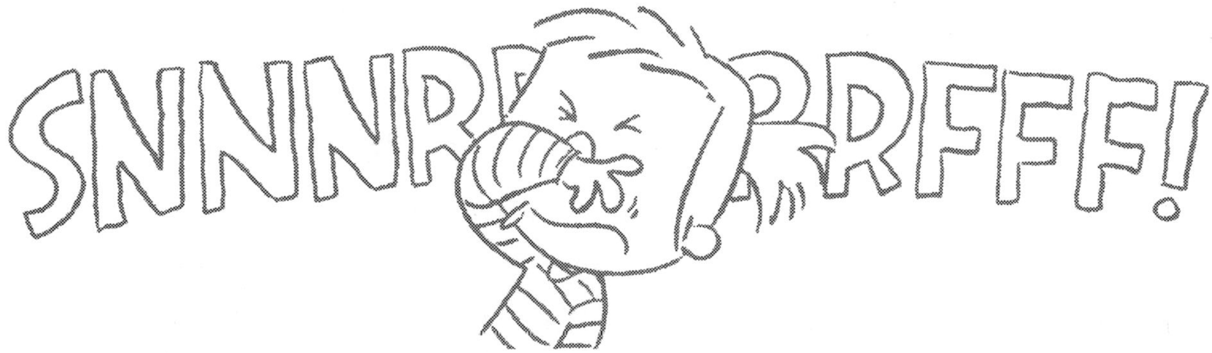
SNNRRRRFFF!

BABY BLUES®
BY RICK KIRKMAN / JERRY SCOTT

WHAT DO YOU THINK?
I LIKE IT.
YOU CAN'T LIKE IT!
WHY NOT?
BECAUSE! YOU'RE A KID! KIDS NEVER LIKE THIS STUFF!
MAYBE WE SHOULD TAKE A VOTE.
GOOD IDEA! EVERYBODY WHO THINKS THIS TASTES GOOD, SAY "AYE"!
AYE!
EVERYBODY WHO WOULD RATHER HAVE PIZZA, SAY "NAY"... NAY!
NAY!
IT'S TOO BAD WREN CAN'T EAT SOLID FOOD YET. SHE COULD BE THE TIE-BREAKER.
YOU DIDN'T SAY ANYTHING ABOUT PIZZA!
THIS IS DINNER, NOT A DEMOCRACY!
KIRKMAN & SCOTT

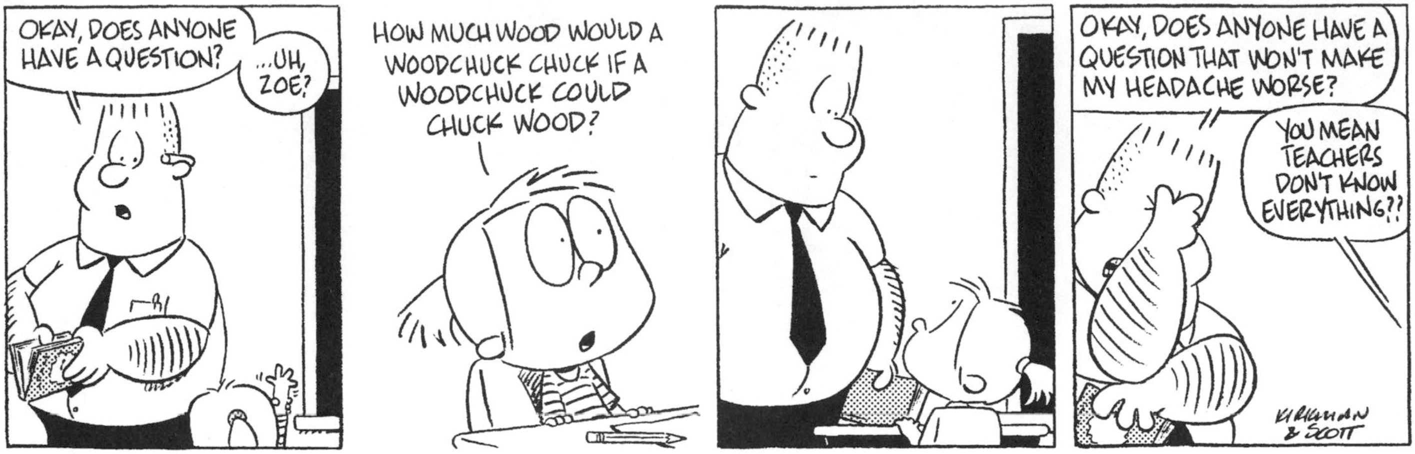
OKAY, DOES ANYONE HAVE A QUESTION?
...UH, ZOE?
HOW MUCH WOOD WOULD A WOODCHUCK CHUCK IF A WOODCHUCK COULD CHUCK WOOD?
OKAY, DOES ANYONE HAVE A QUESTION THAT WON'T MAKE MY HEADACHE WORSE?
YOU MEAN TEACHERS DON'T KNOW EVERYTHING??
KIRKMAN & SCOTT

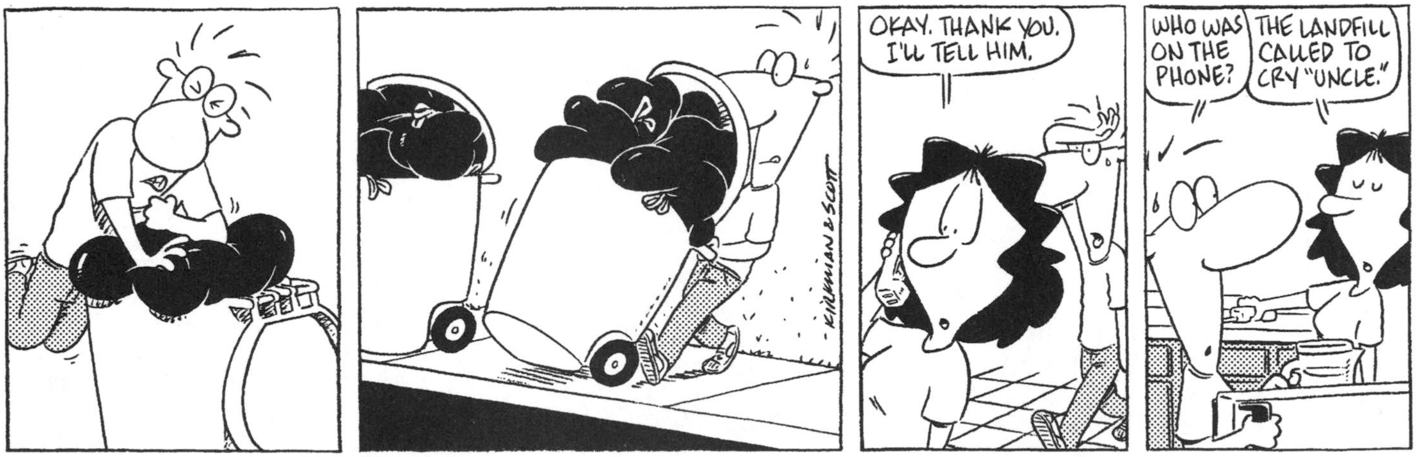
KIRKMAN & SCOTT
OKAY. THANK YOU. I'LL TELL HIM.
WHO WAS ON THE PHONE?
THE LANDFILL CALLED TO CRY "UNCLE."

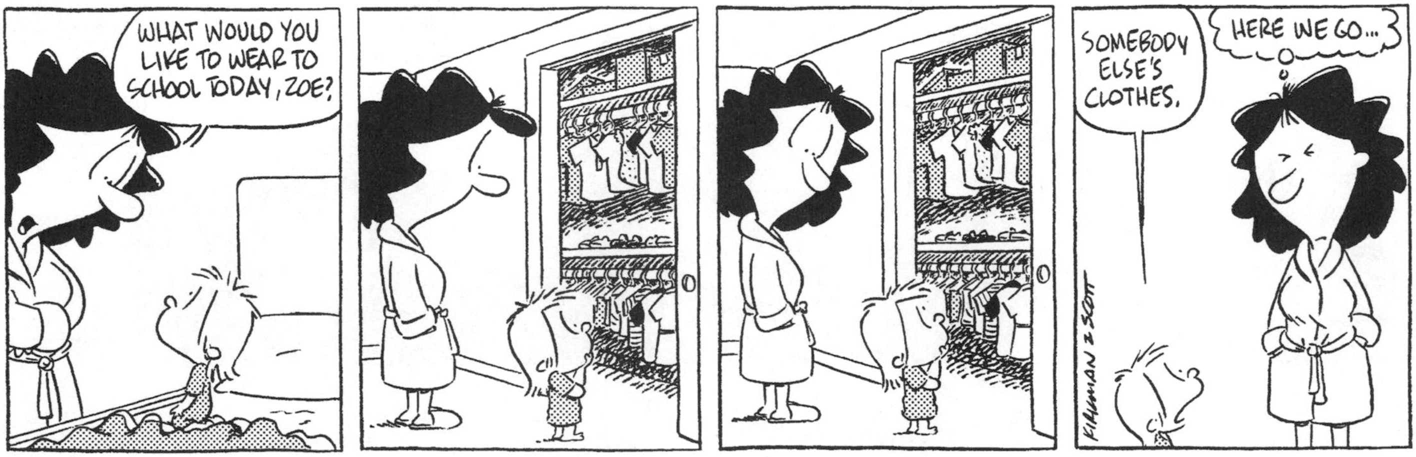
WHAT WOULD YOU LIKE TO WEAR TO SCHOOL TODAY, ZOE?
KIRKMAN & SCOTT
SOMEBODY ELSE'S CLOTHES.
HERE WE GO...

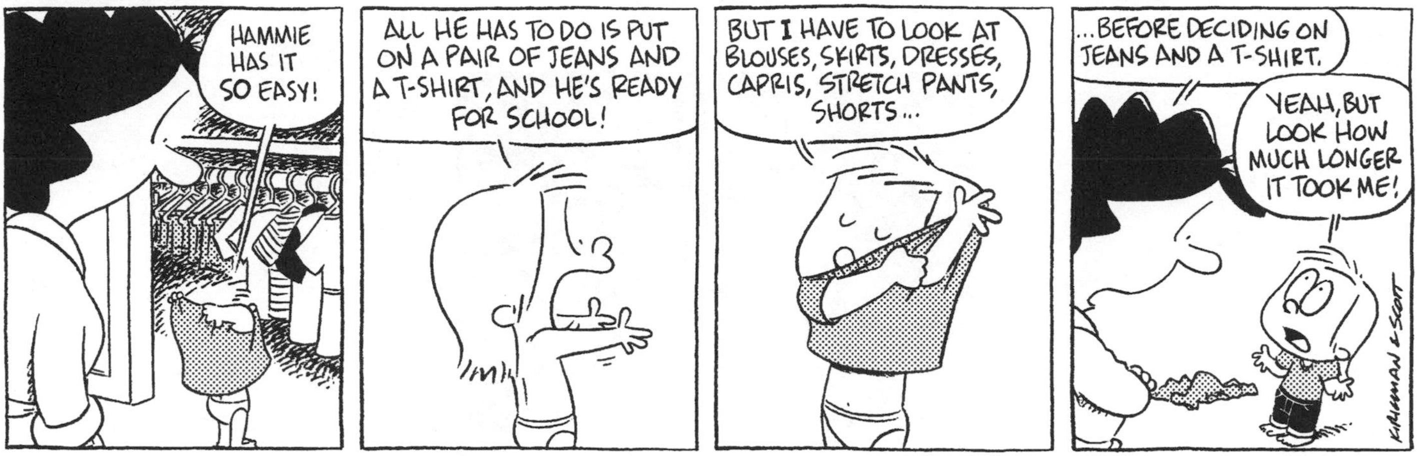
HAMMIE HAS IT SO EASY!
ALL HE HAS TO DO IS PUT ON A PAIR OF JEANS AND A T-SHIRT, AND HE'S READY FOR SCHOOL!
BUT I HAVE TO LOOK AT BLOUSES, SKIRTS, DRESSES, CAPRIS, STRETCH PANTS, SHORTS...
...BEFORE DECIDING ON JEANS AND A T-SHIRT.
YEAH, BUT LOOK HOW MUCH LONGER IT TOOK ME!
KIRKMAN & SCOTT

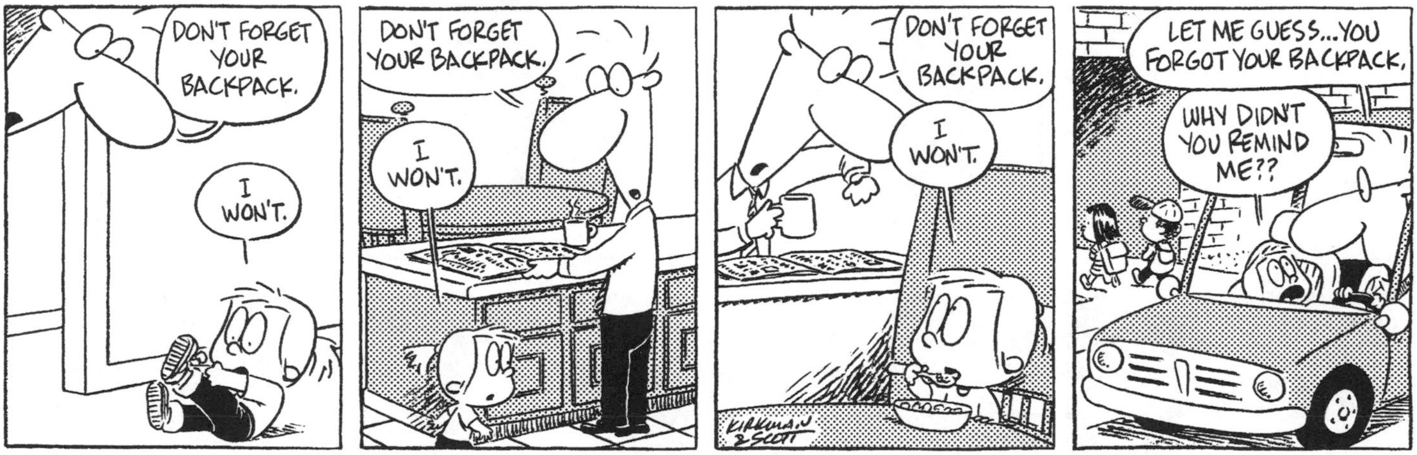
DON'T FORGET YOUR BACKPACK.
I WON'T.
DON'T FORGET YOUR BACKPACK.
I WON'T.
DON'T FORGET YOUR BACKPACK.
I WON'T.
KIRKMAN & SCOTT
LET ME GUESS... YOU FORGOT YOUR BACKPACK.
WHY DIDN'T YOU REMIND ME??

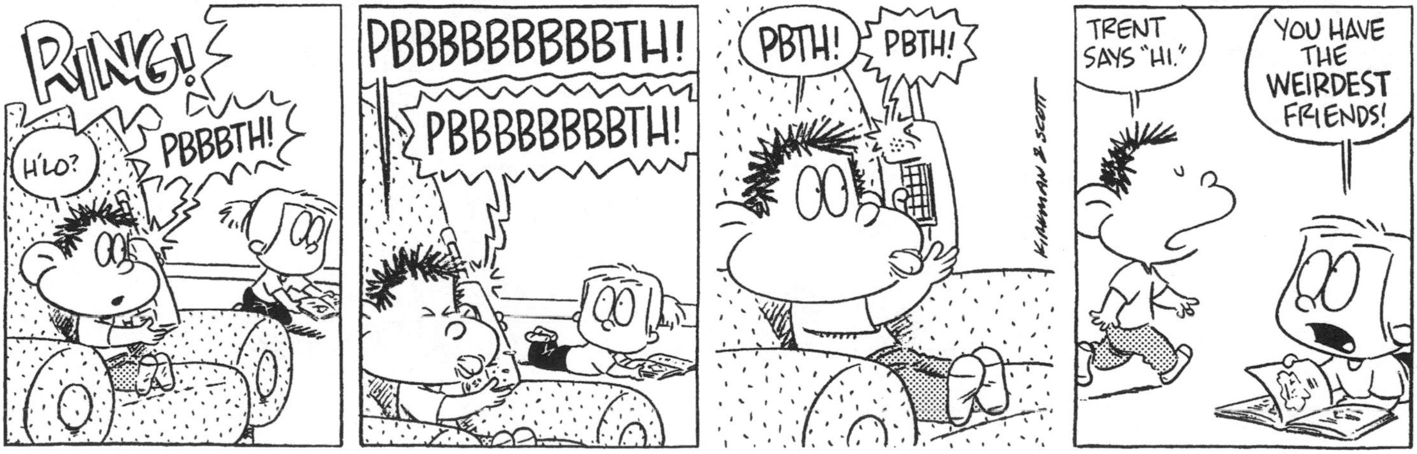
RING!
H'LO?
PBBBTH!
PBBBBBBBBBTH!
PBBBBBBBBTH!
PBTH!
PBTH!
KIRKMAN & SCOTT
TRENT SAYS "HI."
YOU HAVE THE WEIRDEST FRIENDS!

BABY BLUES®
BY RICK KIRKMAN / JERRY SCOTT
THANKS-YOU'VE BEEN GREAT! I'LL BE HERE ALL WEEK!

CAN I HAVE A BOTTLE OF WATER IN MY LUNCH TODAY?
A BOTTLE OF WATER?
YEAH. I DECIDED THAT FROM NOW ON, I'M ONLY GOING TO DRINK WATER OUT OF A PLASTIC BOTTLE.
WHAT'S WRONG WITH YOUR THERMOS CUP?
THERMOS CUPS ARE FOR KIDS. WATER BOTTLES MAKE YOU LOOK MORE GROWN UP.
I SEE.
I'VE GIVEN THIS A LOT OF THOUGHT, SO DON'T TRY TO TALK ME OUT OF IT OR ANYTHING.
WHATEVER YOU SAY. BOTTLED WATER IT IS!
YOU'D THINK YOU'D WANT YOUR MOM TO HAVE A GOOD SENSE OF HUMOR, BUT YOU REALLY DON'T.
KIRKMAN & SCOTT

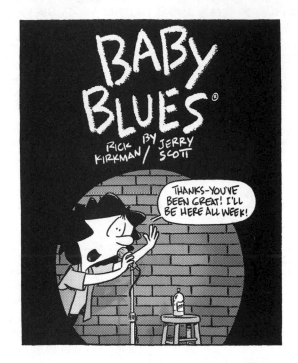

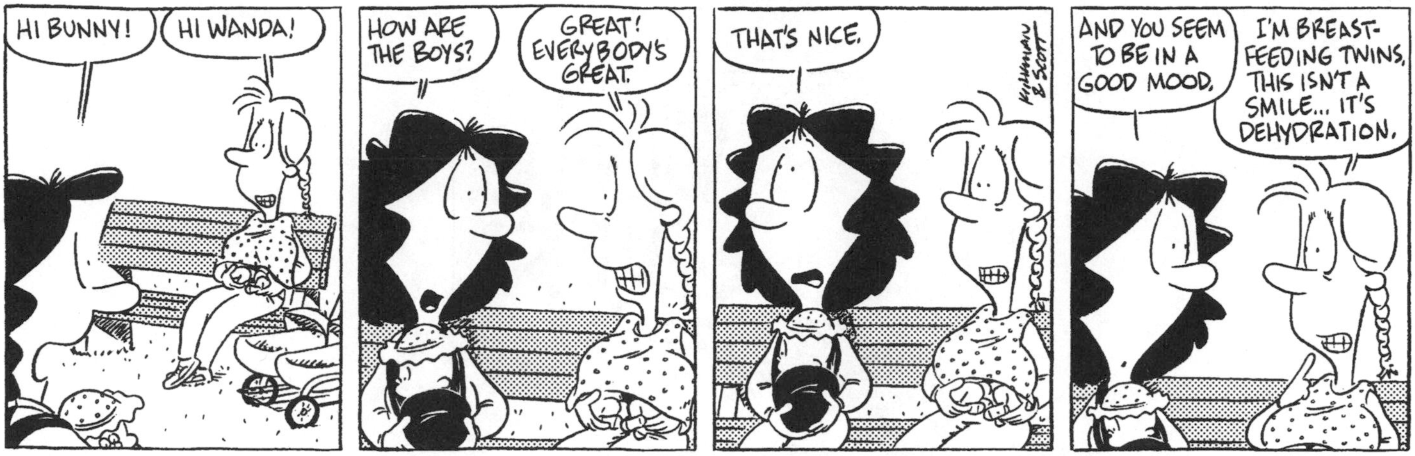
HI BUNNY!
HI WANDA!
HOW ARE THE BOYS?
GREAT! EVERYBODY'S GREAT.
THAT'S NICE.
KIRKMAN & SCOTT
AND YOU SEEM TO BE IN A GOOD MOOD.
I'M BREAST-FEEDING TWINS. THIS ISN'T A SMILE... IT'S DEHYDRATION.

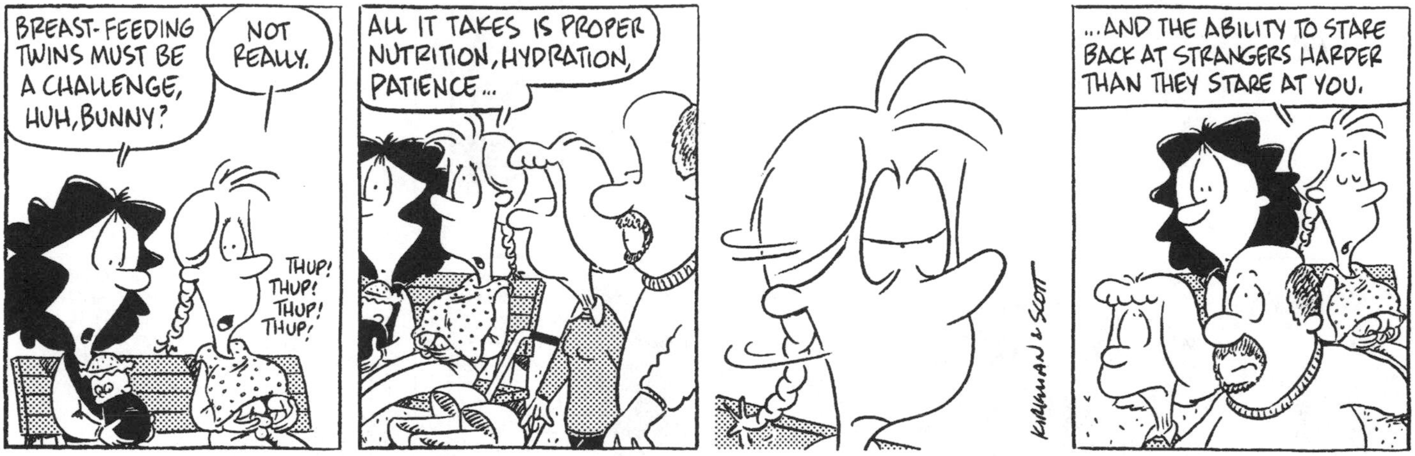
BREAST-FEEDING TWINS MUST BE A CHALLENGE, HUH, BUNNY?
NOT REALLY.
THUP! THUP! THUP! THUP!
ALL IT TAKES IS PROPER NUTRITION, HYDRATION, PATIENCE...
KIRKMAN & SCOTT
...AND THE ABILITY TO STARE BACK AT STRANGERS HARDER THAN THEY STARE AT YOU.

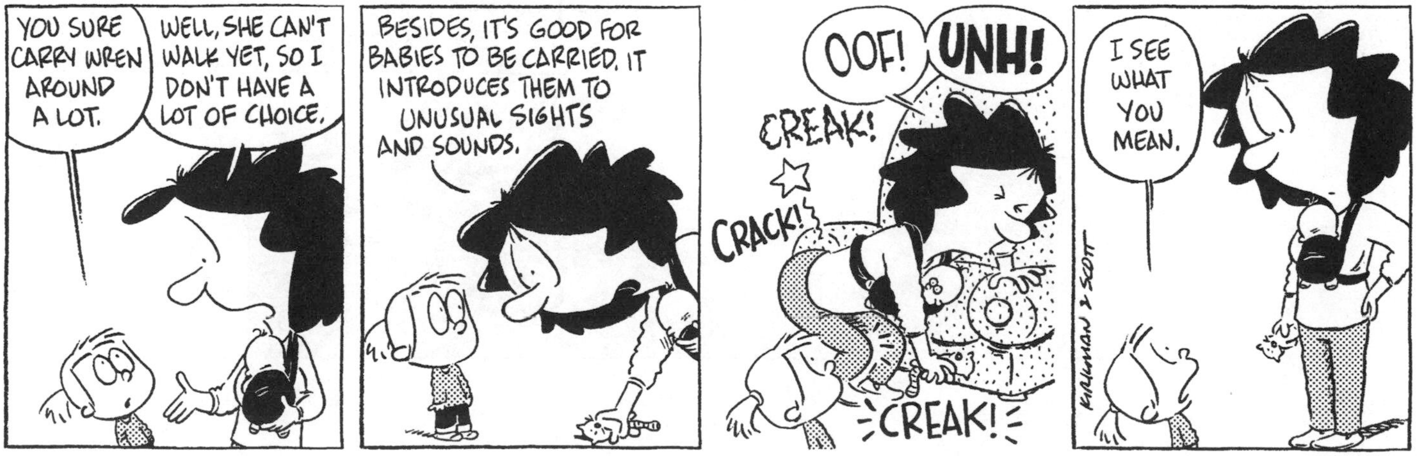
YOU SURE CARRY WREN AROUND A LOT.
WELL, SHE CAN'T WALK YET, SO I DON'T HAVE A LOT OF CHOICE.
BESIDES, IT'S GOOD FOR BABIES TO BE CARRIED. IT INTRODUCES THEM TO UNUSUAL SIGHTS AND SOUNDS.
OOF!
UNH!
CREAK!
CRACK!
CREAK!
KIRKMAN & SCOTT
I SEE WHAT YOU MEAN.

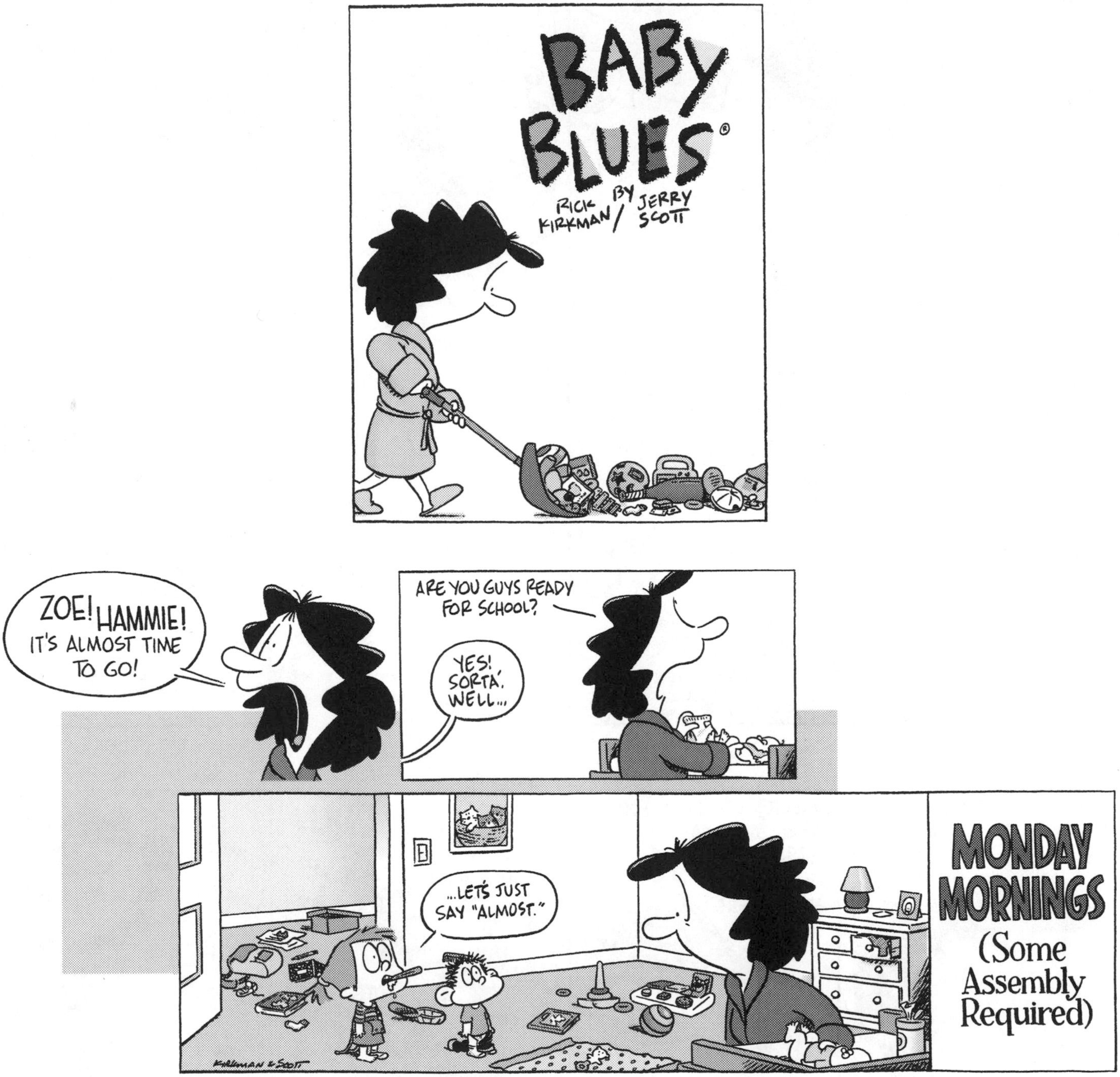
BABY BLUES®
BY RICK KIRKMAN / JERRY SCOTT
ZOE! HAMMIE! IT'S ALMOST TIME TO GO!
ARE YOU GUYS READY FOR SCHOOL?
YES! SORTA'. WELL...
...LET'S JUST SAY "ALMOST."
KIRKMAN & SCOTT
MONDAY MORNINGS
(Some Assembly Required)

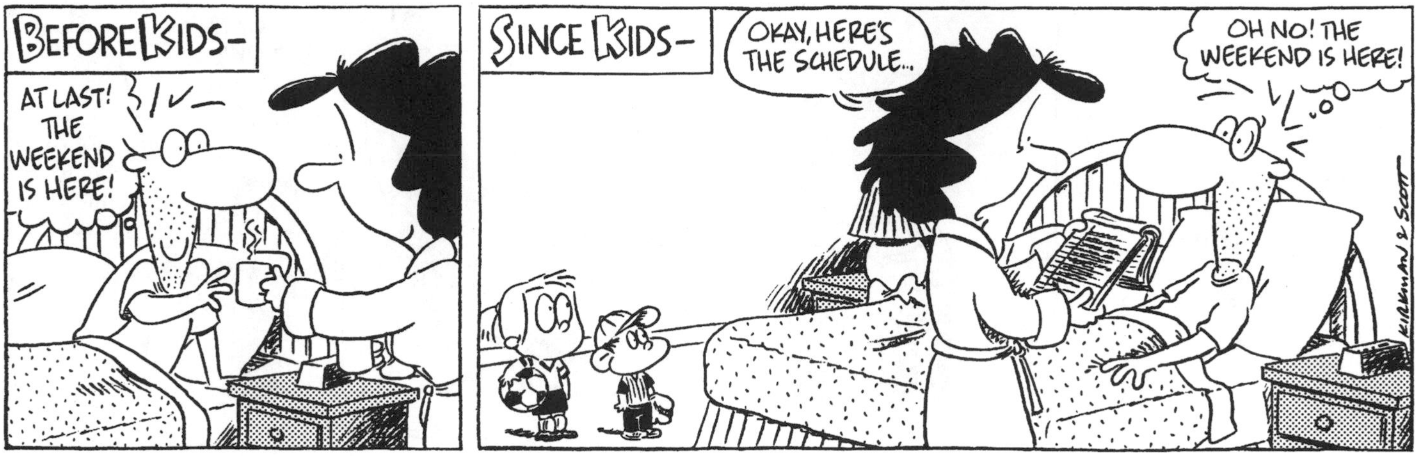
BEFORE KIDS-
AT LAST! THE WEEKEND IS HERE!
SINCE KIDS-
OKAY, HERE'S THE SCHEDULE...
OH NO! THE WEEKEND IS HERE!
KIRKMAN & SCOTT

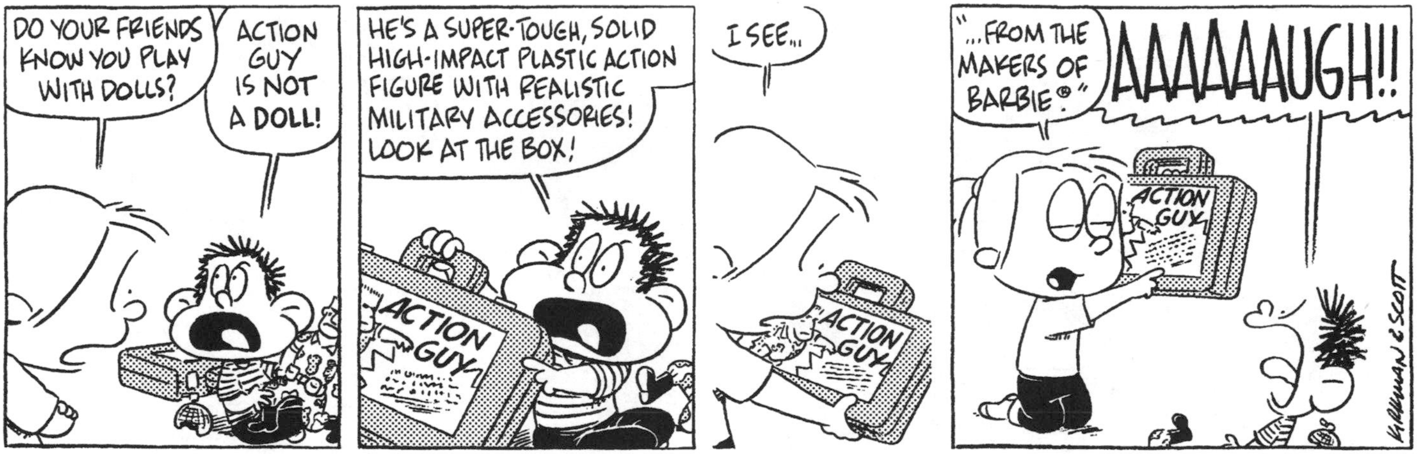
DO YOUR FRIENDS KNOW YOU PLAY WITH DOLLS?
ACTION GUY IS NOT A DOLL!
HE'S A SUPER-TOUGH, SOLID HIGH-IMPACT PLASTIC ACTION FIGURE WITH REALISTIC MILITARY ACCESSORIES! LOOK AT THE BOX!
ACTION GUY
I SEE...
ACTION GUY
"...FROM THE MAKERS OF BARBIE®"
AAAAAAUGH!!
ACTION GUY
KIRKMAN & SCOTT

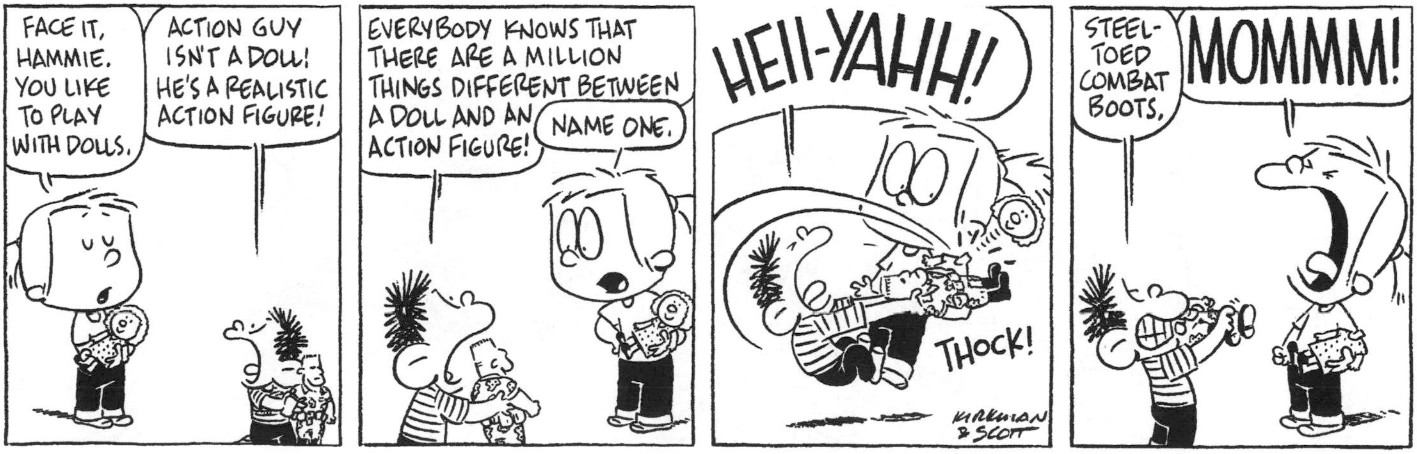
FACE IT, HAMMIE. YOU LIKE TO PLAY WITH DOLLS.
ACTION GUY ISN'T A DOLL! HE'S A REALISTIC ACTION FIGURE!
EVERYBODY KNOWS THAT THERE ARE A MILLION THINGS DIFFERENT BETWEEN A DOLL AND AN ACTION FIGURE!
NAME ONE.
HEII-YAHH!
THOCK!
KIRKMAN & SCOTT
STEEL-TOED COMBAT BOOTS.
MOMMM!

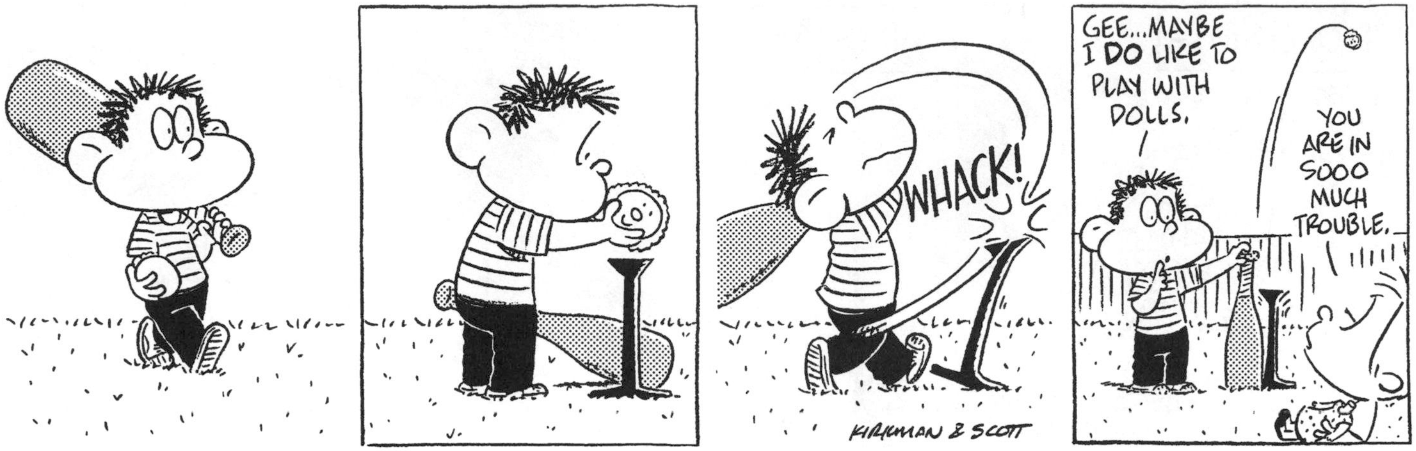
WHACK!
GEE...MAYBE I DO LIKE TO PLAY WITH DOLLS.
YOU ARE IN SOOO MUCH TROUBLE.
KIRKMAN & SCOTT

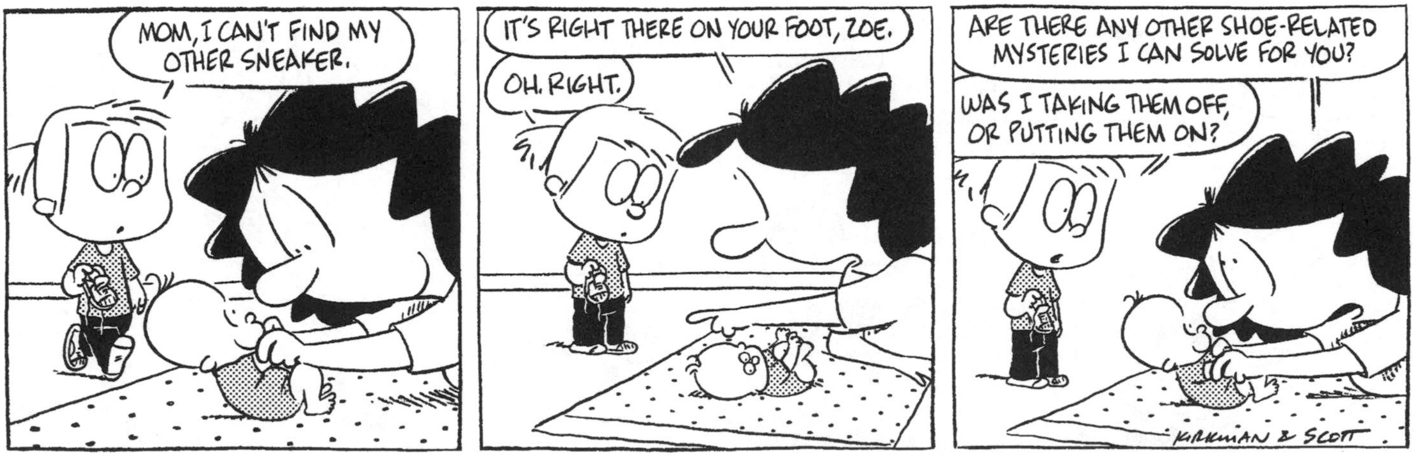
MOM, I CAN'T FIND MY OTHER SNEAKER.
IT'S RIGHT THERE ON YOUR FOOT, ZOE.
OH. RIGHT.
ARE THERE ANY OTHER SHOE-RELATED MYSTERIES I CAN SOLVE FOR YOU?
WAS I TAKING THEM OFF, OR PUTTING THEM ON?
KIRKMAN & SCOTT

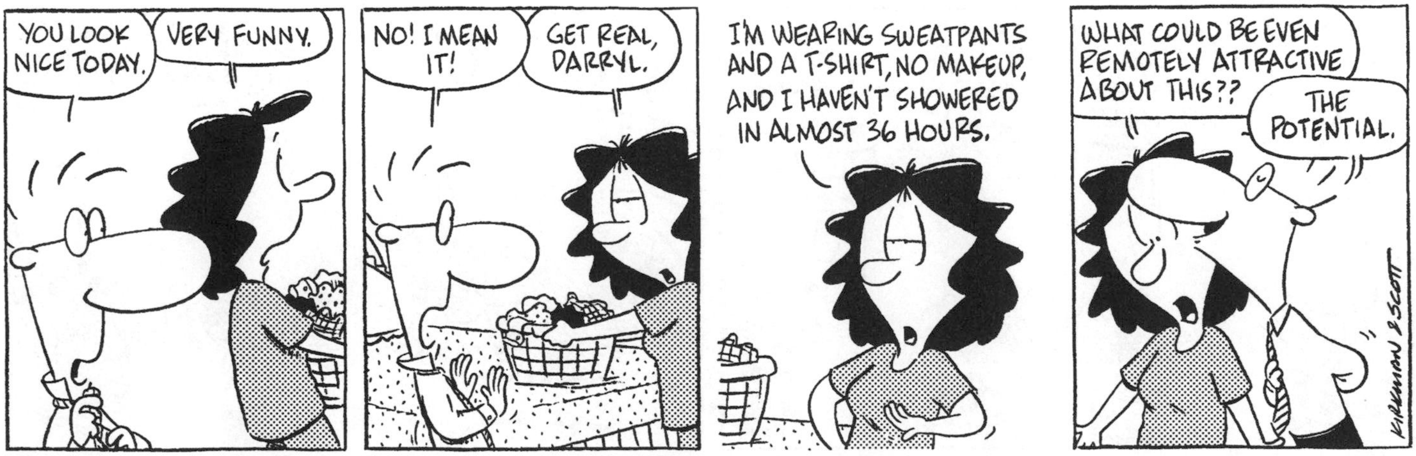
YOU LOOK NICE TODAY.
VERY FUNNY.
NO! I MEAN IT!
GET REAL, DARRYL.
I'M WEARING SWEATPANTS AND A T-SHIRT, NO MAKEUP, AND I HAVEN'T SHOWERED IN ALMOST 36 HOURS.
WHAT COULD BE EVEN REMOTELY ATTRACTIVE ABOUT THIS??
THE POTENTIAL.
KIRKMAN & SCOTT

BABY BLUES®
BY RICK KIRKMAN / JERRY SCOTT

WHATCHA' WATCHING?
SOME NEW SHOW.
THEY GIVE FIVE MARRIED COUPLES COACH-CLASS AIRLINE TICKETS TO A FOREIGN COUNTRY, A WEEK IN A SMALL, STUFFY HOTEL ROOM, MEDIOCRE RESTAURANT MEALS AND A JAM-PACKED SIGHTSEEING SCHEDULE.
THAT DOESN'T SOUND SO BAD... WHAT'S THE CATCH?
THEY HAVE TO BRING THEIR KIDS ALONG.
IT'S CALLED "SURVIVOR: FAMILY VACATION."
IS IT JUST ME, OR ARE TV SHOWS GETTING MEANER?

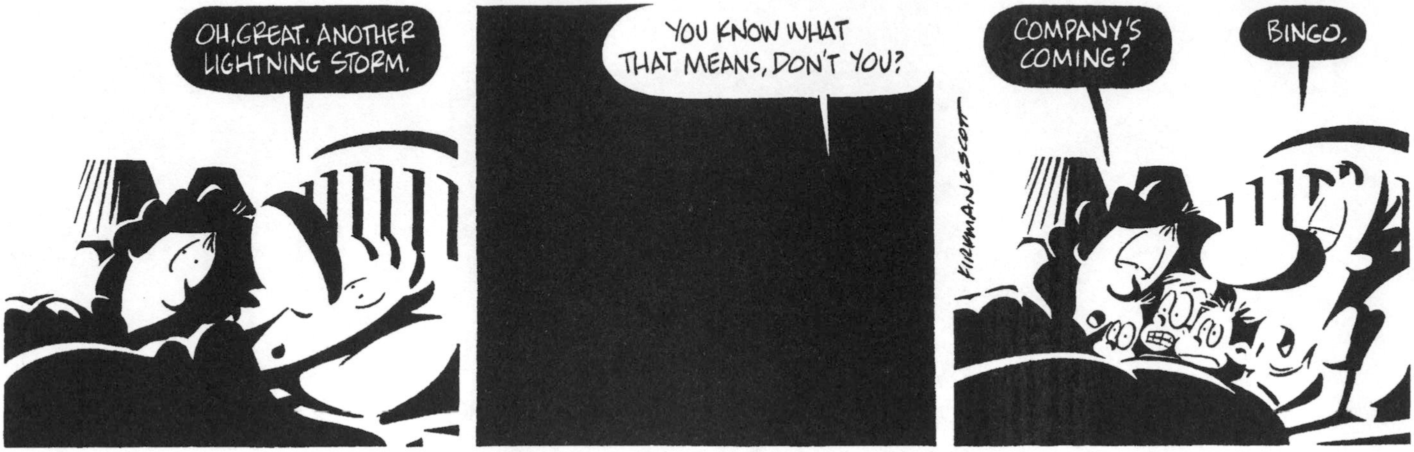
OH, GREAT. ANOTHER LIGHTNING STORM.
YOU KNOW WHAT THAT MEANS, DON'T YOU?
KIRKMAN & SCOTT
COMPANY'S COMING?
BINGO.

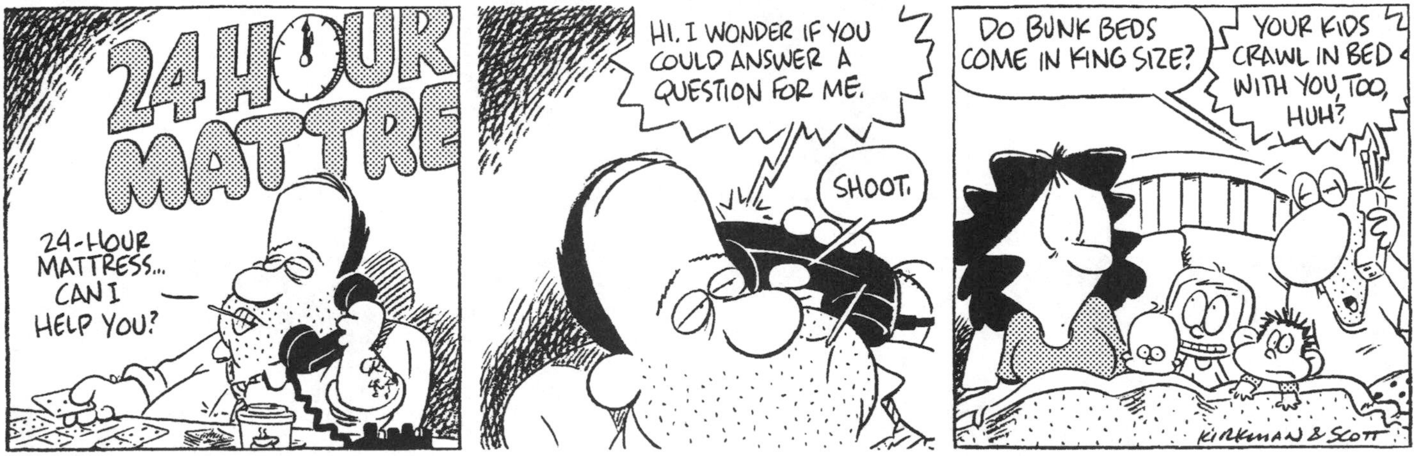
24 HOUR MATTRE
24-HOUR MATTRESS... CAN I HELP YOU?
HI. I WONDER IF YOU COULD ANSWER A QUESTION FOR ME.
SHOOT.
DO BUNK BEDS COME IN KING SIZE?
YOUR KIDS CRAWL IN BED WITH YOU, TOO, HUH?
KIRKMAN & SCOTT

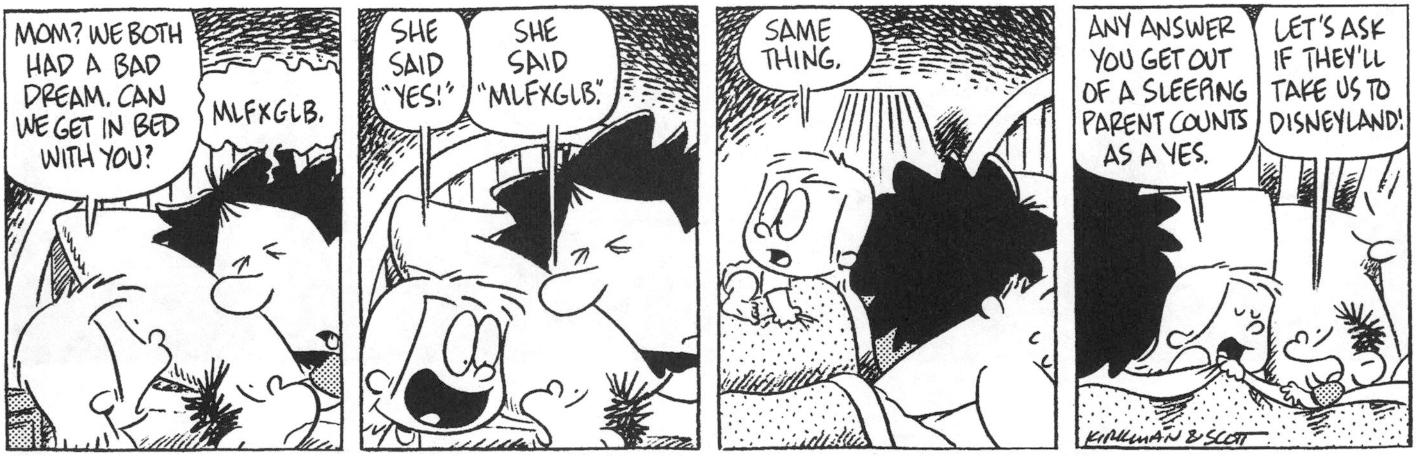
MOM? WE BOTH HAD A BAD DREAM. CAN WE GET IN BED WITH YOU?
MLFXGLB.
SHE SAID "YES!"
SHE SAID "MLFXGLB."
SAME THING.
ANY ANSWER YOU GET OUT OF A SLEEPING PARENT COUNTS AS A YES.
LET'S ASK IF THEY'LL TAKE US TO DISNEYLAND!
KIRKMAN & SCOTT

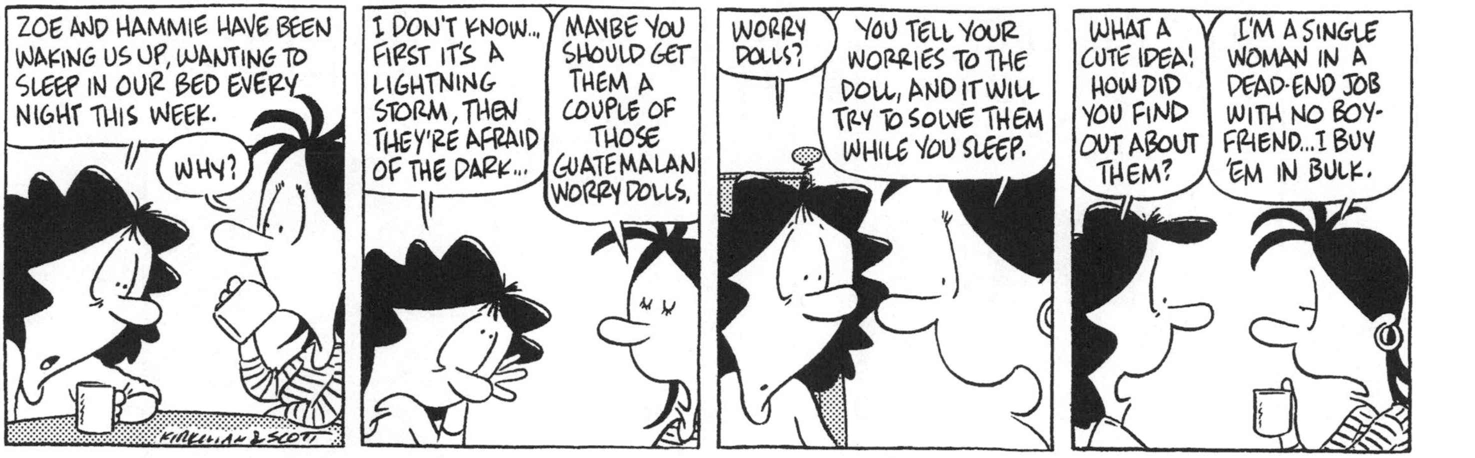
ZOE AND HAMMIE HAVE BEEN WAKING US UP, WANTING TO SLEEP IN OUR BED EVERY NIGHT THIS WEEK.
WHY?
I DON'T KNOW... FIRST IT'S A LIGHTNING STORM, THEN THEY'RE AFRAID OF THE DARK...
MAYBE YOU SHOULD GET THEM A COUPLE OF THOSE GUATEMALAN WORRY DOLLS.
WORRY DOLLS?
YOU TELL YOUR WORRIES TO THE DOLL, AND IT WILL TRY TO SOLVE THEM WHILE YOU SLEEP.
WHAT A CUTE IDEA! HOW DID YOU FIND OUT ABOUT THEM?
I'M A SINGLE WOMAN IN A DEAD-END JOB WITH NO BOY-FRIEND... I BUY 'EM IN BULK.
KIRKMAN & SCOTT

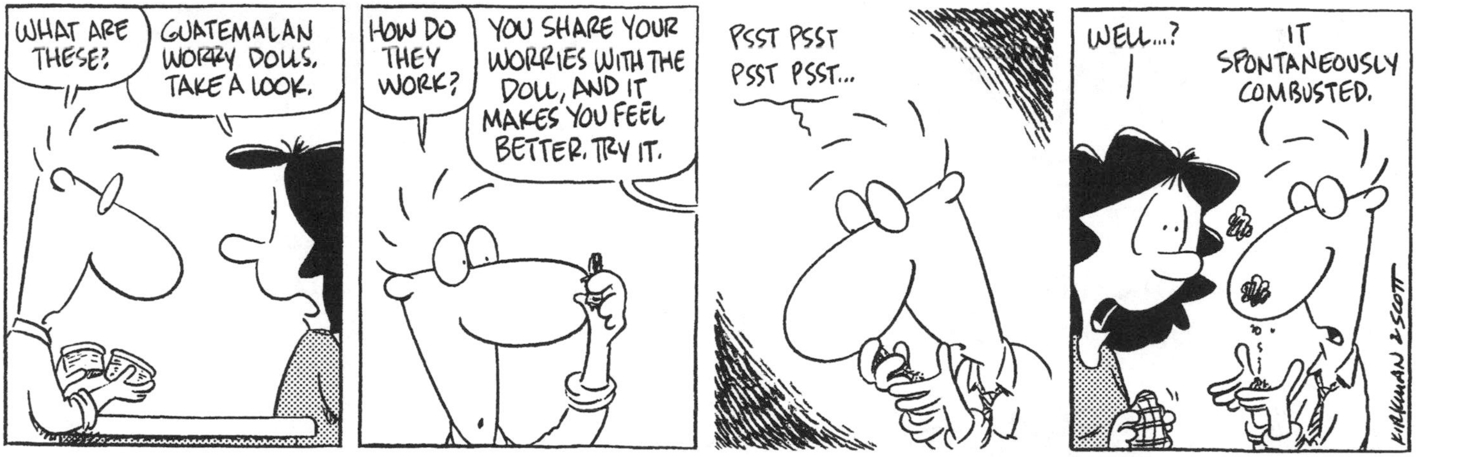
WHAT ARE THESE?
GUATEMALAN WORRY DOLLS. TAKE A LOOK.
HOW DO THEY WORK?
YOU SHARE YOUR WORRIES WITH THE DOLL, AND IT MAKES YOU FEEL BETTER. TRY IT.
PSST PSST PSST PSST...
WELL...?
IT SPONTANEOUSLY COMBUSTED.
KIRKMAN & SCOTT

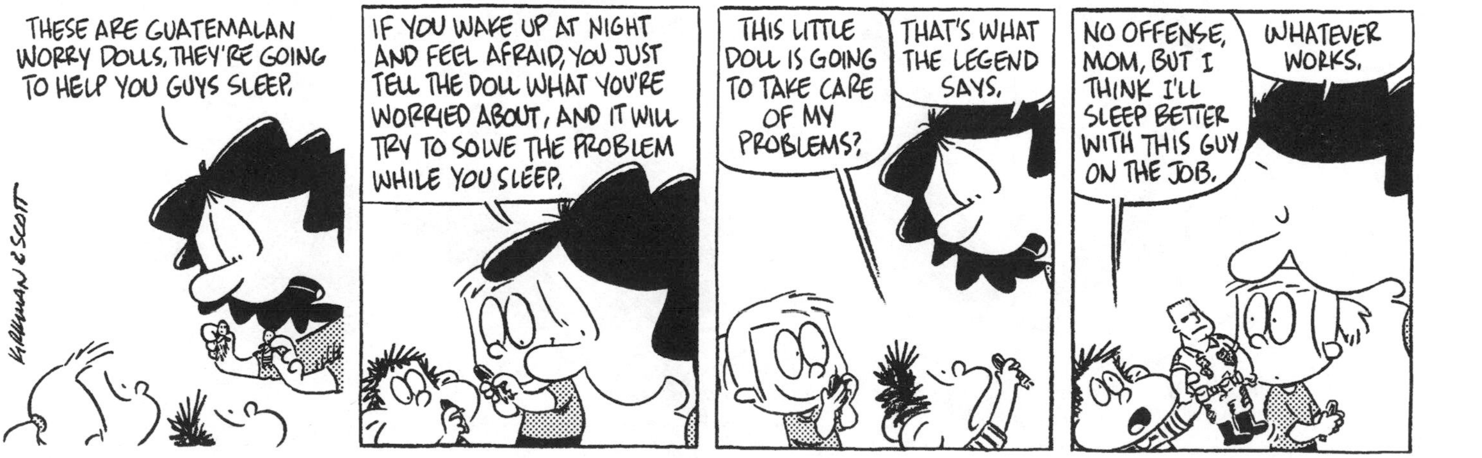
THESE ARE GUATEMALAN WORRY DOLLS. THEY'RE GOING TO HELP YOU GUYS SLEEP.
KIRKMAN & SCOTT
IF YOU WAKE UP AT NIGHT AND FEEL AFRAID, YOU JUST TELL THE DOLL WHAT YOU'RE WORRIED ABOUT, AND IT WILL TRY TO SOLVE THE PROBLEM WHILE YOU SLEEP.
THIS LITTLE DOLL IS GOING TO TAKE CARE OF MY PROBLEMS?
THAT'S WHAT THE LEGEND SAYS.
NO OFFENSE, MOM, BUT I THINK I'LL SLEEP BETTER WITH THIS GUY ON THE JOB.
WHATEVER WORKS.

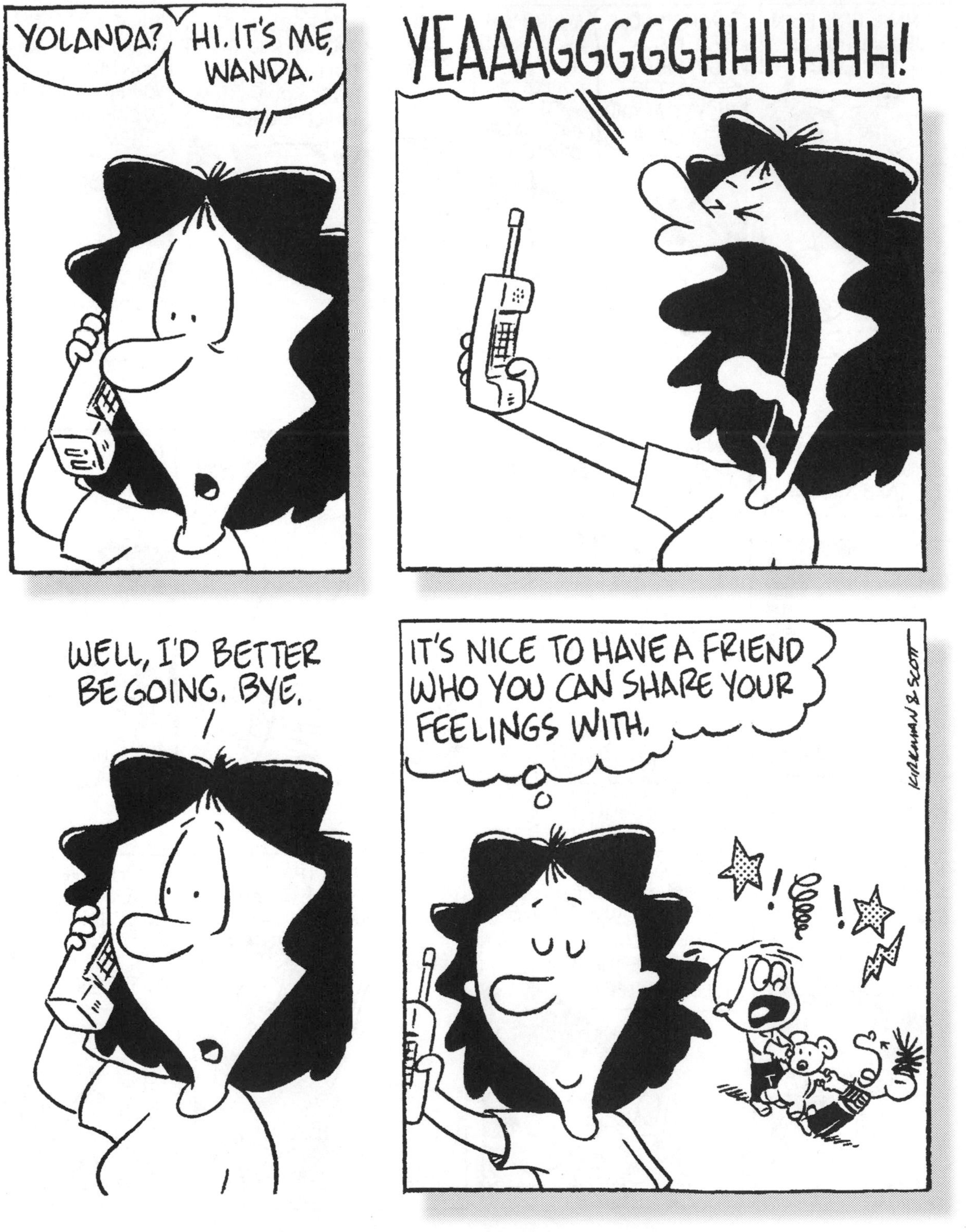
YOLANDA?
HI. IT'S ME, WANDA.
YEAAAGGGGHHHHHH!
WELL, I'D BETTER BE GOING. BYE.
IT'S NICE TO HAVE A FRIEND WHO YOU CAN SHARE YOUR FEELINGS WITH.
KIRKMAN & SCOTT

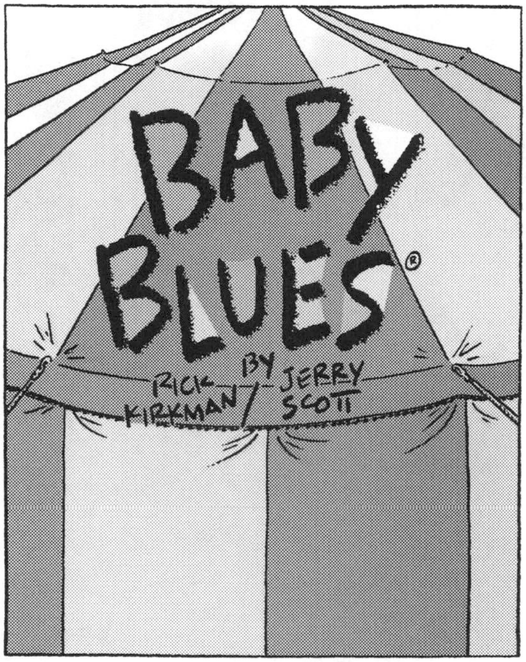
BABY BLUES®
BY RICK KIRKMAN / JERRY SCOTT

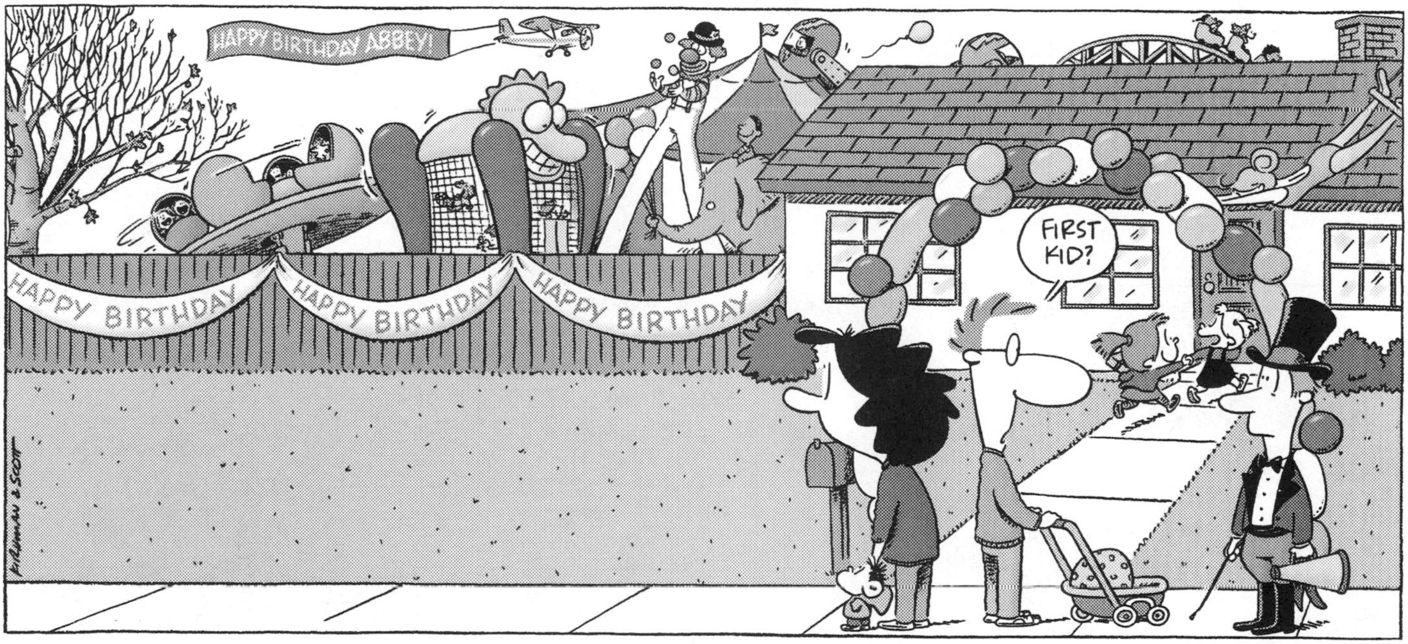
HAPPY BIRTHDAY ABBEY!
HAPPY BIRTHDAY
HAPPY BIRTHDAY
HAPPY BIRTHDAY
FIRST KID?

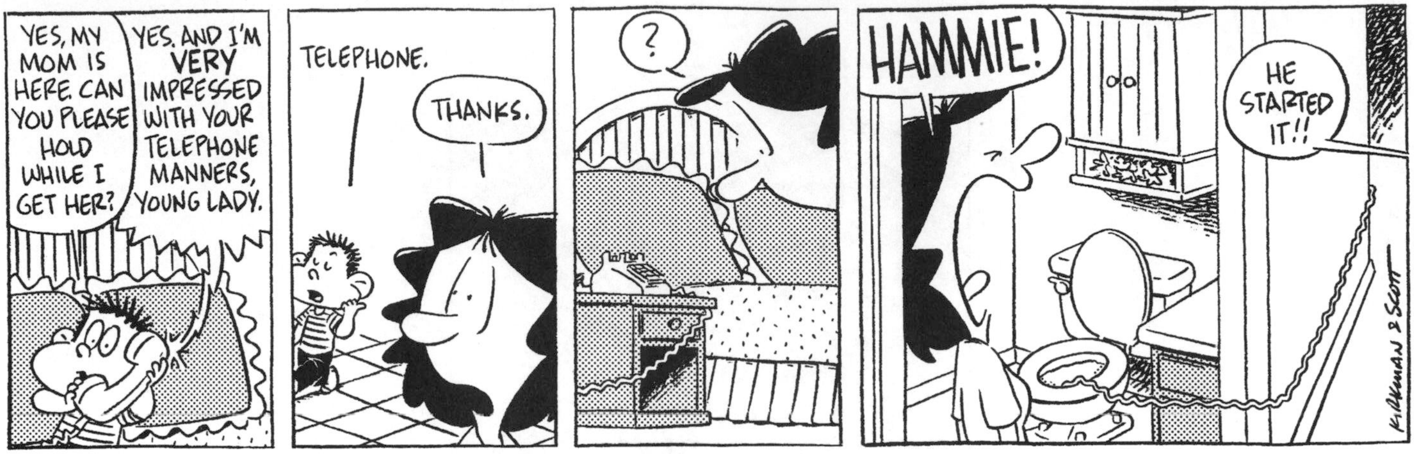
YES, MY MOM IS HERE. CAN YOU PLEASE HOLD WHILE I GET HER?
YES. AND I'M VERY IMPRESSED WITH YOUR TELEPHONE MANNERS, YOUNG LADY.
TELEPHONE.
THANKS.
?
HAMMIE!
HE STARTED IT!!
KIRKMAN & SCOTT

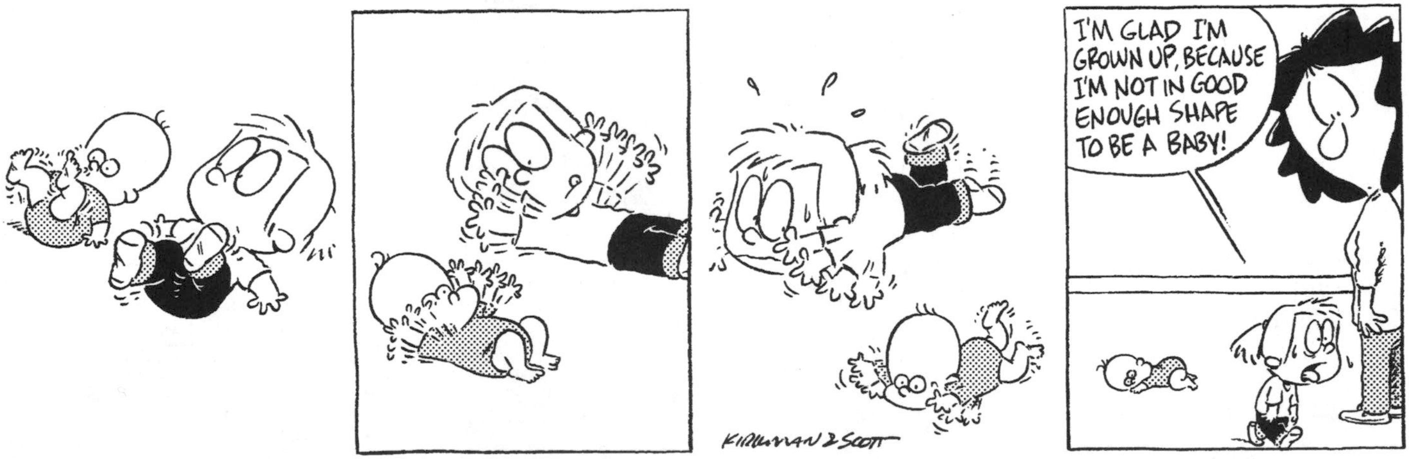
KIRKMAN & SCOTT
I'M GLAD I'M GROWN UP, BECAUSE I'M NOT IN GOOD ENOUGH SHAPE TO BE A BABY!

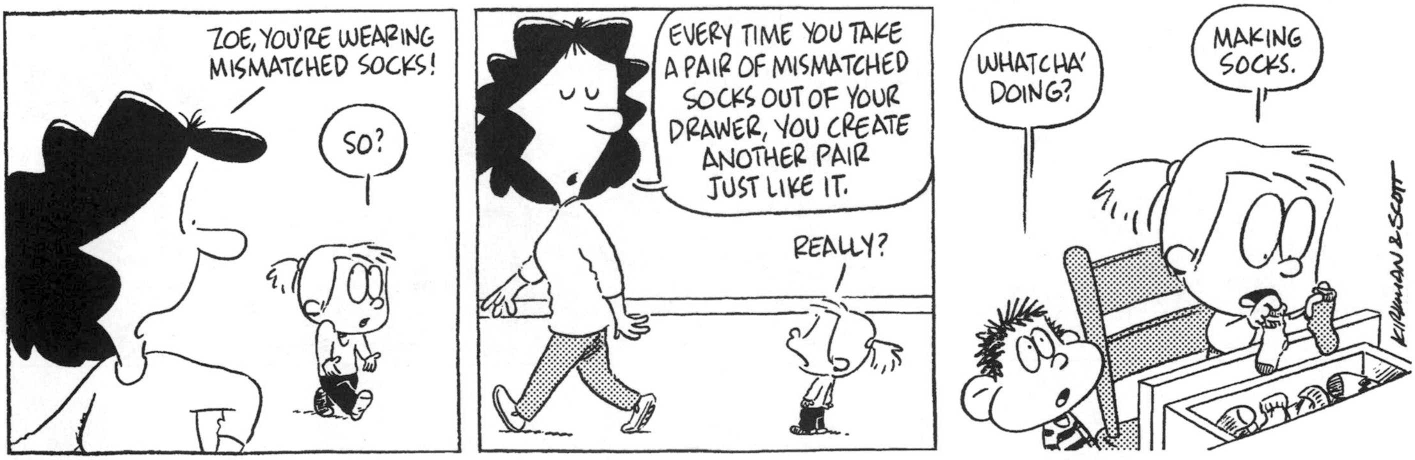
ZOE, YOU'RE WEARING MISMATCHED SOCKS!
SO?
EVERY TIME YOU TAKE A PAIR OF MISMATCHED SOCKS OUT OF YOUR DRAWER, YOU CREATE ANOTHER PAIR JUST LIKE IT.
REALLY?
WHATCHA' DOING?
MAKING SOCKS.
KIRKMAN & SCOTT

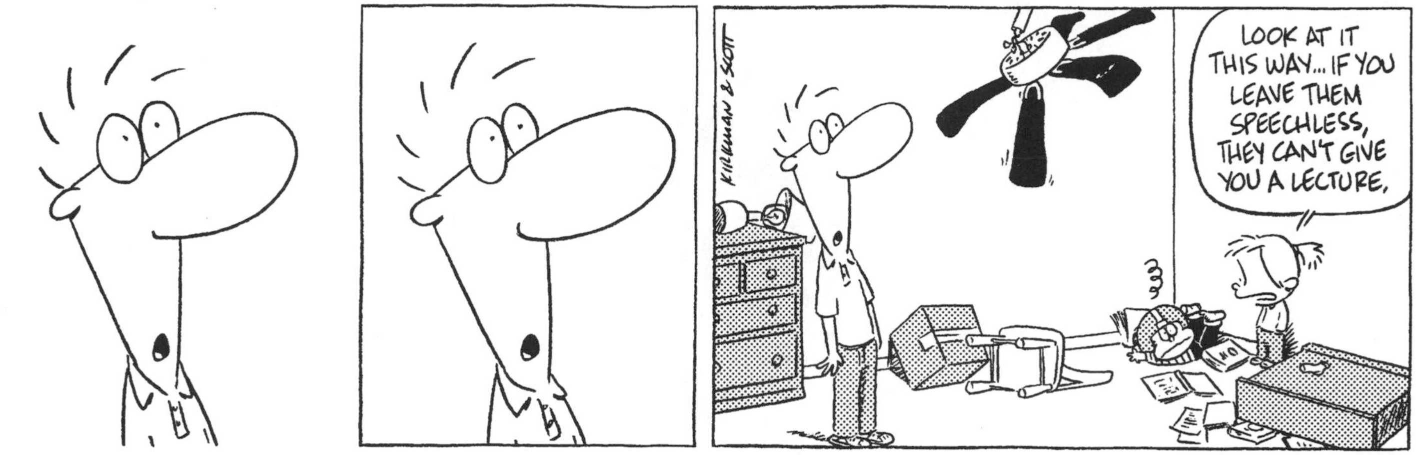
KIRKMAN & SCOTT
LOOK AT IT THIS WAY... IF YOU LEAVE THEM SPEECHLESS, THEY CAN'T GIVE YOU A LECTURE.

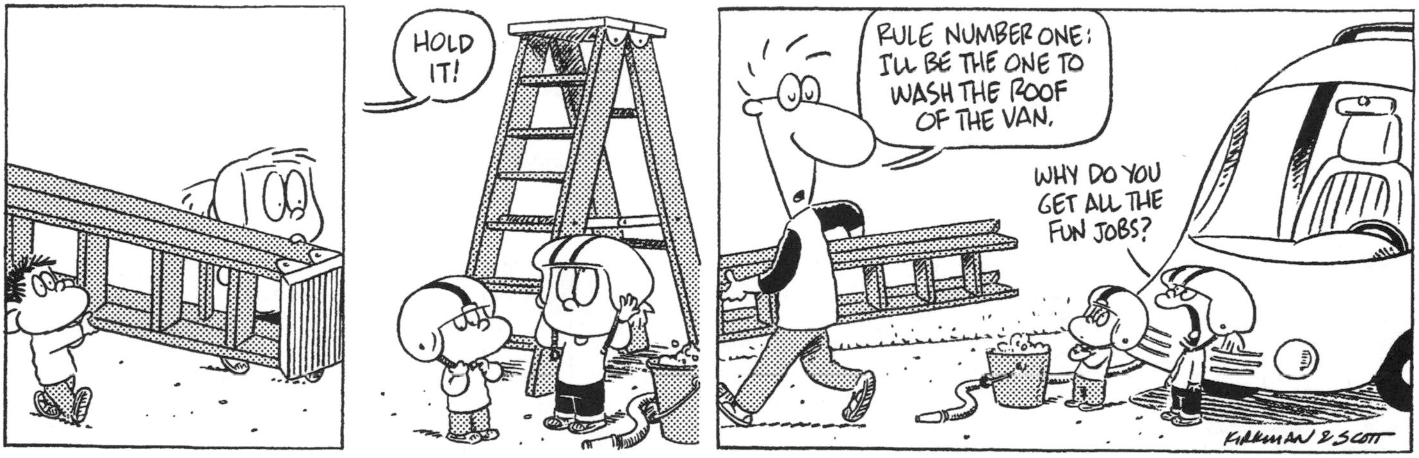
HOLD IT!
RULE NUMBER ONE: I'LL BE THE ONE TO WASH THE ROOF OF THE VAN.
WHY DO YOU GET ALL THE FUN JOBS?
KIRKMAN & SCOTT

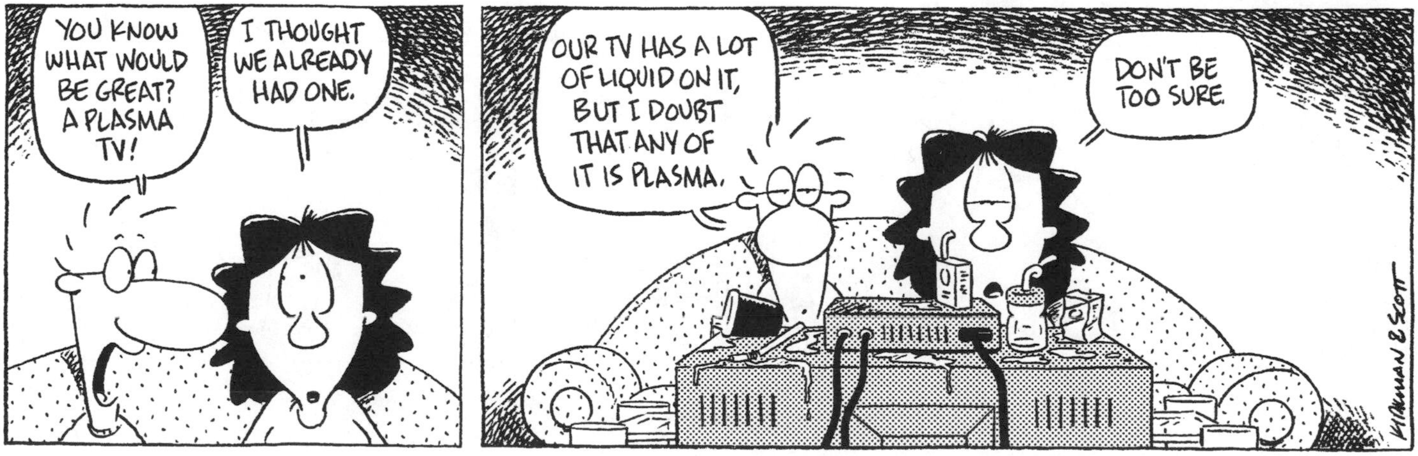
YOU KNOW WHAT WOULD BE GREAT? A PLASMA TV!
I THOUGHT WE ALREADY HAD ONE.
OUR TV HAS A LOT OF LIQUID ON IT, BUT I DOUBT THAT ANY OF IT IS PLASMA.
DON'T BE TOO SURE.
KIRKMAN & SCOTT

BABY BLUES®

BY RICK KIRKMAN / JERRY SCOTT

OKAY, FEET TOGETHER... BACK STRAIGHT... STAND UP TALL...

WOW, HAMMIE! YOU'VE GROWN AN INCH!

OR NOT.

HUH?

YOU WERE HOLDING THE RULER CROOKED.

WHAT?

PLUS, THE PENCIL WAS TILTED UP, SO YOUR MEASUREMENT IS PROBABLY WAY OFF.

BUT HEY, IF YOU GUYS WANT TO THINK THAT HE GREW AN INCH, WHO AM I TO ARGUE?

SO HOW'S THE GROWTH PROGRESS?

HAMMIE IS THIS MUCH TALLER, AND ZOE IS THIS MUCH MORE ANNOYING.

NO! THIS MUCH!

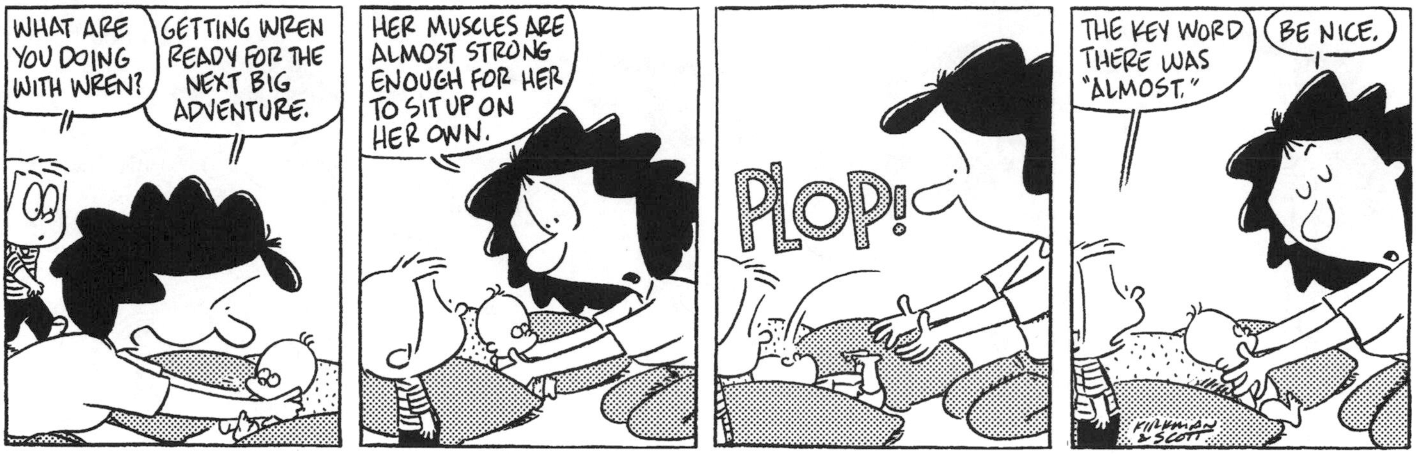
WHAT ARE YOU DOING WITH WREN?
GETTING WREN READY FOR THE NEXT BIG ADVENTURE.
HER MUSCLES ARE ALMOST STRONG ENOUGH FOR HER TO SIT UP ON HER OWN.
PLOP!
THE KEY WORD THERE WAS "ALMOST."
BE NICE.
KIRKMAN & SCOTT

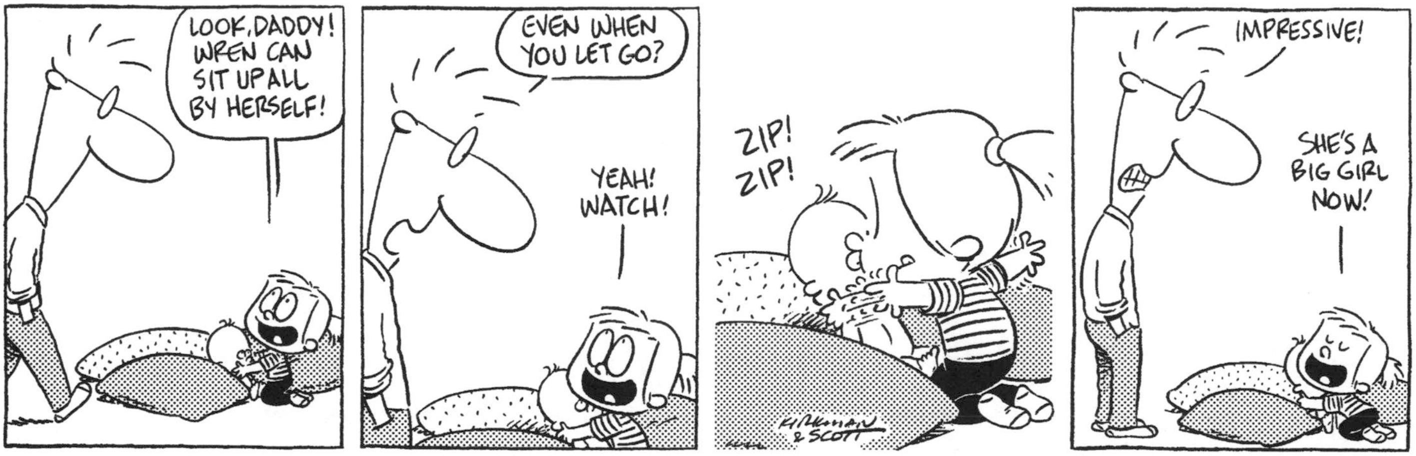
LOOK, DADDY! WREN CAN SIT UP ALL BY HERSELF!
EVEN WHEN YOU LET GO?
YEAH! WATCH!
ZIP! ZIP!
KIRKMAN & SCOTT
IMPRESSIVE!
SHE'S A BIG GIRL NOW!

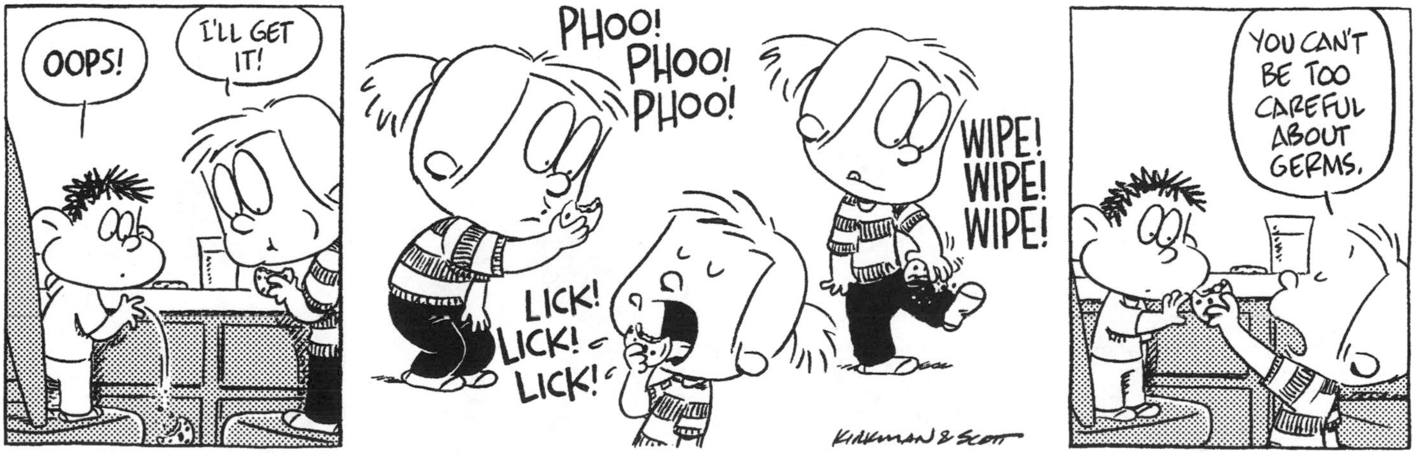
OOPS!
I'LL GET IT!
PHOO! PHOO! PHOO!
LICK! LICK! LICK!
WIPE! WIPE! WIPE!
KIRKMAN & SCOTT
YOU CAN'T BE TOO CAREFUL ABOUT GERMS.

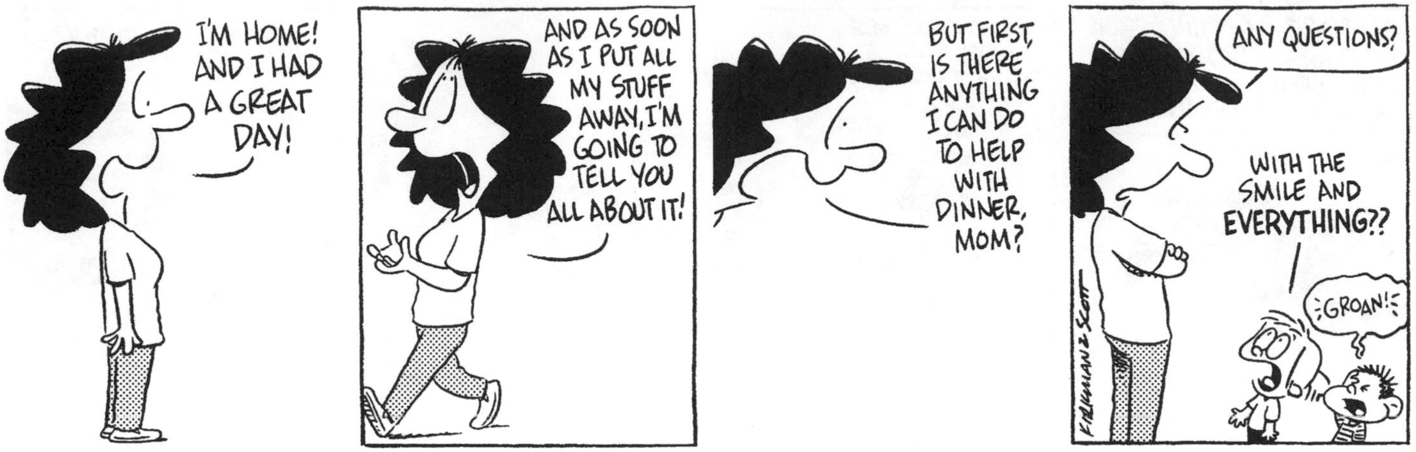
I'M HOME! AND I HAD A GREAT DAY!
AND AS SOON AS I PUT ALL MY STUFF AWAY, I'M GOING TO TELL YOU ALL ABOUT IT!
BUT FIRST, IS THERE ANYTHING I CAN DO TO HELP WITH DINNER, MOM?
ANY QUESTIONS?
WITH THE SMILE AND EVERYTHING??
GROAN!

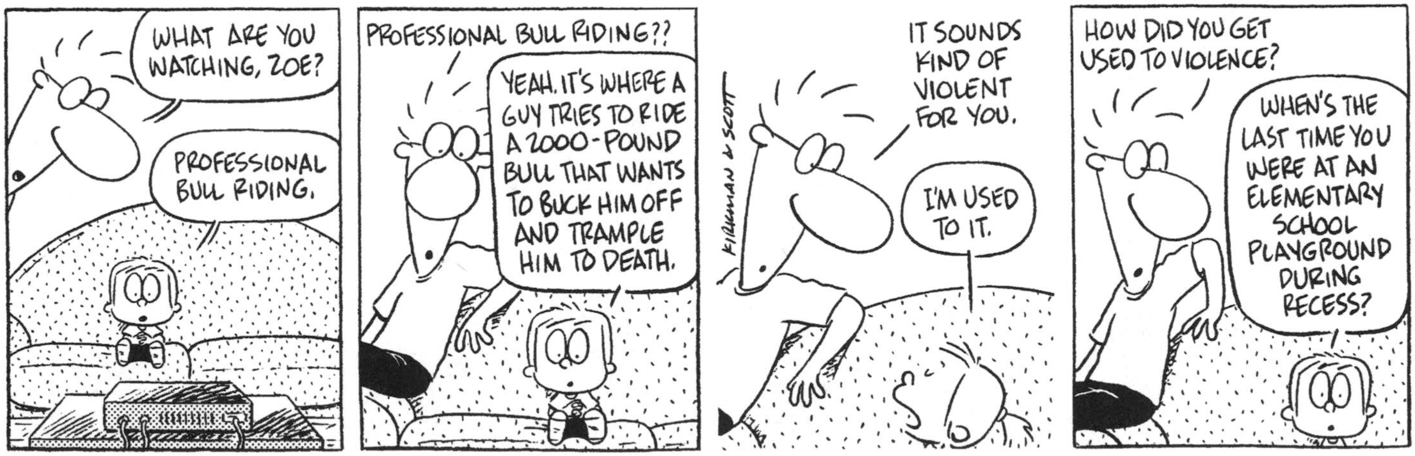
WHAT ARE YOU WATCHING, ZOE?
PROFESSIONAL BULL RIDING.
PROFESSIONAL BULL RIDING??
YEAH. IT'S WHERE A GUY TRIES TO RIDE A 2000-POUND BULL THAT WANTS TO BUCK HIM OFF AND TRAMPLE HIM TO DEATH.
IT SOUNDS KIND OF VIOLENT FOR YOU.
I'M USED TO IT.
HOW DID YOU GET USED TO VIOLENCE?
WHEN'S THE LAST TIME YOU WERE AT AN ELEMENTARY SCHOOL PLAYGROUND DURING RECESS?

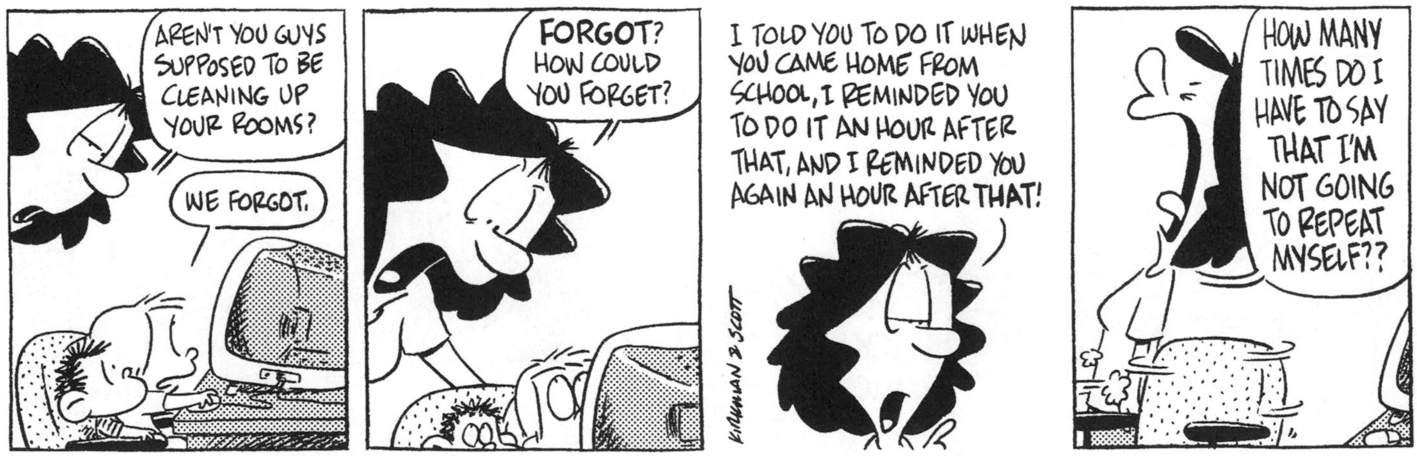
AREN'T YOU GUYS SUPPOSED TO BE CLEANING UP YOUR ROOMS?
WE FORGOT.
FORGOT? HOW COULD YOU FORGET?
I TOLD YOU TO DO IT WHEN YOU CAME HOME FROM SCHOOL, I REMINDED YOU TO DO IT AN HOUR AFTER THAT, AND I REMINDED YOU AGAIN AN HOUR AFTER THAT!
HOW MANY TIMES DO I HAVE TO SAY THAT I'M NOT GOING TO REPEAT MYSELF??

BABY BLUES®
BY RICK KIRKMAN / JERRY SCOTT

TSK! WHAT A MESS!
YOU SAID IT!
ICK! POPCORN... POTATO CHIP CRUMBS... RAISINS...
KIRKMAN & SCOTT
HEY! AN M&M!
WHAT ARE YOU DOING? HOW LONG HAS THAT BEEN ON THE FLOOR?
CRUNCH! CRUNCH! I DUNNO.
WANDA, THE FIVE SECOND RULE CLEARLY STATES:
Any food object that has been on the floor longer than five seconds is no longer edible, and should be thrown away.
SO?
SO... YOU'RE VIOLATING THE FIVE SECOND RULE!
YOU'RE OBVIOUSLY NOT FAMILIAR WITH THE CHOCOLATE AMENDMENT.

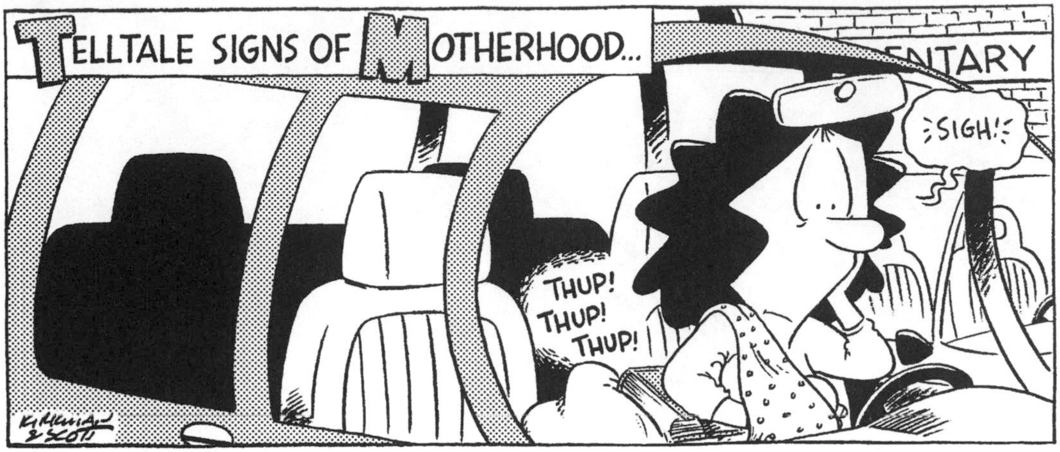
TELLTALE SIGNS OF MOTHERHOOD...
ENTARY
SIGH!
THUP! THUP! THUP!
KIRKMAN & SCOTT

Breast-feeding your baby in the elementary school parking lot while using a bag of dirty soccer uniforms and a Harry Potter book for a nursing pillow.

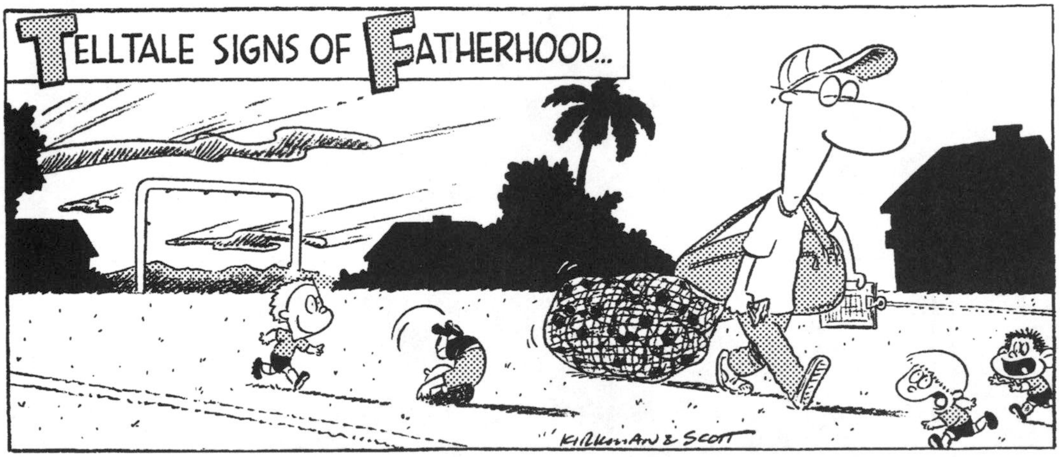
TELLTALE SIGNS OF FATHERHOOD...
KIRKMAN & SCOTT

Your entire weekend of spectator sports didn't involve a single athlete over the age of six.

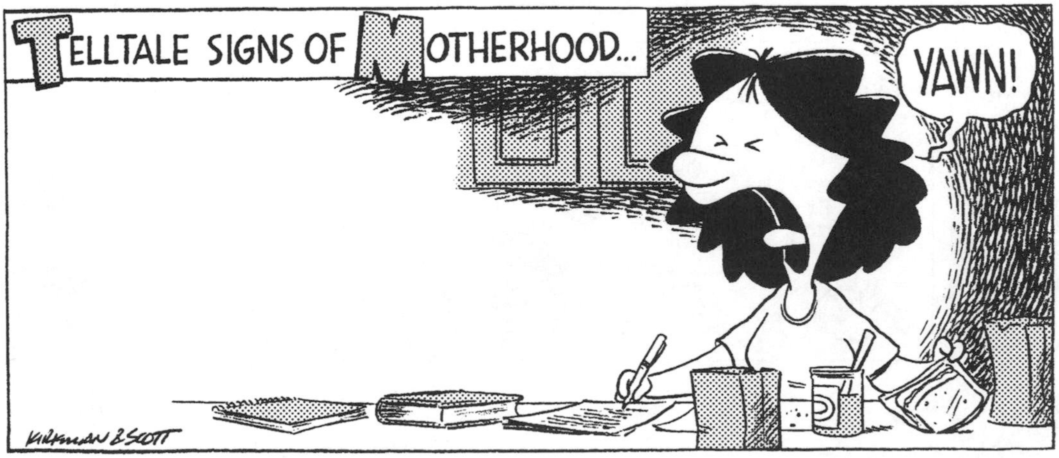
TELLTALE SIGNS OF MOTHERHOOD...
YAWN!
KIRKMAN & SCOTT

The phrase "Ready for Bed" means that all you have to do is pack tomorrow's lunches, check homework, fill out permission forms for a field trip, straighten up the living room and fold two loads of laundry.

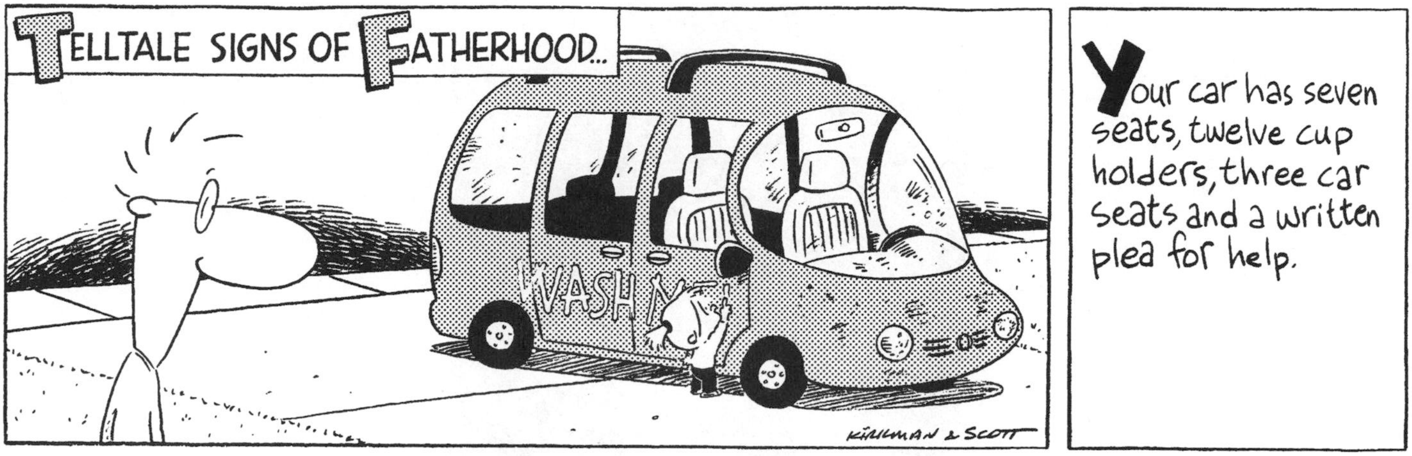
TELLTALE SIGNS OF FATHERHOOD...
KIRKMAN & SCOTT
Your car has seven seats, twelve cup holders, three car seats and a written plea for help.

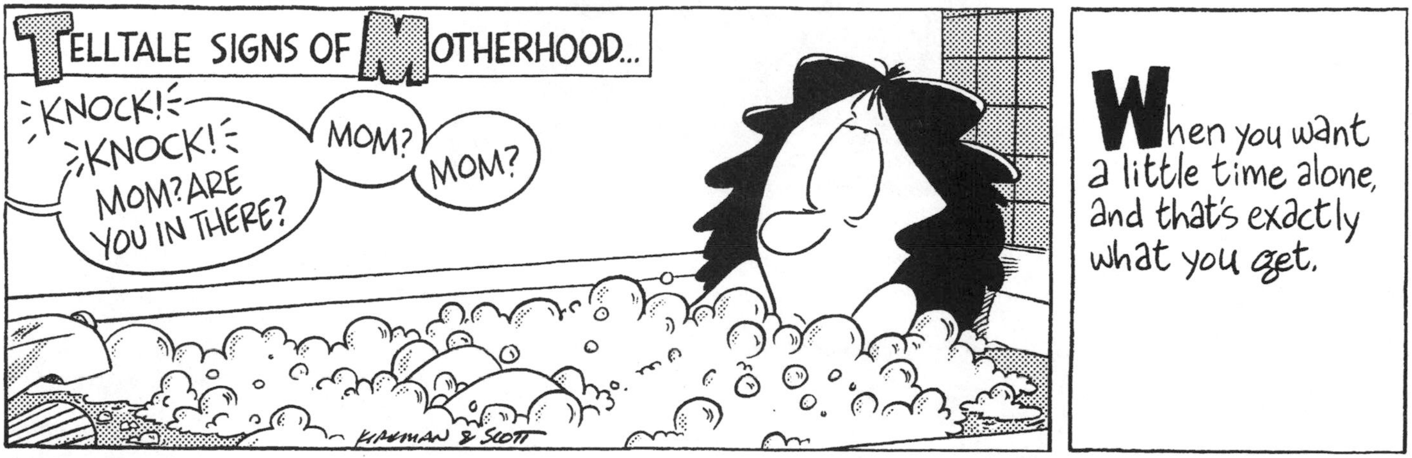
TELLTALE SIGNS OF MOTHERHOOD...
KNOCK! KNOCK! MOM? ARE YOU IN THERE?
MOM?
MOM?
KIRKMAN & SCOTT
When you want a little time alone, and that's exactly what you get.

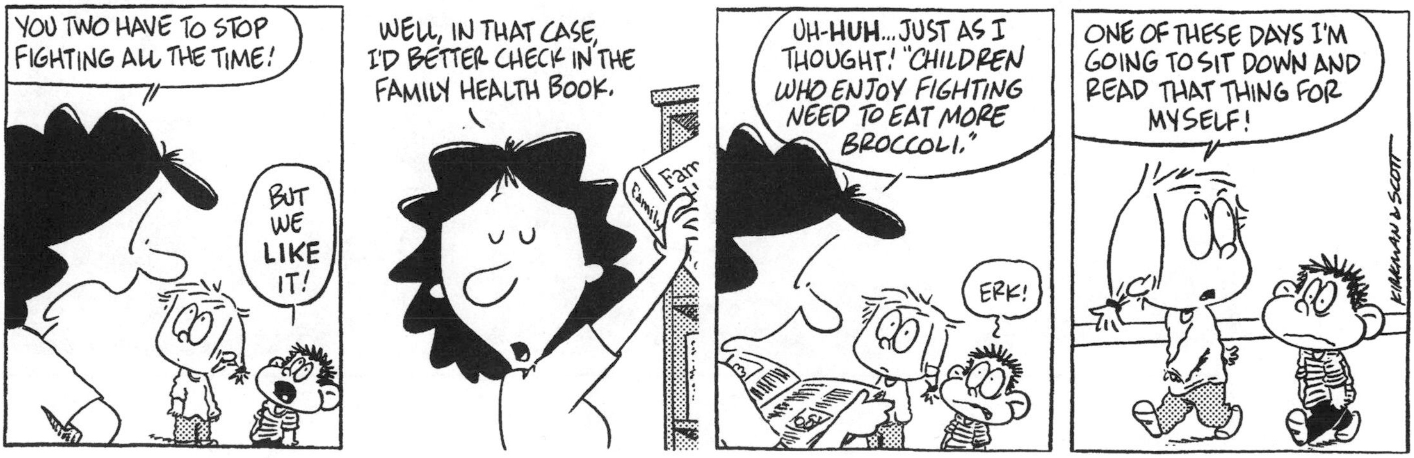
YOU TWO HAVE TO STOP FIGHTING ALL THE TIME!
BUT WE LIKE IT!
WELL, IN THAT CASE, I'D BETTER CHECK IN THE FAMILY HEALTH BOOK.
UH-HUH... JUST AS I THOUGHT! "CHILDREN WHO ENJOY FIGHTING NEED TO EAT MORE BROCCOLI."
ERK!
ONE OF THESE DAYS I'M GOING TO SIT DOWN AND READ THAT THING FOR MYSELF!
KIRKMAN & SCOTT

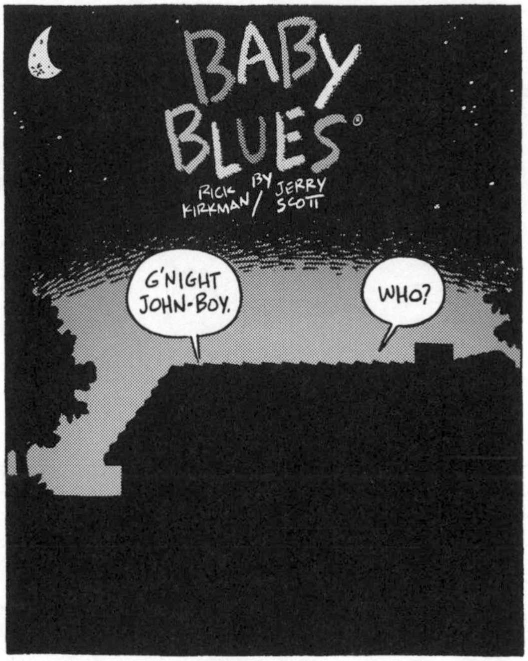
BABY BLUES®
BY RICK KIRKMAN / JERRY SCOTT
G'NIGHT JOHN-BOY.
WHO?

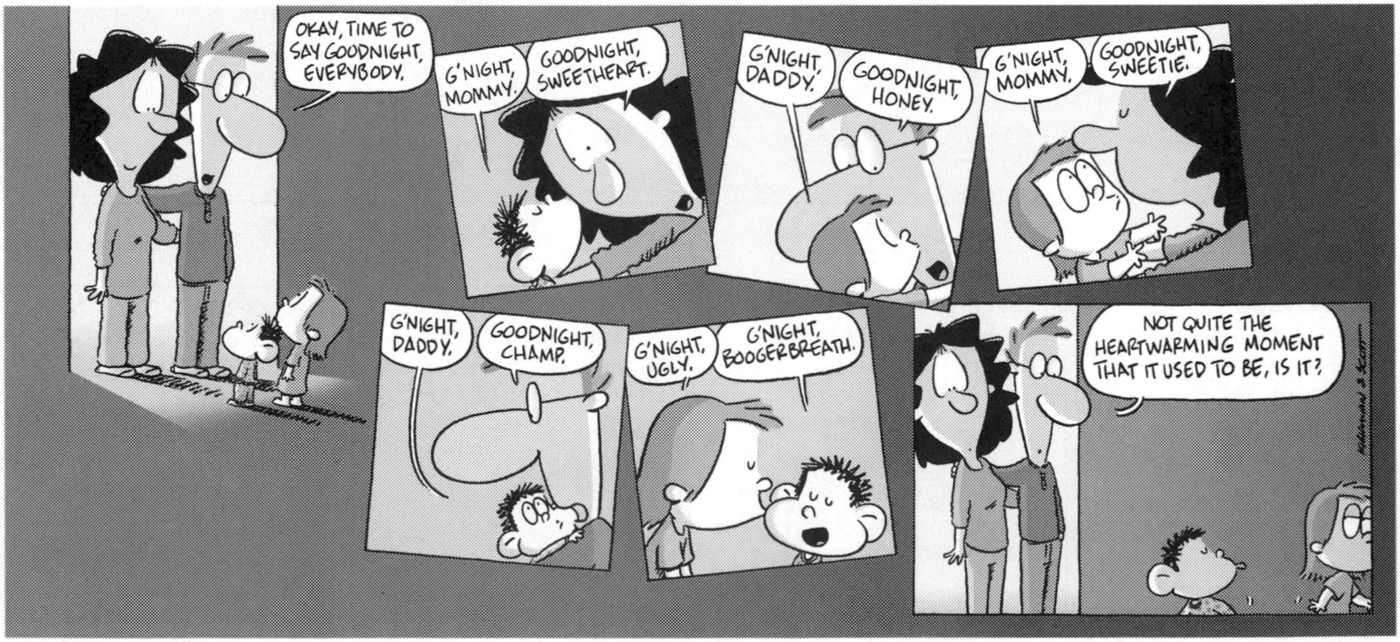
OKAY, TIME TO SAY GOODNIGHT, EVERYBODY.
G'NIGHT, MOMMY.
GOODNIGHT, SWEETHEART.
G'NIGHT, DADDY.
GOODNIGHT, HONEY.
G'NIGHT, MOMMY.
GOODNIGHT, SWEETIE.
G'NIGHT, DADDY.
GOODNIGHT, CHAMP.
G'NIGHT, UGLY.
G'NIGHT, BOOGERBREATH.
NOT QUITE THE HEARTWARMING MOMENT THAT IT USED TO BE, IS IT?

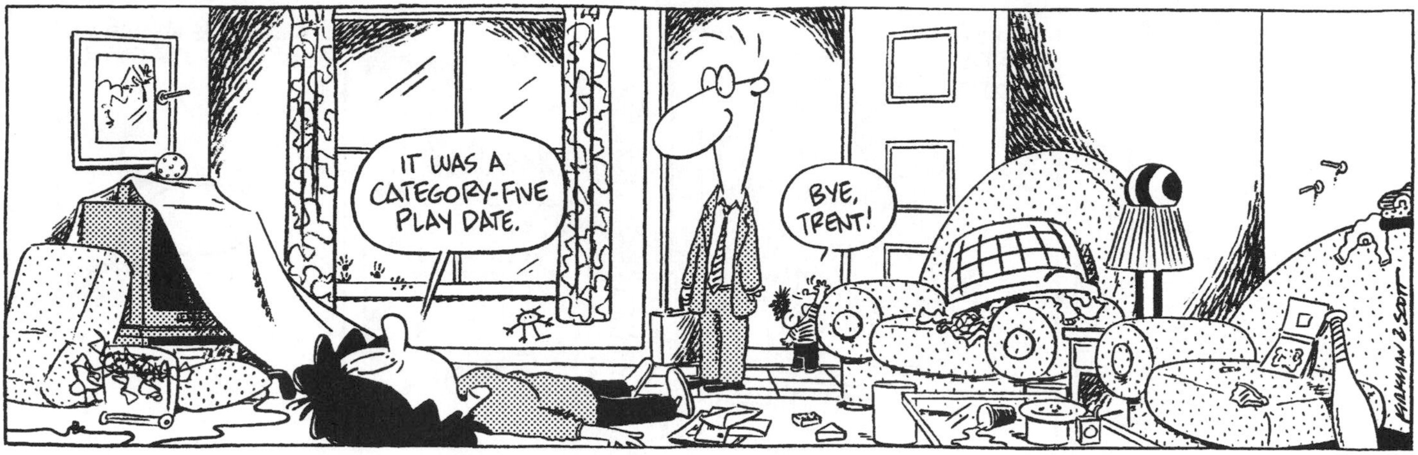
IT WAS A CATEGORY-FIVE PLAY DATE.
BYE, TRENT!
KIRKMAN & SCOTT

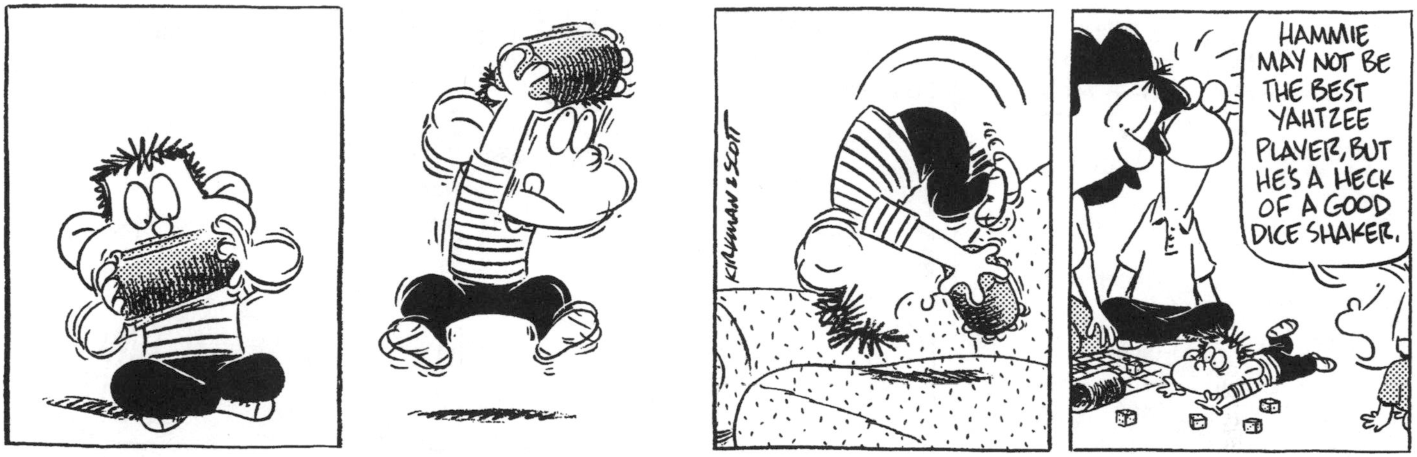
KIRKMAN & SCOTT
HAMMIE MAY NOT BE THE BEST YAHTZEE PLAYER, BUT HE'S A HECK OF A GOOD DICE SHAKER.

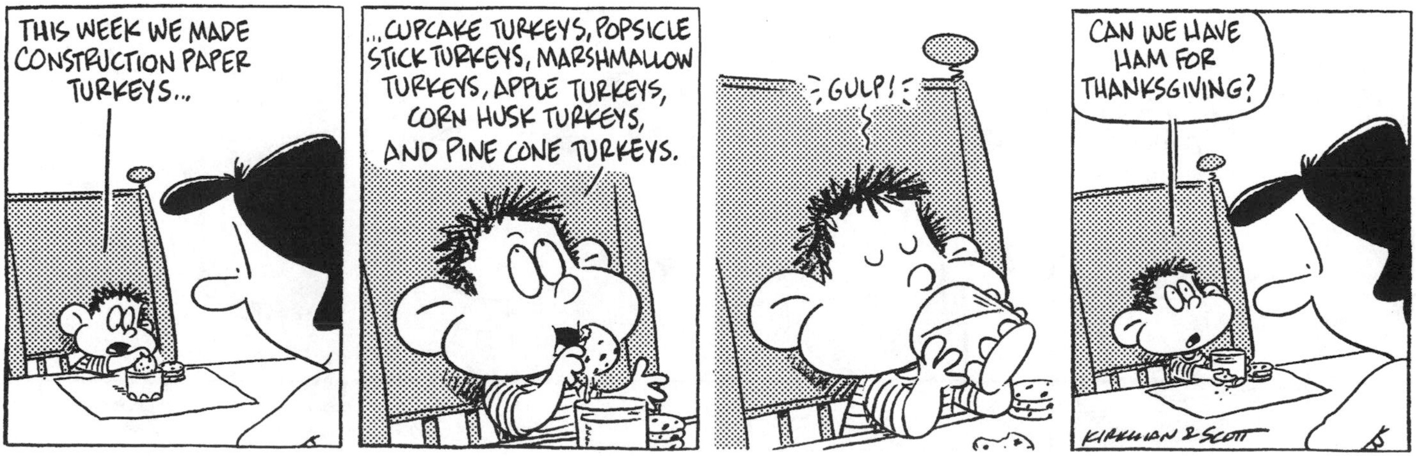
THIS WEEK WE MADE CONSTRUCTION PAPER TURKEYS...
...CUPCAKE TURKEYS, POPSICLE STICK TURKEYS, MARSHMALLOW TURKEYS, APPLE TURKEYS, CORN HUSK TURKEYS, AND PINE CONE TURKEYS.
GULP!
CAN WE HAVE HAM FOR THANKSGIVING?
KIRKMAN & SCOTT

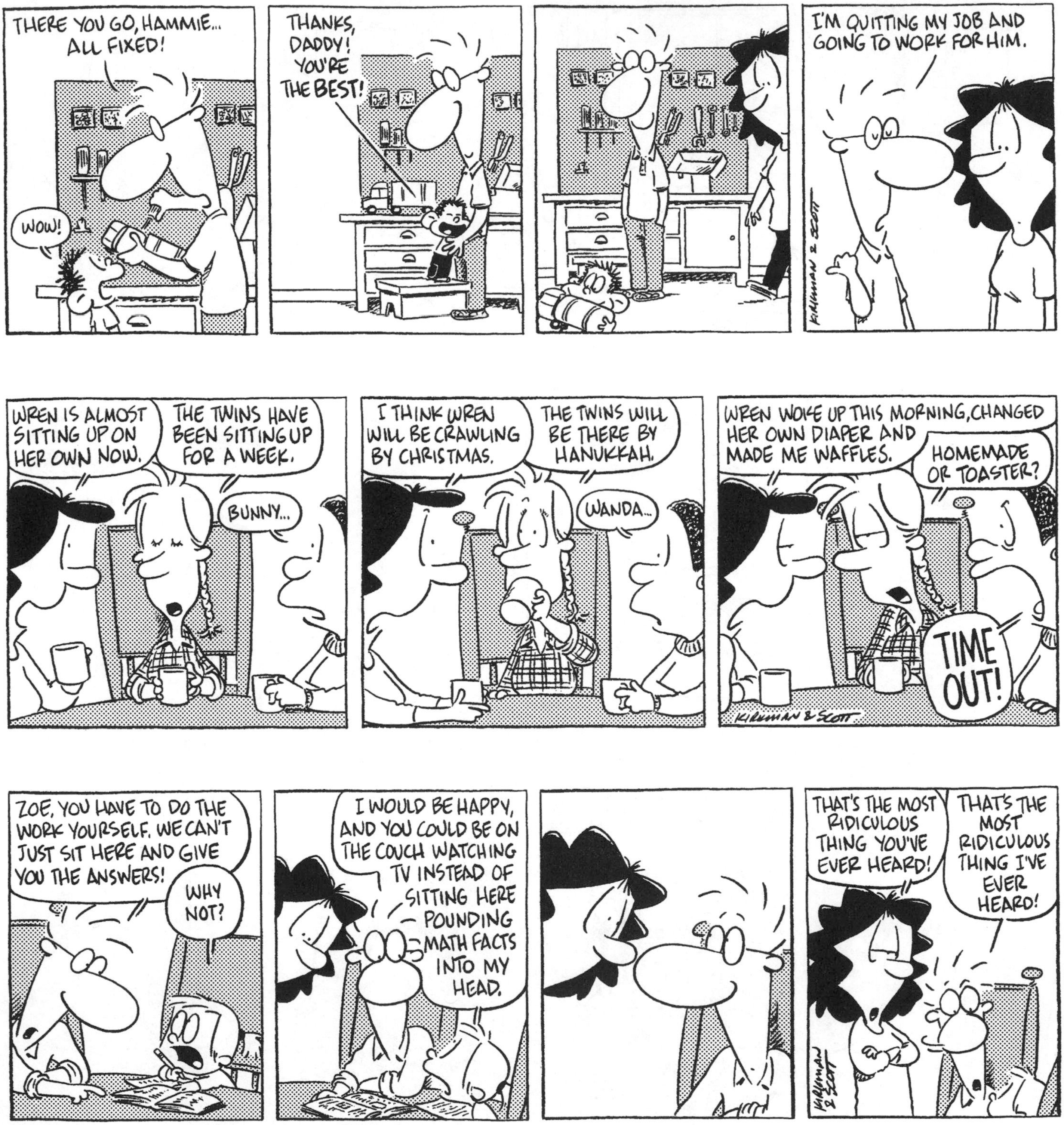
THERE YOU GO, HAMMIE... ALL FIXED!
WOW!
THANKS, DADDY! YOU'RE THE BEST!
I'M QUITTING MY JOB AND GOING TO WORK FOR HIM.
KIRKMAN & SCOTT
WREN IS ALMOST SITTING UP ON HER OWN NOW.
THE TWINS HAVE BEEN SITTING UP FOR A WEEK.
BUNNY...
I THINK WREN WILL BE CRAWLING BY CHRISTMAS.
THE TWINS WILL BE THERE BY HANUKKAH.
WANDA...
WREN WOKE UP THIS MORNING, CHANGED HER OWN DIAPER AND MADE ME WAFFLES.
HOMEMADE OR TOASTER?
TIME OUT!
KIRKMAN & SCOTT
ZOE, YOU HAVE TO DO THE WORK YOURSELF. WE CAN'T JUST SIT HERE AND GIVE YOU THE ANSWERS!
WHY NOT?
I WOULD BE HAPPY, AND YOU COULD BE ON THE COUCH WATCHING TV INSTEAD OF SITTING HERE POUNDING MATH FACTS INTO MY HEAD.
THAT'S THE MOST RIDICULOUS THING YOU'VE EVER HEARD!
THAT'S THE MOST RIDICULOUS THING I'VE EVER HEARD!
KIRKMAN & SCOTT

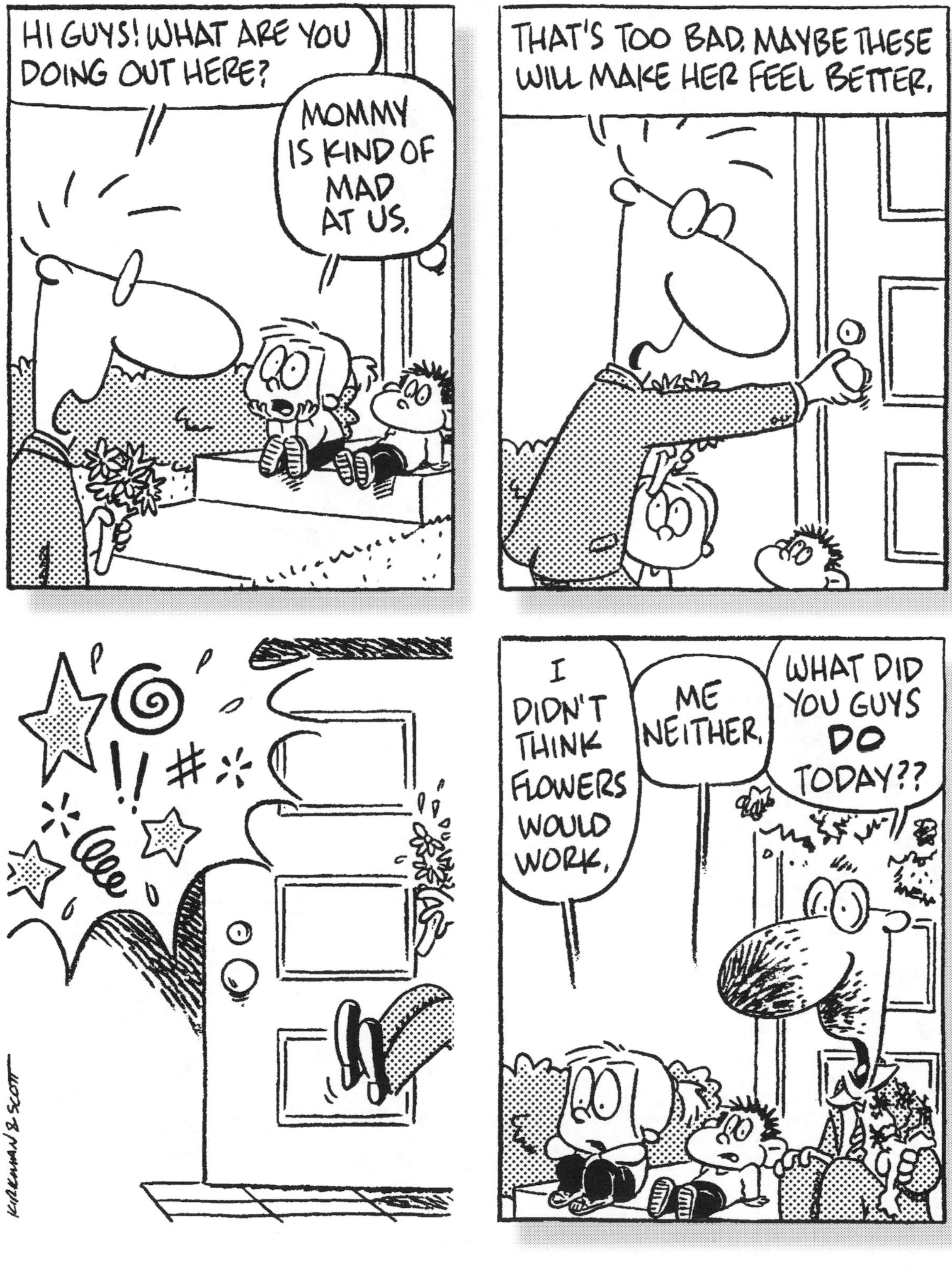
HI GUYS! WHAT ARE YOU DOING OUT HERE?
MOMMY IS KIND OF MAD AT US.
THAT'S TOO BAD. MAYBE THESE WILL MAKE HER FEEL BETTER.
KIRKMAN & SCOTT
I DIDN'T THINK FLOWERS WOULD WORK.
ME NEITHER.
WHAT DID YOU GUYS **DO** TODAY??

BABY BLUES®

RICK KIRKMAN / BY JERRY SCOTT

DIAPER TIME!

NOW??

DARRYL! THE BABY NEEDS TO BE CHANGED!

DARRYL...?

GOOD NEWS, HONEY! I THINK I'VE FIGURED OUT THE PROBLEM WITH THE REMOTE!

I JUST NEED TO HOLD THESE TWO TINY CIRCUITS TOGETHER FOR THREE MORE MINUTES WHILE THE GLUE DRIES, AND THEN I'LL BE HAPPY TO CHANGE WREN'S DIAPER.

UNLESS THAT'S TOO LONG TO MAKE THE POOR THING WAIT...

NEVER MIND. I'LL DO IT.

THAT'S THE SECOND LOAD I'VE BEEN HANDED IN THE LAST MINUTE AND A HALF.

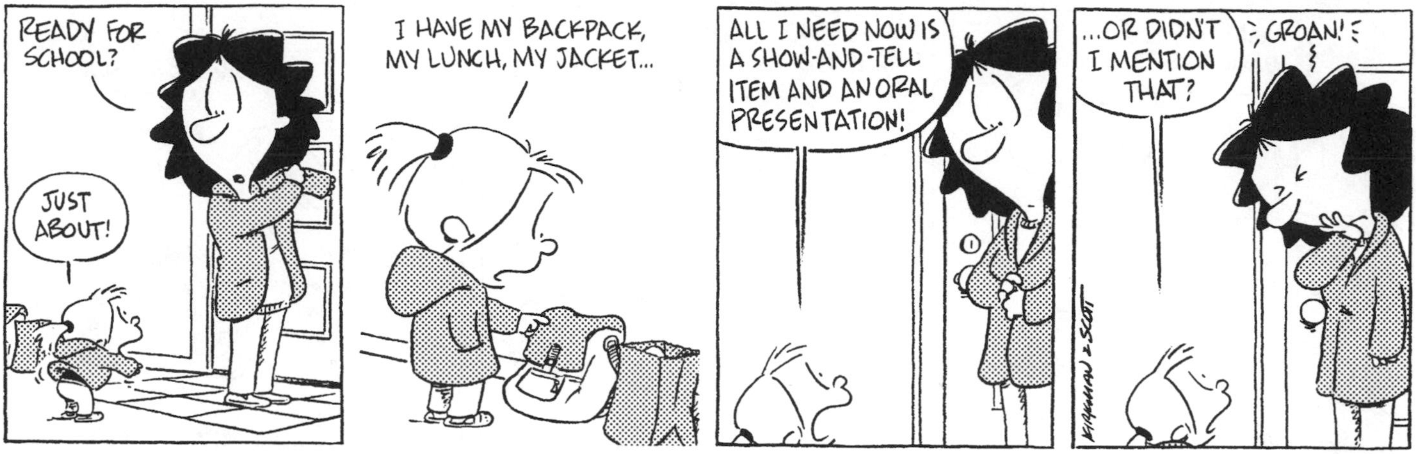
READY FOR SCHOOL?
JUST ABOUT!
I HAVE MY BACKPACK, MY LUNCH, MY JACKET...
ALL I NEED NOW IS A SHOW-AND-TELL ITEM AND AN ORAL PRESENTATION!
...OR DIDN'T I MENTION THAT?
GROAN!
KIRKMAN & SCOTT

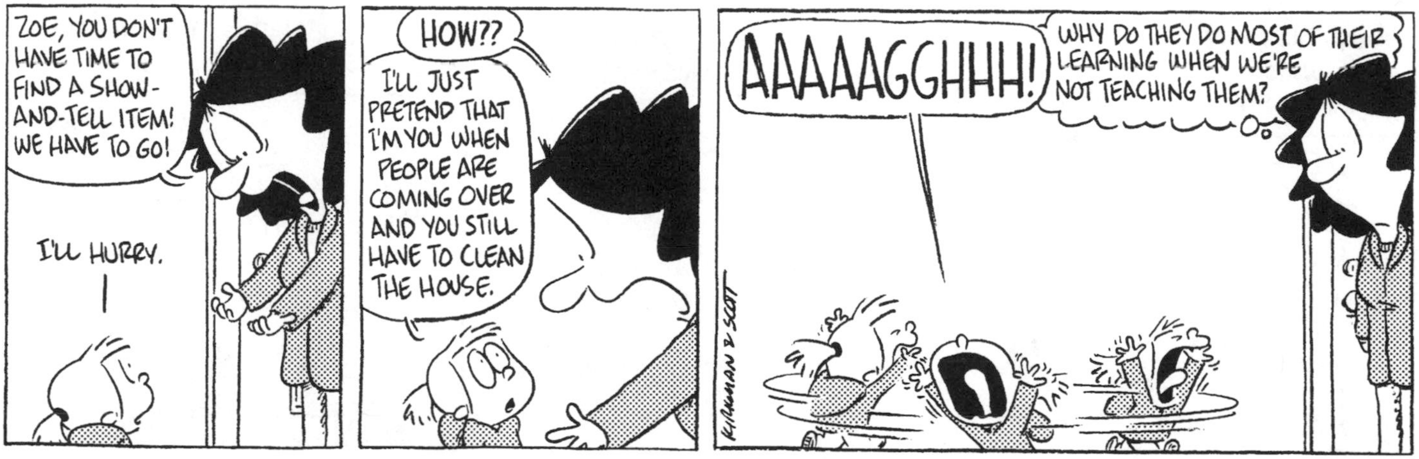
ZOE, YOU DON'T HAVE TIME TO FIND A SHOW-AND-TELL ITEM! WE HAVE TO GO!
I'LL HURRY.
HOW??
I'LL JUST PRETEND THAT I'M YOU WHEN PEOPLE ARE COMING OVER AND YOU STILL HAVE TO CLEAN THE HOUSE.
AAAAAGGHHH!
WHY DO THEY DO MOST OF THEIR LEARNING WHEN WE'RE NOT TEACHING THEM?
KIRKMAN & SCOTT

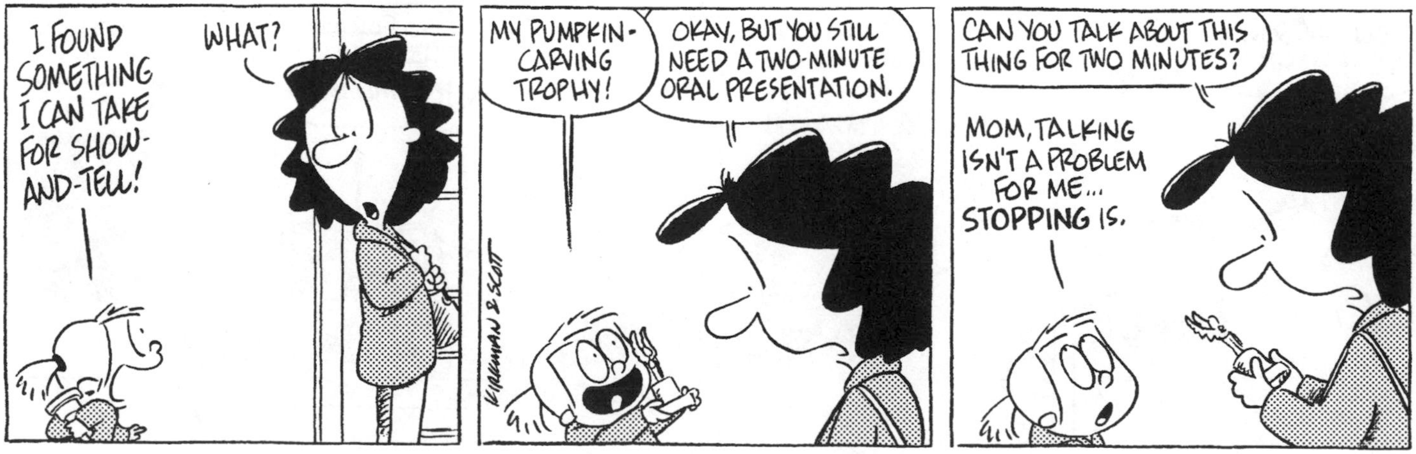
I FOUND SOMETHING I CAN TAKE FOR SHOW-AND-TELL!
WHAT?
MY PUMPKIN-CARVING TROPHY!
OKAY, BUT YOU STILL NEED A TWO-MINUTE ORAL PRESENTATION.
CAN YOU TALK ABOUT THIS THING FOR TWO MINUTES?
MOM, TALKING ISN'T A PROBLEM FOR ME... STOPPING IS.
KIRKMAN & SCOTT

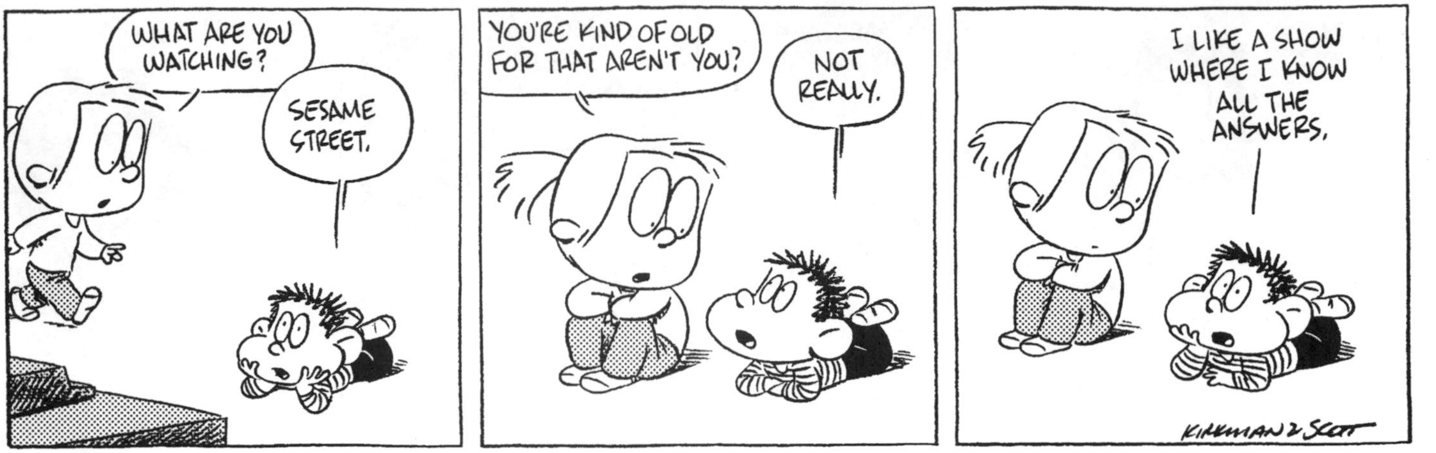
WHAT ARE YOU WATCHING?
SESAME STREET.
YOU'RE KIND OF OLD FOR THAT AREN'T YOU?
NOT REALLY.
I LIKE A SHOW WHERE I KNOW ALL THE ANSWERS.
KIRKMAN & SCOTT

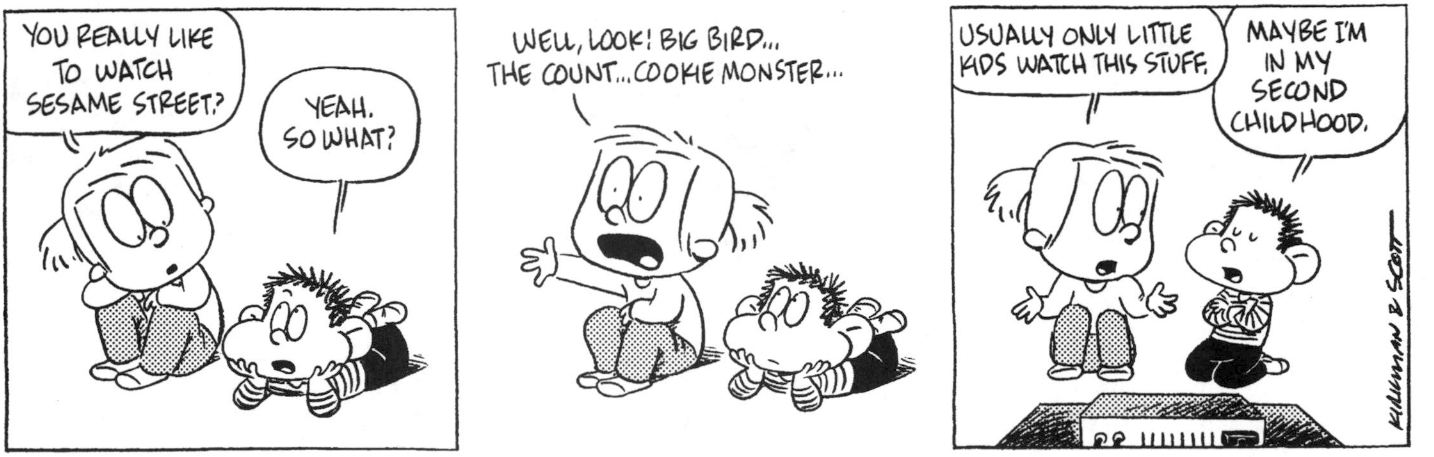
YOU REALLY LIKE TO WATCH SESAME STREET?
YEAH. SO WHAT?
WELL, LOOK! BIG BIRD... THE COUNT... COOKIE MONSTER...
USUALLY ONLY LITTLE KIDS WATCH THIS STUFF.
MAYBE I'M IN MY SECOND CHILDHOOD.
KIRKMAN & SCOTT

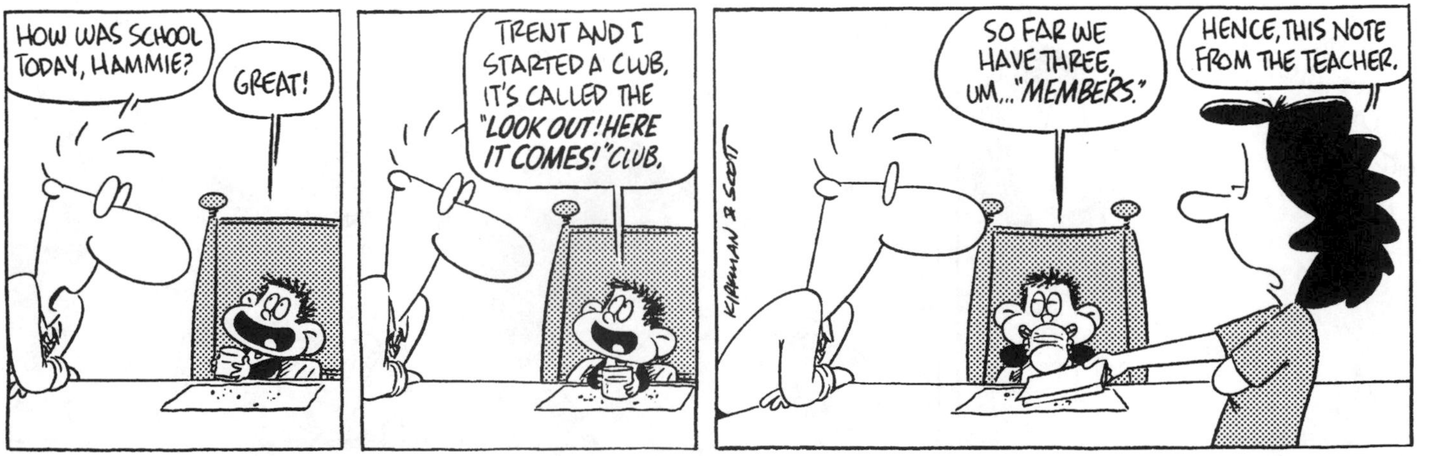
HOW WAS SCHOOL TODAY, HAMMIE?
GREAT!
TRENT AND I STARTED A CLUB. IT'S CALLED THE "LOOK OUT! HERE IT COMES!" CLUB.
KIRKMAN & SCOTT
SO FAR WE HAVE THREE, UM... "MEMBERS."
HENCE, THIS NOTE FROM THE TEACHER.

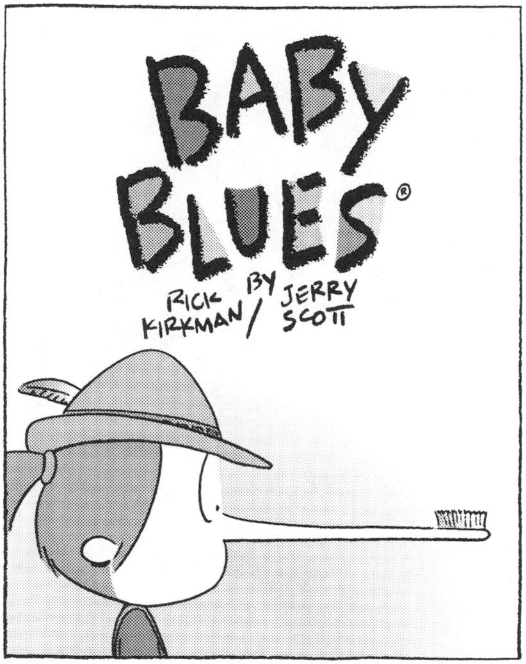
BABY BLUES®
BY
RICK KIRKMAN / JERRY SCOTT

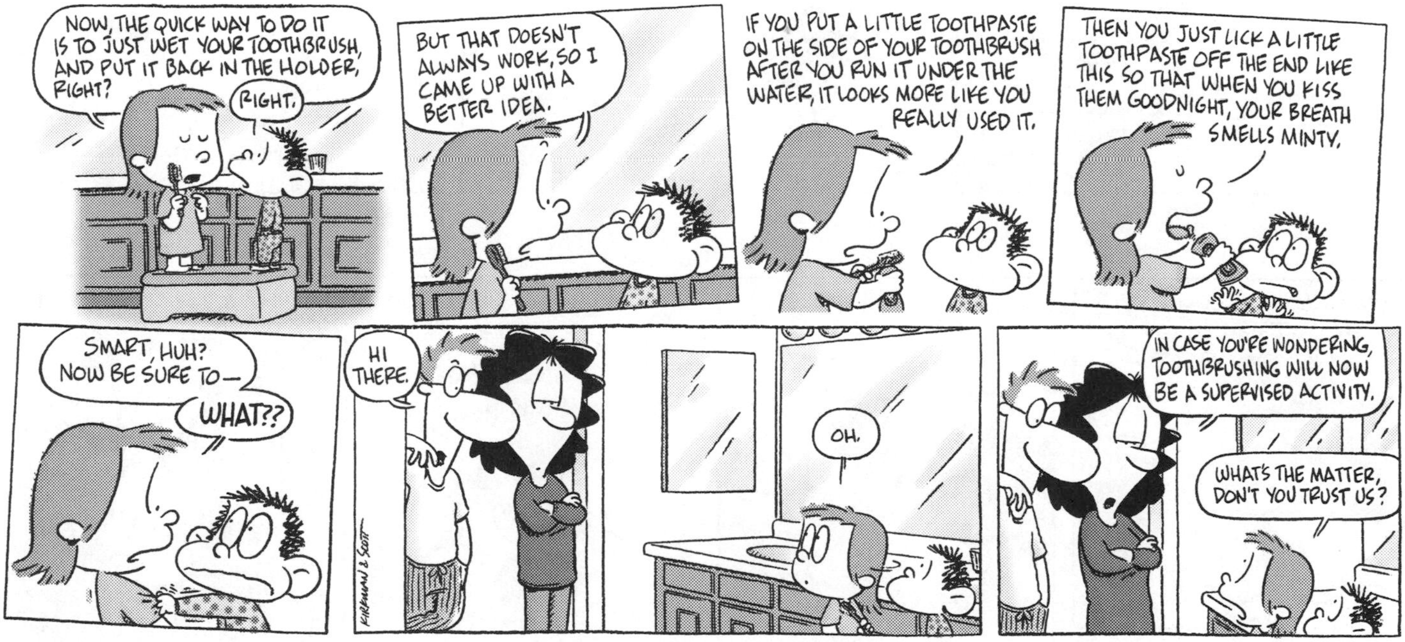
NOW, THE QUICK WAY TO DO IT IS TO JUST WET YOUR TOOTHBRUSH, AND PUT IT BACK IN THE HOLDER, RIGHT?
RIGHT.
BUT THAT DOESN'T ALWAYS WORK, SO I CAME UP WITH A BETTER IDEA.
IF YOU PUT A LITTLE TOOTHPASTE ON THE SIDE OF YOUR TOOTHBRUSH AFTER YOU RUN IT UNDER THE WATER, IT LOOKS MORE LIKE YOU REALLY USED IT.
THEN YOU JUST LICK A LITTLE TOOTHPASTE OFF THE END LIKE THIS SO THAT WHEN YOU KISS THEM GOODNIGHT, YOUR BREATH SMELLS MINTY.
SMART, HUH? NOW BE SURE TO—
WHAT??
HI THERE.
KIRKMAN & SCOTT
OH.
IN CASE YOU'RE WONDERING, TOOTHBRUSHING WILL NOW BE A SUPERVISED ACTIVITY.
WHAT'S THE MATTER, DON'T YOU TRUST US?

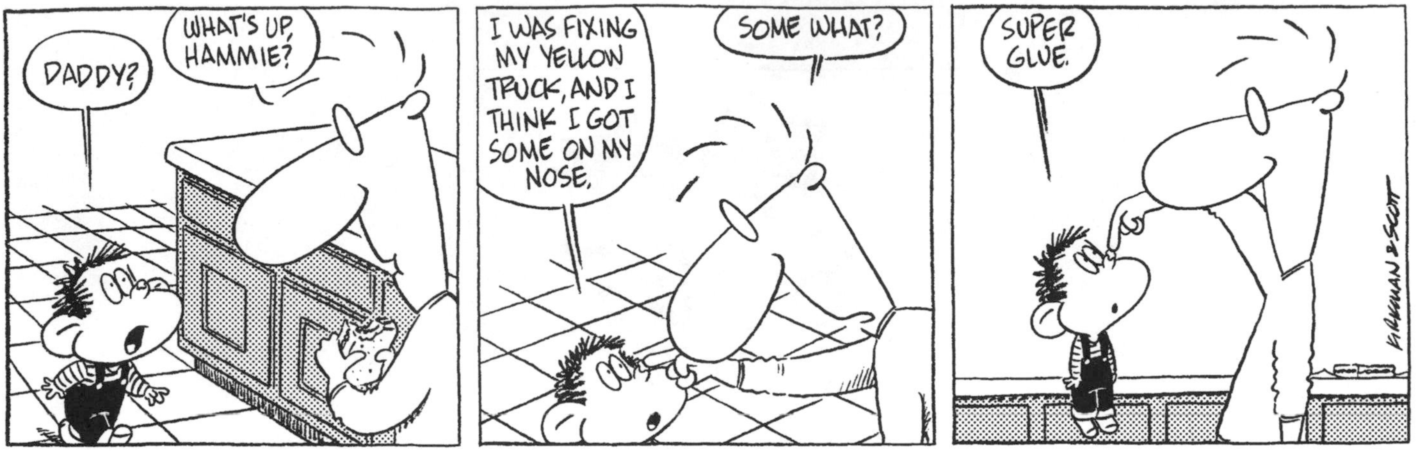
DADDY?
WHAT'S UP, HAMMIE?
I WAS FIXING MY YELLOW TRUCK, AND I THINK I GOT SOME ON MY NOSE.
SOME WHAT?
SUPER GLUE.
KIRKMAN & SCOTT

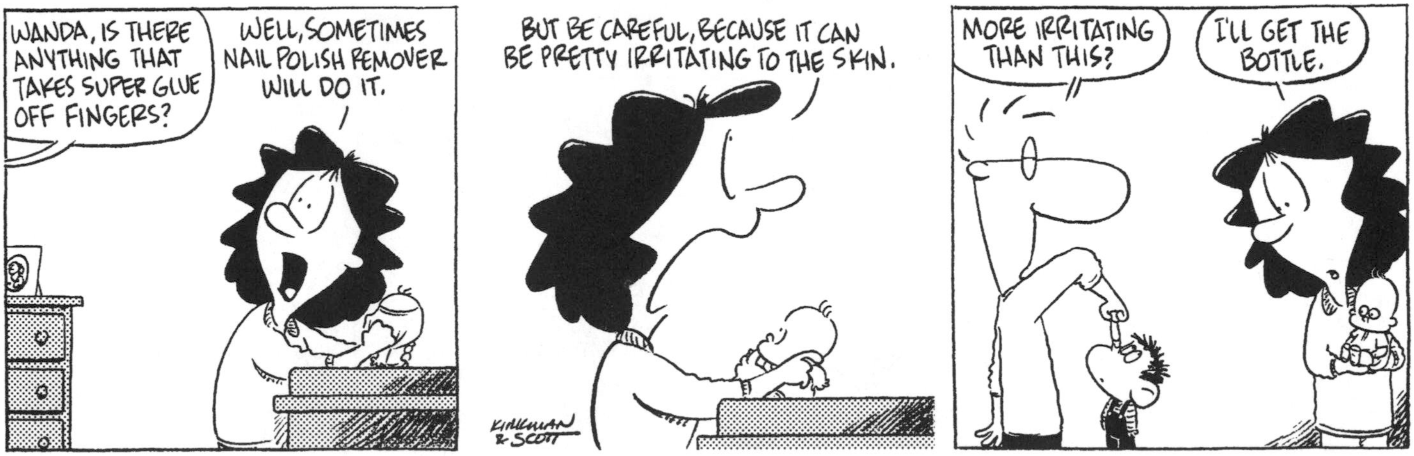
WANDA, IS THERE ANYTHING THAT TAKES SUPER GLUE OFF FINGERS?
WELL, SOMETIMES NAIL POLISH REMOVER WILL DO IT.
BUT BE CAREFUL, BECAUSE IT CAN BE PRETTY IRRITATING TO THE SKIN.
KIRKMAN & SCOTT
MORE IRRITATING THAN THIS?
I'LL GET THE BOTTLE.

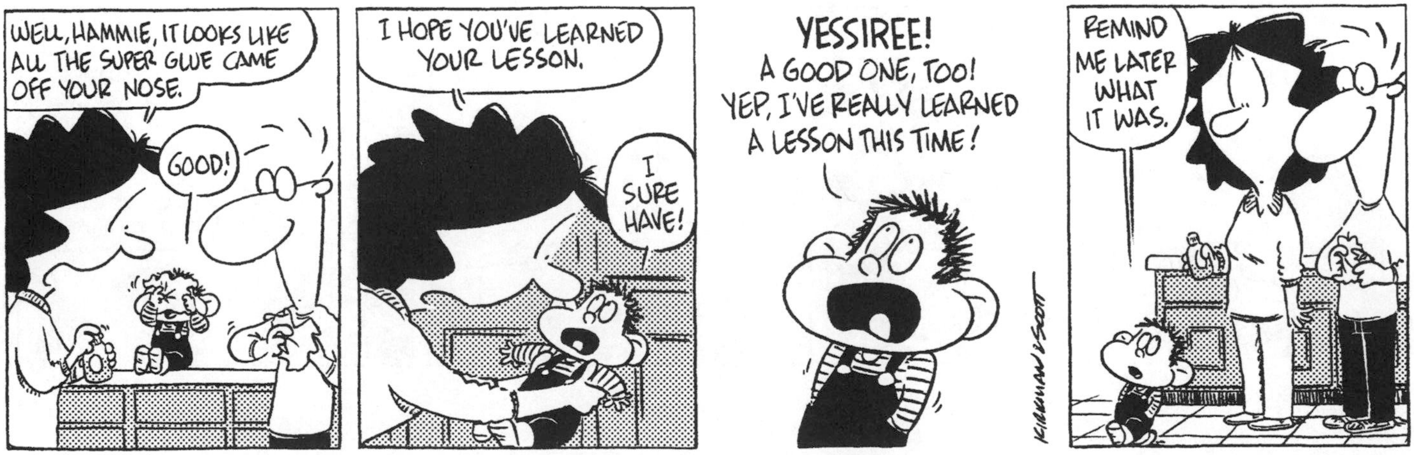
WELL, HAMMIE, IT LOOKS LIKE ALL THE SUPER GLUE CAME OFF YOUR NOSE.
GOOD!
I HOPE YOU'VE LEARNED YOUR LESSON.
I SURE HAVE!
YESSIREE!
A GOOD ONE, TOO!
YEP, I'VE REALLY LEARNED A LESSON THIS TIME!
KIRKMAN & SCOTT
REMIND ME LATER WHAT IT WAS.

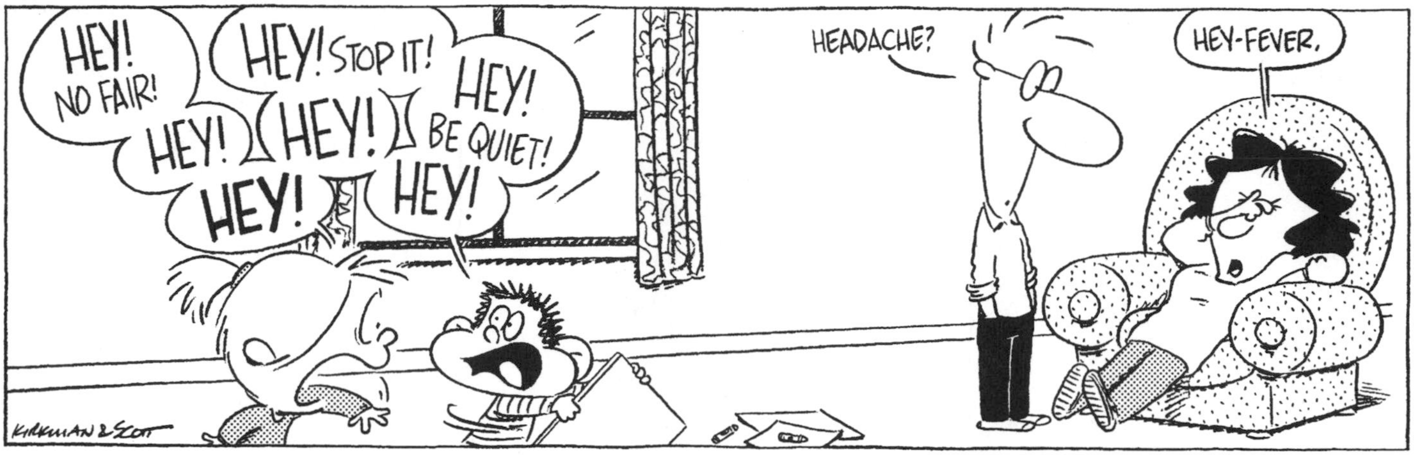
HEY! NO FAIR!
HEY! STOP IT!
HEY! BE QUIET!
HEY!
(HEY!)
HEY!
HEY!
KIRKMAN & SCOTT
HEADACHE?
HEY-FEVER.

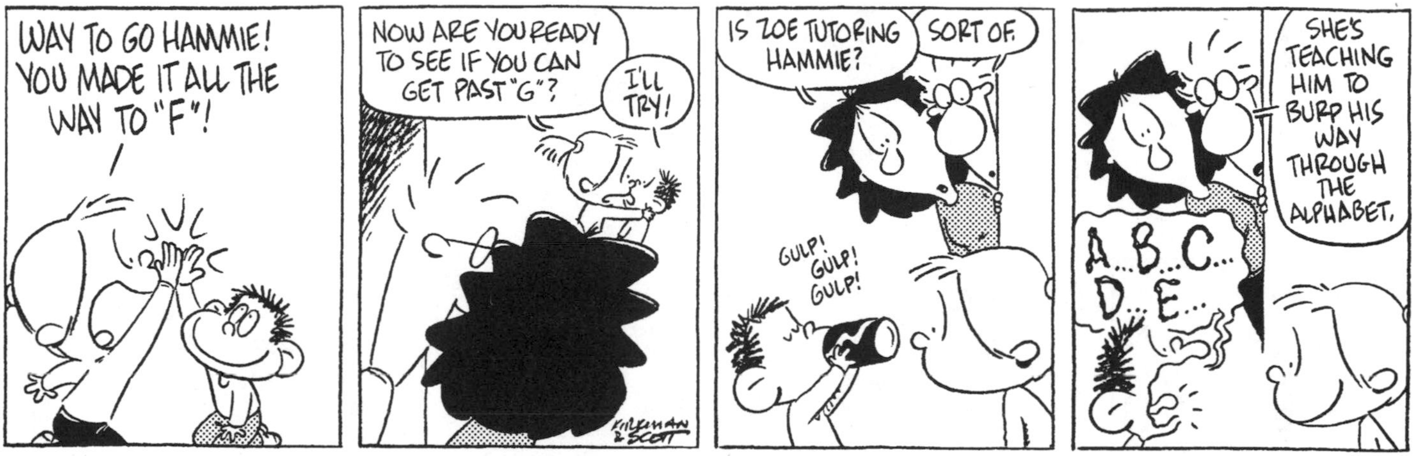
WAY TO GO HAMMIE! YOU MADE IT ALL THE WAY TO "F"!
NOW ARE YOU READY TO SEE IF YOU CAN GET PAST "G"?
I'LL TRY!
KIRKMAN & SCOTT
IS ZOE TUTORING HAMMIE?
SORT OF.
GULP! GULP! GULP!
SHE'S TEACHING HIM TO BURP HIS WAY THROUGH THE ALPHABET.
A...B...C... D...E...

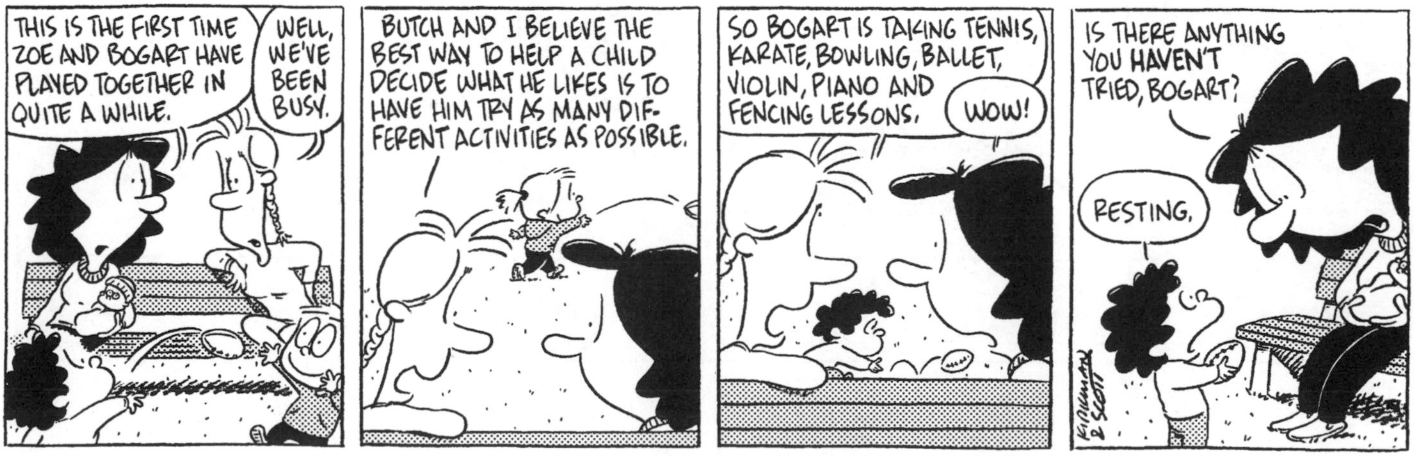
THIS IS THE FIRST TIME ZOE AND BOGART HAVE PLAYED TOGETHER IN QUITE A WHILE.
WELL, WE'VE BEEN BUSY.
BUTCH AND I BELIEVE THE BEST WAY TO HELP A CHILD DECIDE WHAT HE LIKES IS TO HAVE HIM TRY AS MANY DIFFERENT ACTIVITIES AS POSSIBLE.
SO BOGART IS TAKING TENNIS, KARATE, BOWLING, BALLET, VIOLIN, PIANO AND FENCING LESSONS.
WOW!
IS THERE ANYTHING YOU HAVEN'T TRIED, BOGART?
RESTING.
KIRKMAN & SCOTT

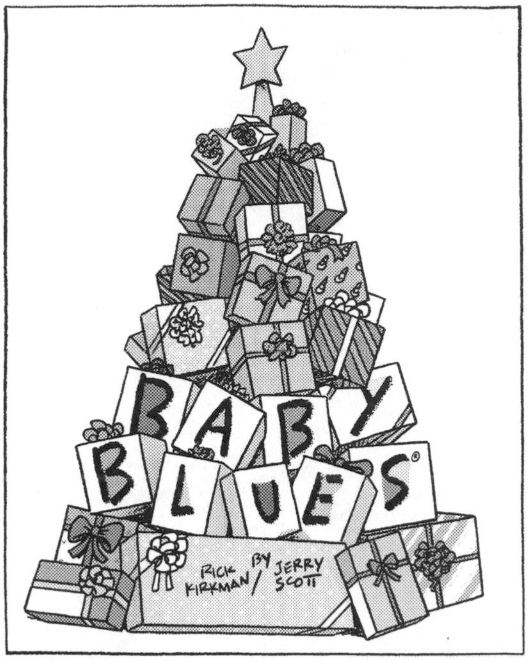
BABY BLUES®
BY RICK KIRKMAN / JERRY SCOTT

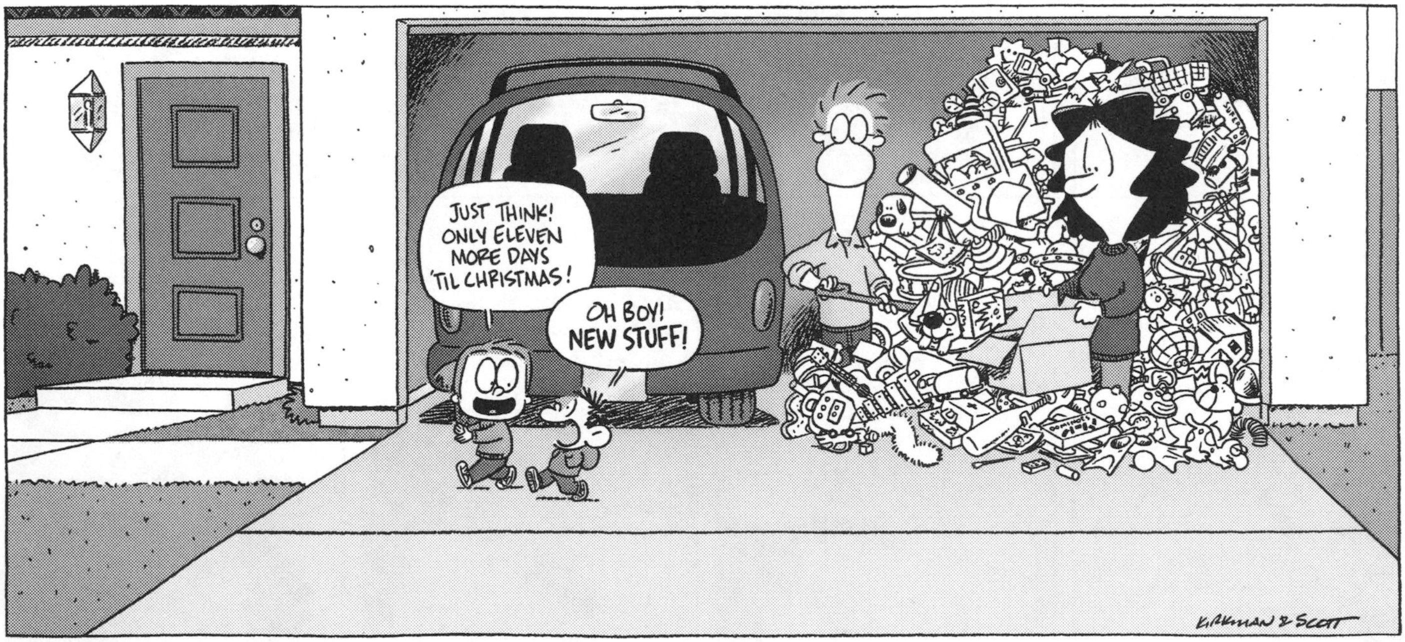
JUST THINK! ONLY ELEVEN MORE DAYS 'TIL CHRISTMAS!
OH BOY! NEW STUFF!
KIRKMAN & SCOTT

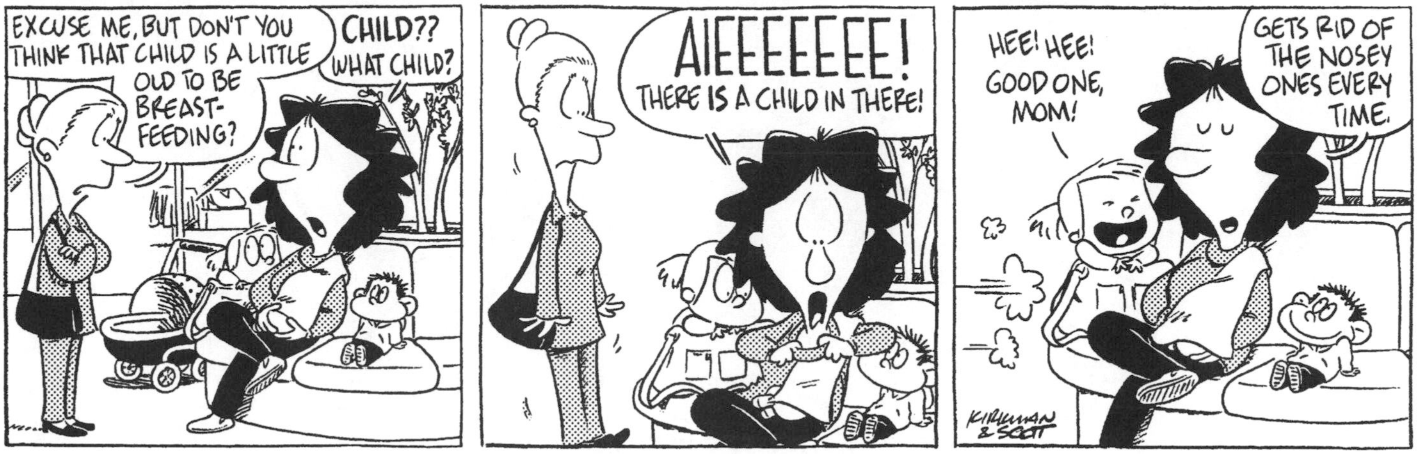
EXCUSE ME, BUT DON'T YOU THINK THAT CHILD IS A LITTLE OLD TO BE BREAST-FEEDING?
CHILD?? WHAT CHILD?
AIEEEEEEEE! THERE IS A CHILD IN THERE!
HEE! HEE! GOOD ONE, MOM!
GETS RID OF THE NOSEY ONES EVERY TIME.
KIRKMAN & SCOTT

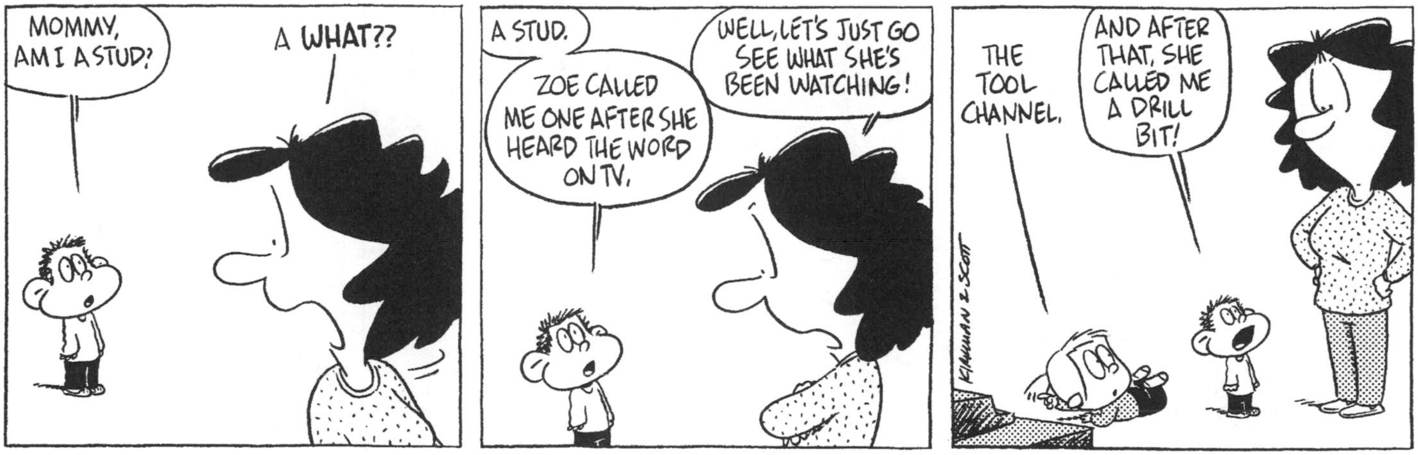
MOMMY, AM I A STUD?
A WHAT??
A STUD.
ZOE CALLED ME ONE AFTER SHE HEARD THE WORD ON TV.
WELL, LET'S JUST GO SEE WHAT SHE'S BEEN WATCHING!
THE TOOL CHANNEL.
AND AFTER THAT, SHE CALLED ME A DRILL BIT!
KIRKMAN & SCOTT

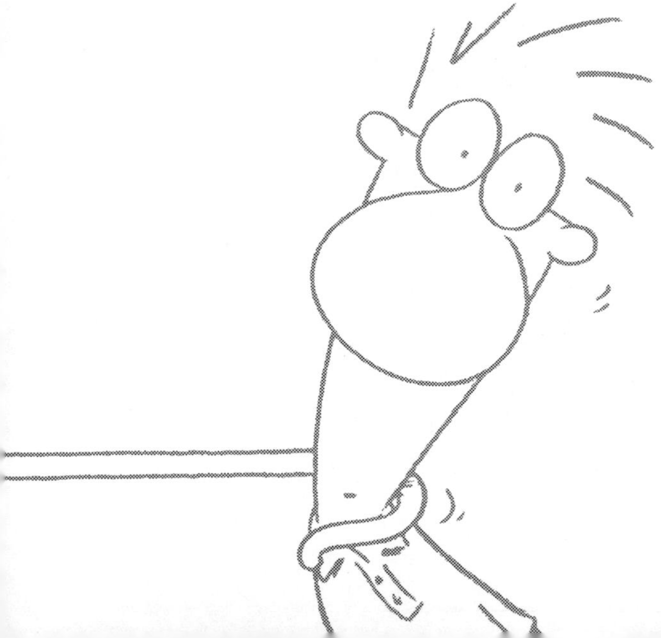

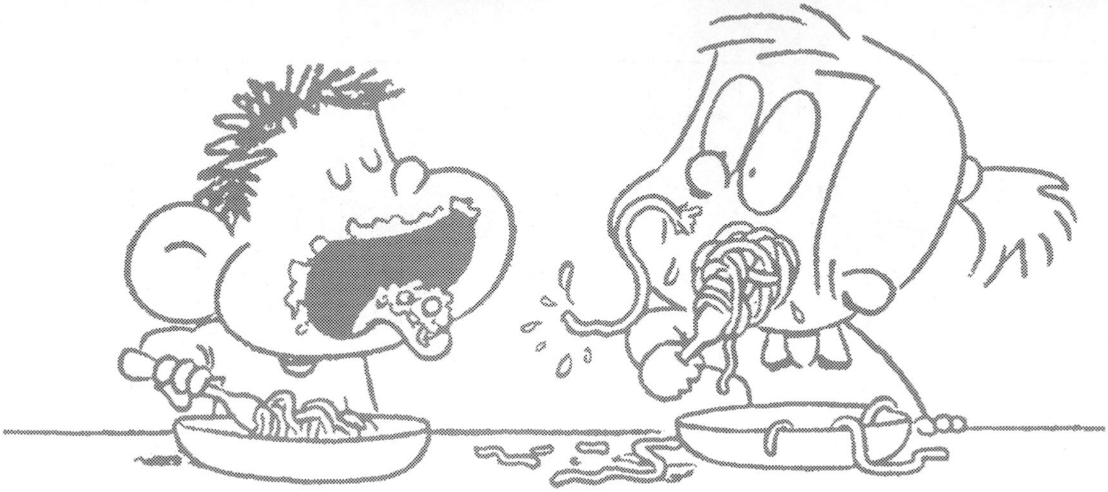

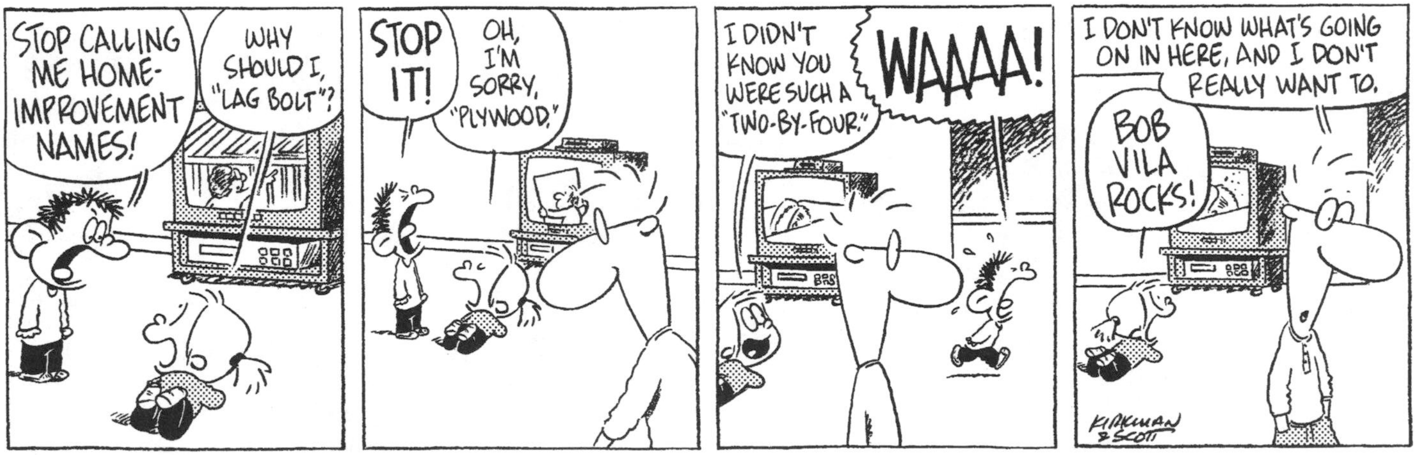
STOP CALLING ME HOME-IMPROVEMENT NAMES!
WHY SHOULD I, "LAG BOLT"?
STOP IT!
OH, I'M SORRY, "PLYWOOD."
I DIDN'T KNOW YOU WERE SUCH A "TWO-BY-FOUR."
WAAAA!
I DON'T KNOW WHAT'S GOING ON IN HERE, AND I DON'T REALLY WANT TO.
BOB VILA ROCKS!
KIRKMAN & SCOTT

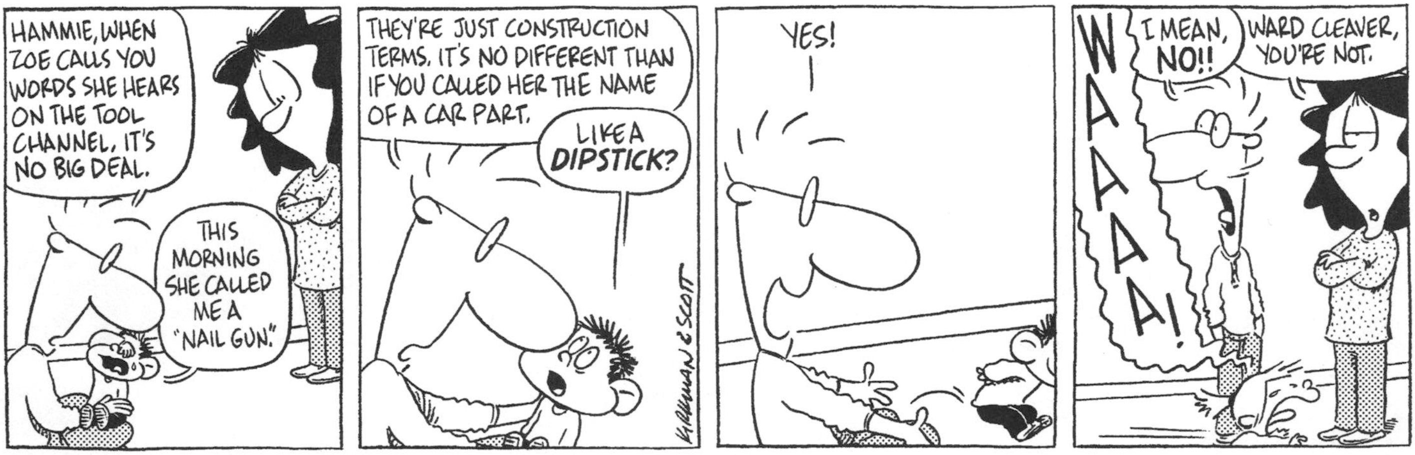
HAMMIE, WHEN ZOE CALLS YOU WORDS SHE HEARS ON THE TOOL CHANNEL, IT'S NO BIG DEAL.
THIS MORNING SHE CALLED ME A "NAIL GUN."
THEY'RE JUST CONSTRUCTION TERMS. IT'S NO DIFFERENT THAN IF YOU CALLED HER THE NAME OF A CAR PART.
LIKE A DIPSTICK?
KIRKMAN & SCOTT
YES!
I MEAN, NO!!
WARD CLEAVER, YOU'RE NOT.
WAAAAA!

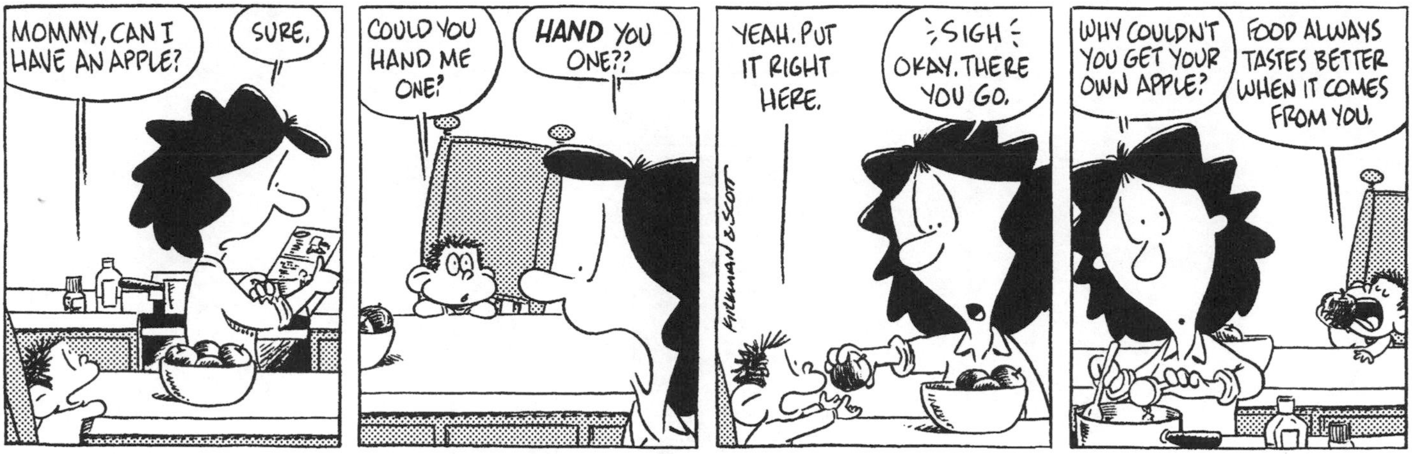
MOMMY, CAN I HAVE AN APPLE?
SURE.
COULD YOU HAND ME ONE?
HAND YOU ONE??
KIRKMAN & SCOTT
YEAH. PUT IT RIGHT HERE.
SIGH
OKAY. THERE YOU GO.
WHY COULDN'T YOU GET YOUR OWN APPLE?
FOOD ALWAYS TASTES BETTER WHEN IT COMES FROM YOU.

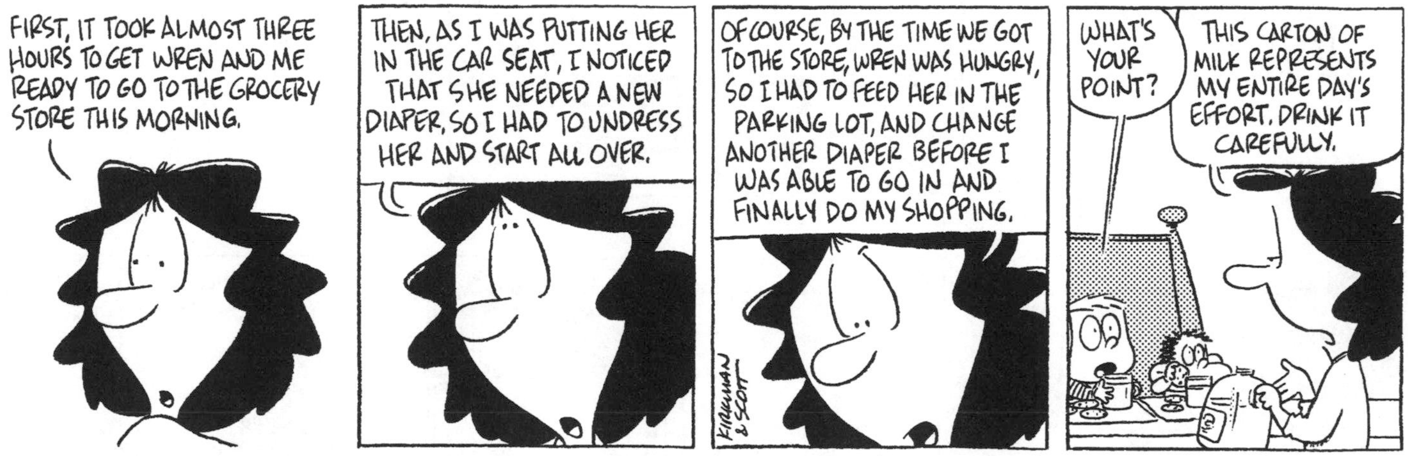
FIRST, IT TOOK ALMOST THREE HOURS TO GET WREN AND ME READY TO GO TO THE GROCERY STORE THIS MORNING.
THEN, AS I WAS PUTTING HER IN THE CAR SEAT, I NOTICED THAT SHE NEEDED A NEW DIAPER, SO I HAD TO UNDRESS HER AND START ALL OVER.
OF COURSE, BY THE TIME WE GOT TO THE STORE, WREN WAS HUNGRY, SO I HAD TO FEED HER IN THE PARKING LOT, AND CHANGE ANOTHER DIAPER BEFORE I WAS ABLE TO GO IN AND FINALLY DO MY SHOPPING.
KIRKMAN & SCOTT
WHAT'S YOUR POINT?
THIS CARTON OF MILK REPRESENTS MY ENTIRE DAY'S EFFORT. DRINK IT CAREFULLY.

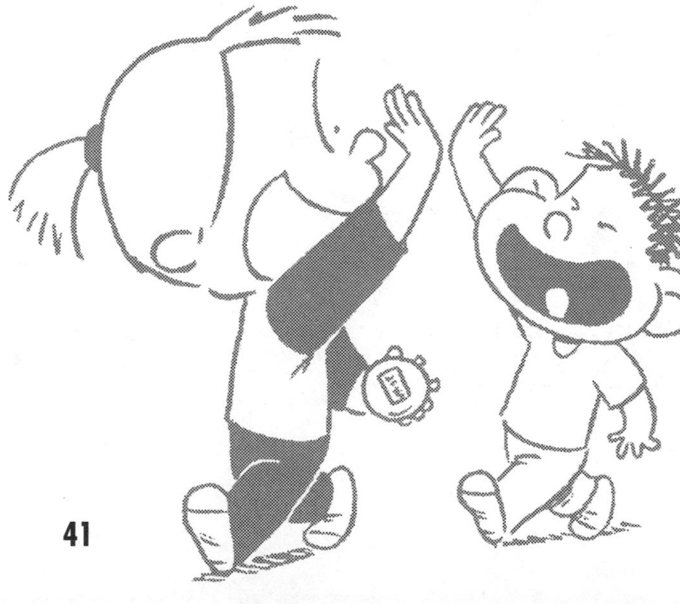

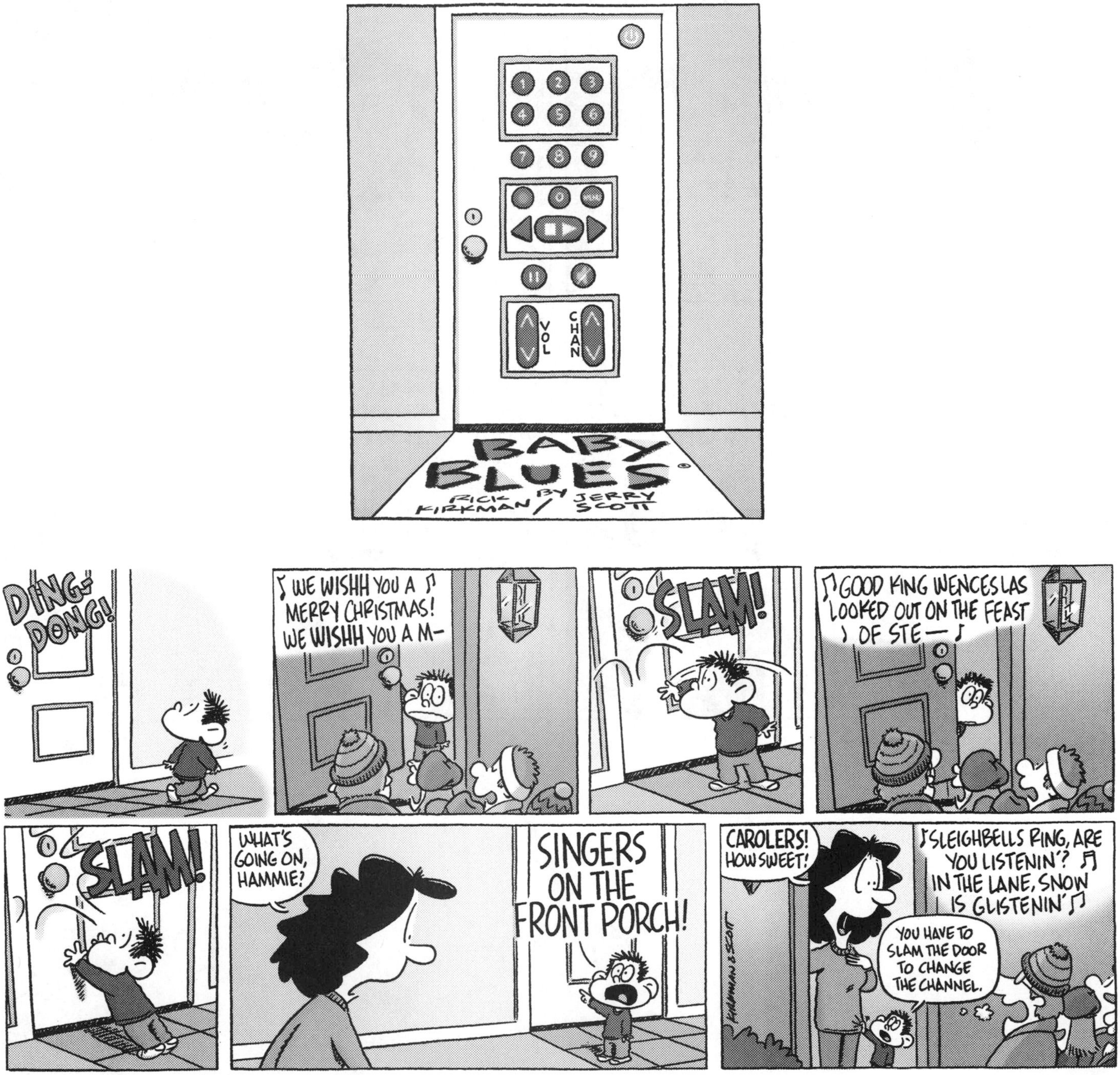
VOL
CHAN
BABY BLUES®
BY RICK KIRKMAN / JERRY SCOTT
DING-DONG!
WE WISHH YOU A MERRY CHRISTMAS! WE WISHH YOU A M—
SLAM!
GOOD KING WENCESLAS LOOKED OUT ON THE FEAST OF STE—
SLAM!
WHAT'S GOING ON, HAMMIE?
SINGERS ON THE FRONT PORCH!
CAROLERS! HOW SWEET!
SLEIGHBELLS RING, ARE YOU LISTENIN'? IN THE LANE, SNOW IS GLISTENIN'
YOU HAVE TO SLAM THE DOOR TO CHANGE THE CHANNEL.

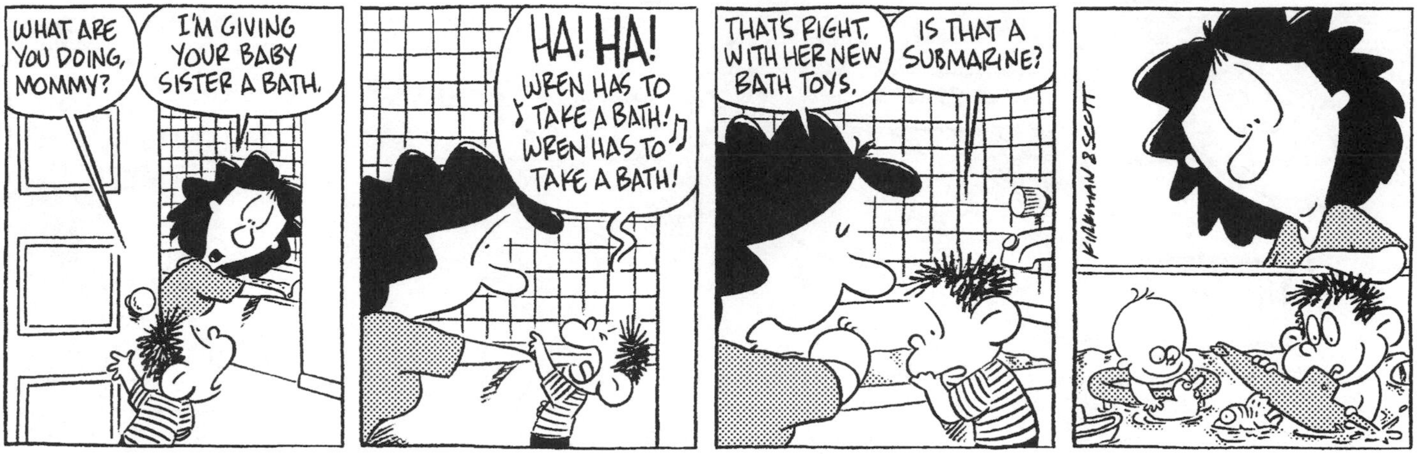
WHAT ARE YOU DOING, MOMMY?
I'M GIVING YOUR BABY SISTER A BATH.
HA! HA! WREN HAS TO TAKE A BATH! WREN HAS TO TAKE A BATH!
THAT'S RIGHT, WITH HER NEW BATH TOYS.
IS THAT A SUBMARINE?
KIRKMAN & SCOTT

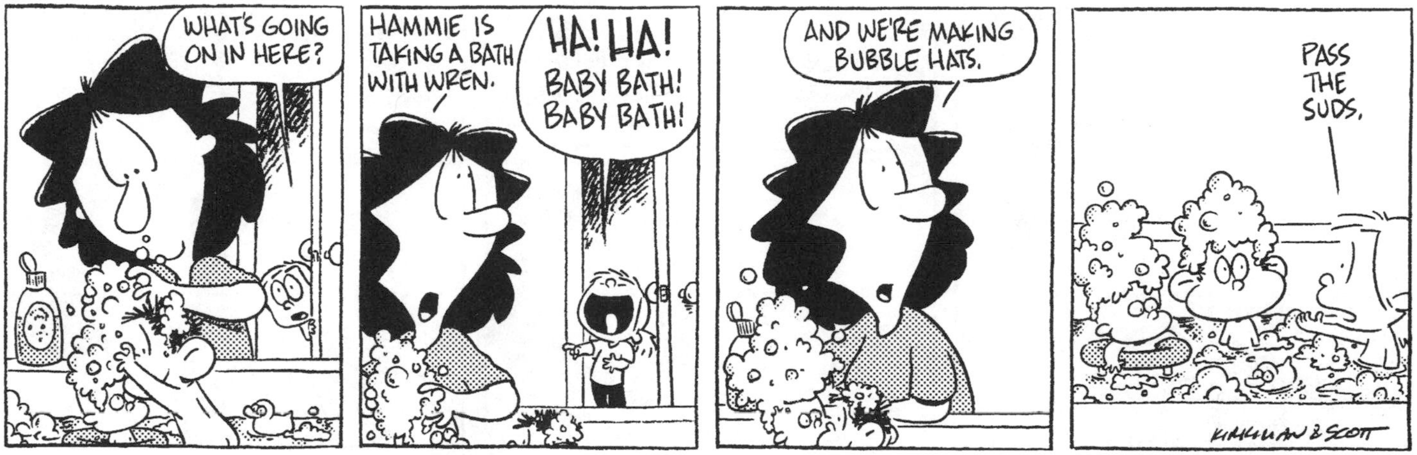
WHAT'S GOING ON IN HERE?
HAMMIE IS TAKING A BATH WITH WREN.
HA! HA! BABY BATH! BABY BATH!
AND WE'RE MAKING BUBBLE HATS.
PASS THE SUDS.
KIRKMAN & SCOTT

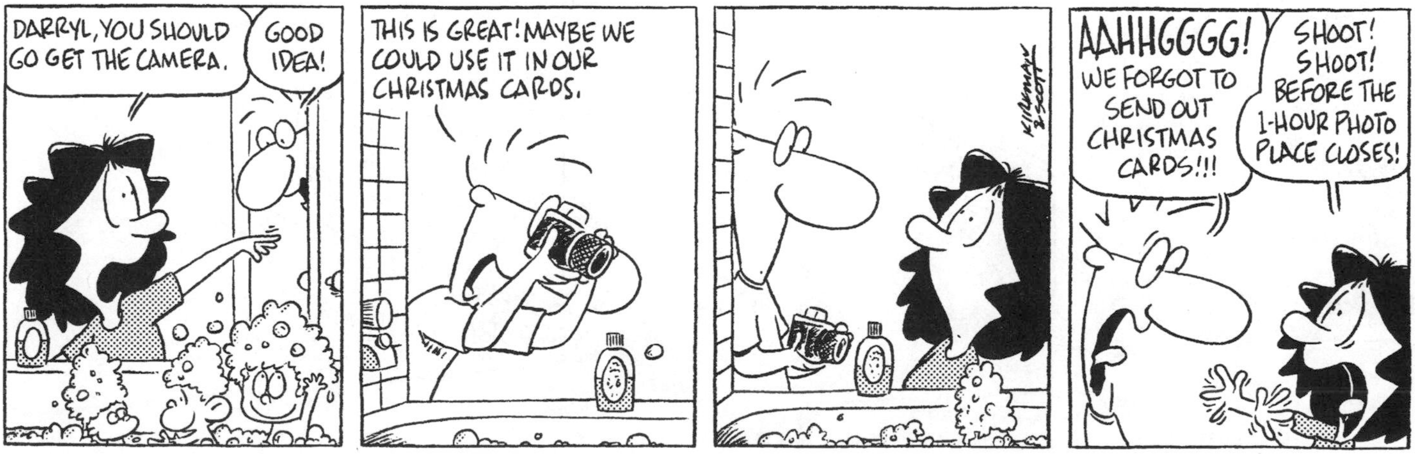
DARRYL, YOU SHOULD GO GET THE CAMERA.
GOOD IDEA!
THIS IS GREAT! MAYBE WE COULD USE IT IN OUR CHRISTMAS CARDS.
KIRKMAN & SCOTT
AAHHGGGG! WE FORGOT TO SEND OUT CHRISTMAS CARDS!!!
SHOOT! SHOOT! BEFORE THE 1-HOUR PHOTO PLACE CLOSES!

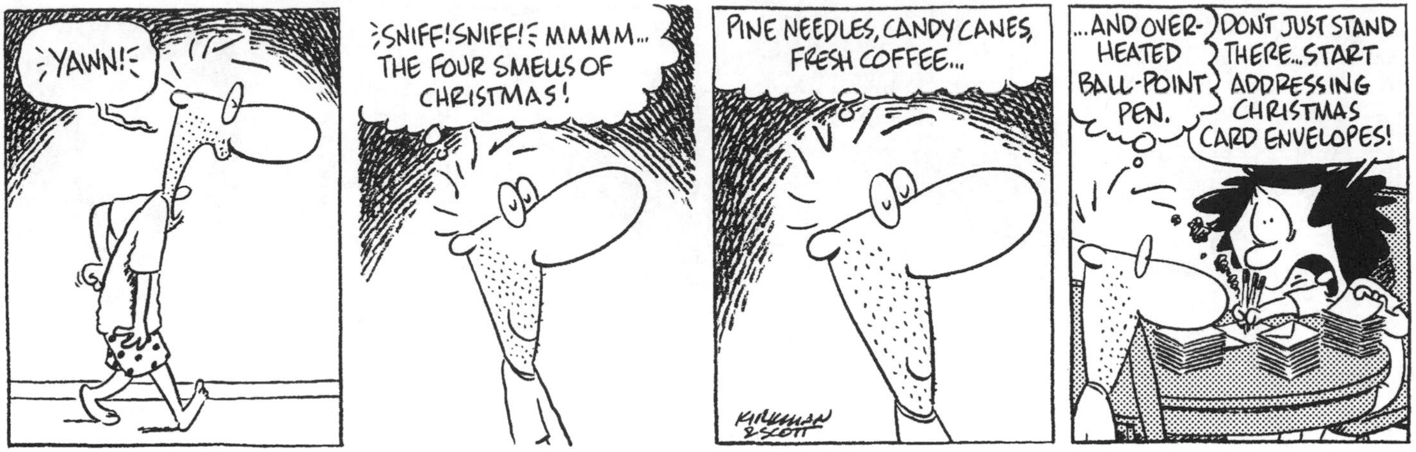
YAWN!
SNIFF! SNIFF! MMMM... THE FOUR SMELLS OF CHRISTMAS!
PINE NEEDLES, CANDY CANES, FRESH COFFEE...
KIRKMAN & SCOTT
...AND OVER-HEATED BALL-POINT PEN.
DON'T JUST STAND THERE...START ADDRESSING CHRISTMAS CARD ENVELOPES!

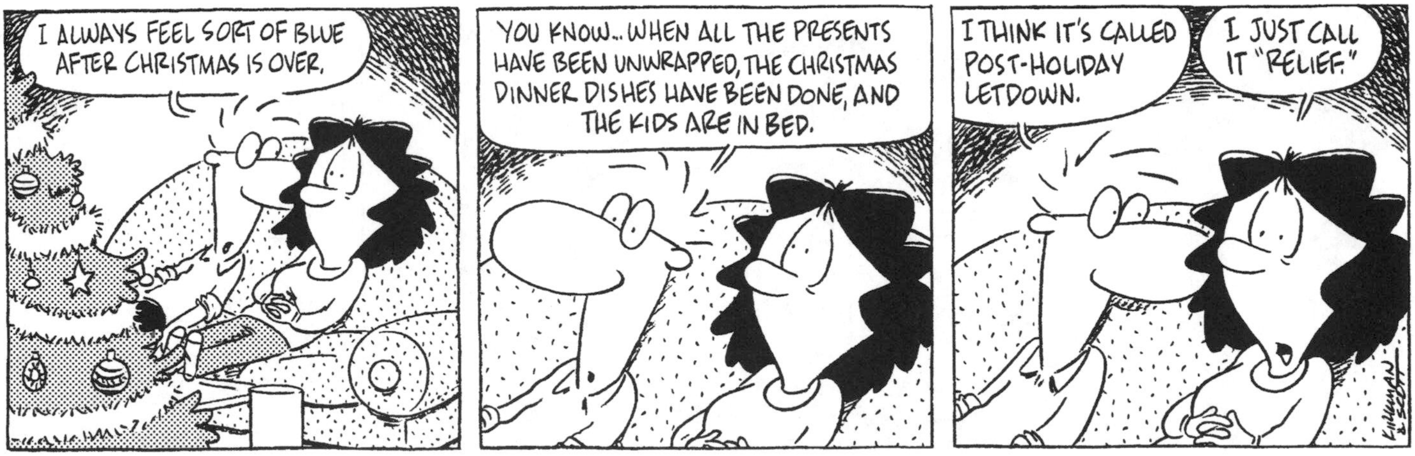
I ALWAYS FEEL SORT OF BLUE AFTER CHRISTMAS IS OVER.
YOU KNOW... WHEN ALL THE PRESENTS HAVE BEEN UNWRAPPED, THE CHRISTMAS DINNER DISHES HAVE BEEN DONE, AND THE KIDS ARE IN BED.
I THINK IT'S CALLED POST-HOLIDAY LETDOWN.
I JUST CALL IT "RELIEF."
KIRKMAN & SCOTT

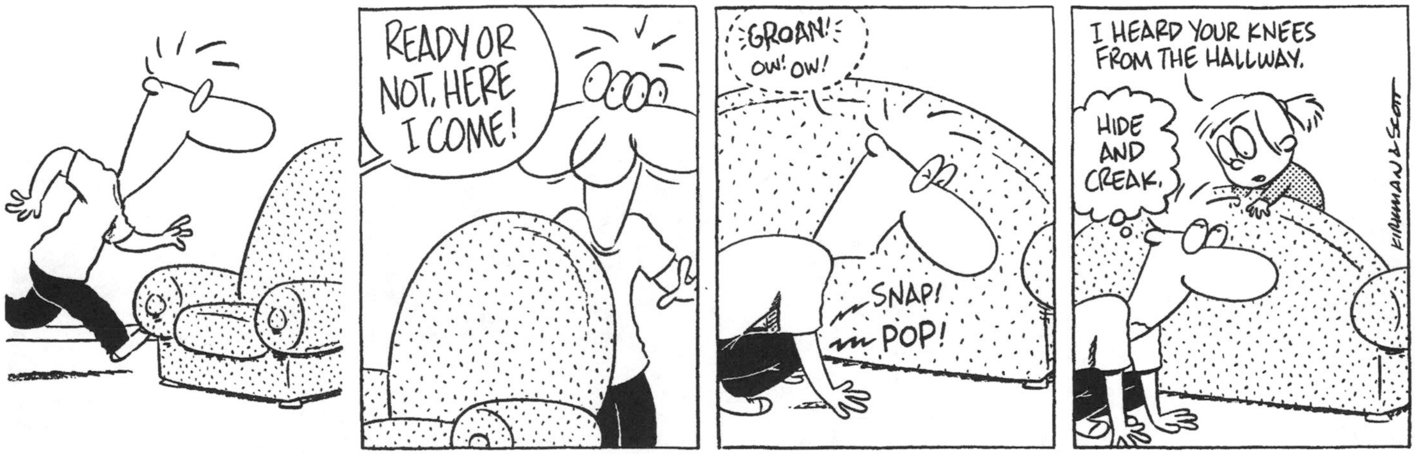
READY OR NOT, HERE I COME!
GROAN! OW! OW!
SNAP!
POP!
I HEARD YOUR KNEES FROM THE HALLWAY.
HIDE AND CREAK.
KIRKMAN & SCOTT

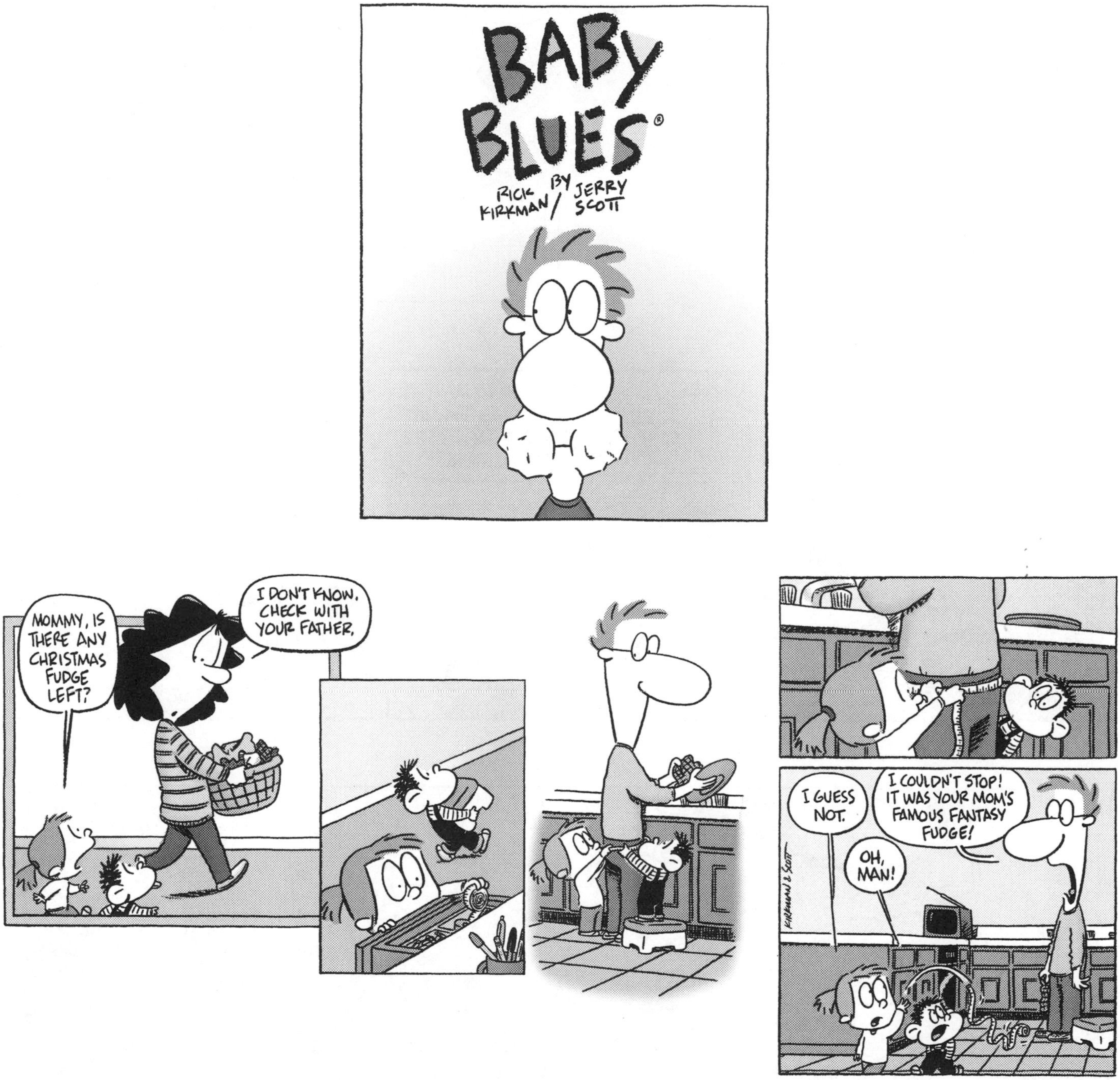
BABY BLUES®
BY RICK KIRKMAN / JERRY SCOTT
MOMMY, IS THERE ANY CHRISTMAS FUDGE LEFT?
I DON'T KNOW. CHECK WITH YOUR FATHER.
I GUESS NOT.
I COULDN'T STOP! IT WAS YOUR MOM'S FAMOUS FANTASY FUDGE!
OH, MAN!

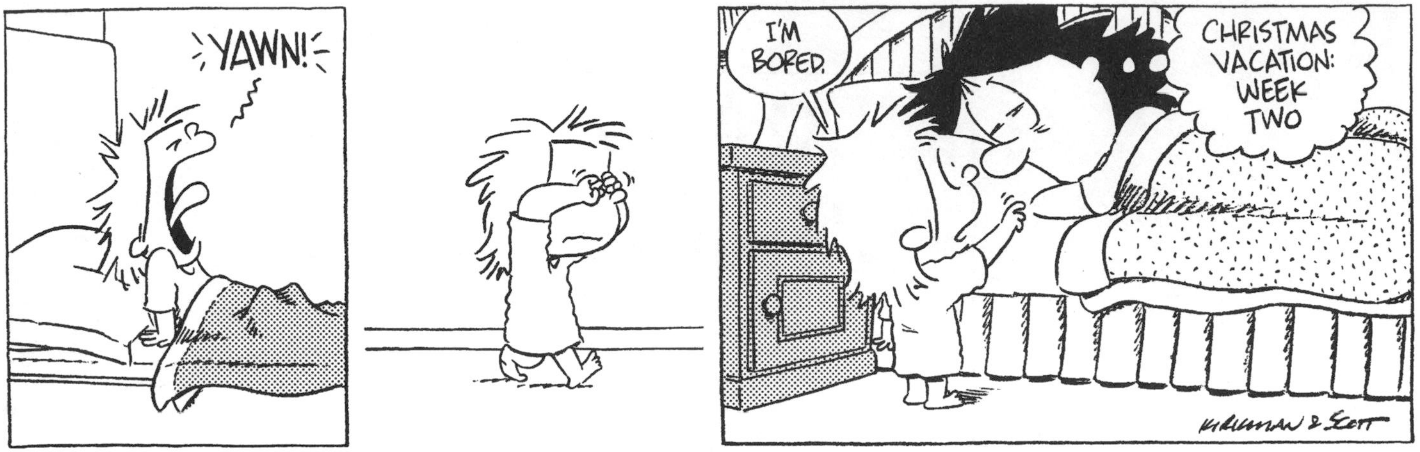
YAWN!
I'M BORED.
CHRISTMAS VACATION: WEEK TWO
KIRKMAN & SCOTT

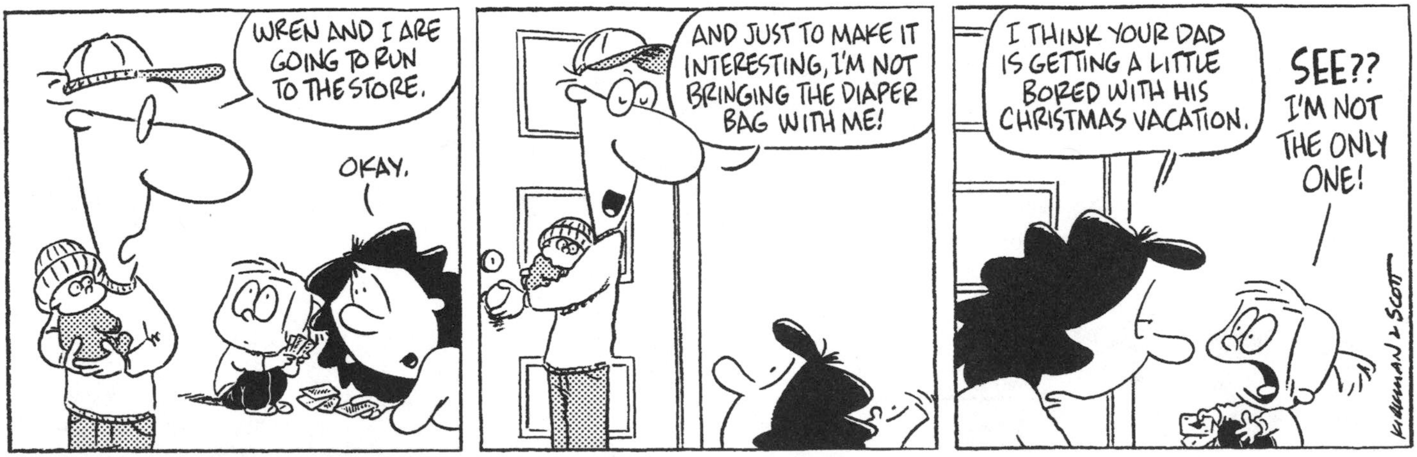
WREN AND I ARE GOING TO RUN TO THE STORE.
OKAY.
AND JUST TO MAKE IT INTERESTING, I'M NOT BRINGING THE DIAPER BAG WITH ME!
I THINK YOUR DAD IS GETTING A LITTLE BORED WITH HIS CHRISTMAS VACATION.
SEE?? I'M NOT THE ONLY ONE!
KIRKMAN & SCOTT

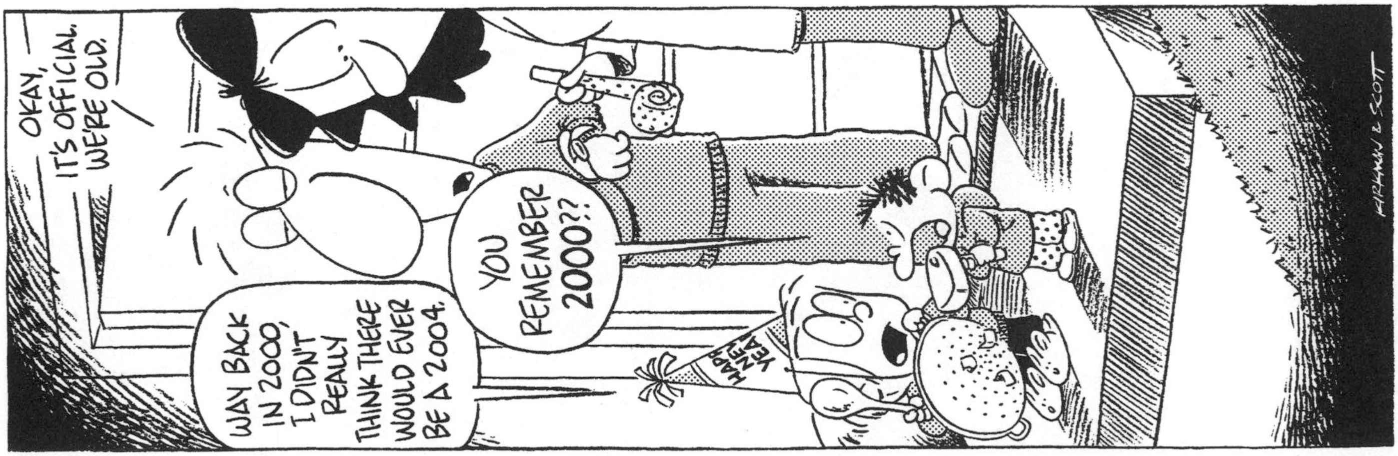
WAY BACK IN 2000, I DIDN'T REALLY THINK THERE WOULD EVER BE A 2004.
YOU REMEMBER 2000??
OKAY, IT'S OFFICIAL. WE'RE OLD.
KIRKMAN & SCOTT

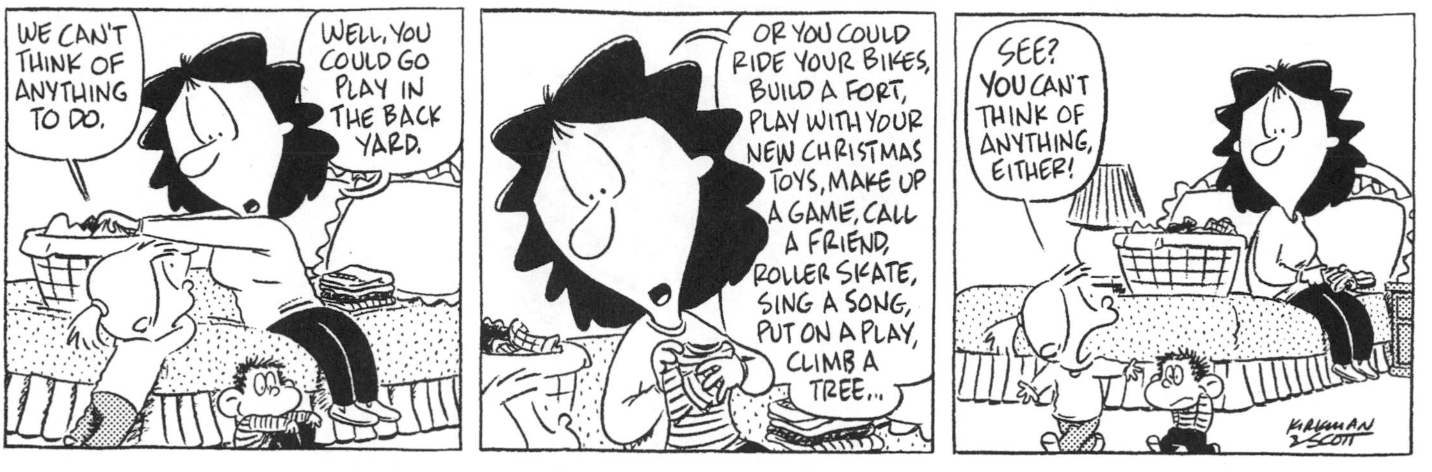
WE CAN'T THINK OF ANYTHING TO DO.
WELL, YOU COULD GO PLAY IN THE BACK YARD.
OR YOU COULD RIDE YOUR BIKES, BUILD A FORT, PLAY WITH YOUR NEW CHRISTMAS TOYS, MAKE UP A GAME, CALL A FRIEND, ROLLER SKATE, SING A SONG, PUT ON A PLAY, CLIMB A TREE...
SEE? **YOU** CAN'T THINK OF ANYTHING, EITHER!
KIRKMAN & SCOTT

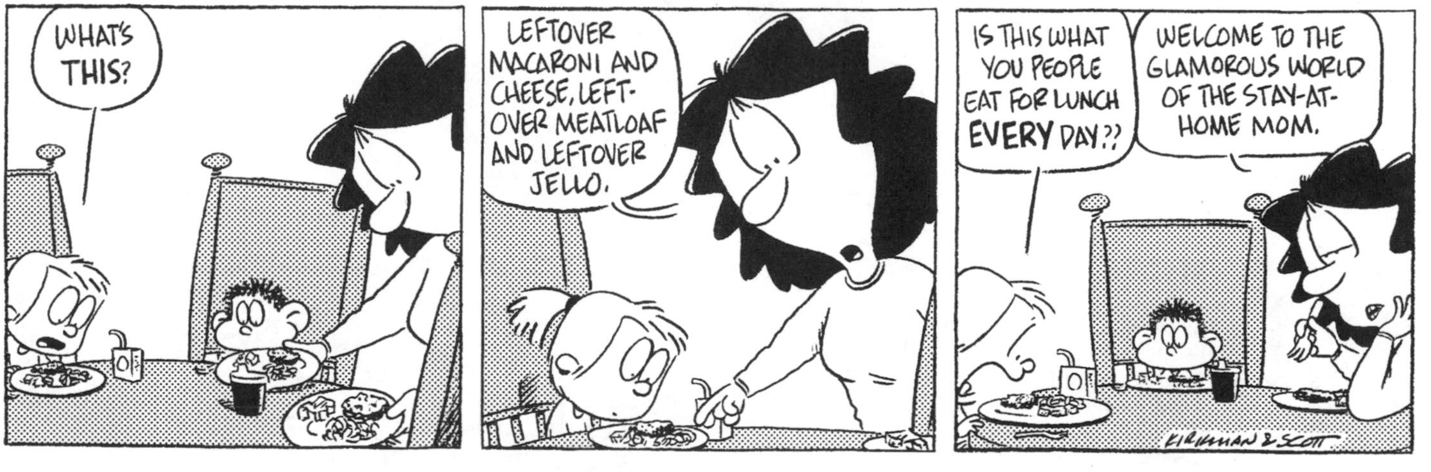
WHAT'S **THIS**?
LEFTOVER MACARONI AND CHEESE, LEFT-OVER MEATLOAF AND LEFTOVER JELLO.
IS THIS WHAT YOU PEOPLE EAT FOR LUNCH **EVERY** DAY??
WELCOME TO THE GLAMOROUS WORLD OF THE STAY-AT-HOME MOM.
KIRKMAN & SCOTT

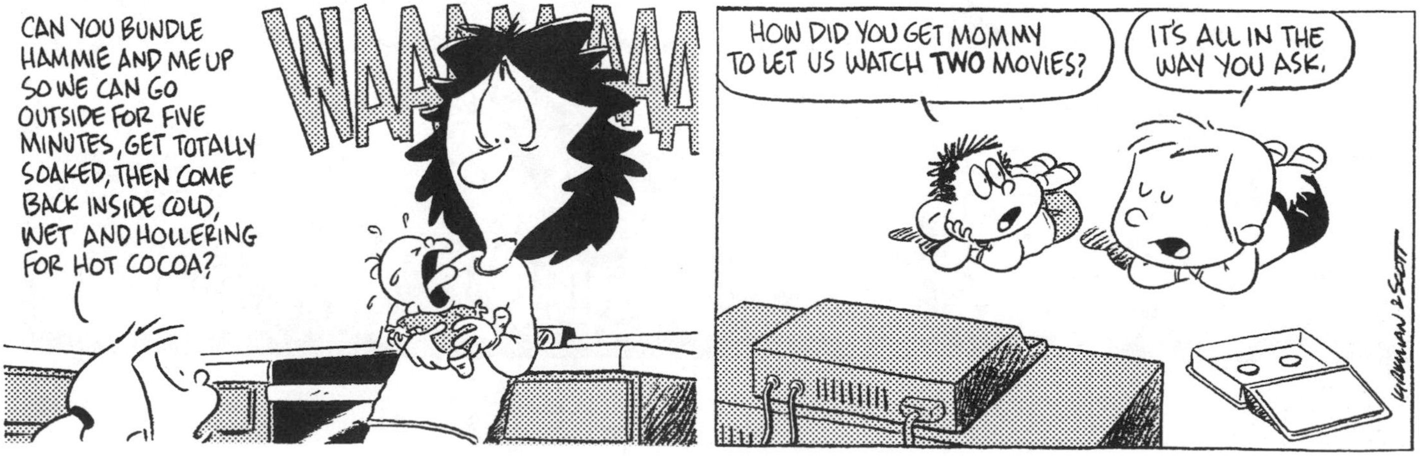
CAN YOU BUNDLE HAMMIE AND ME UP SO WE CAN GO OUTSIDE FOR FIVE MINUTES, GET TOTALLY SOAKED, THEN COME BACK INSIDE COLD, WET AND HOLLERING FOR HOT COCOA?
WAAAAAAA
HOW DID YOU GET MOMMY TO LET US WATCH **TWO** MOVIES?
IT'S ALL IN THE WAY YOU ASK.
KIRKMAN & SCOTT

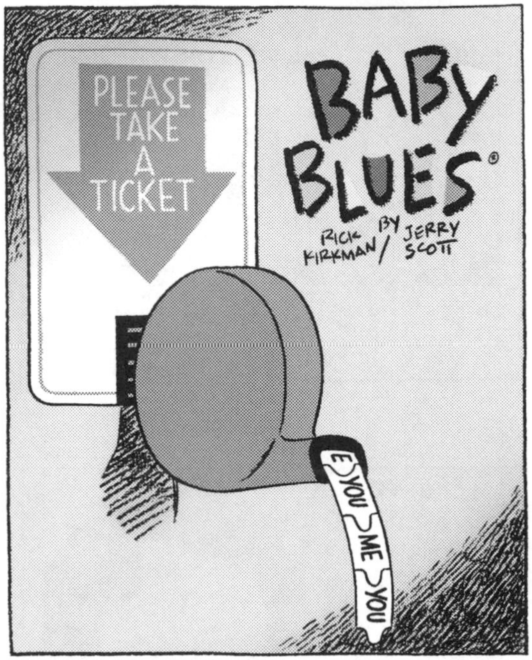
PLEASE TAKE A TICKET
BABY BLUES®
BY RICK KIRKMAN / JERRY SCOTT
YOU ME YOU

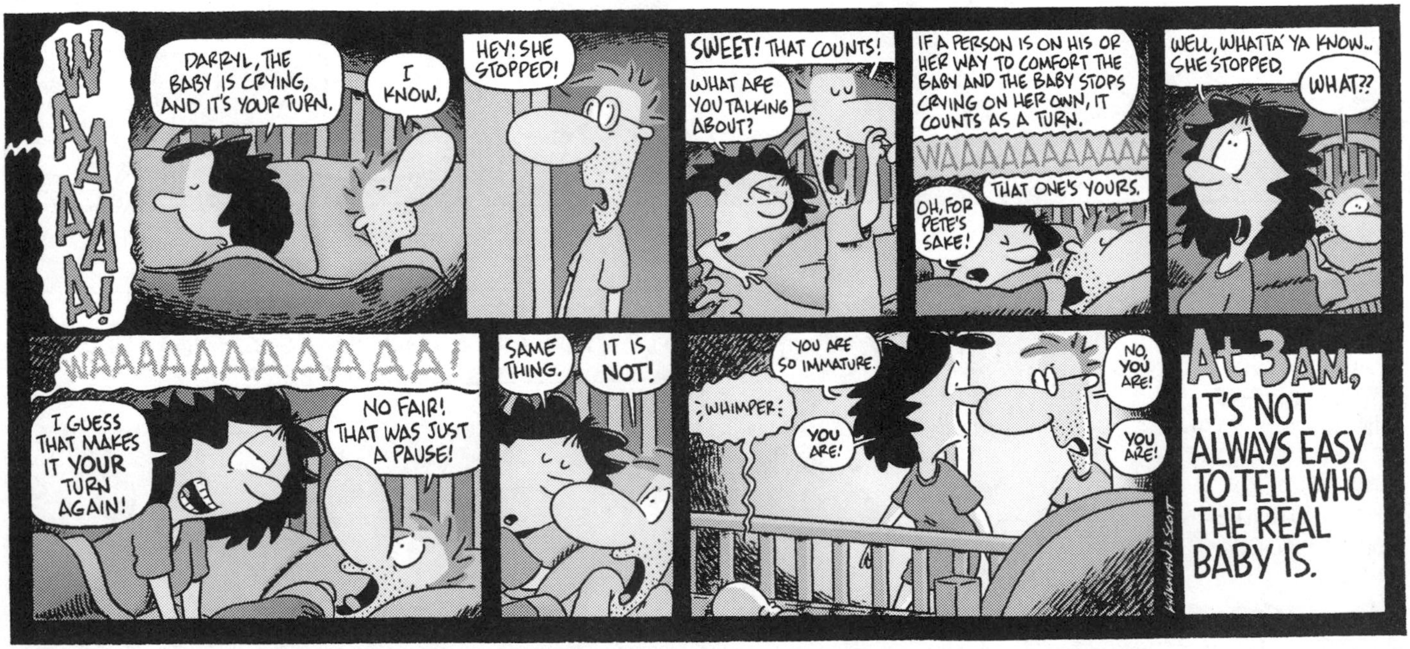
WAAAA!
DARRYL, THE BABY IS CRYING, AND IT'S YOUR TURN.
I KNOW.
HEY! SHE STOPPED!
SWEET! THAT COUNTS!
WHAT ARE YOU TALKING ABOUT?
IF A PERSON IS ON HIS OR HER WAY TO COMFORT THE BABY AND THE BABY STOPS CRYING ON HER OWN, IT COUNTS AS A TURN.
WAAAAAAAAAAA
THAT ONE'S YOURS.
OH, FOR PETE'S SAKE!
WELL, WHATTA' YA KNOW.. SHE STOPPED.
WHAT??
WAAAAAAAAAAAA!
I GUESS THAT MAKES IT YOUR TURN AGAIN!
NO FAIR! THAT WAS JUST A PAUSE!
SAME THING.
IT IS NOT!
YOU ARE SO IMMATURE.
NO, YOU ARE!
WHIMPER
YOU ARE!
YOU ARE!
At 3AM, IT'S NOT ALWAYS EASY TO TELL WHO THE REAL BABY IS.

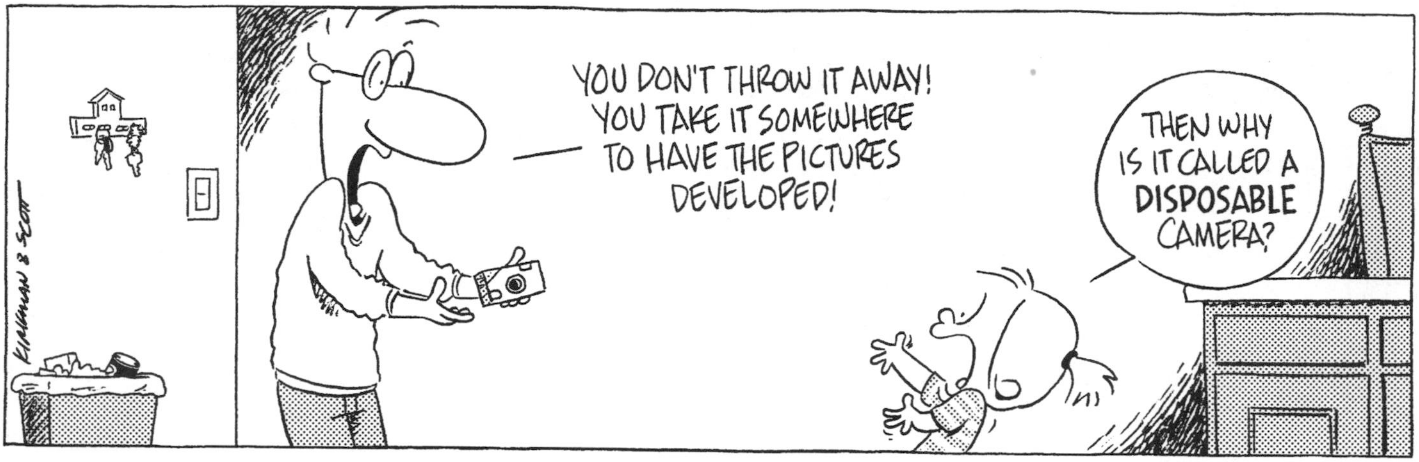
KIRKMAN & SCOTT
YOU DON'T THROW IT AWAY! YOU TAKE IT SOMEWHERE TO HAVE THE PICTURES DEVELOPED!
THEN WHY IS IT CALLED A **DISPOSABLE** CAMERA?

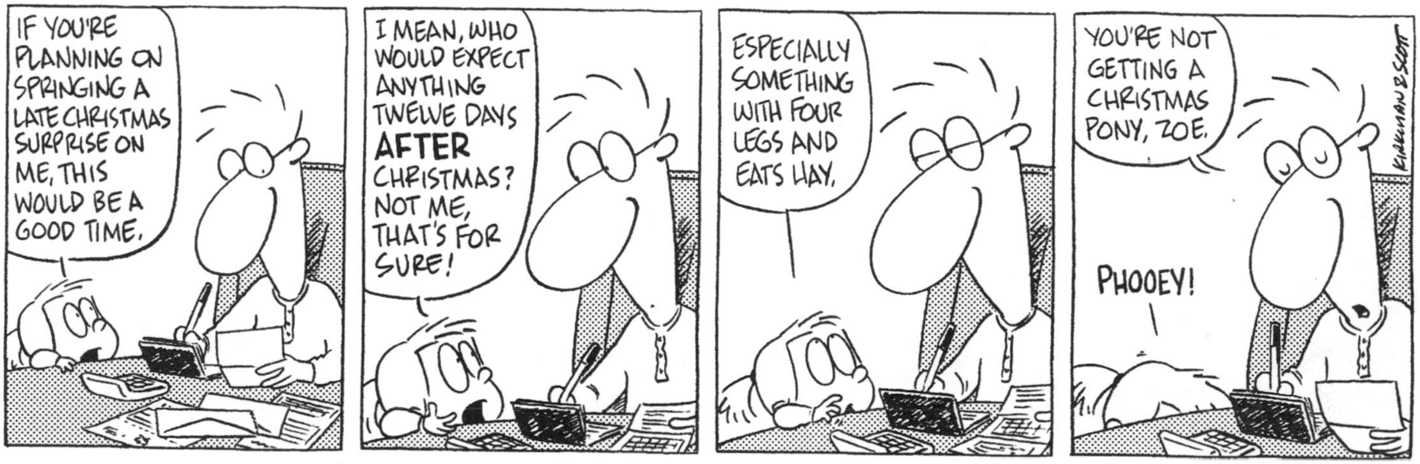
IF YOU'RE PLANNING ON SPRINGING A LATE CHRISTMAS SURPRISE ON ME, THIS WOULD BE A GOOD TIME.
I MEAN, WHO WOULD EXPECT ANYTHING TWELVE DAYS **AFTER** CHRISTMAS? NOT ME, THAT'S FOR SURE!
ESPECIALLY SOMETHING WITH FOUR LEGS AND EATS HAY.
YOU'RE NOT GETTING A CHRISTMAS PONY, ZOE.
PHOOEY!
KIRKMAN & SCOTT

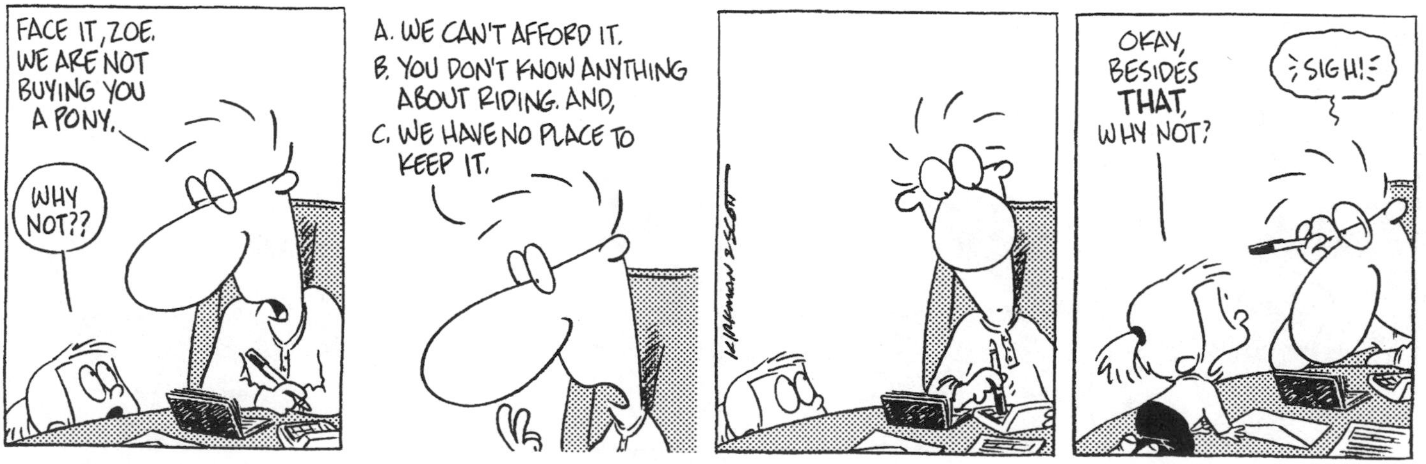
FACE IT, ZOE. WE ARE NOT BUYING YOU A PONY.
WHY NOT??
A. WE CAN'T AFFORD IT.
B. YOU DON'T KNOW ANYTHING ABOUT RIDING. AND,
C. WE HAVE NO PLACE TO KEEP IT.
KIRKMAN & SCOTT
OKAY, BESIDES **THAT**, WHY NOT?
SIGH!

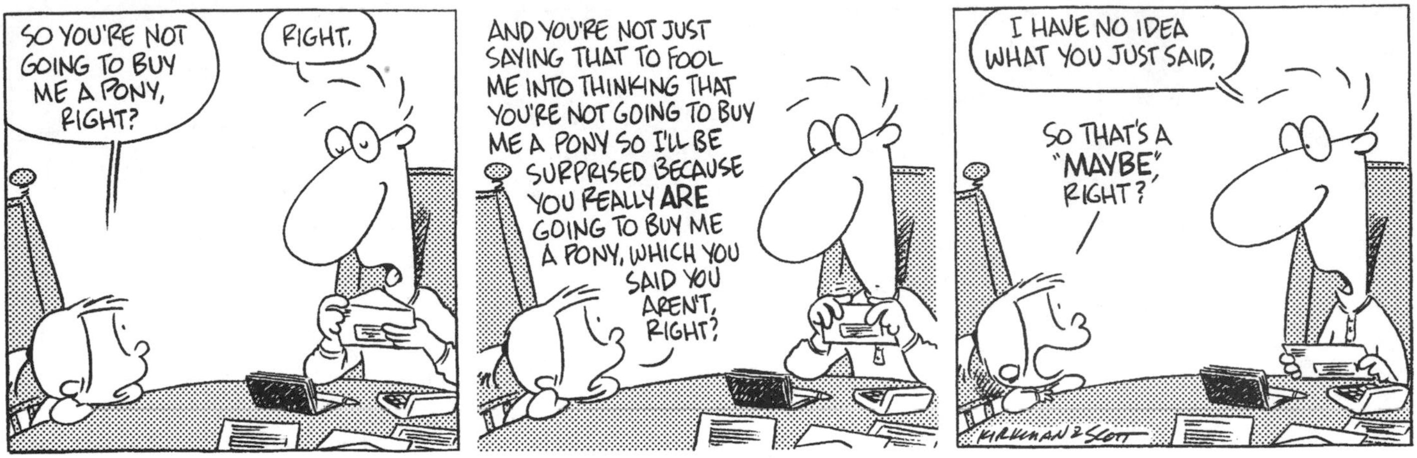
SO YOU'RE NOT GOING TO BUY ME A PONY, RIGHT?
RIGHT.
AND YOU'RE NOT JUST SAYING THAT TO FOOL ME INTO THINKING THAT YOU'RE NOT GOING TO BUY ME A PONY SO I'LL BE SURPRISED BECAUSE YOU REALLY **ARE** GOING TO BUY ME A PONY, WHICH YOU SAID YOU AREN'T, RIGHT?
I HAVE NO IDEA WHAT YOU JUST SAID.
SO THAT'S A "**MAYBE**," RIGHT?

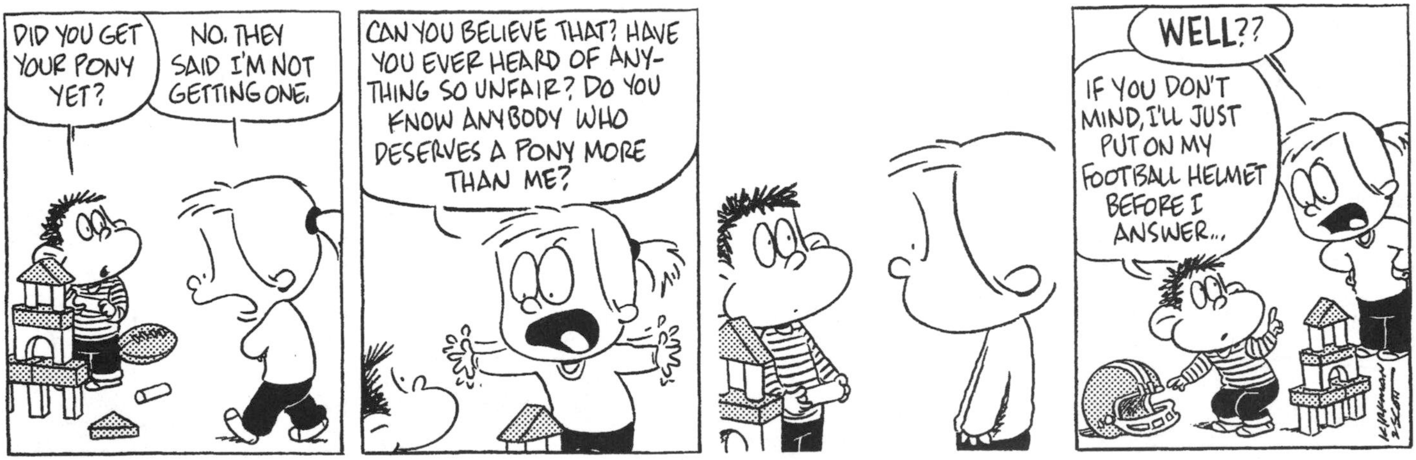
DID YOU GET YOUR PONY YET?
NO. THEY SAID I'M NOT GETTING ONE.
CAN YOU BELIEVE THAT? HAVE YOU EVER HEARD OF ANYTHING SO UNFAIR? DO YOU KNOW ANYBODY WHO DESERVES A PONY MORE THAN ME?
WELL??
IF YOU DON'T MIND, I'LL JUST PUT ON MY FOOTBALL HELMET BEFORE I ANSWER...

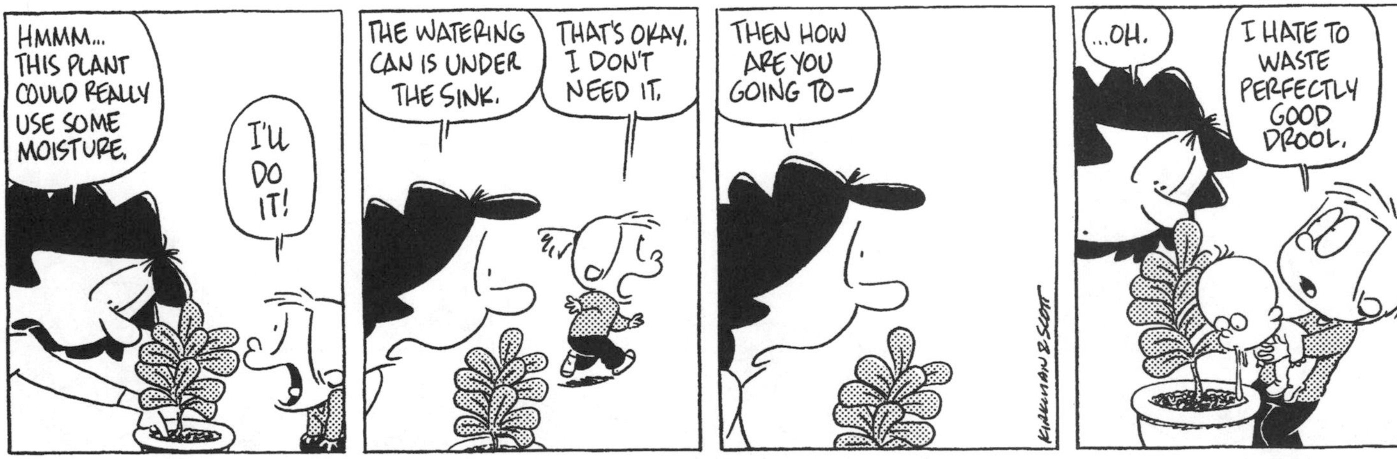
HMMM... THIS PLANT COULD REALLY USE SOME MOISTURE.
I'LL DO IT!
THE WATERING CAN IS UNDER THE SINK.
THAT'S OKAY. I DON'T NEED IT.
THEN HOW ARE YOU GOING TO—
...OH.
I HATE TO WASTE PERFECTLY GOOD DROOL.

BABY BLUES®
BY RICK KIRKMAN / JERRY SCOTT

GLOOP!
SNNNR
RFFF!
BLORP!
EWWWWW!
GROSS!!
GAAA!
FWIP!

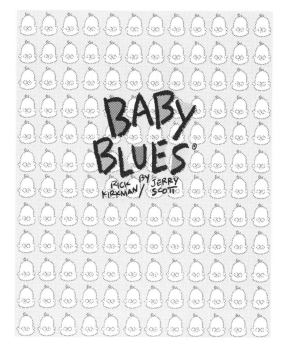

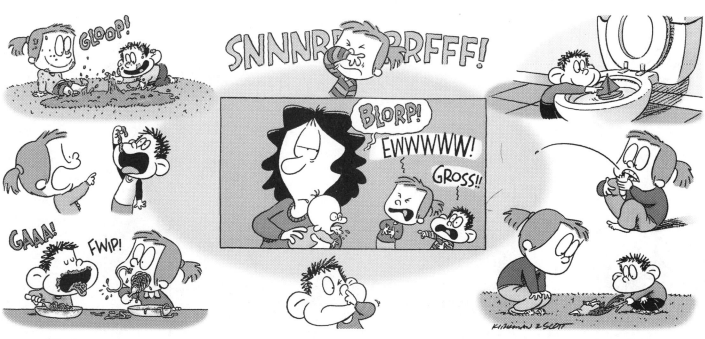

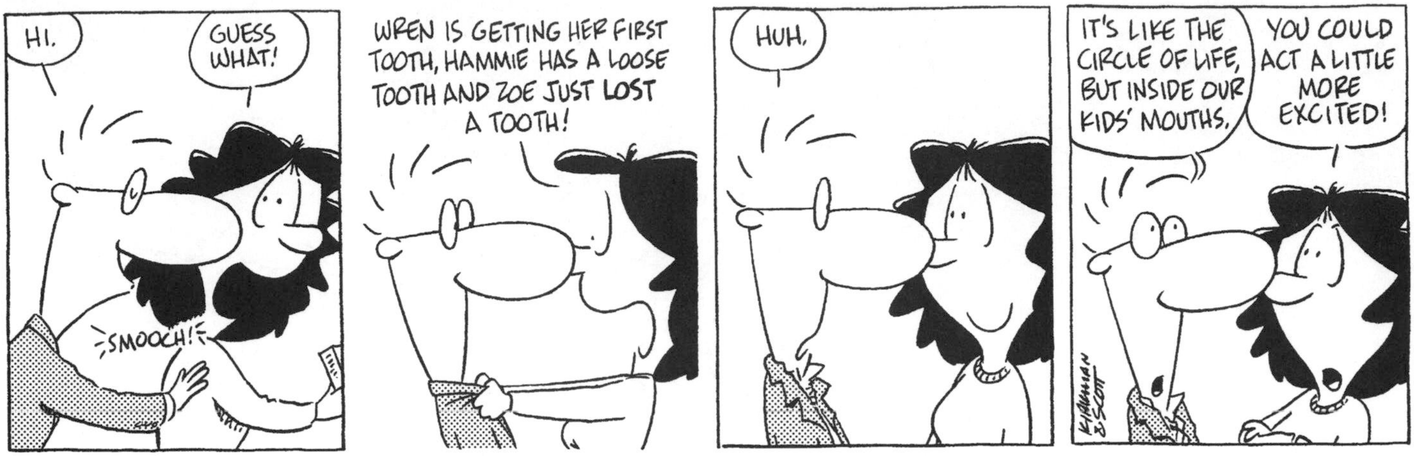
HI.
GUESS WHAT!
SMOOCH!
WREN IS GETTING HER FIRST TOOTH, HAMMIE HAS A LOOSE TOOTH AND ZOE JUST LOST A TOOTH!
HUH.
IT'S LIKE THE CIRCLE OF LIFE, BUT INSIDE OUR KIDS' MOUTHS.
YOU COULD ACT A LITTLE MORE EXCITED!

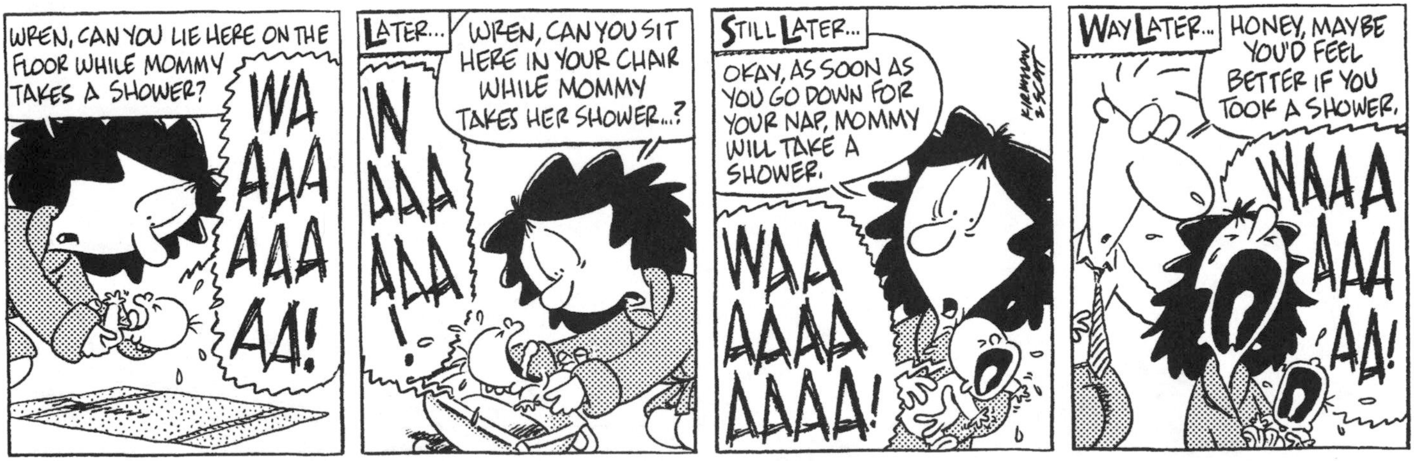
WREN, CAN YOU LIE HERE ON THE FLOOR WHILE MOMMY TAKES A SHOWER?
WAAAAAAAAAA!
LATER...
WREN, CAN YOU SIT HERE IN YOUR CHAIR WHILE MOMMY TAKES HER SHOWER...?
WAAAAAA!
STILL LATER...
OKAY, AS SOON AS YOU GO DOWN FOR YOUR NAP, MOMMY WILL TAKE A SHOWER.
WAAAAAAAAAAA!
WAY LATER...
HONEY, MAYBE YOU'D FEEL BETTER IF YOU TOOK A SHOWER.
WAAAAAAAA!

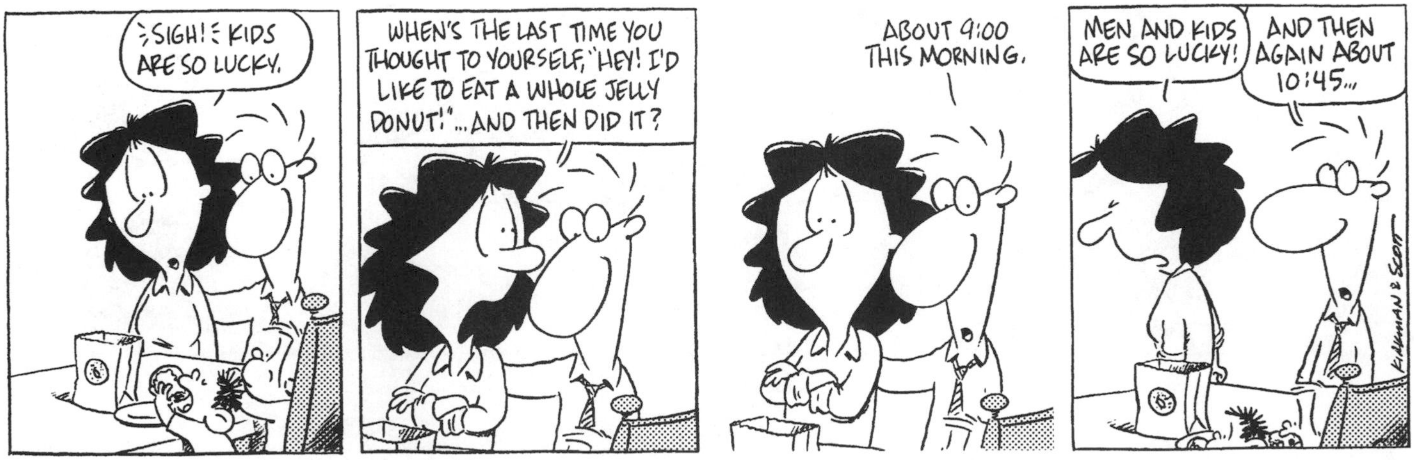
SIGH! KIDS ARE SO LUCKY.
WHEN'S THE LAST TIME YOU THOUGHT TO YOURSELF, "HEY! I'D LIKE TO EAT A WHOLE JELLY DONUT!"... AND THEN DID IT?
ABOUT 9:00 THIS MORNING.
MEN AND KIDS ARE SO LUCKY!
AND THEN AGAIN ABOUT 10:45...

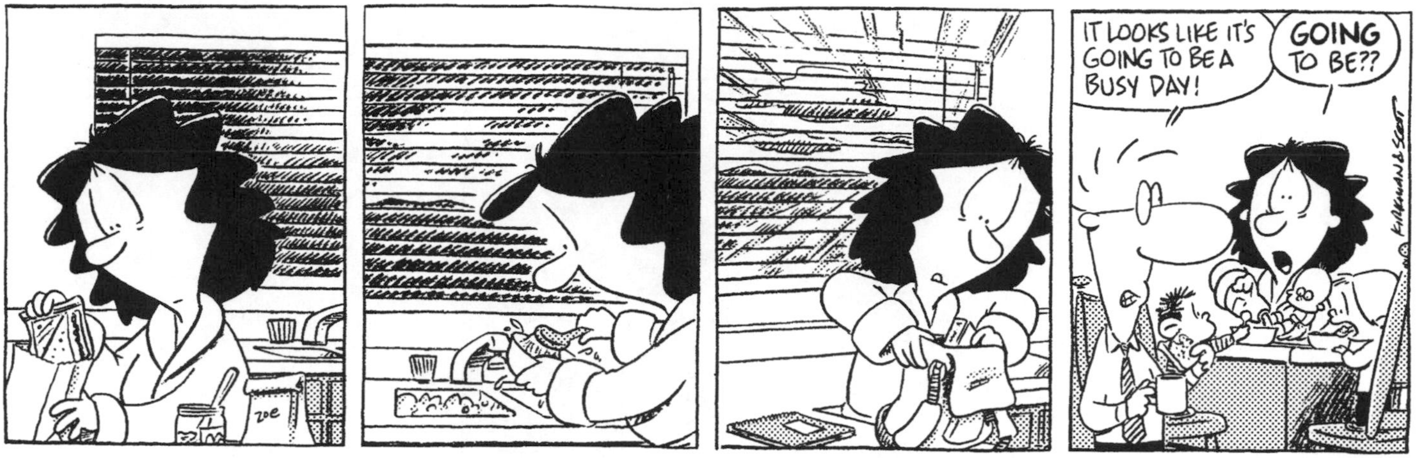
ZOE
IT LOOKS LIKE IT'S GOING TO BE A BUSY DAY!
GOING TO BE??
KIRKMAN & SCOTT

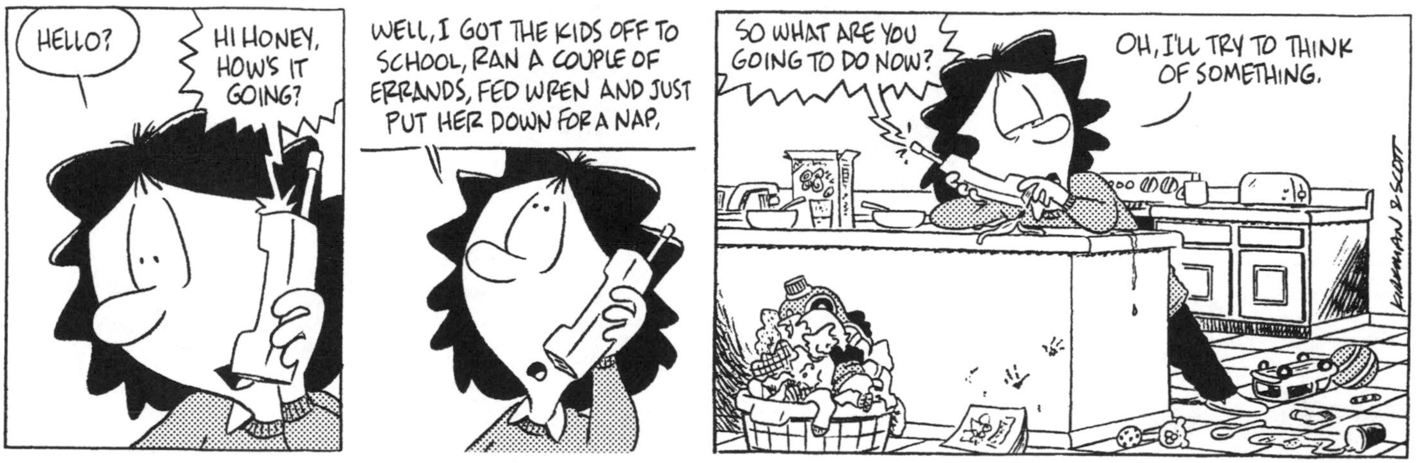
HELLO?
HI HONEY, HOW'S IT GOING?
WELL, I GOT THE KIDS OFF TO SCHOOL, RAN A COUPLE OF ERRANDS, FED WREN AND JUST PUT HER DOWN FOR A NAP.
SO WHAT ARE YOU GOING TO DO NOW?
OH, I'LL TRY TO THINK OF SOMETHING.
KIRKMAN & SCOTT

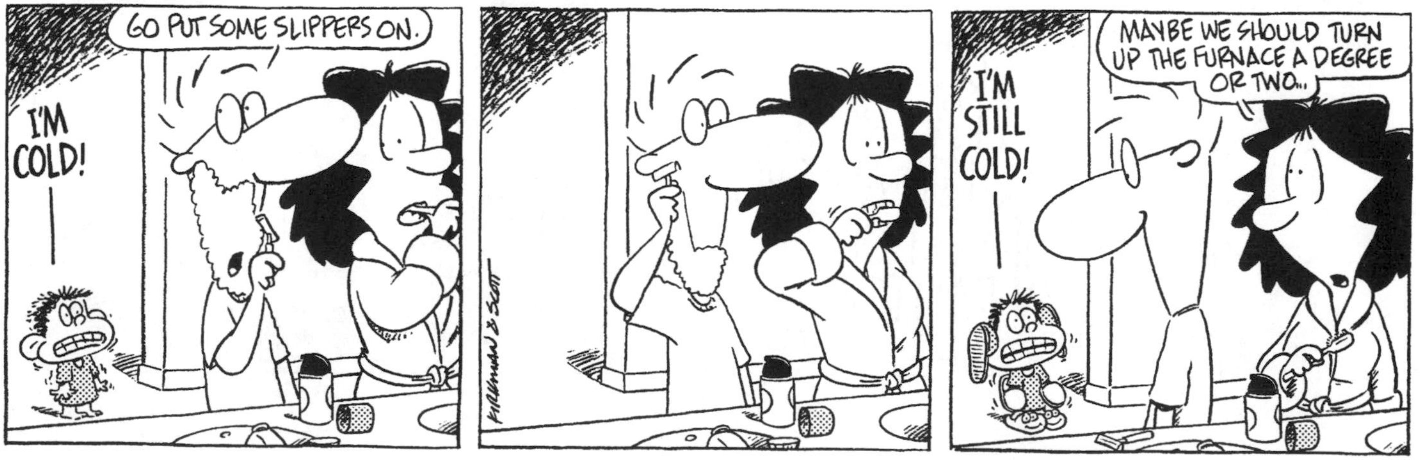
I'M COLD!
GO PUT SOME SLIPPERS ON.
KIRKMAN & SCOTT
I'M STILL COLD!
MAYBE WE SHOULD TURN UP THE FURNACE A DEGREE OR TWO...

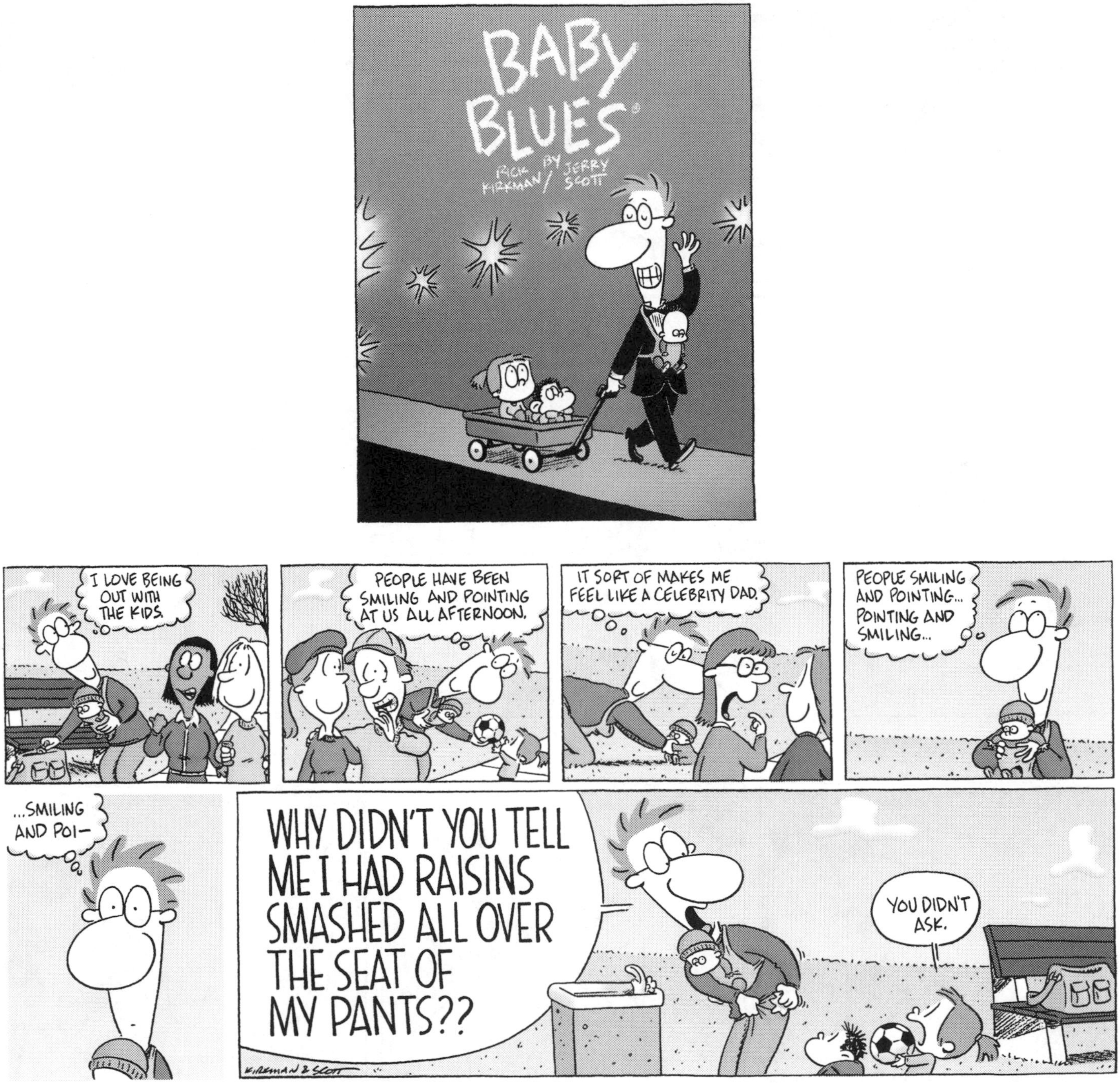
BABY BLUES
BY RICK KIRKMAN / JERRY SCOTT
I LOVE BEING OUT WITH THE KIDS.
PEOPLE HAVE BEEN SMILING AND POINTING AT US ALL AFTERNOON.
IT SORT OF MAKES ME FEEL LIKE A CELEBRITY DAD.
PEOPLE SMILING AND POINTING... POINTING AND SMILING...
...SMILING AND POI–
WHY DIDN'T YOU TELL ME I HAD RAISINS SMASHED ALL OVER THE SEAT OF MY PANTS??
YOU DIDN'T ASK.
KIRKMAN & SCOTT

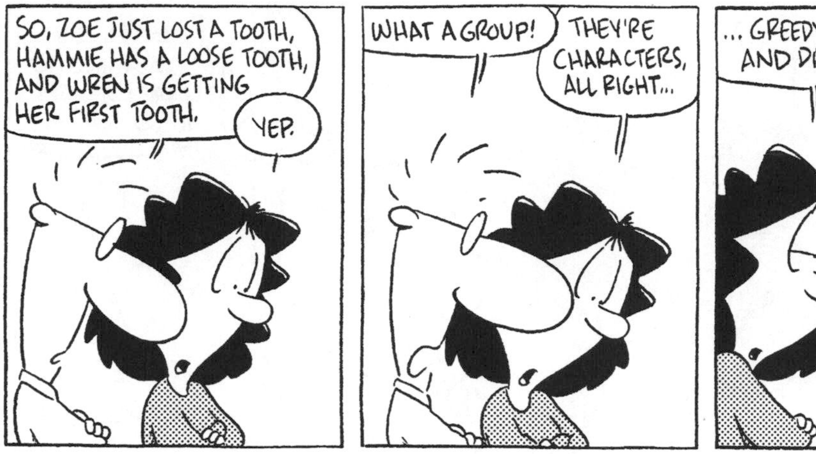
SO, ZOE JUST LOST A TOOTH, HAMMIE HAS A LOOSE TOOTH, AND WREN IS GETTING HER FIRST TOOTH.
YEP.
WHAT A GROUP!
THEY'RE CHARACTERS, ALL RIGHT...
... GREEDY, WIGGLY AND DROOLY.
AND WHEN YOU TURN SEVEN, THE TOOTH FAIRY STOPS LEAVING YOU COINS AND STARTS LEAVING YOU FOLDING MONEY!
NO FAIR!
WIGGLE! WIGGLE! WIGGLE!
DRIP! DRIP! DRIP!
KIRKMAN & SCOTT

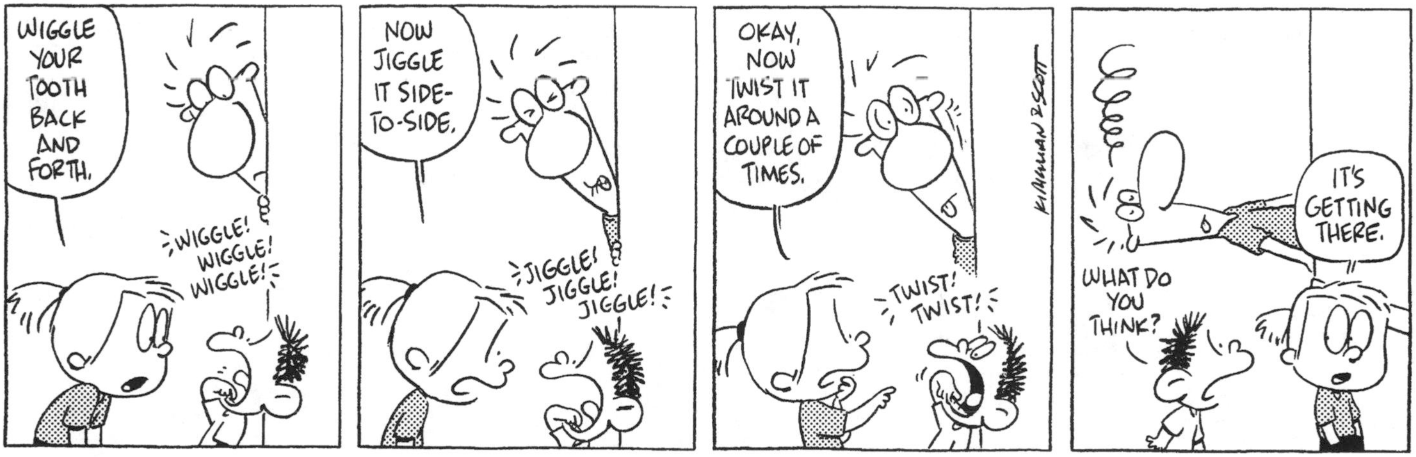
WIGGLE YOUR TOOTH BACK AND FORTH.
WIGGLE! WIGGLE! WIGGLE!
NOW JIGGLE IT SIDE-TO-SIDE.
JIGGLE! JIGGLE! JIGGLE!
OKAY, NOW TWIST IT AROUND A COUPLE OF TIMES.
TWIST! TWIST!
KIRKMAN & SCOTT
WHAT DO YOU THINK?
IT'S GETTING THERE.

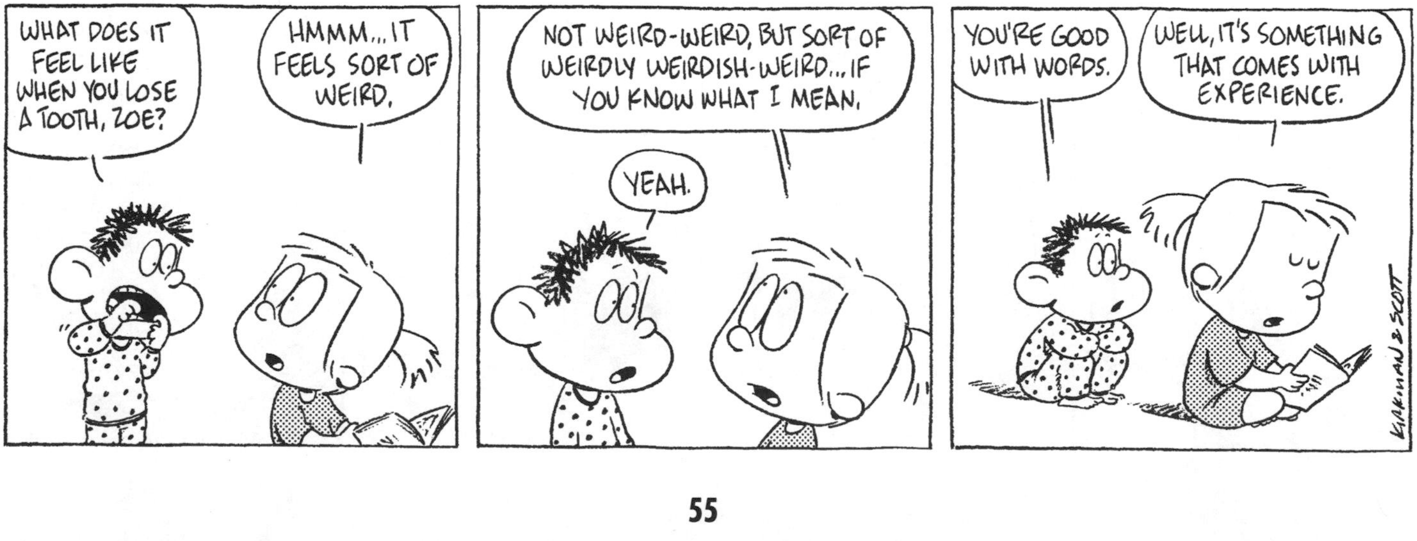
WHAT DOES IT FEEL LIKE WHEN YOU LOSE A TOOTH, ZOE?
HMMM... IT FEELS SORT OF WEIRD.
NOT WEIRD-WEIRD, BUT SORT OF WEIRDLY WEIRDISH-WEIRD... IF YOU KNOW WHAT I MEAN.
YEAH.
YOU'RE GOOD WITH WORDS.
WELL, IT'S SOMETHING THAT COMES WITH EXPERIENCE.
KIRKMAN & SCOTT

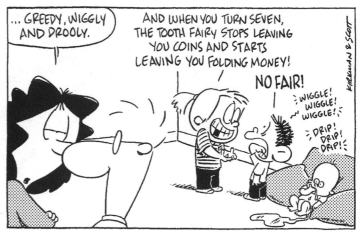

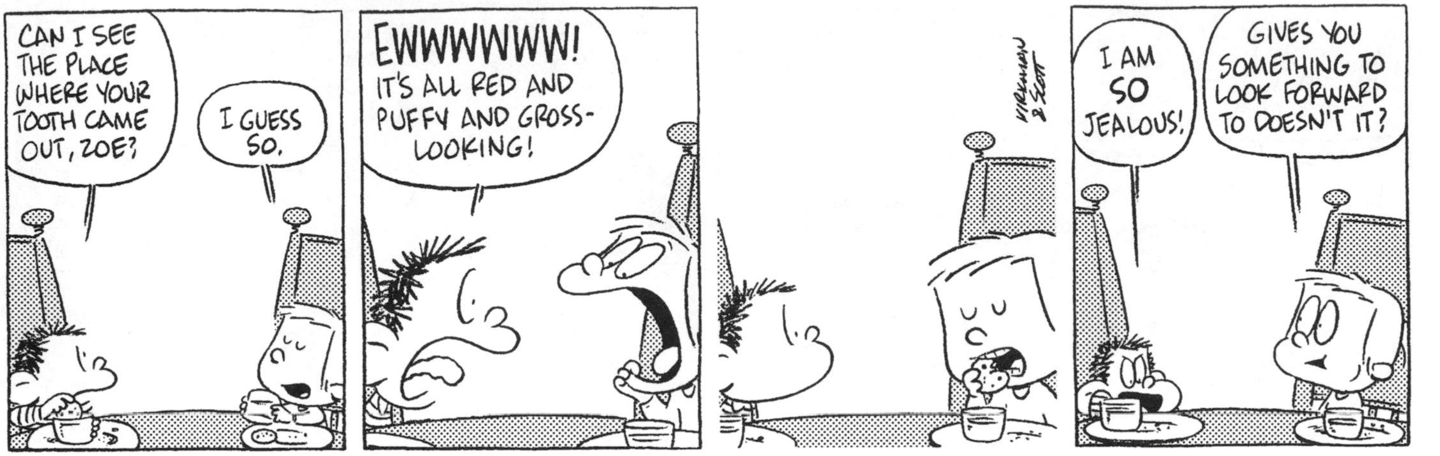
CAN I SEE THE PLACE WHERE YOUR TOOTH CAME OUT, ZOE?
I GUESS SO.
EWWWWWW! IT'S ALL RED AND PUFFY AND GROSS-LOOKING!
I AM SO JEALOUS!
GIVES YOU SOMETHING TO LOOK FORWARD TO DOESN'T IT?

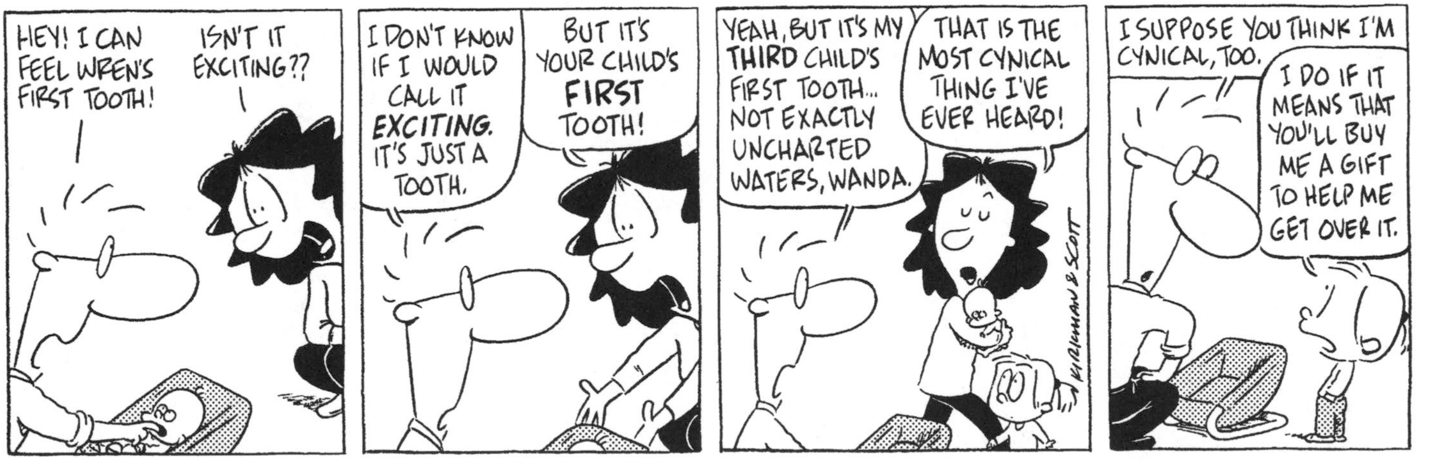
HEY! I CAN FEEL WREN'S FIRST TOOTH!
ISN'T IT EXCITING??
I DON'T KNOW IF I WOULD CALL IT EXCITING. IT'S JUST A TOOTH.
BUT IT'S YOUR CHILD'S FIRST TOOTH!
YEAH, BUT IT'S MY THIRD CHILD'S FIRST TOOTH... NOT EXACTLY UNCHARTED WATERS, WANDA.
THAT IS THE MOST CYNICAL THING I'VE EVER HEARD!
I SUPPOSE YOU THINK I'M CYNICAL, TOO.
I DO IF IT MEANS THAT YOU'LL BUY ME A GIFT TO HELP ME GET OVER IT.

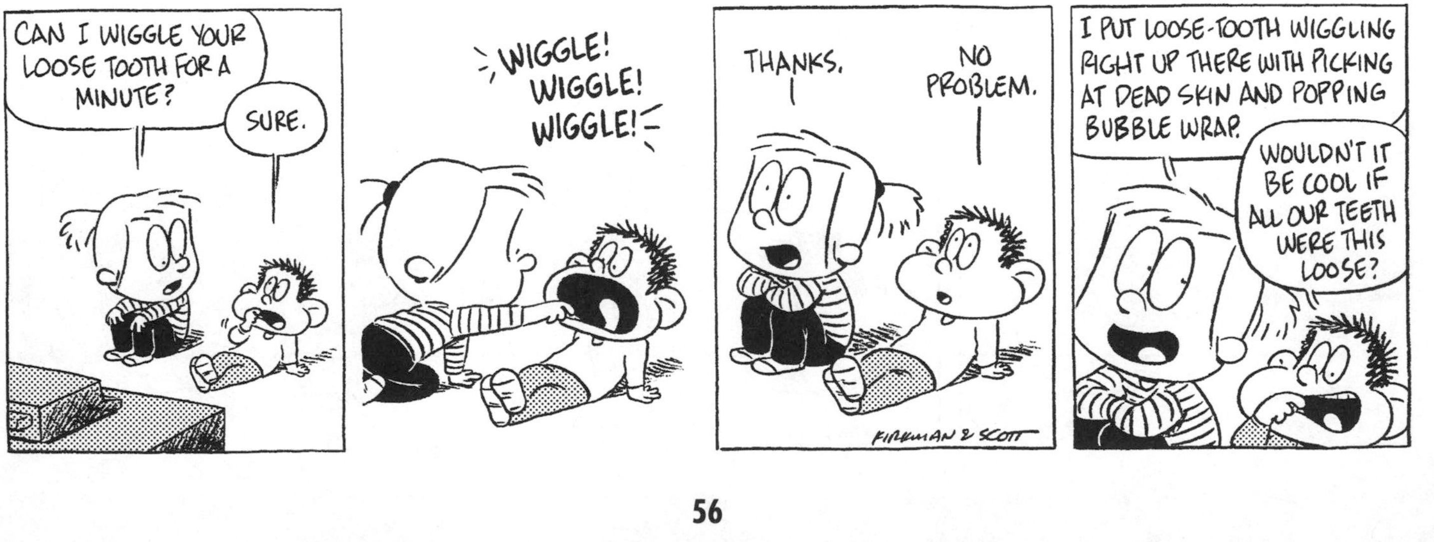
CAN I WIGGLE YOUR LOOSE TOOTH FOR A MINUTE?
SURE.
WIGGLE! WIGGLE! WIGGLE!
THANKS.
NO PROBLEM.
KIRKMAN & SCOTT
I PUT LOOSE-TOOTH WIGGLING RIGHT UP THERE WITH PICKING AT DEAD SKIN AND POPPING BUBBLE WRAP.
WOULDN'T IT BE COOL IF ALL OUR TEETH WERE THIS LOOSE?

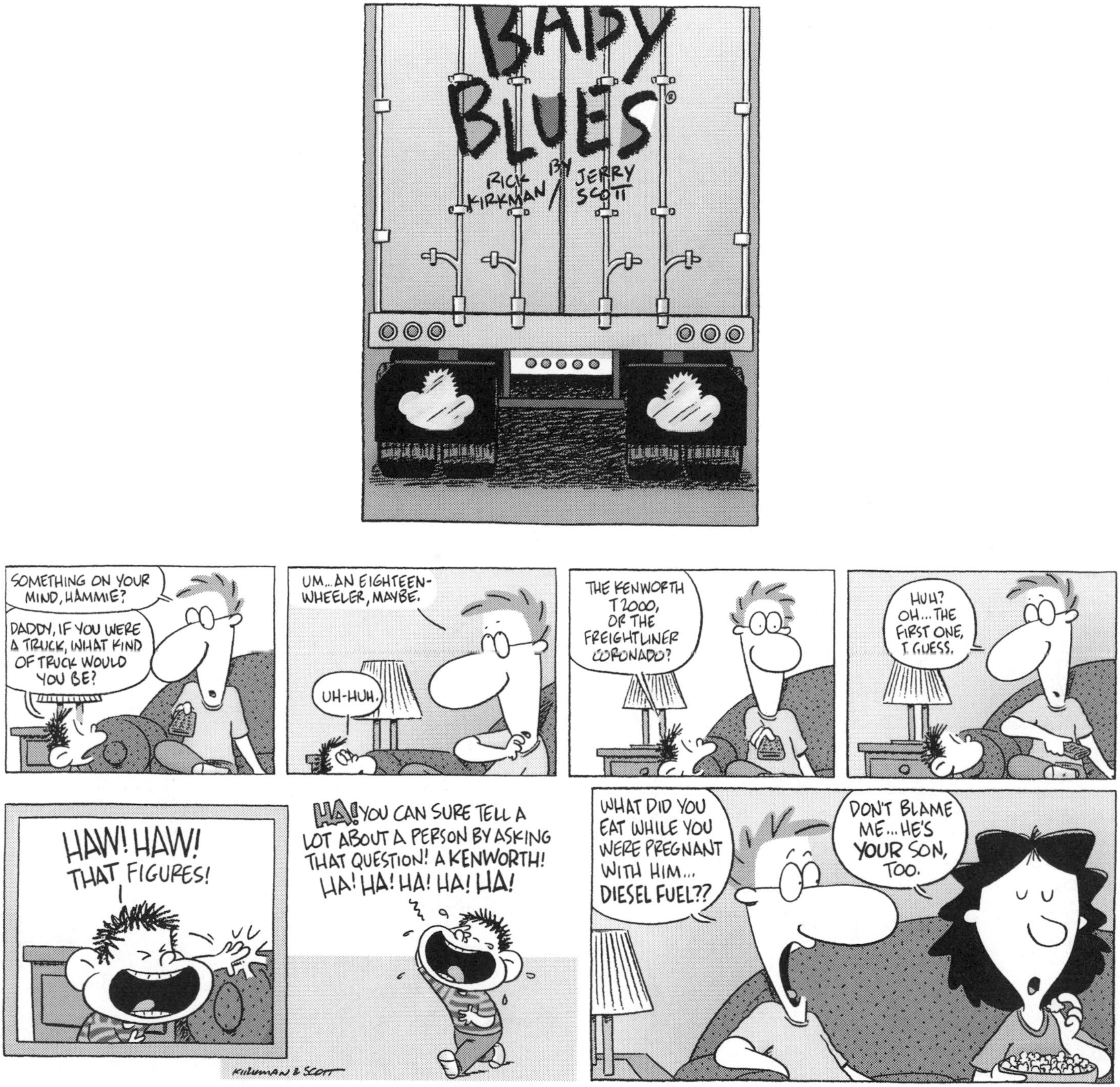
BABY BLUES®
BY RICK KIRKMAN / JERRY SCOTT
SOMETHING ON YOUR MIND, HAMMIE?
DADDY, IF YOU WERE A TRUCK, WHAT KIND OF TRUCK WOULD YOU BE?
UM... AN EIGHTEEN-WHEELER, MAYBE.
UH-HUH.
THE KENWORTH T2000, OR THE FREIGHTLINER CORONADO?
HUH? OH... THE FIRST ONE, I GUESS.
HAW! HAW! THAT FIGURES!
HA! YOU CAN SURE TELL A LOT ABOUT A PERSON BY ASKING THAT QUESTION! A KENWORTH! HA! HA! HA! HA! HA!
KIRKMAN & SCOTT
WHAT DID YOU EAT WHILE YOU WERE PREGNANT WITH HIM... DIESEL FUEL??
DON'T BLAME ME... HE'S YOUR SON, TOO.

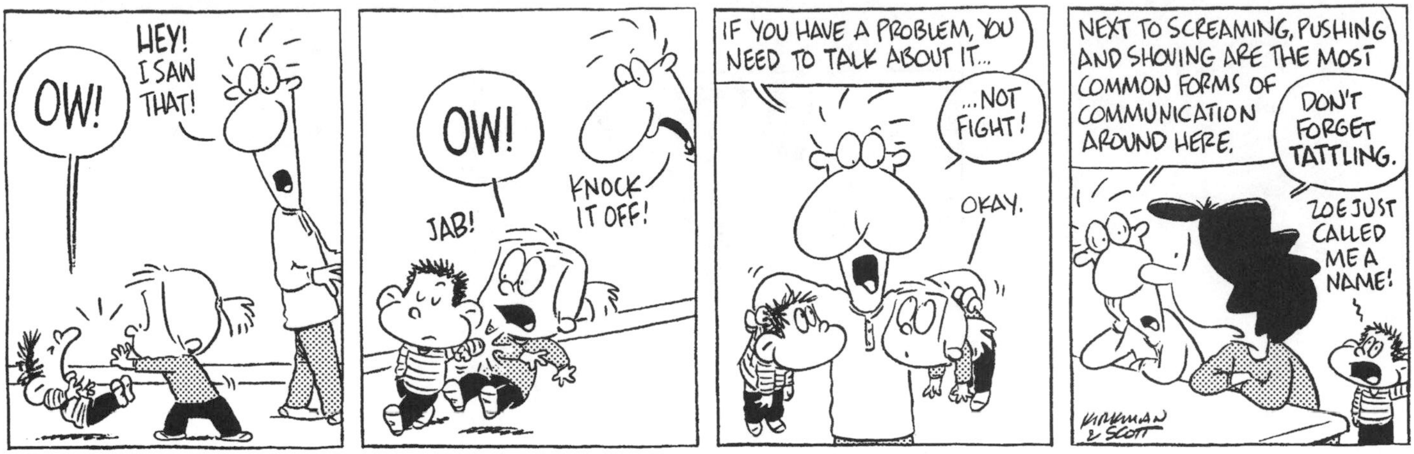
OW!
HEY! I SAW THAT!
OW!
JAB!
KNOCK IT OFF!
IF YOU HAVE A PROBLEM, YOU NEED TO TALK ABOUT IT...
...NOT FIGHT!
OKAY.
NEXT TO SCREAMING, PUSHING AND SHOVING ARE THE MOST COMMON FORMS OF COMMUNICATION AROUND HERE.
DON'T FORGET TATTLING.
ZOE JUST CALLED ME A NAME!
KIRKMAN & SCOTT

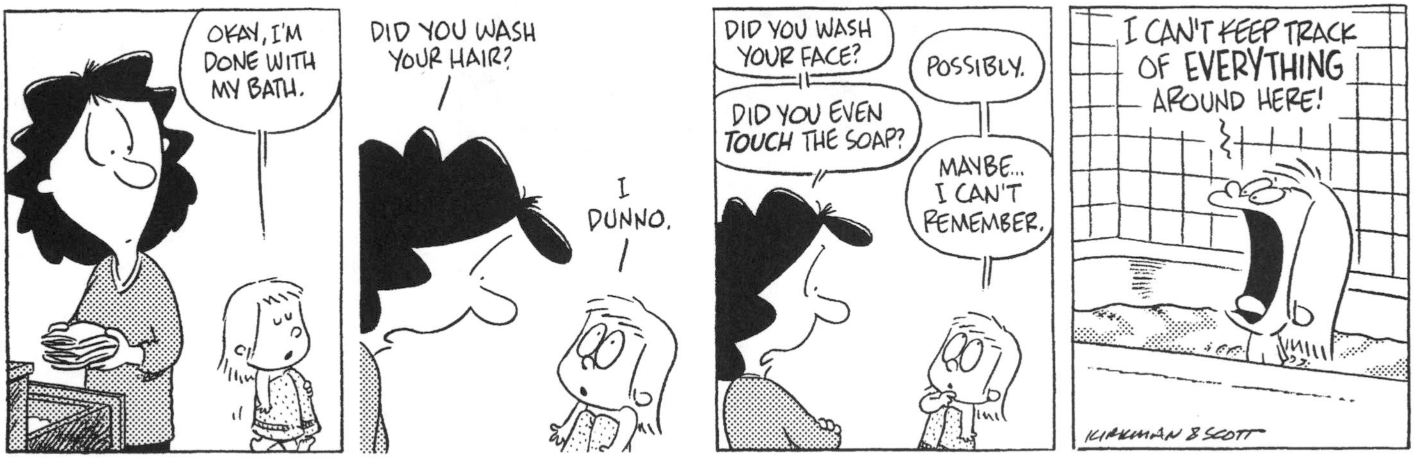
OKAY, I'M DONE WITH MY BATH.
DID YOU WASH YOUR HAIR?
I DUNNO.
DID YOU WASH YOUR FACE?
DID YOU EVEN TOUCH THE SOAP?
POSSIBLY.
MAYBE... I CAN'T REMEMBER.
I CAN'T KEEP TRACK OF EVERYTHING AROUND HERE!
KIRKMAN & SCOTT

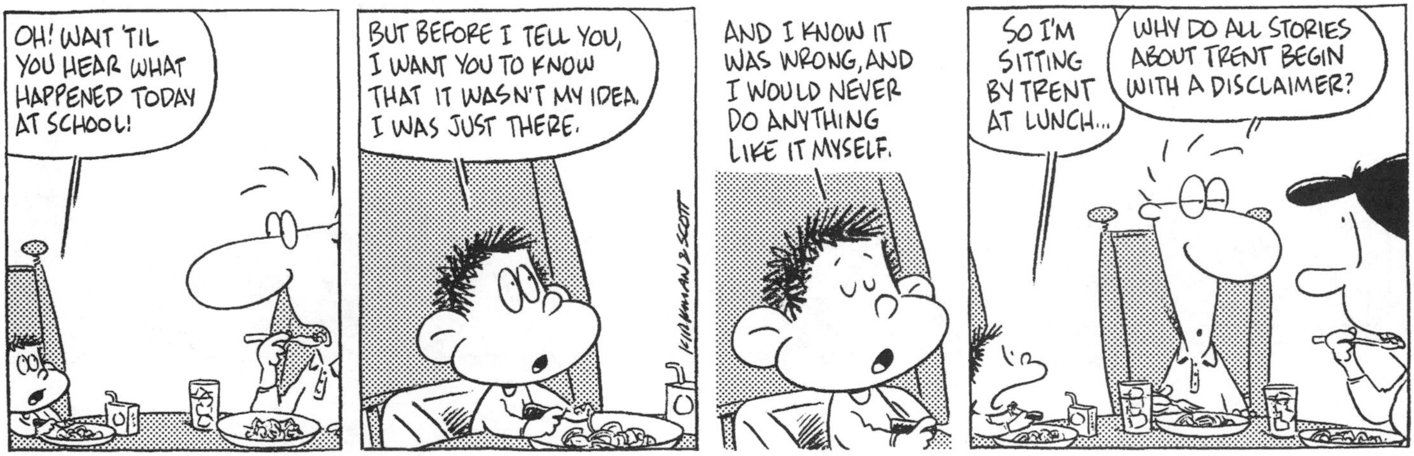
OH! WAIT 'TIL YOU HEAR WHAT HAPPENED TODAY AT SCHOOL!
BUT BEFORE I TELL YOU, I WANT YOU TO KNOW THAT IT WASN'T MY IDEA. I WAS JUST THERE.
KIRKMAN & SCOTT
AND I KNOW IT WAS WRONG, AND I WOULD NEVER DO ANYTHING LIKE IT MYSELF.
SO I'M SITTING BY TRENT AT LUNCH...
WHY DO ALL STORIES ABOUT TRENT BEGIN WITH A DISCLAIMER?

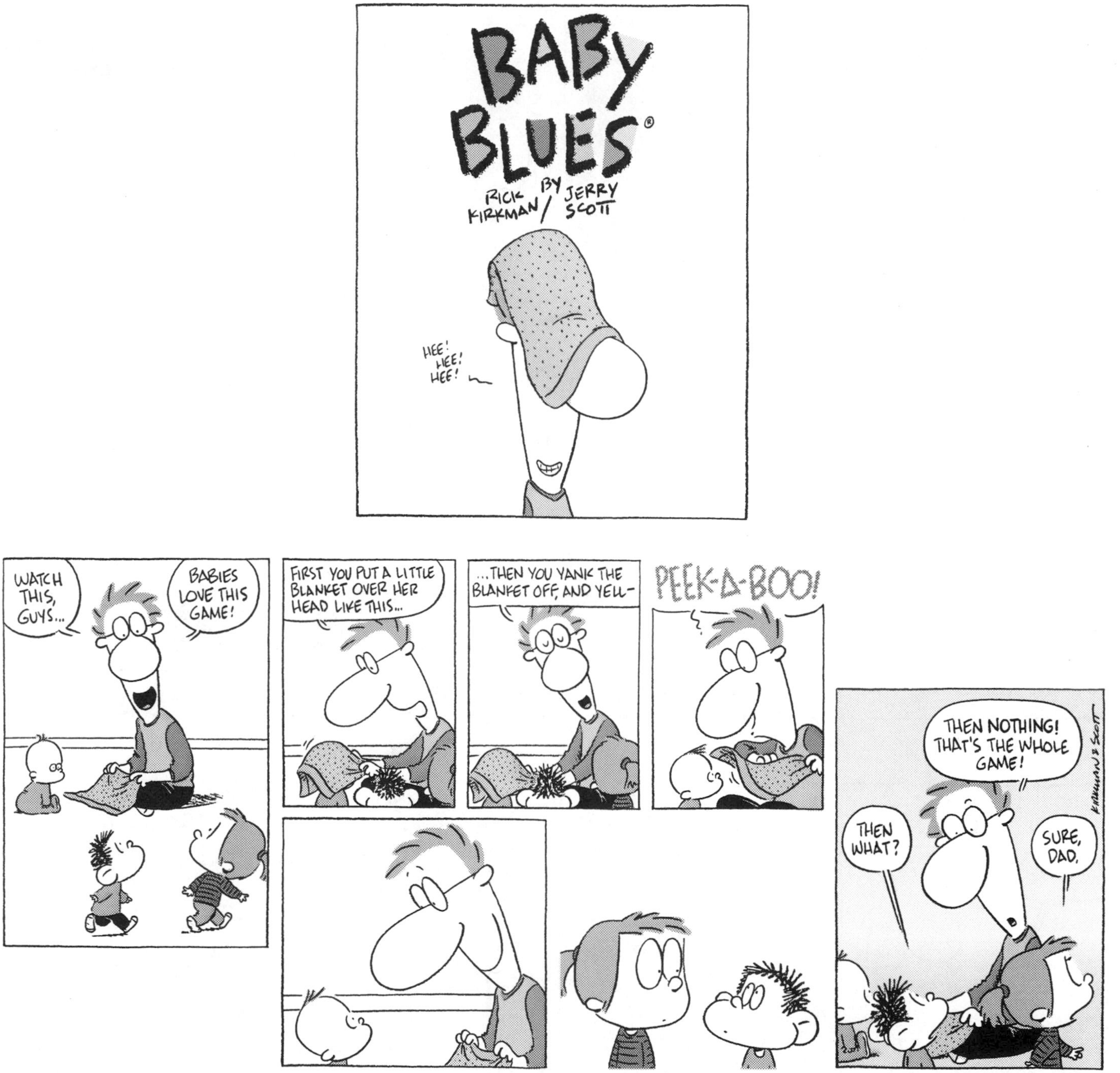
BABY BLUES®
BY RICK KIRKMAN / JERRY SCOTT
HEE! HEE! HEE!
WATCH THIS, GUYS...
BABIES LOVE THIS GAME!
FIRST YOU PUT A LITTLE BLANKET OVER HER HEAD LIKE THIS...
...THEN YOU YANK THE BLANKET OFF, AND YELL-
PEEK-A-BOO!
THEN WHAT?
THEN NOTHING! THAT'S THE WHOLE GAME!
SURE, DAD.

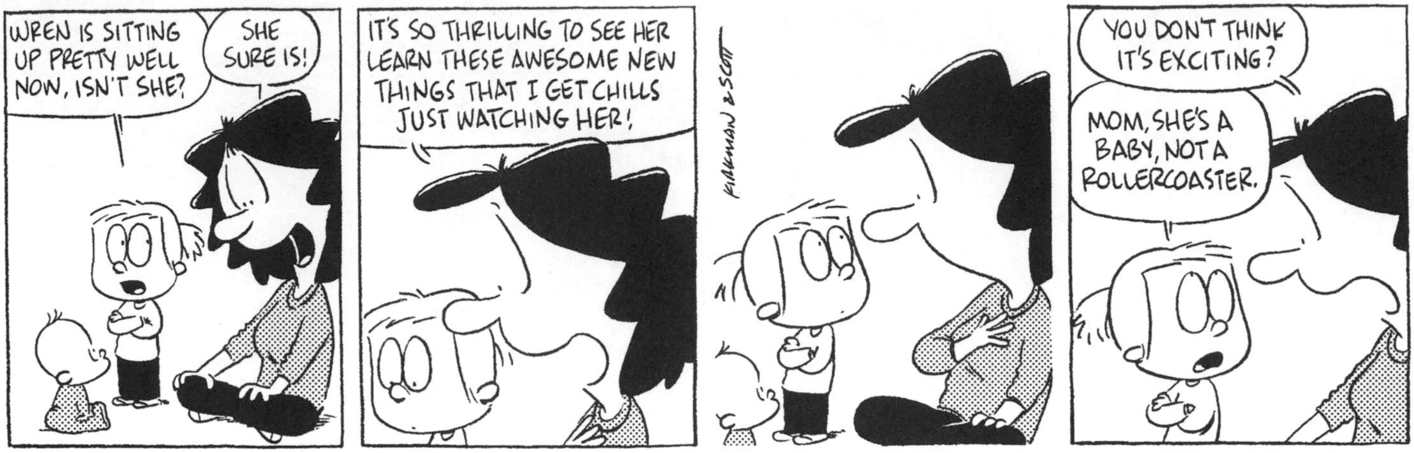
WREN IS SITTING UP PRETTY WELL NOW, ISN'T SHE?
SHE SURE IS!
IT'S SO THRILLING TO SEE HER LEARN THESE AWESOME NEW THINGS THAT I GET CHILLS JUST WATCHING HER!
KIRKMAN & SCOTT
YOU DON'T THINK IT'S EXCITING?
MOM, SHE'S A BABY, NOT A ROLLERCOASTER.

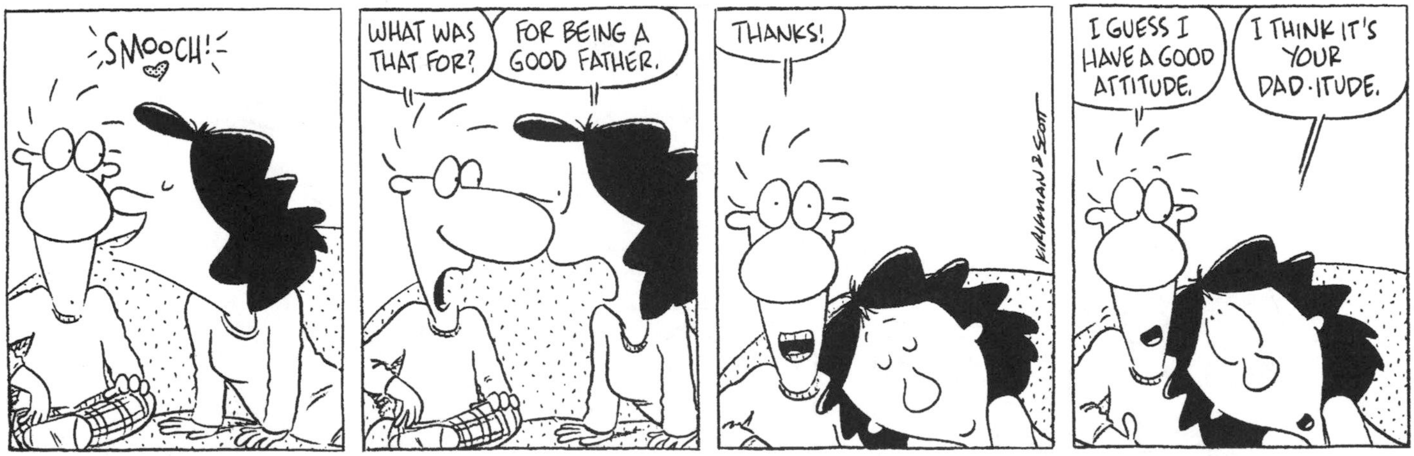
SMOOCH!
WHAT WAS THAT FOR?
FOR BEING A GOOD FATHER.
THANKS!
KIRKMAN & SCOTT
I GUESS I HAVE A GOOD ATTITUDE.
I THINK IT'S YOUR DAD·ITUDE.

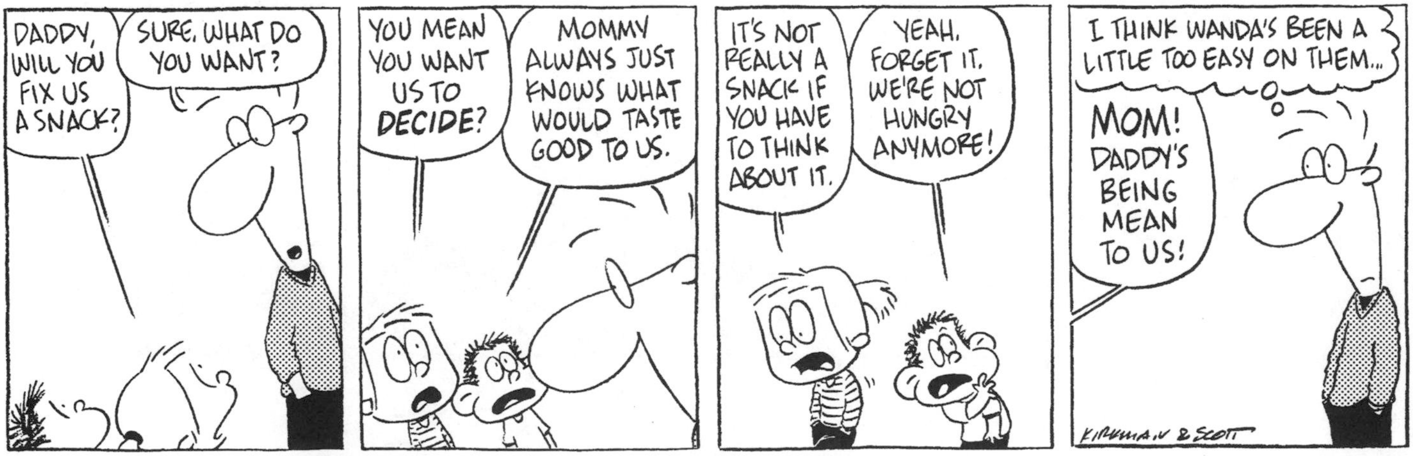
DADDY, WILL YOU FIX US A SNACK?
SURE. WHAT DO YOU WANT?
YOU MEAN YOU WANT US TO DECIDE?
MOMMY ALWAYS JUST KNOWS WHAT WOULD TASTE GOOD TO US.
IT'S NOT REALLY A SNACK IF YOU HAVE TO THINK ABOUT IT.
YEAH. FORGET IT. WE'RE NOT HUNGRY ANYMORE!
I THINK WANDA'S BEEN A LITTLE TOO EASY ON THEM...
MOM! DADDY'S BEING MEAN TO US!
KIRKMAN & SCOTT

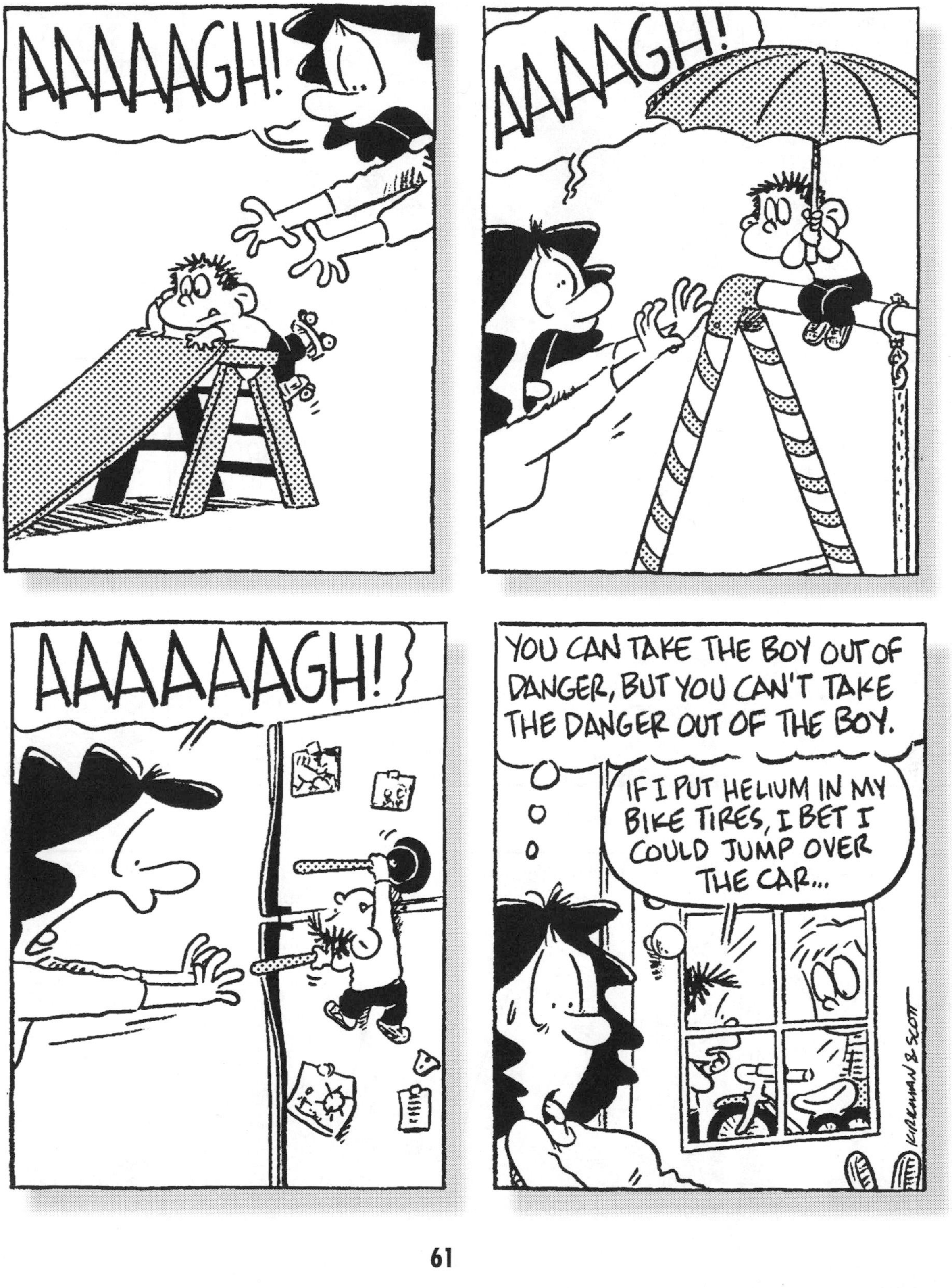
AAAAAGH!
AAAAGH!
AAAAAAGH!
YOU CAN TAKE THE BOY OUT OF DANGER, BUT YOU CAN'T TAKE THE DANGER OUT OF THE BOY.
IF I PUT HELIUM IN MY BIKE TIRES, I BET I COULD JUMP OVER THE CAR...
KIRKMAN & SCOTT

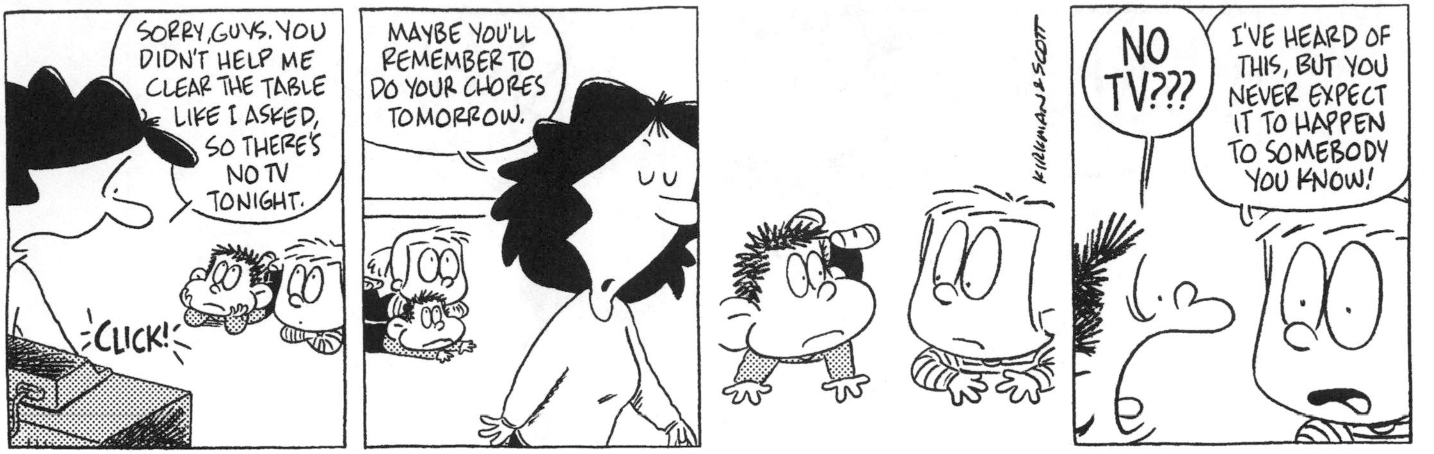
SORRY, GUYS. YOU DIDN'T HELP ME CLEAR THE TABLE LIKE I ASKED, SO THERE'S NO TV TONIGHT.
CLICK!
MAYBE YOU'LL REMEMBER TO DO YOUR CHORES TOMORROW.
KIRKMAN & SCOTT
NO TV???
I'VE HEARD OF THIS, BUT YOU NEVER EXPECT IT TO HAPPEN TO SOMEBODY YOU KNOW!

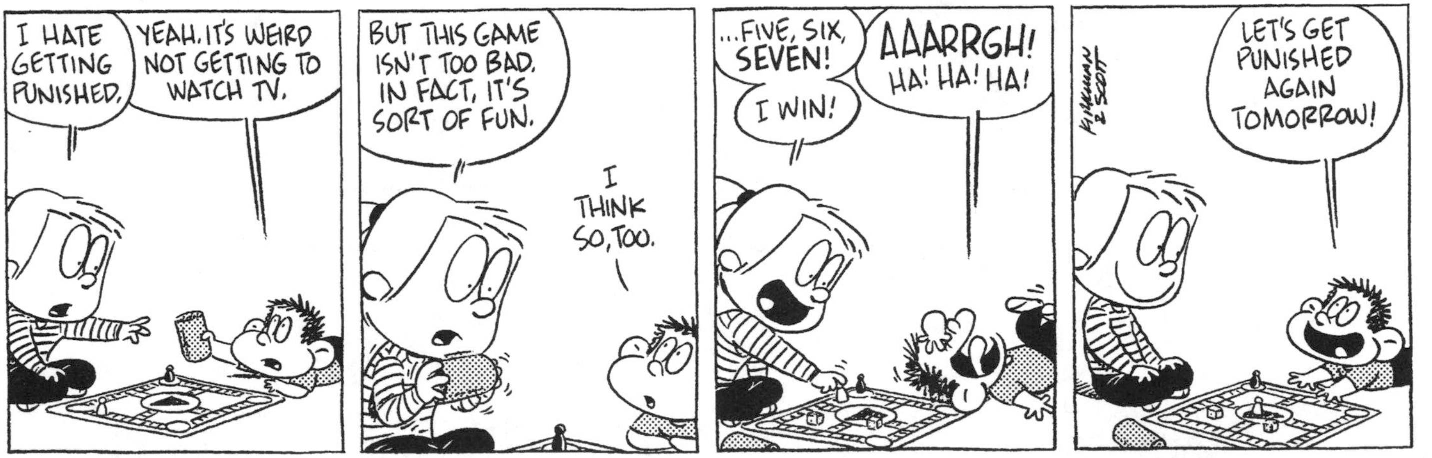
I HATE GETTING PUNISHED.
YEAH. IT'S WEIRD NOT GETTING TO WATCH TV.
BUT THIS GAME ISN'T TOO BAD. IN FACT, IT'S SORT OF FUN.
I THINK SO, TOO.
...FIVE, SIX, SEVEN!
I WIN!
AAARRGH! HA! HA! HA!
KIRKMAN & SCOTT
LET'S GET PUNISHED AGAIN TOMORROW!

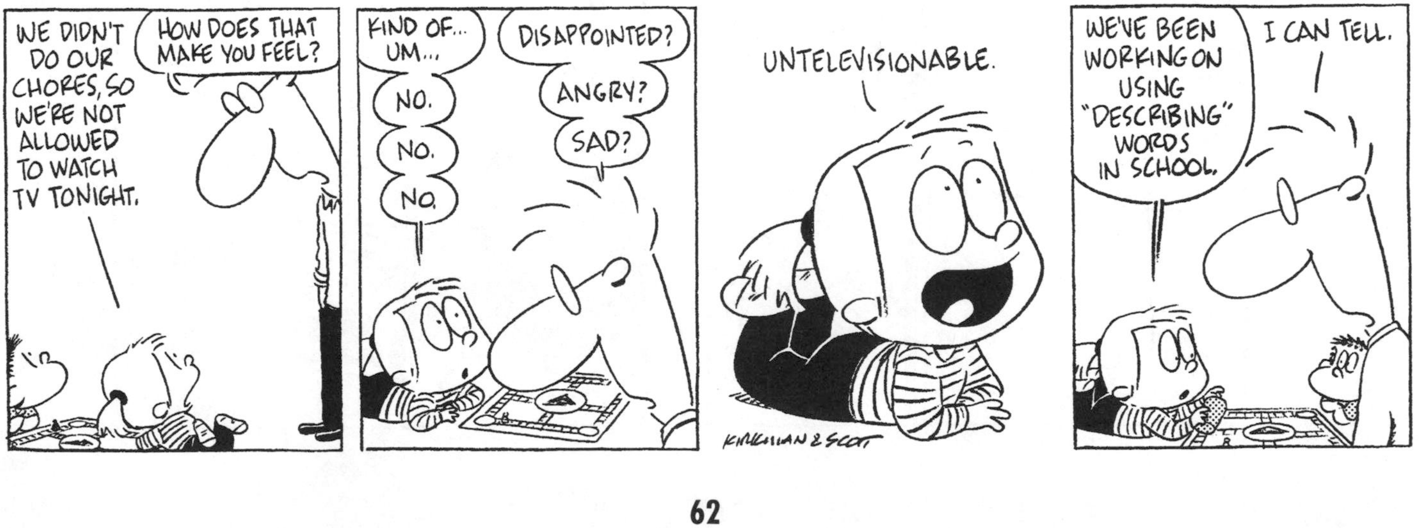
WE DIDN'T DO OUR CHORES, SO WE'RE NOT ALLOWED TO WATCH TV TONIGHT.
HOW DOES THAT MAKE YOU FEEL?
KIND OF... UM...
DISAPPOINTED?
NO.
ANGRY?
NO.
SAD?
NO.
UNTELEVISIONABLE.
KIRKMAN & SCOTT
WE'VE BEEN WORKING ON USING "DESCRIBING" WORDS IN SCHOOL.
I CAN TELL.

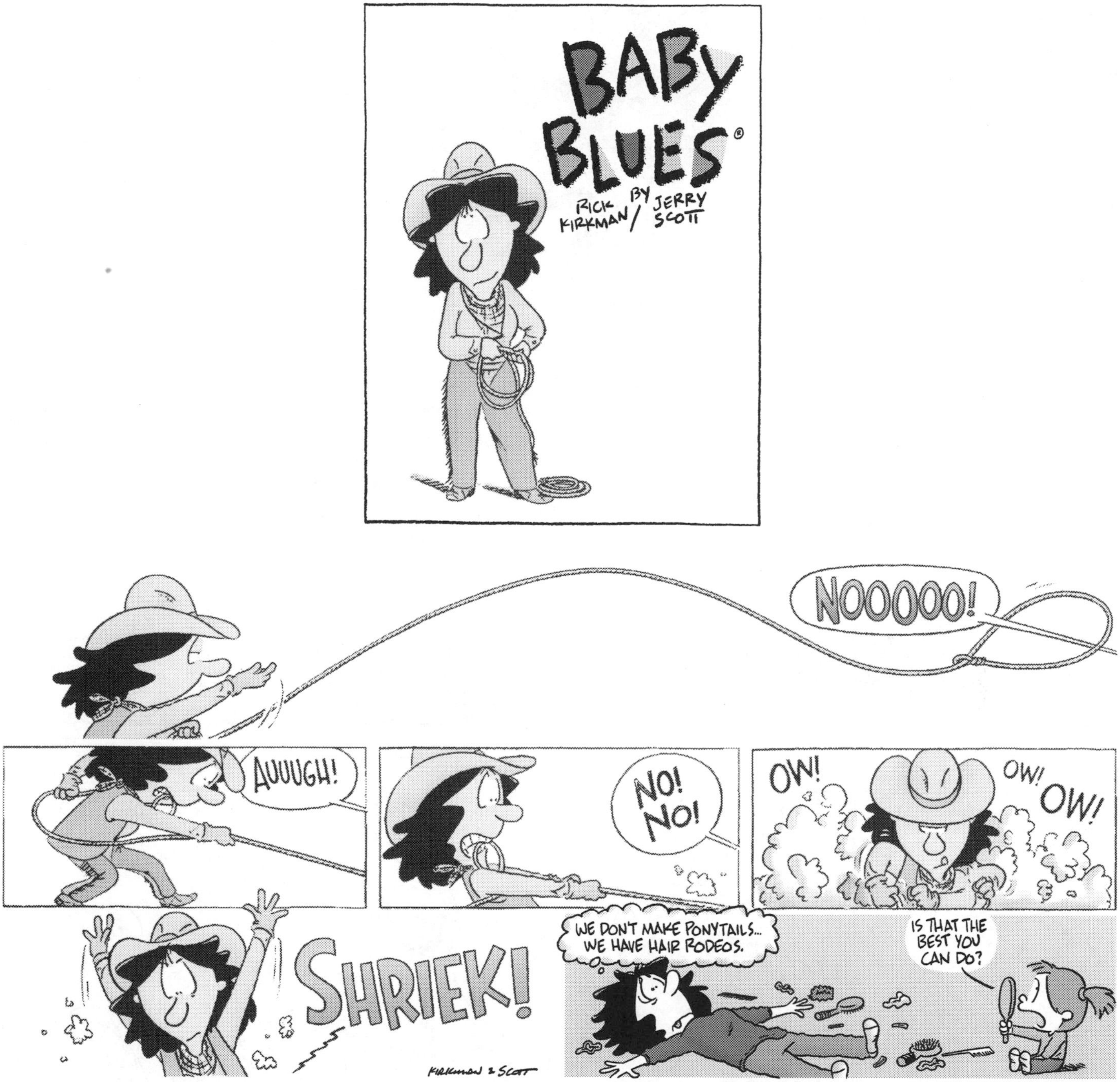
BABY BLUES®
BY RICK KIRKMAN / JERRY SCOTT
NOOOOO!
AUUUGH!
NO! NO!
OW!
OW! OW!
SHRIEK!
KIRKMAN & SCOTT
WE DON'T MAKE PONYTAILS... WE HAVE HAIR RODEOS.
IS THAT THE BEST YOU CAN DO?

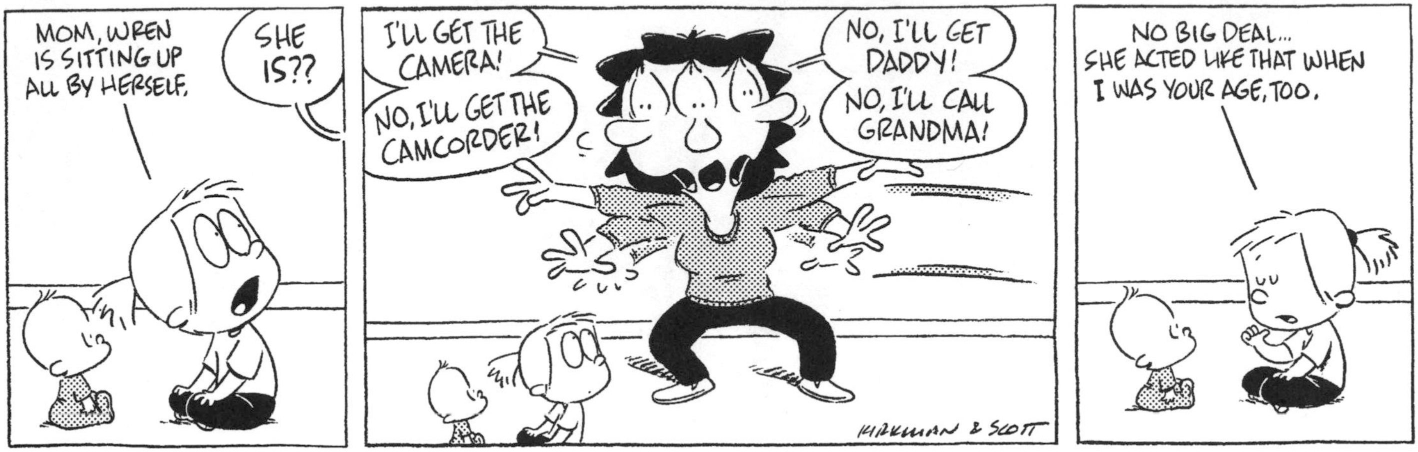
MOM, WREN IS SITTING UP ALL BY HERSELF.
SHE IS??
I'LL GET THE CAMERA!
NO, I'LL GET THE CAMCORDER!
NO, I'LL GET DADDY!
NO, I'LL CALL GRANDMA!
KIRKMAN & SCOTT
NO BIG DEAL... SHE ACTED LIKE THAT WHEN I WAS YOUR AGE, TOO.

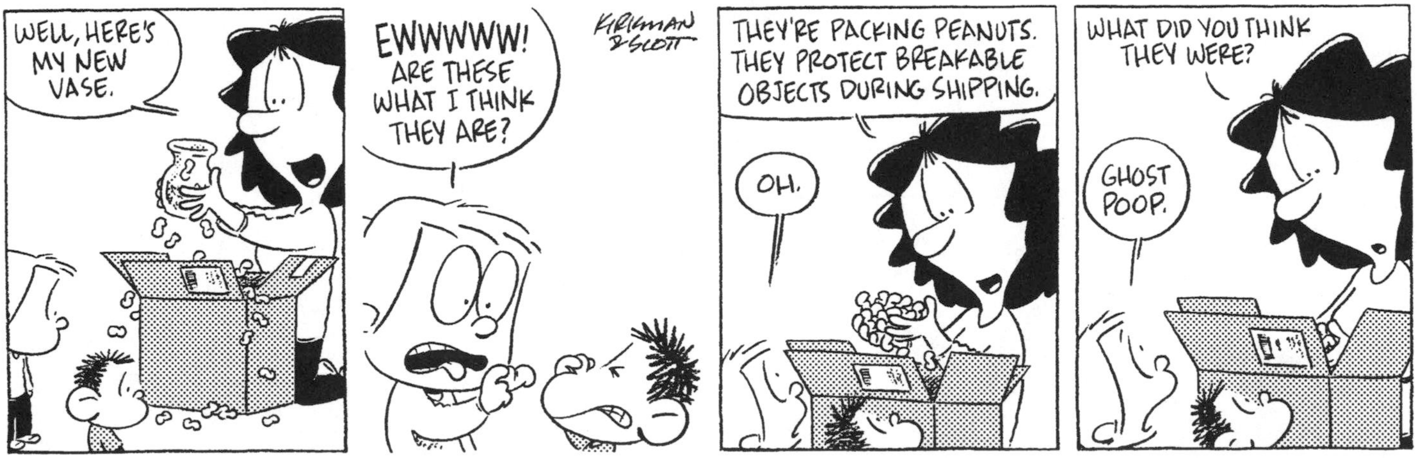
WELL, HERE'S MY NEW VASE.
EWWWWW! ARE THESE WHAT I THINK THEY ARE?
KIRKMAN & SCOTT
THEY'RE PACKING PEANUTS. THEY PROTECT BREAKABLE OBJECTS DURING SHIPPING.
OH.
WHAT DID YOU THINK THEY WERE?
GHOST POOP.

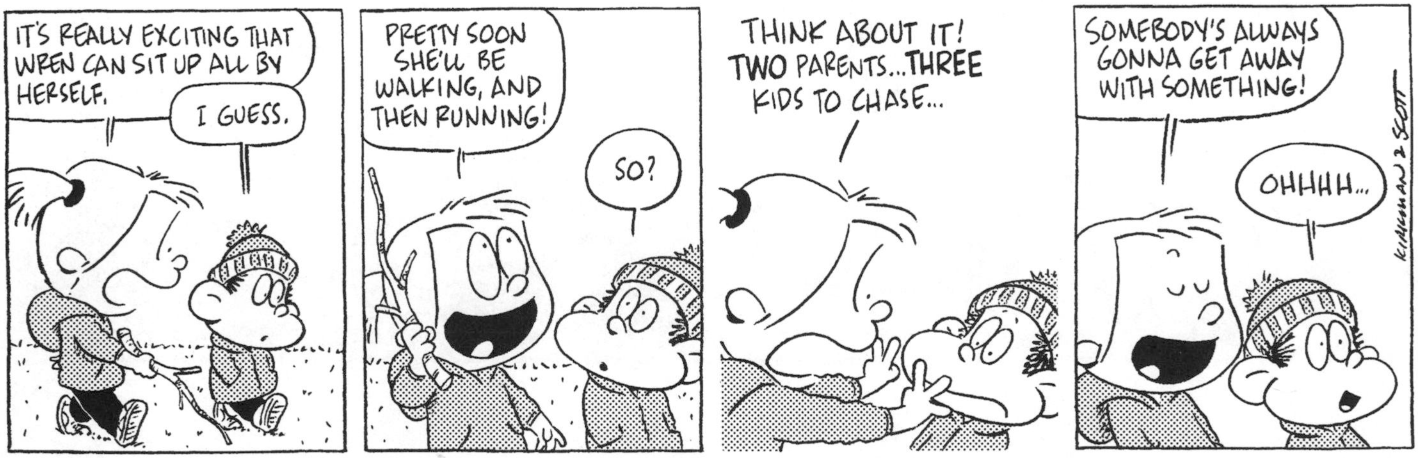
IT'S REALLY EXCITING THAT WREN CAN SIT UP ALL BY HERSELF.
I GUESS.
PRETTY SOON SHE'LL BE WALKING, AND THEN RUNNING!
SO?
THINK ABOUT IT! TWO PARENTS...THREE KIDS TO CHASE...
SOMEBODY'S ALWAYS GONNA GET AWAY WITH SOMETHING!
OHHHH...
KIRKMAN & SCOTT

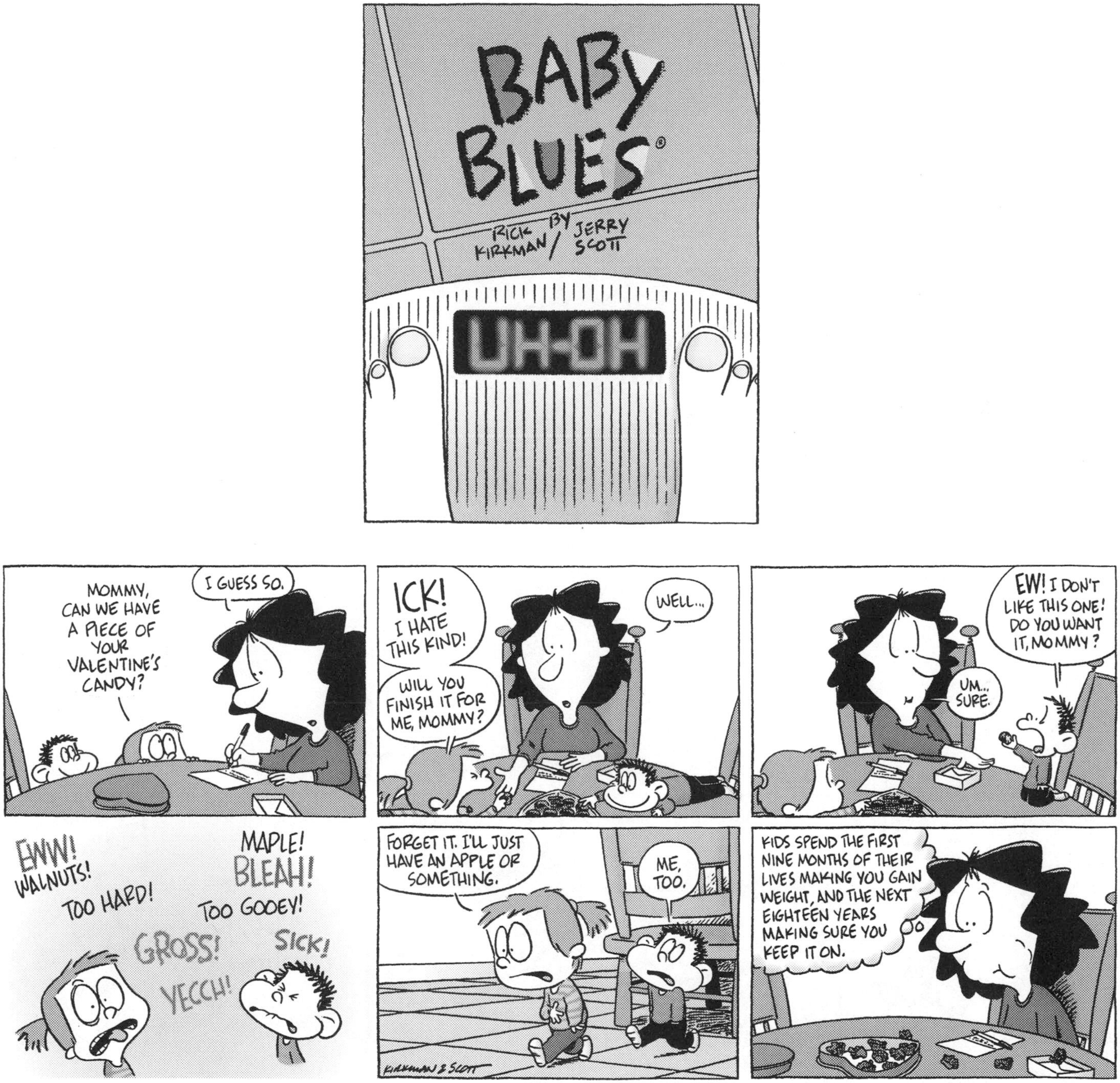
BABY BLUES®
BY RICK KIRKMAN / JERRY SCOTT
UH-OH
MOMMY, CAN WE HAVE A PIECE OF YOUR VALENTINE'S CANDY?
I GUESS SO.
ICK! I HATE THIS KIND!
WILL YOU FINISH IT FOR ME, MOMMY?
WELL...
EW! I DON'T LIKE THIS ONE! DO YOU WANT IT, MOMMY?
UM... SURE.
EWW! WALNUTS!
TOO HARD!
MAPLE! BLEAH!
TOO GOOEY!
GROSS!
SICK!
YECCH!
FORGET IT. I'LL JUST HAVE AN APPLE OR SOMETHING.
ME, TOO.
KIRKMAN & SCOTT
KIDS SPEND THE FIRST NINE MONTHS OF THEIR LIVES MAKING YOU GAIN WEIGHT, AND THE NEXT EIGHTEEN YEARS MAKING SURE YOU KEEP IT ON.

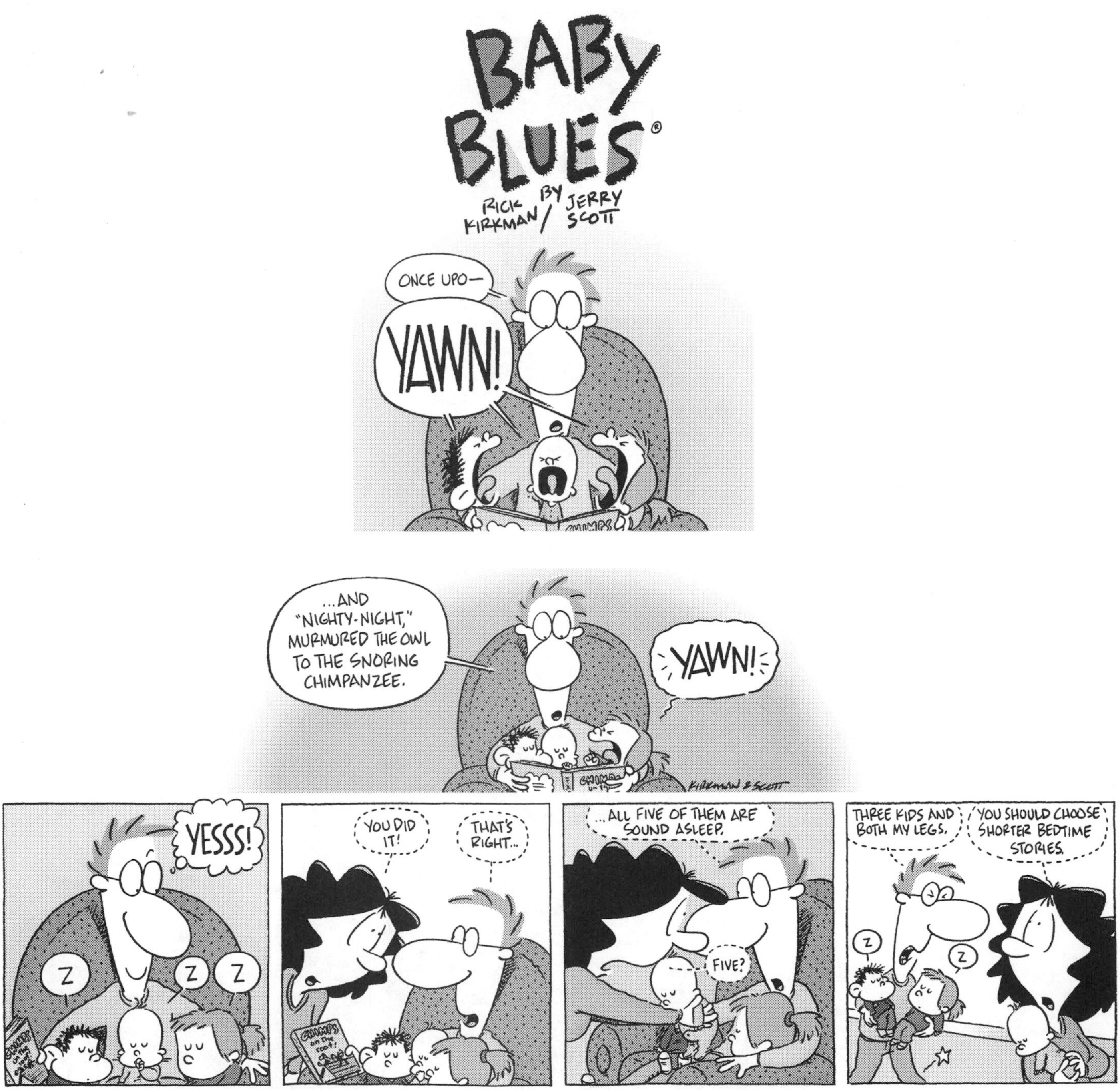
BABY BLUES®
BY RICK KIRKMAN / JERRY SCOTT
ONCE UPO—
YAWN!
...AND "NIGHTY-NIGHT," MURMURED THE OWL TO THE SNORING CHIMPANZEE.
YAWN!
KIRKMAN & SCOTT
YESSS!
Z
Z
Z
YOU DID IT!
THAT'S RIGHT...
...ALL FIVE OF THEM ARE SOUND ASLEEP.
FIVE?
THREE KIDS AND BOTH MY LEGS.
YOU SHOULD CHOOSE SHORTER BEDTIME STORIES.
Z
Z

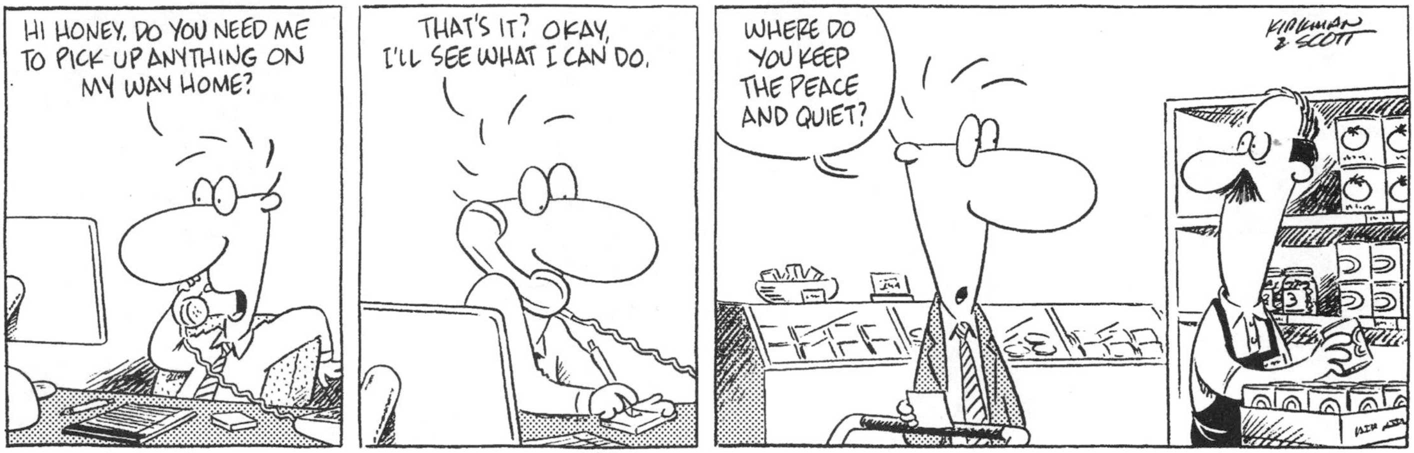
HI HONEY. DO YOU NEED ME TO PICK UP ANYTHING ON MY WAY HOME?
THAT'S IT? OKAY, I'LL SEE WHAT I CAN DO.
WHERE DO YOU KEEP THE PEACE AND QUIET?
KIRKMAN & SCOTT

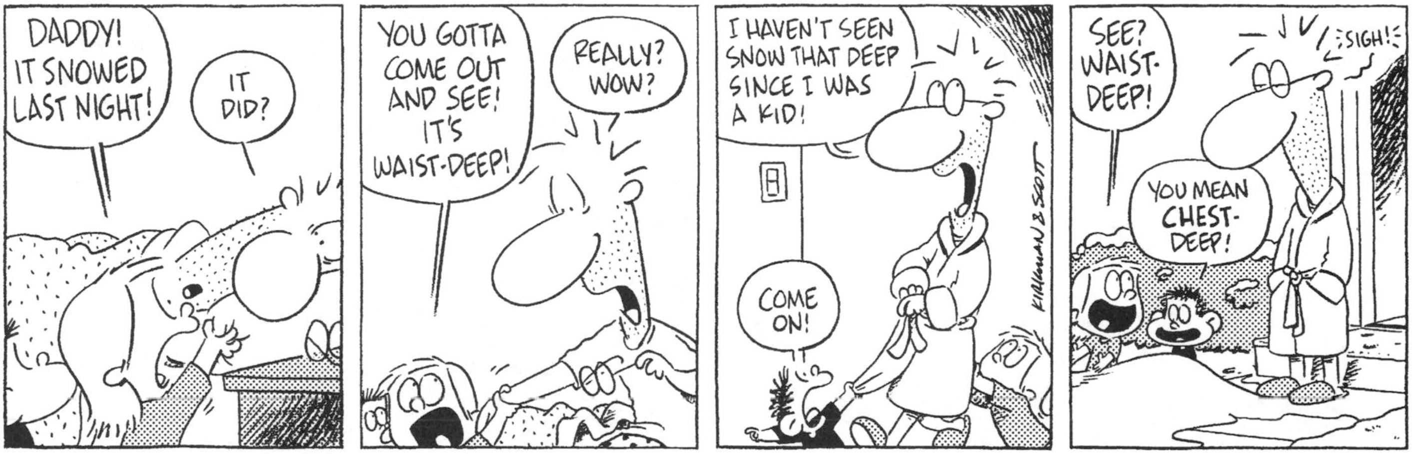
DADDY! IT SNOWED LAST NIGHT!
IT DID?
YOU GOTTA COME OUT AND SEE! IT'S WAIST-DEEP!
REALLY? WOW?
I HAVEN'T SEEN SNOW THAT DEEP SINCE I WAS A KID!
COME ON!
KIRKMAN & SCOTT
SEE? WAIST-DEEP!
SIGH!
YOU MEAN CHEST-DEEP!

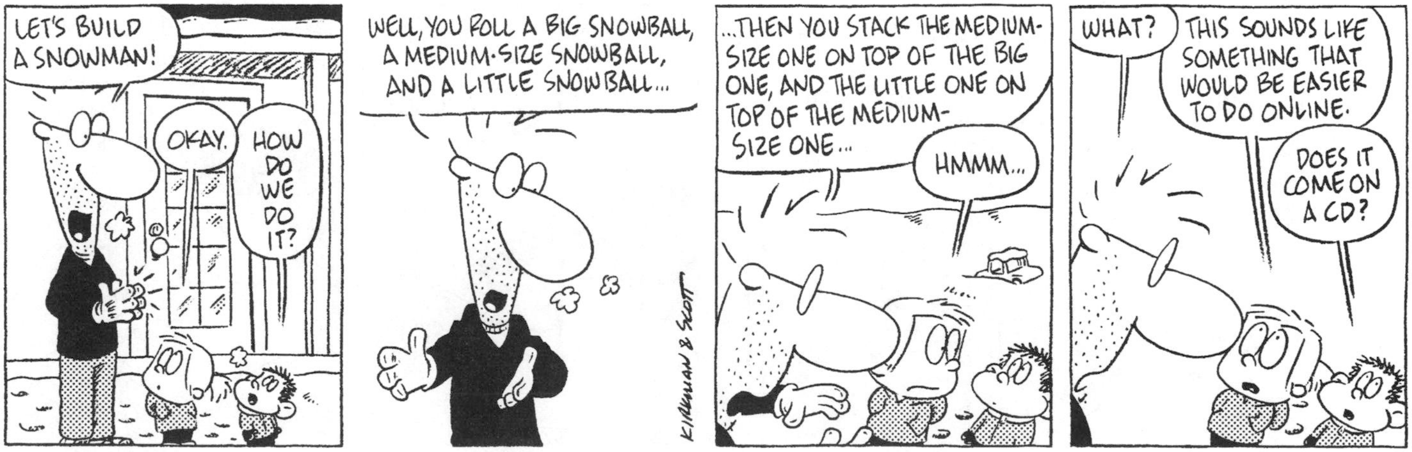
LET'S BUILD A SNOWMAN!
OKAY.
HOW DO WE DO IT?
WELL, YOU ROLL A BIG SNOWBALL, A MEDIUM-SIZE SNOWBALL, AND A LITTLE SNOWBALL...
KIRKMAN & SCOTT
...THEN YOU STACK THE MEDIUM-SIZE ONE ON TOP OF THE BIG ONE, AND THE LITTLE ONE ON TOP OF THE MEDIUM-SIZE ONE...
HMMM...
WHAT?
THIS SOUNDS LIKE SOMETHING THAT WOULD BE EASIER TO DO ONLINE.
DOES IT COME ON A CD?

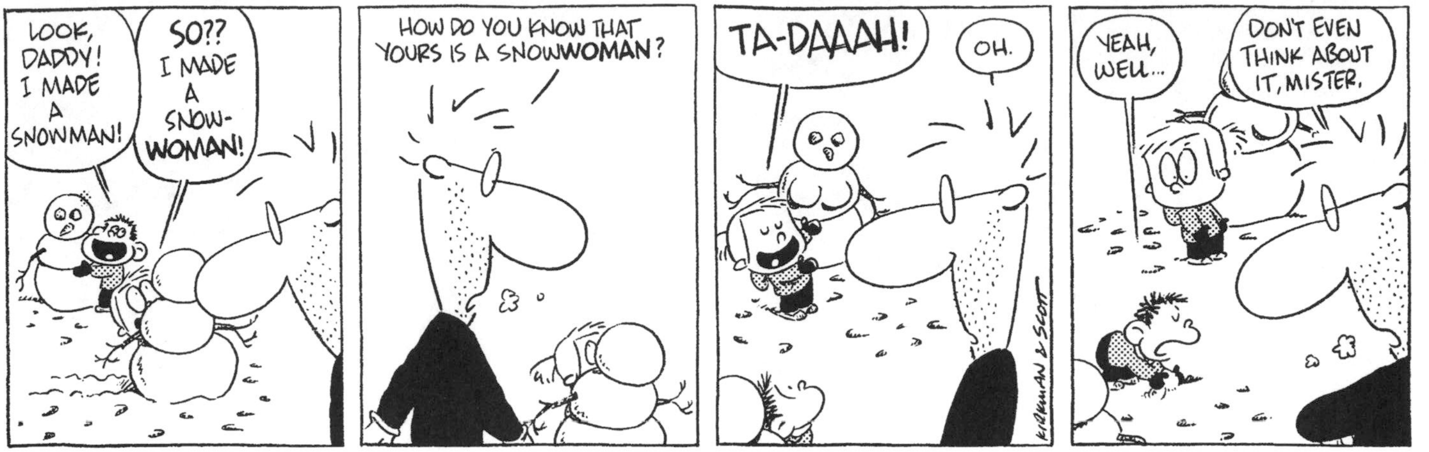
LOOK, DADDY! I MADE A SNOWMAN!
SO?? I MADE A SNOW-WOMAN!
HOW DO YOU KNOW THAT YOURS IS A SNOWWOMAN?
TA-DAAAH!
OH.
KIRKMAN & SCOTT
YEAH, WELL...
DON'T EVEN THINK ABOUT IT, MISTER.

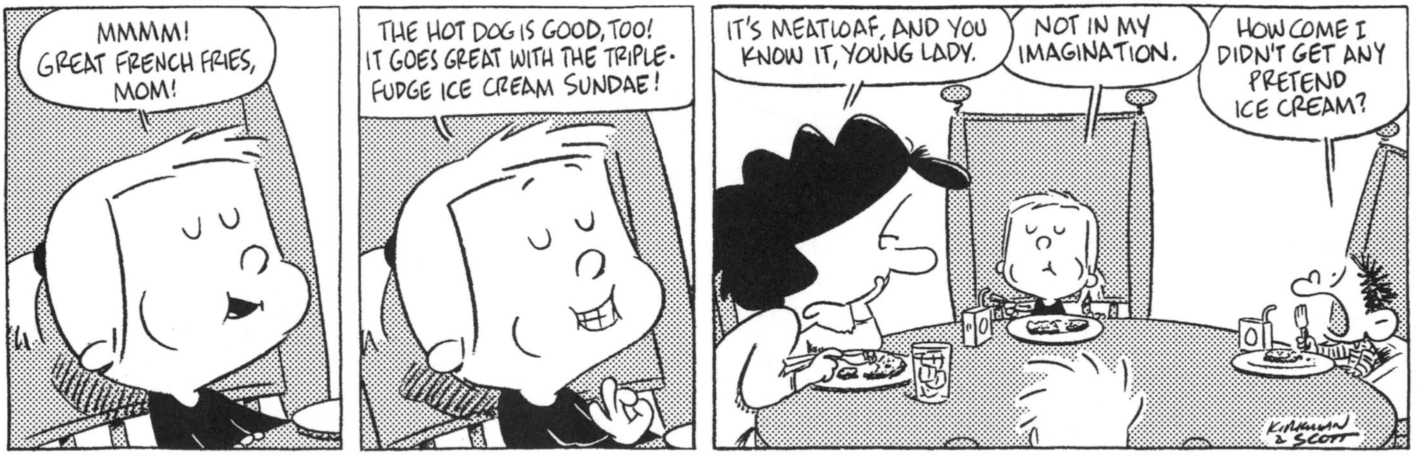
MMMM! GREAT FRENCH FRIES, MOM!
THE HOT DOG IS GOOD, TOO! IT GOES GREAT WITH THE TRIPLE-FUDGE ICE CREAM SUNDAE!
IT'S MEATLOAF, AND YOU KNOW IT, YOUNG LADY.
NOT IN MY IMAGINATION.
HOW COME I DIDN'T GET ANY PRETEND ICE CREAM?
KIRKMAN & SCOTT

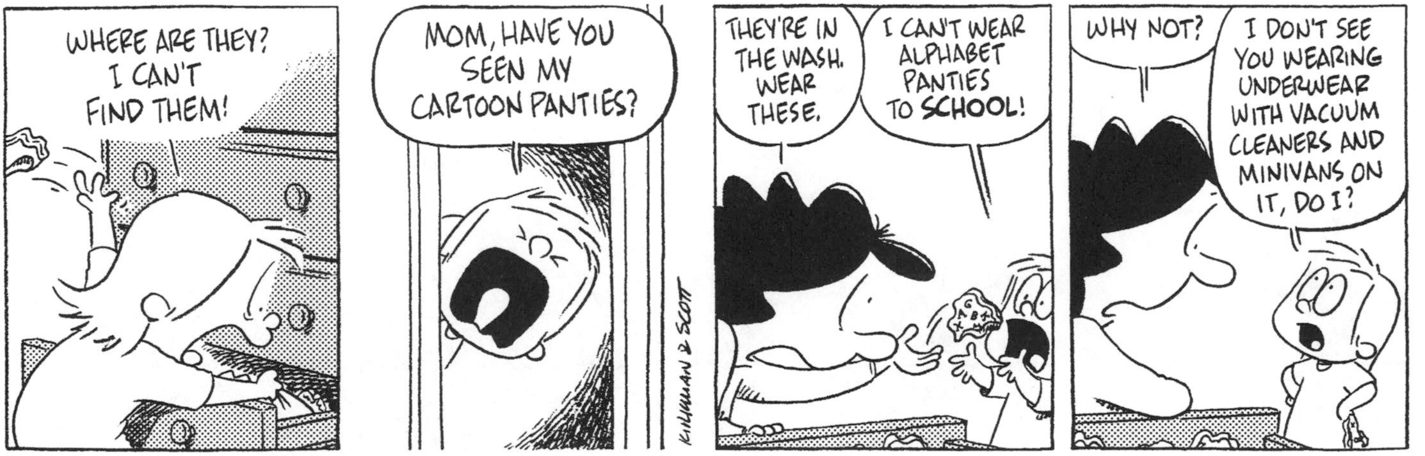
WHERE ARE THEY? I CAN'T FIND THEM!
MOM, HAVE YOU SEEN MY CARTOON PANTIES?
KIRKMAN & SCOTT
THEY'RE IN THE WASH. WEAR THESE.
I CAN'T WEAR ALPHABET PANTIES TO SCHOOL!
WHY NOT?
I DON'T SEE YOU WEARING UNDERWEAR WITH VACUUM CLEANERS AND MINIVANS ON IT, DO I?

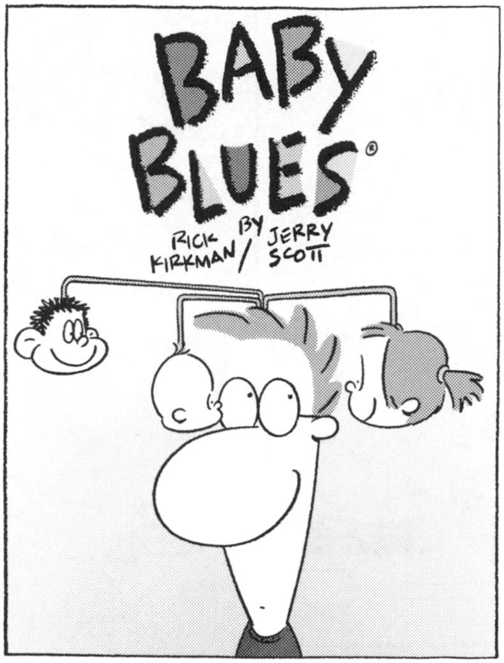
BABY BLUES®
BY
RICK KIRKMAN / JERRY SCOTT

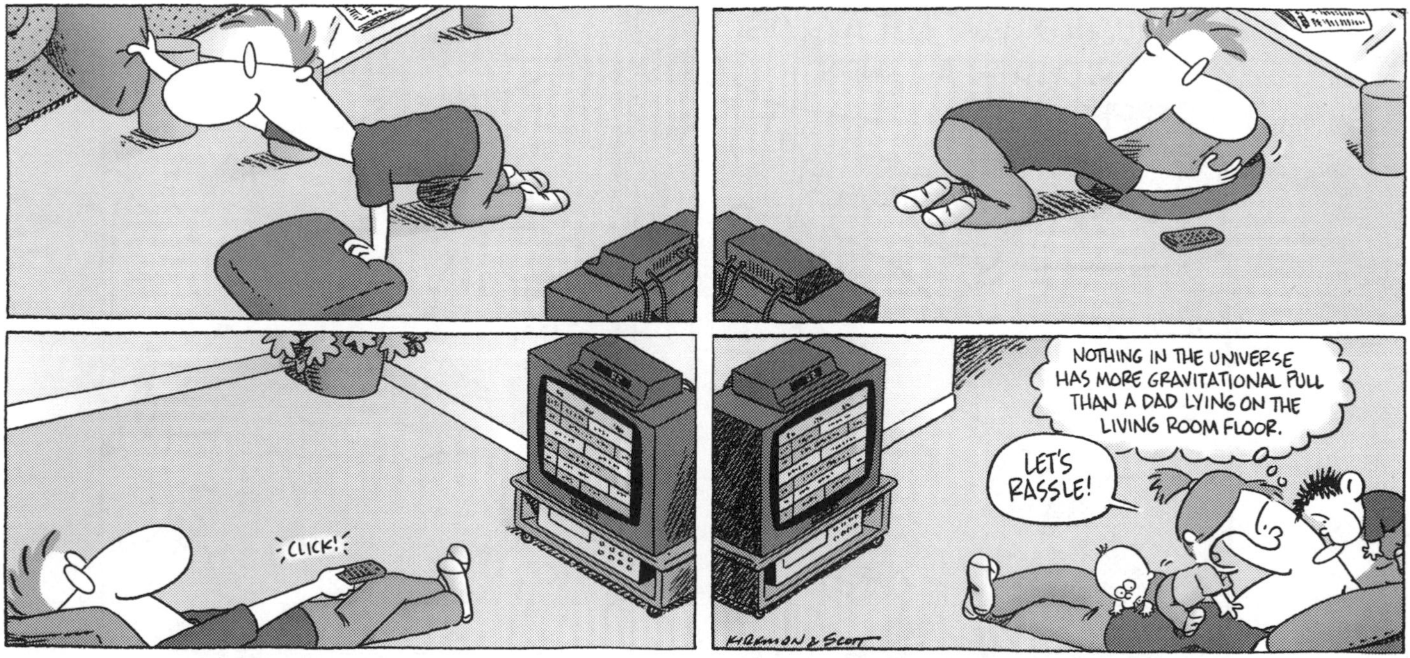
CLICK!
NOTHING IN THE UNIVERSE HAS MORE GRAVITATIONAL PULL THAN A DAD LYING ON THE LIVING ROOM FLOOR.
LET'S RASSLE!
KIRKMAN & SCOTT

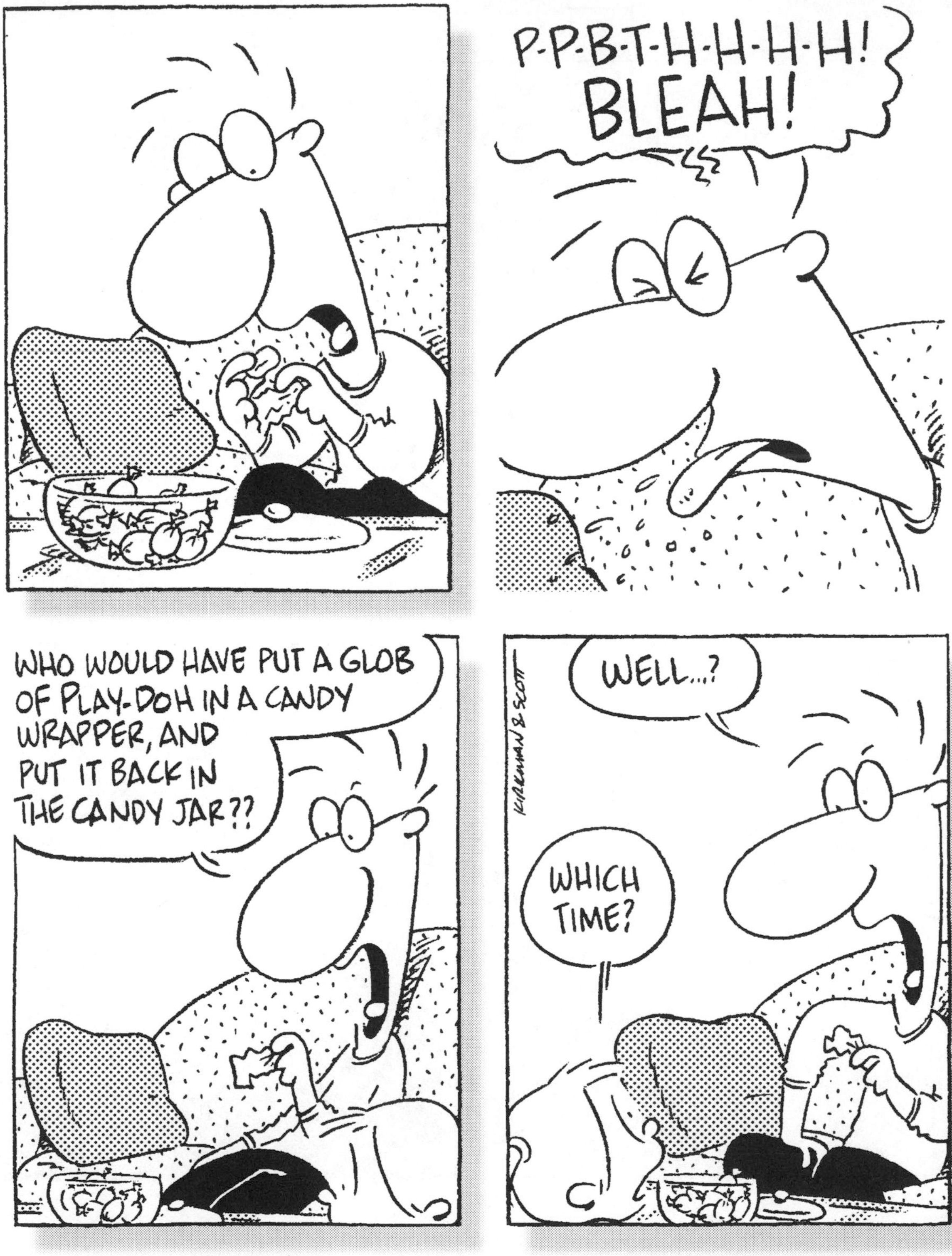
P-P-B-T-H-H-H-H!
BLEAH!
WHO WOULD HAVE PUT A GLOB OF PLAY-DOH IN A CANDY WRAPPER, AND PUT IT BACK IN THE CANDY JAR??
KIRKMAN & SCOTT
WELL...?
WHICH TIME?

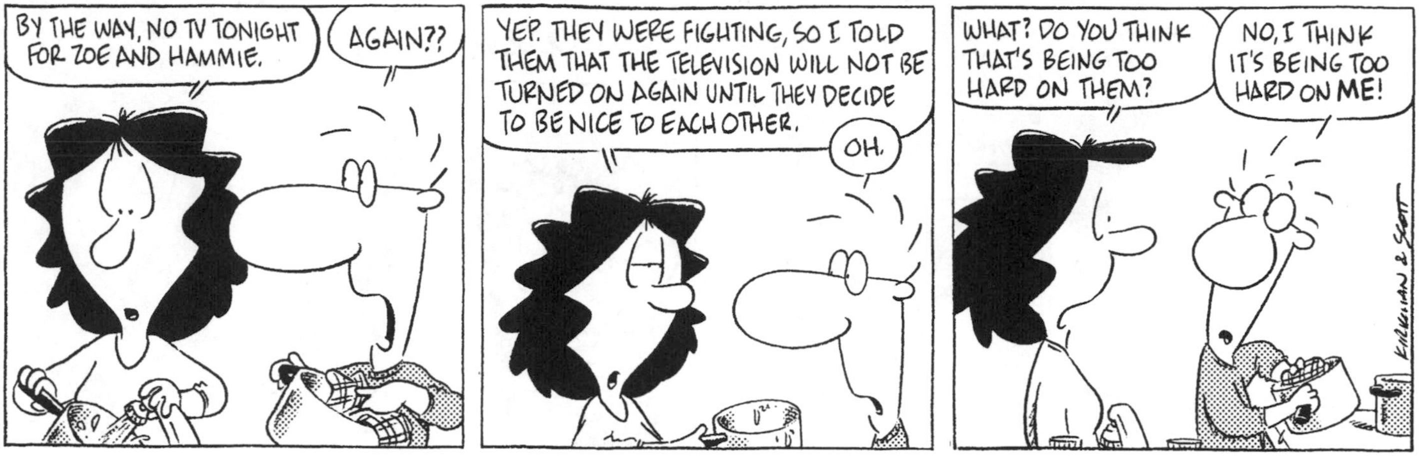
BY THE WAY, NO TV TONIGHT FOR ZOE AND HAMMIE.
AGAIN??
YEP. THEY WERE FIGHTING, SO I TOLD THEM THAT THE TELEVISION WILL NOT BE TURNED ON AGAIN UNTIL THEY DECIDE TO BE NICE TO EACH OTHER.
OH.
WHAT? DO YOU THINK THAT'S BEING TOO HARD ON THEM?
NO, I THINK IT'S BEING TOO HARD ON ME!
KIRKMAN & SCOTT

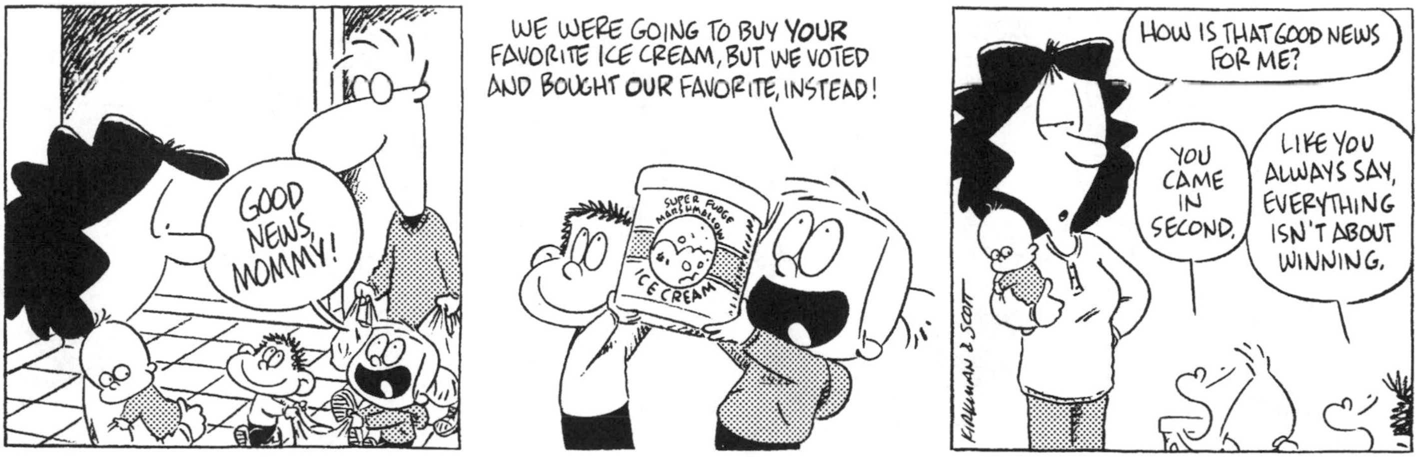
GOOD NEWS, MOMMY!
WE WERE GOING TO BUY YOUR FAVORITE ICE CREAM, BUT WE VOTED AND BOUGHT OUR FAVORITE, INSTEAD!
SUPER FUDGE MARSHMALLOW
ICE CREAM
HOW IS THAT GOOD NEWS FOR ME?
YOU CAME IN SECOND.
LIKE YOU ALWAYS SAY, EVERYTHING ISN'T ABOUT WINNING.
KIRKMAN & SCOTT

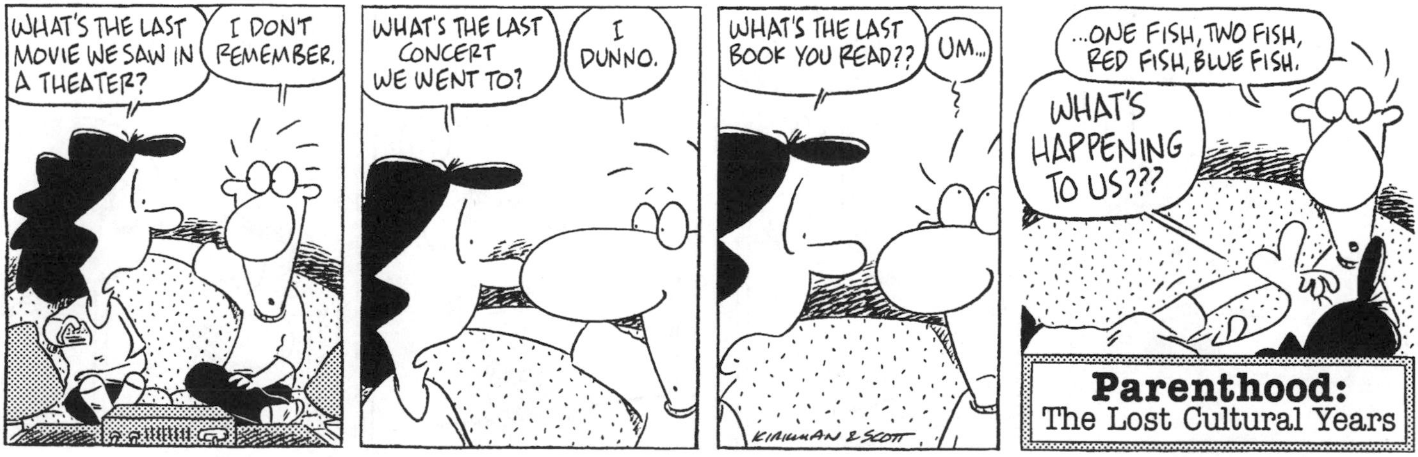
WHAT'S THE LAST MOVIE WE SAW IN A THEATER?
I DON'T REMEMBER.
WHAT'S THE LAST CONCERT WE WENT TO?
I DUNNO.
WHAT'S THE LAST BOOK YOU READ??
UM...
KIRKMAN & SCOTT
...ONE FISH, TWO FISH, RED FISH, BLUE FISH.
WHAT'S HAPPENING TO US???
Parenthood: The Lost Cultural Years

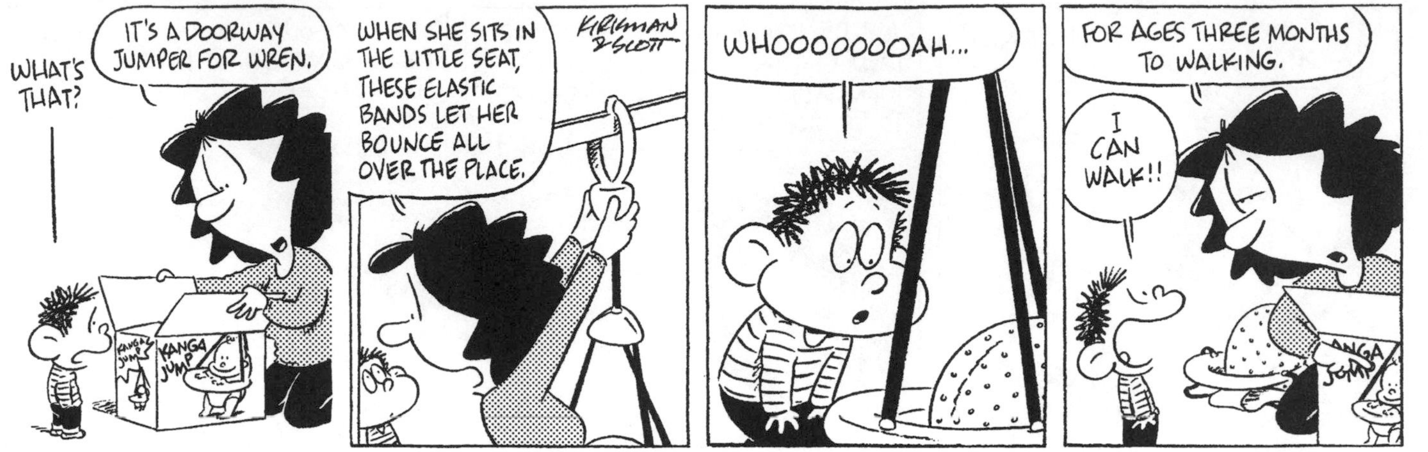
WHAT'S THAT?
IT'S A DOORWAY JUMPER FOR WREN.
KANGA JUMP
WHEN SHE SITS IN THE LITTLE SEAT, THESE ELASTIC BANDS LET HER BOUNCE ALL OVER THE PLACE.
KIRKMAN & SCOTT
WHOOOOOOOOAH...
FOR AGES THREE MONTHS TO WALKING.
I CAN WALK!!

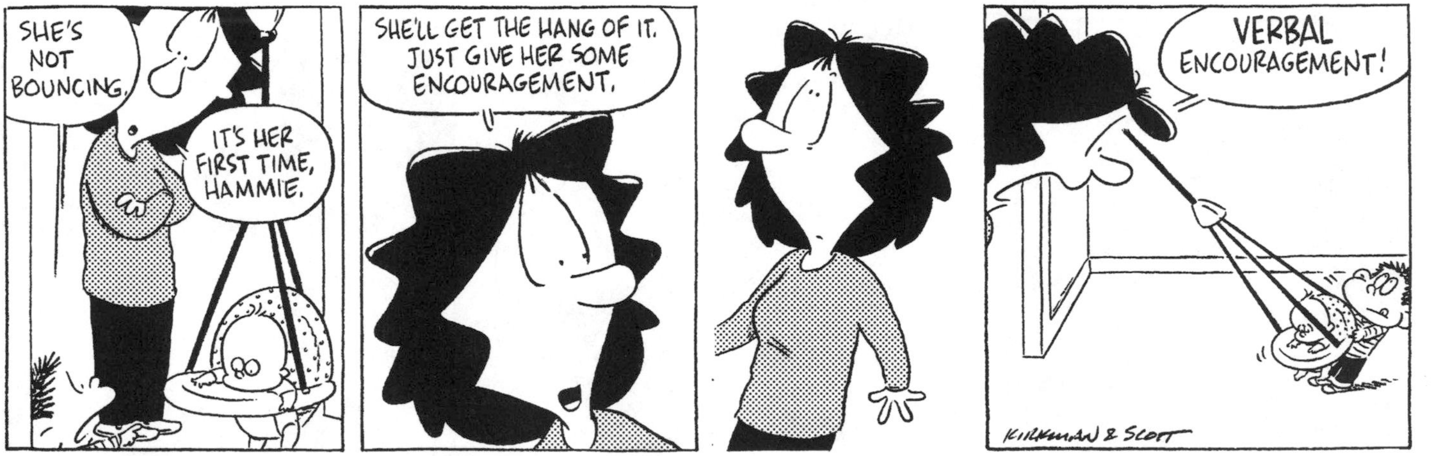
SHE'S NOT BOUNCING.
IT'S HER FIRST TIME, HAMMIE.
SHE'LL GET THE HANG OF IT. JUST GIVE HER SOME ENCOURAGEMENT.
VERBAL ENCOURAGEMENT!
KIRKMAN & SCOTT

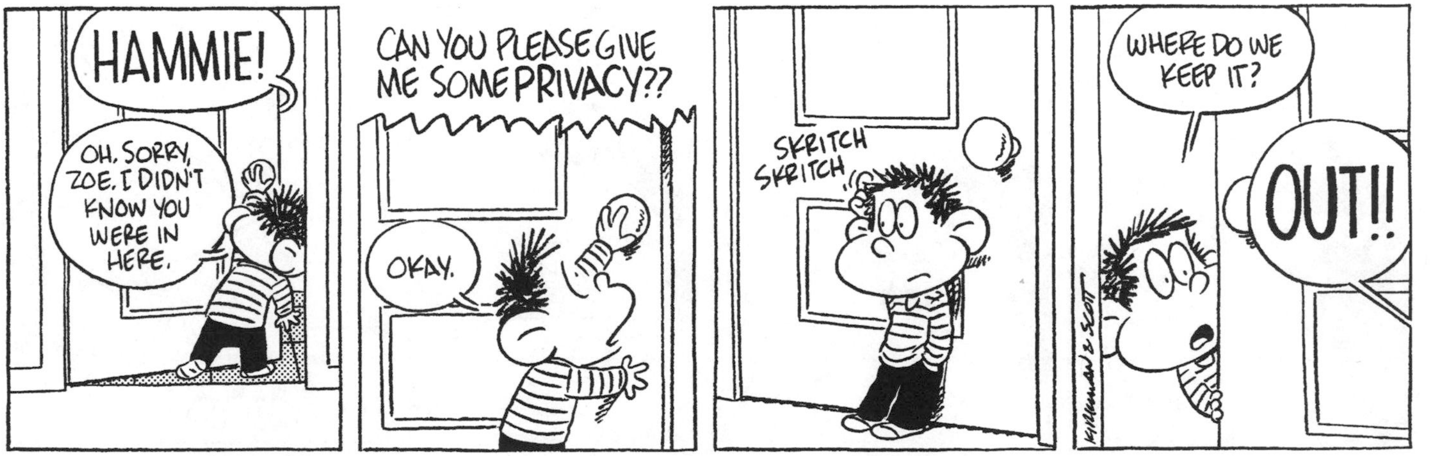
HAMMIE!
OH. SORRY, ZOE. I DIDN'T KNOW YOU WERE IN HERE.
CAN YOU PLEASE GIVE ME SOME PRIVACY??
OKAY.
SKRITCH SKRITCH
WHERE DO WE KEEP IT?
OUT!!
KIRKMAN & SCOTT

BABY BLUES®
BY RICK KIRKMAN / JERRY SCOTT

GREEN TEA...
...A LITTLE MILK...
...LEMON... SWEETENER... MINT...
...AND A TOUCH OF TABASCO.
IS THAT GOOD?
S-I-I-I-P! NOT REALLY.
KIRKMAN & SCOTT
THEN WHY DID YOU-?
IT'S THE ONLY THING I CAN DRINK AROUND HERE WITHOUT A KID ASKING FOR A SIP.
YUK!

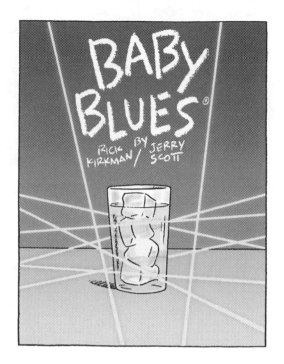

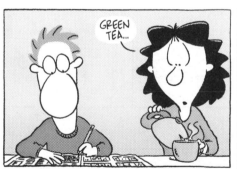

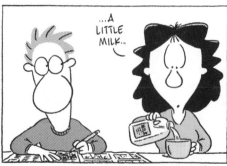

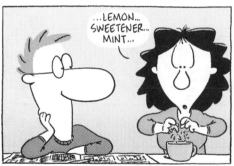

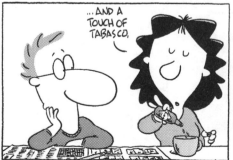

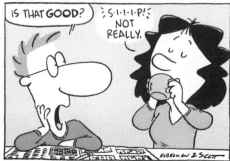

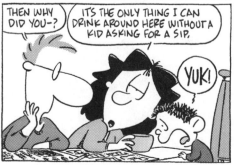

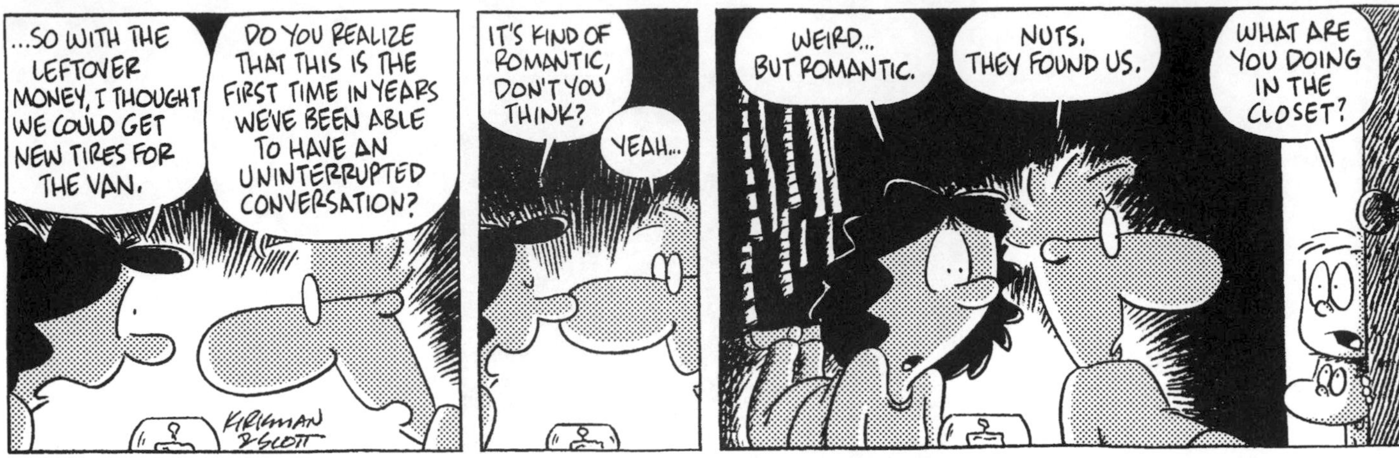
...SO WITH THE LEFTOVER MONEY, I THOUGHT WE COULD GET NEW TIRES FOR THE VAN.
DO YOU REALIZE THAT THIS IS THE FIRST TIME IN YEARS WE'VE BEEN ABLE TO HAVE AN UNINTERRUPTED CONVERSATION?
IT'S KIND OF ROMANTIC, DON'T YOU THINK?
YEAH...
WEIRD... BUT ROMANTIC.
NUTS. THEY FOUND US.
WHAT ARE YOU DOING IN THE CLOSET?

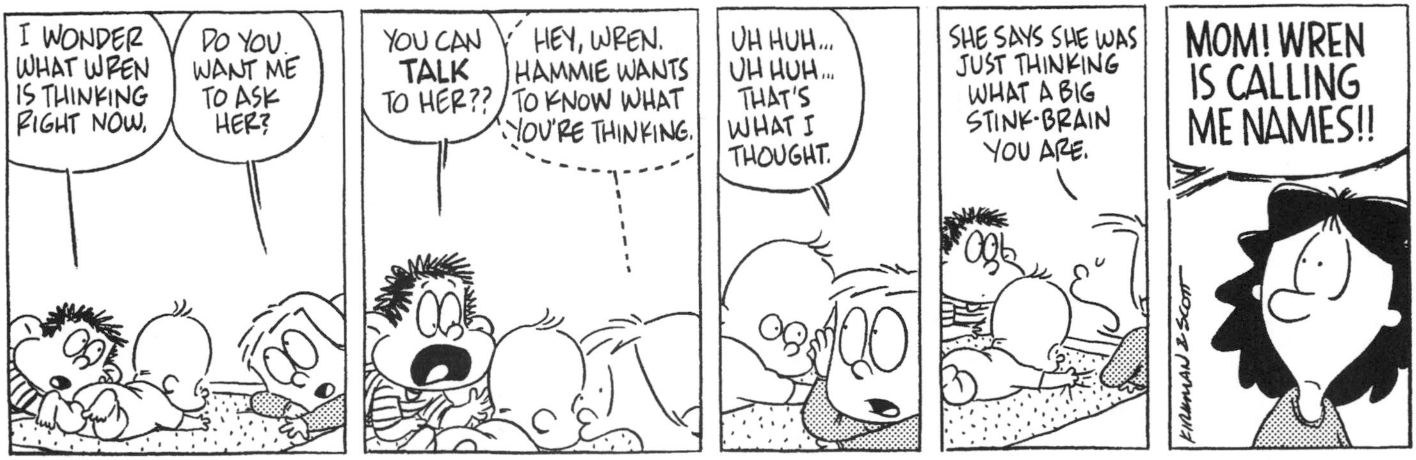
I WONDER WHAT WREN IS THINKING RIGHT NOW.
DO YOU WANT ME TO ASK HER?
YOU CAN **TALK** TO HER??
HEY, WREN. HAMMIE WANTS TO KNOW WHAT YOU'RE THINKING.
UH HUH... UH HUH... THAT'S WHAT I THOUGHT.
SHE SAYS SHE WAS JUST THINKING WHAT A BIG STINK-BRAIN YOU ARE.
MOM! WREN IS CALLING ME NAMES!!

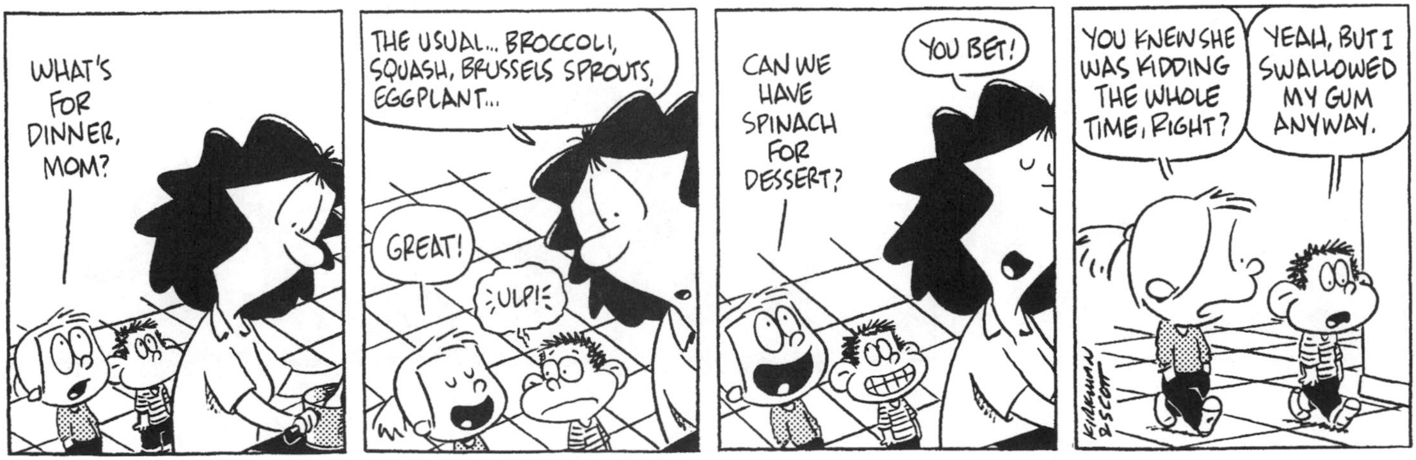
WHAT'S FOR DINNER, MOM?
THE USUAL... BROCCOLI, SQUASH, BRUSSELS SPROUTS, EGGPLANT...
GREAT!
ULP!
CAN WE HAVE SPINACH FOR DESSERT?
YOU BET!
YOU KNEW SHE WAS KIDDING THE WHOLE TIME, RIGHT?
YEAH, BUT I SWALLOWED MY GUM ANYWAY.

BABY BLUES®
BY RICK KIRKMAN / JERRY SCOTT

WHAT ARE YOU WORKING ON, ZOE?
HOMEWORK.
ON A GROCERY BAG??
SWEETHEART, THE LIGHT IN HERE IS SO DIM, YOU CAN HARDLY SEE!
CLICK!
AND YOU CALL THIS A PENCIL? IT'S JUST A STUB!
YOUR WHOLE STUDY ENVIRONMENT NEEDS IMPROVEMENT. LET ME HELP.
LET'S START WITH A STACK OF CLEAN, CRISP NOTEBOOK PAPER AND A NEW, RAZOR-SHARP PENCIL WITH A FRESH, PINK ERASER...
...ADD NICE STRONG LIGHT OVER YOUR LEFT SHOULDER, GOOD POSTURE, AND PRESTO! ISN'T THAT BETTER?
I GUESS SO.
KIRKMAN & SCOTT
SO...WHAT'S THE ASSIGNMENT?
WE'RE SUPPOSED TO WRITE A POEM ON A GROCERY BAG IN THE DARK WITH A DULL PENCIL STUB.

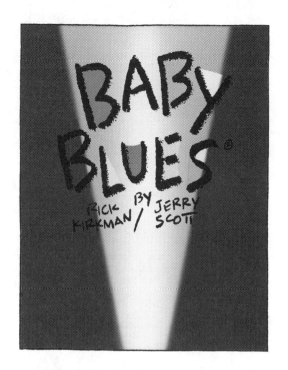

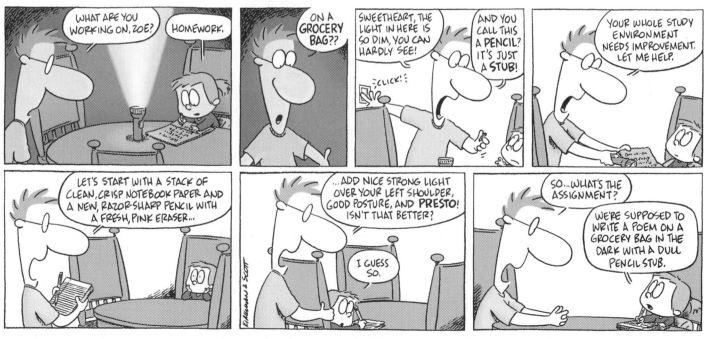

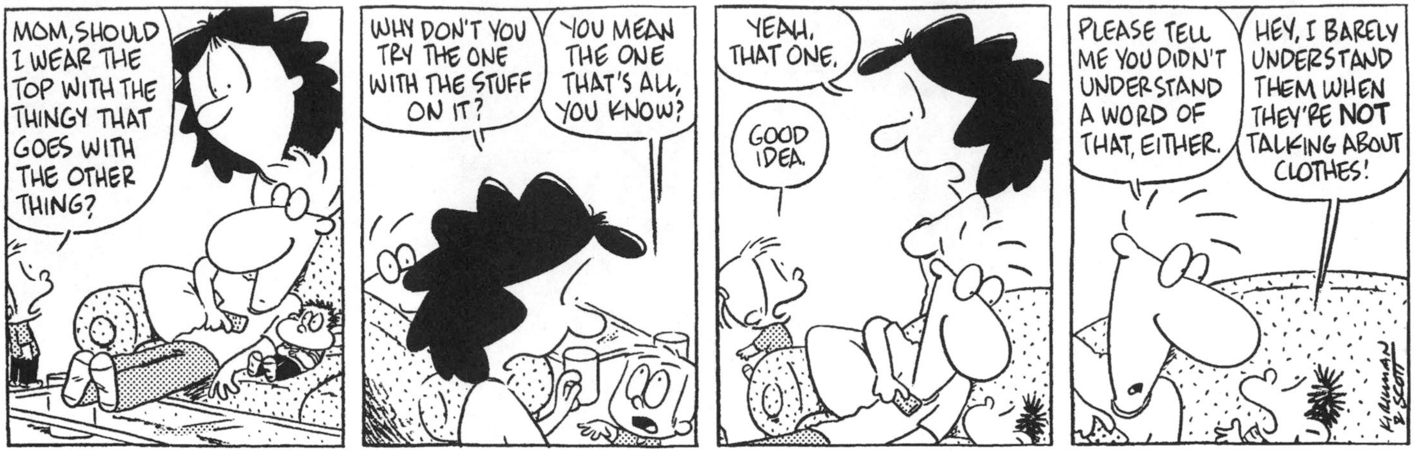
MOM, SHOULD I WEAR THE TOP WITH THE THINGY THAT GOES WITH THE OTHER THING?
WHY DON'T YOU TRY THE ONE WITH THE STUFF ON IT?
YOU MEAN THE ONE THAT'S ALL, YOU KNOW?
YEAH, THAT ONE.
GOOD IDEA.
PLEASE TELL ME YOU DIDN'T UNDERSTAND A WORD OF THAT, EITHER.
HEY, I BARELY UNDERSTAND THEM WHEN THEY'RE **NOT** TALKING ABOUT CLOTHES!
KIRKMAN & SCOTT

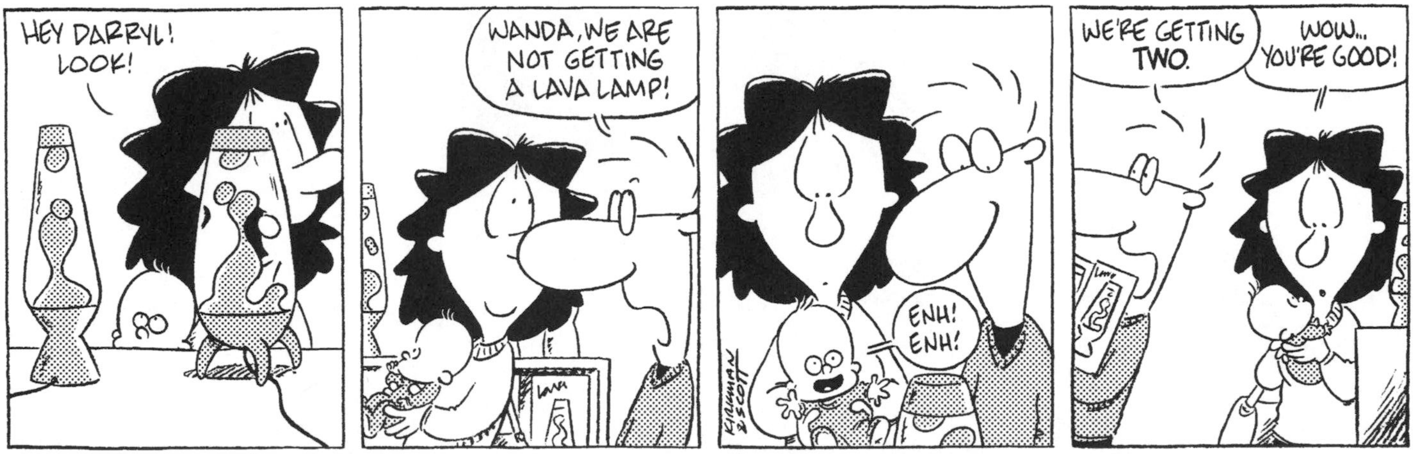
HEY DARRYL! LOOK!
WANDA, WE ARE NOT GETTING A LAVA LAMP!
KIRKMAN & SCOTT
ENH! ENH!
WE'RE GETTING **TWO**.
WOW... YOU'RE GOOD!

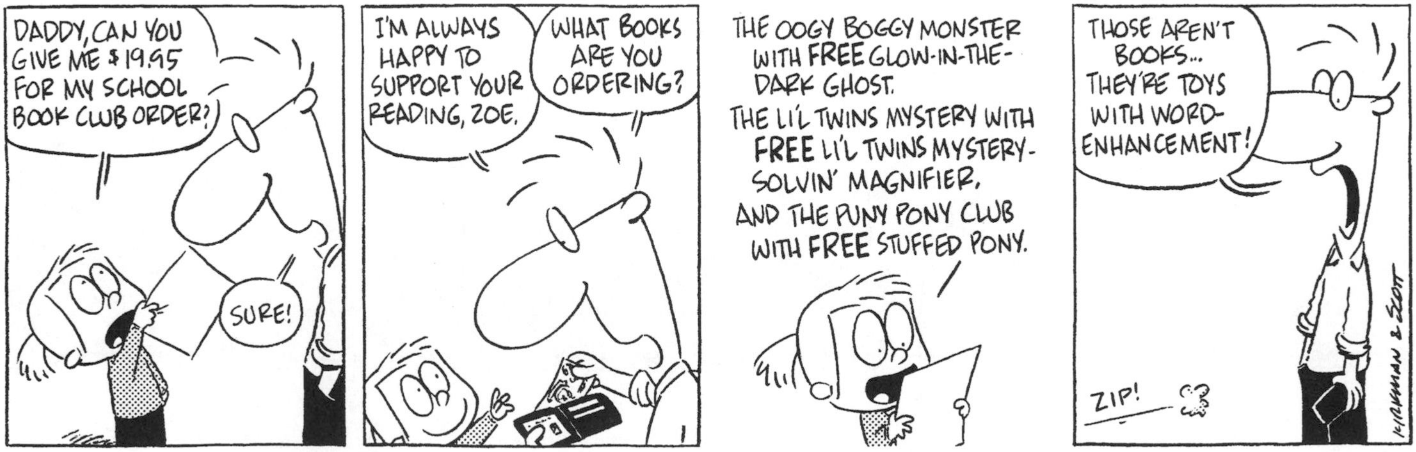
DADDY, CAN YOU GIVE ME $19.95 FOR MY SCHOOL BOOK CLUB ORDER?
SURE!
I'M ALWAYS HAPPY TO SUPPORT YOUR READING, ZOE.
WHAT BOOKS ARE YOU ORDERING?
THE OOGY BOGGY MONSTER WITH **FREE** GLOW-IN-THE-DARK GHOST. THE LI'L TWINS MYSTERY WITH **FREE** LI'L TWINS MYSTERY-SOLVIN' MAGNIFIER, AND THE PUNY PONY CLUB WITH **FREE** STUFFED PONY.
THOSE AREN'T BOOKS... THEY'RE TOYS WITH WORD-ENHANCEMENT!
ZIP!
KIRKMAN & SCOTT

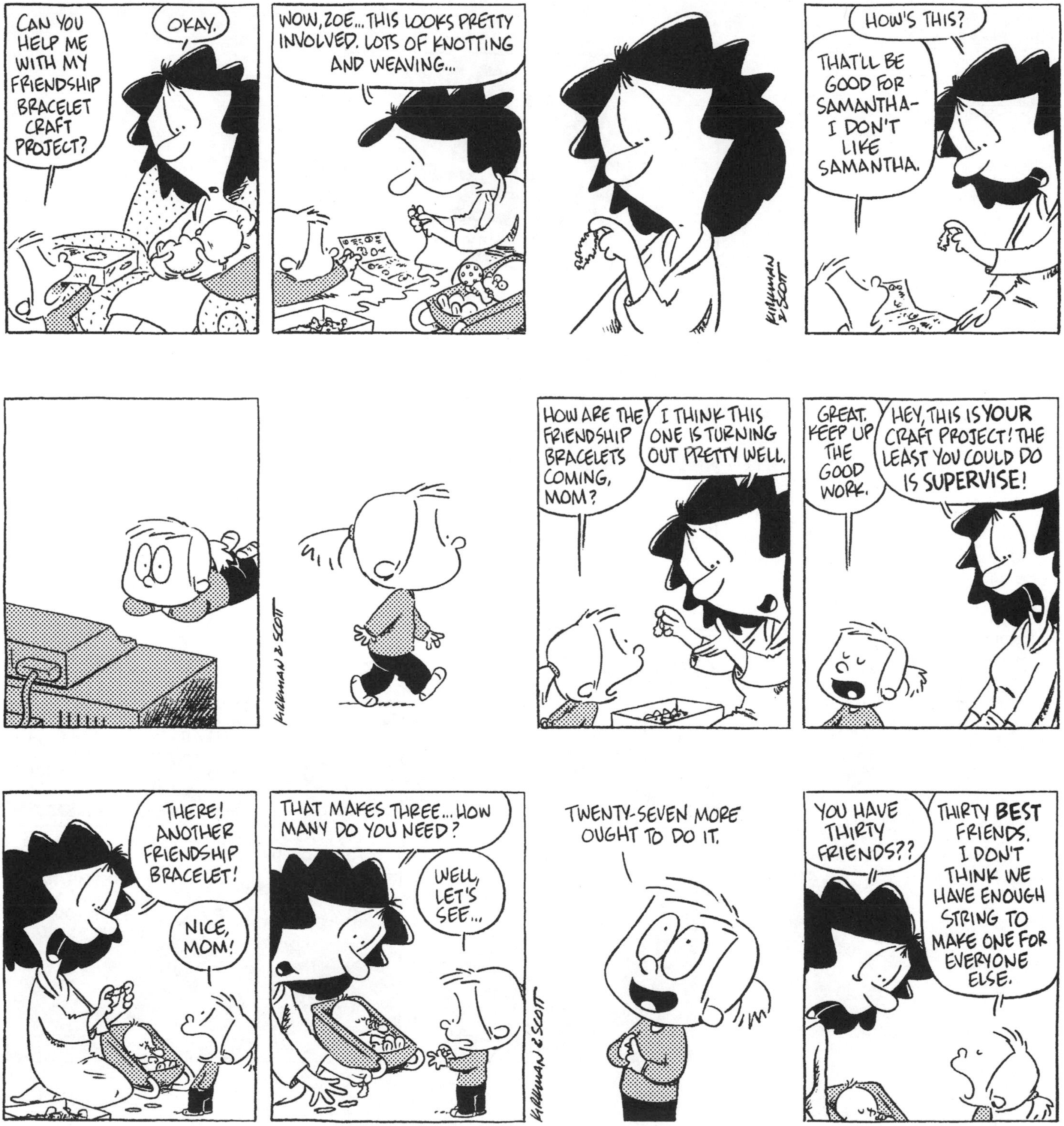
CAN YOU HELP ME WITH MY FRIENDSHIP BRACELET CRAFT PROJECT?
OKAY.
WOW, ZOE... THIS LOOKS PRETTY INVOLVED. LOTS OF KNOTTING AND WEAVING...
HOW'S THIS?
THAT'LL BE GOOD FOR SAMANTHA- I DON'T LIKE SAMANTHA.
KIRKMAN & SCOTT
KIRKMAN & SCOTT
HOW ARE THE FRIENDSHIP BRACELETS COMING, MOM?
I THINK THIS ONE IS TURNING OUT PRETTY WELL.
GREAT. KEEP UP THE GOOD WORK.
HEY, THIS IS YOUR CRAFT PROJECT! THE LEAST YOU COULD DO IS SUPERVISE!
THERE! ANOTHER FRIENDSHIP BRACELET!
NICE, MOM!
THAT MAKES THREE... HOW MANY DO YOU NEED?
WELL, LET'S SEE...
KIRKMAN & SCOTT
TWENTY-SEVEN MORE OUGHT TO DO IT.
YOU HAVE THIRTY FRIENDS??
THIRTY BEST FRIENDS. I DON'T THINK WE HAVE ENOUGH STRING TO MAKE ONE FOR EVERYONE ELSE.

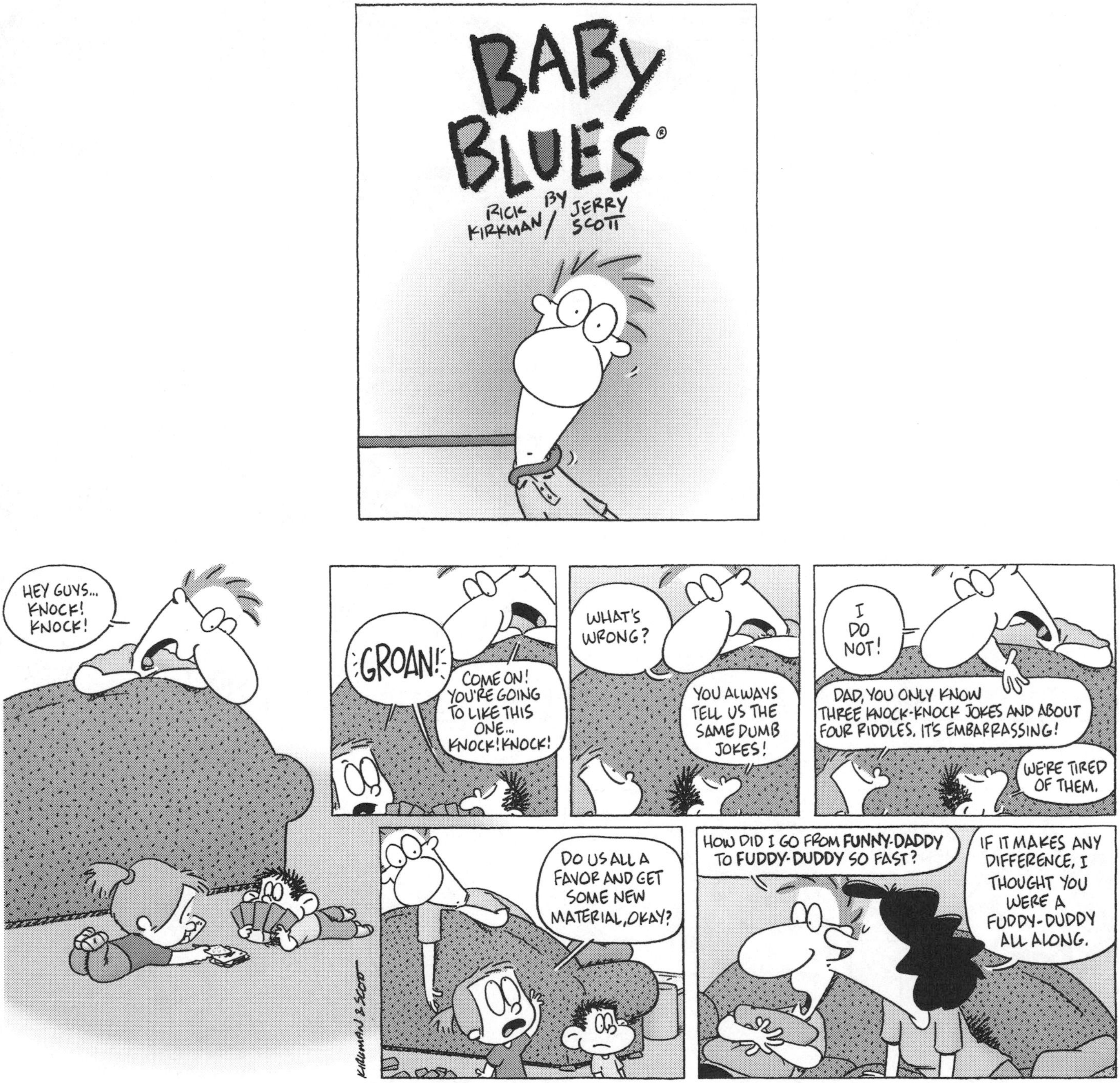
BABY BLUES®
BY RICK KIRKMAN / JERRY SCOTT
HEY GUYS... KNOCK! KNOCK!
GROAN!
COME ON! YOU'RE GOING TO LIKE THIS ONE... KNOCK! KNOCK!
WHAT'S WRONG?
YOU ALWAYS TELL US THE SAME DUMB JOKES!
I DO NOT!
DAD, YOU ONLY KNOW THREE KNOCK-KNOCK JOKES AND ABOUT FOUR RIDDLES. IT'S EMBARRASSING!
WE'RE TIRED OF THEM.
DO US ALL A FAVOR AND GET SOME NEW MATERIAL, OKAY?
HOW DID I GO FROM FUNNY-DADDY TO FUDDY-DUDDY SO FAST?
IF IT MAKES ANY DIFFERENCE, I THOUGHT YOU WERE A FUDDY-DUDDY ALL ALONG.
KIRKMAN & SCOTT

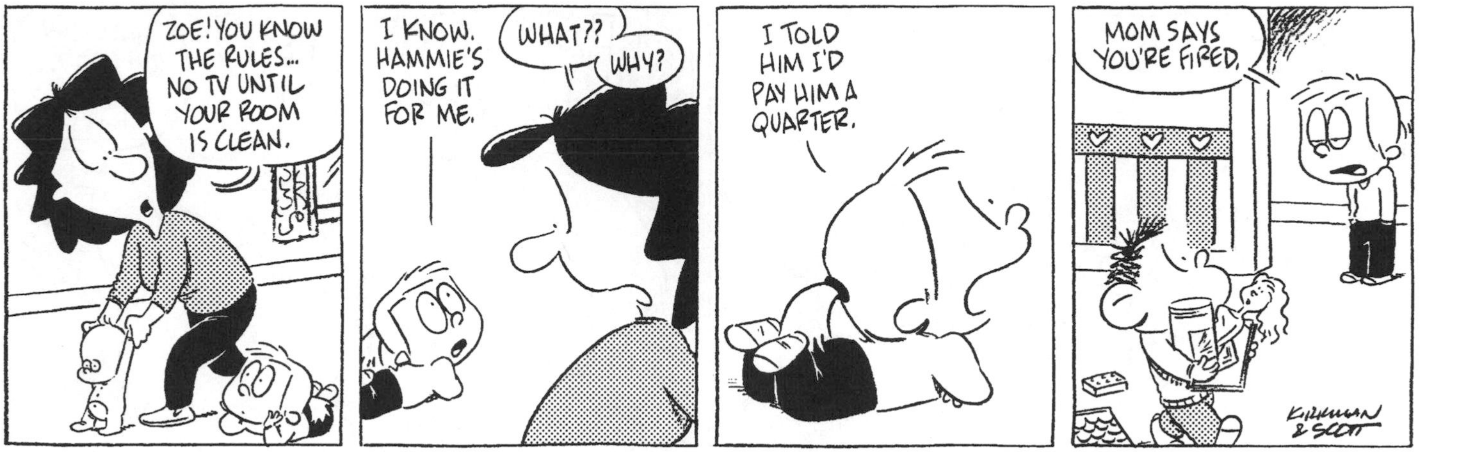
ZOE! YOU KNOW THE RULES... NO TV UNTIL YOUR ROOM IS CLEAN.
I KNOW. HAMMIE'S DOING IT FOR ME.
WHAT??
WHY?
I TOLD HIM I'D PAY HIM A QUARTER.
MOM SAYS YOU'RE FIRED.
KIRKMAN & SCOTT

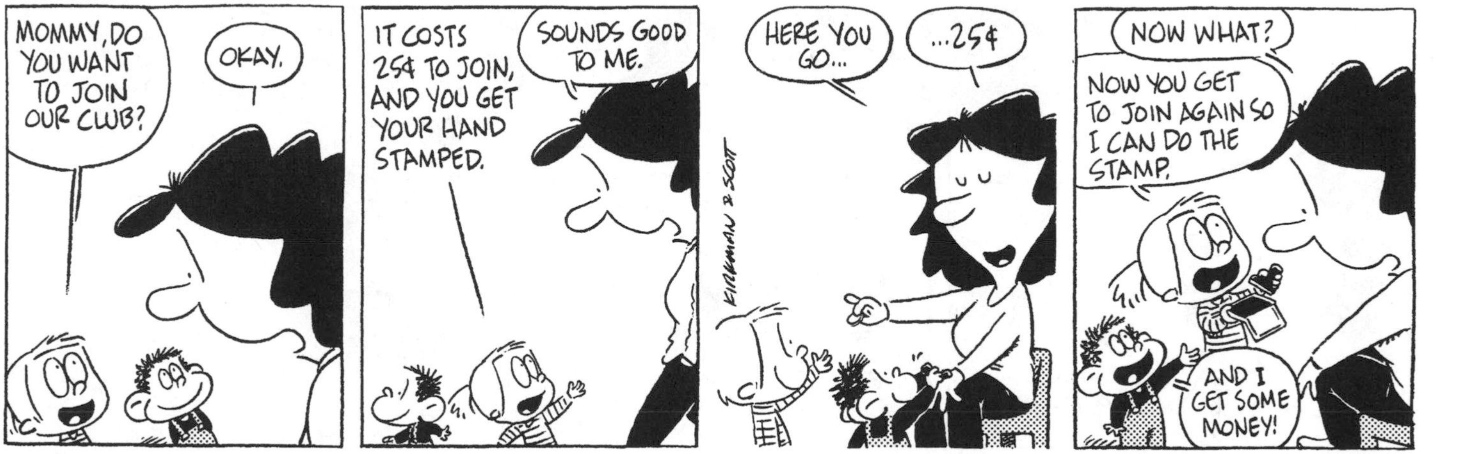
MOMMY, DO YOU WANT TO JOIN OUR CLUB?
OKAY.
IT COSTS 25¢ TO JOIN, AND YOU GET YOUR HAND STAMPED.
SOUNDS GOOD TO ME.
KIRKMAN & SCOTT
HERE YOU GO...
...25¢
NOW WHAT?
NOW YOU GET TO JOIN AGAIN SO I CAN DO THE STAMP.
AND I GET SOME MONEY!

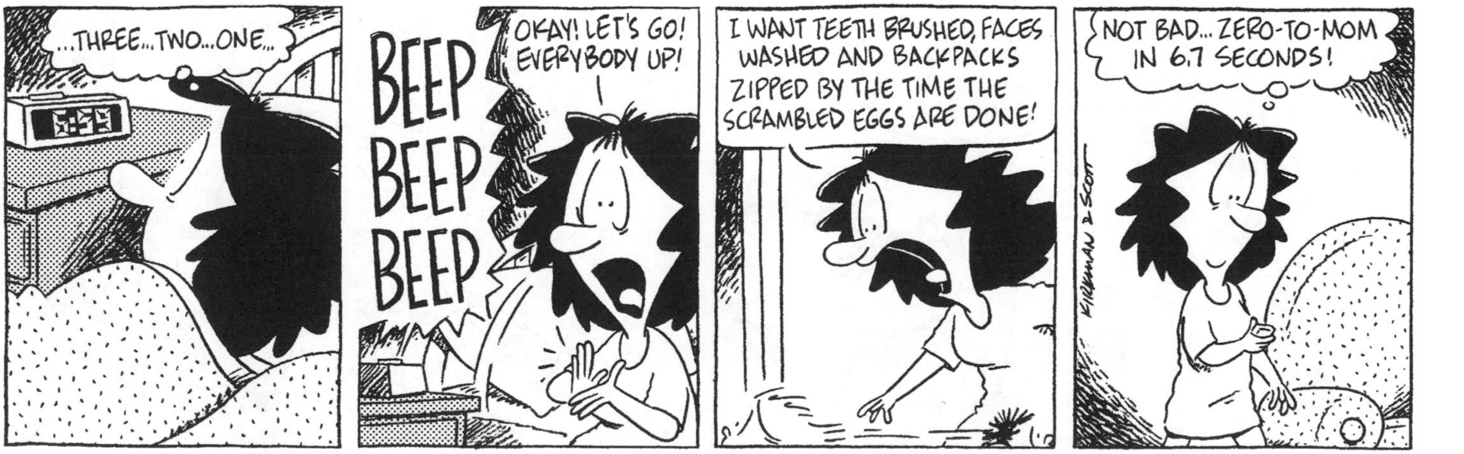
...THREE...TWO...ONE...
BEEP BEEP BEEP
OKAY! LET'S GO! EVERYBODY UP!
I WANT TEETH BRUSHED, FACES WASHED AND BACKPACKS ZIPPED BY THE TIME THE SCRAMBLED EGGS ARE DONE!
KIRKMAN & SCOTT
NOT BAD... ZERO-TO-MOM IN 6.7 SECONDS!

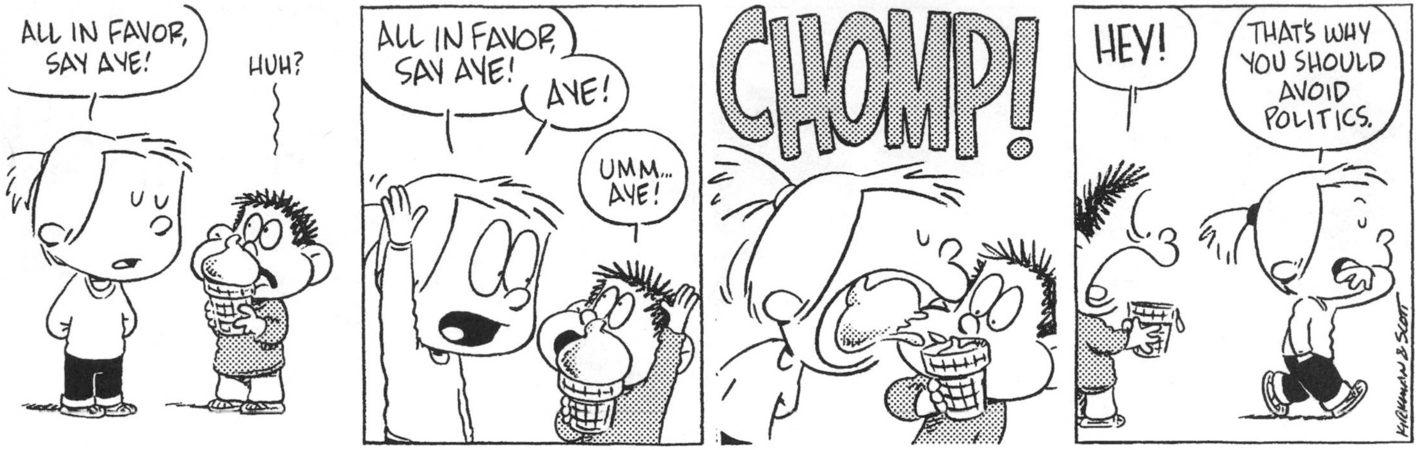
ALL IN FAVOR, SAY AYE!
HUH?
ALL IN FAVOR, SAY AYE!
AYE!
UMM... AYE!
CHOMP!
HEY!
THAT'S WHY YOU SHOULD AVOID POLITICS.
KIRKMAN & SCOTT

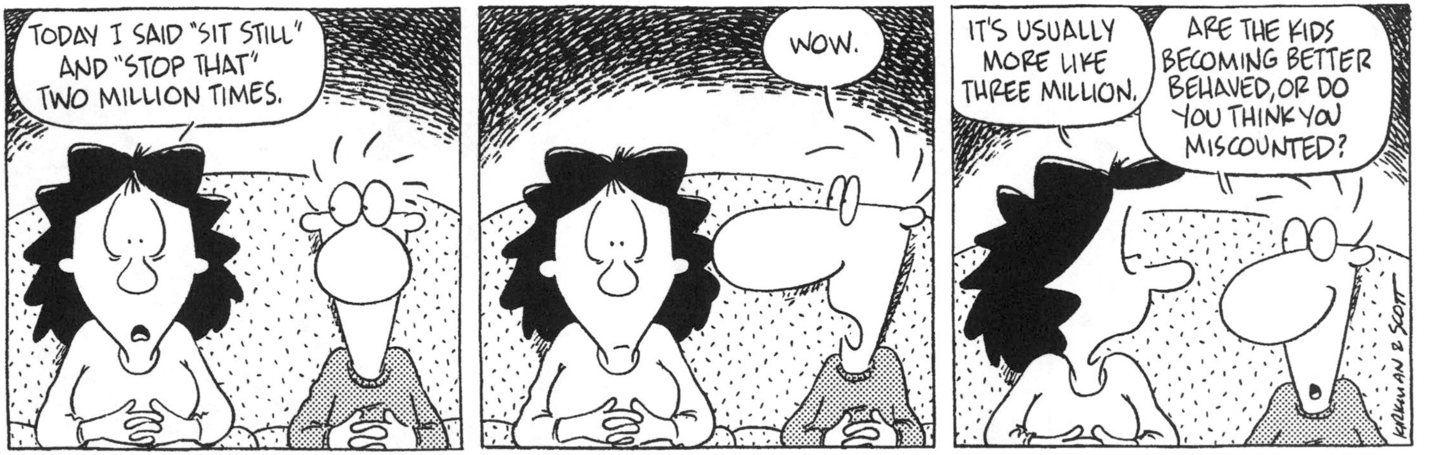
TODAY I SAID "SIT STILL" AND "STOP THAT" TWO MILLION TIMES.
WOW.
IT'S USUALLY MORE LIKE THREE MILLION.
ARE THE KIDS BECOMING BETTER BEHAVED, OR DO YOU THINK YOU MISCOUNTED?
KIRKMAN & SCOTT

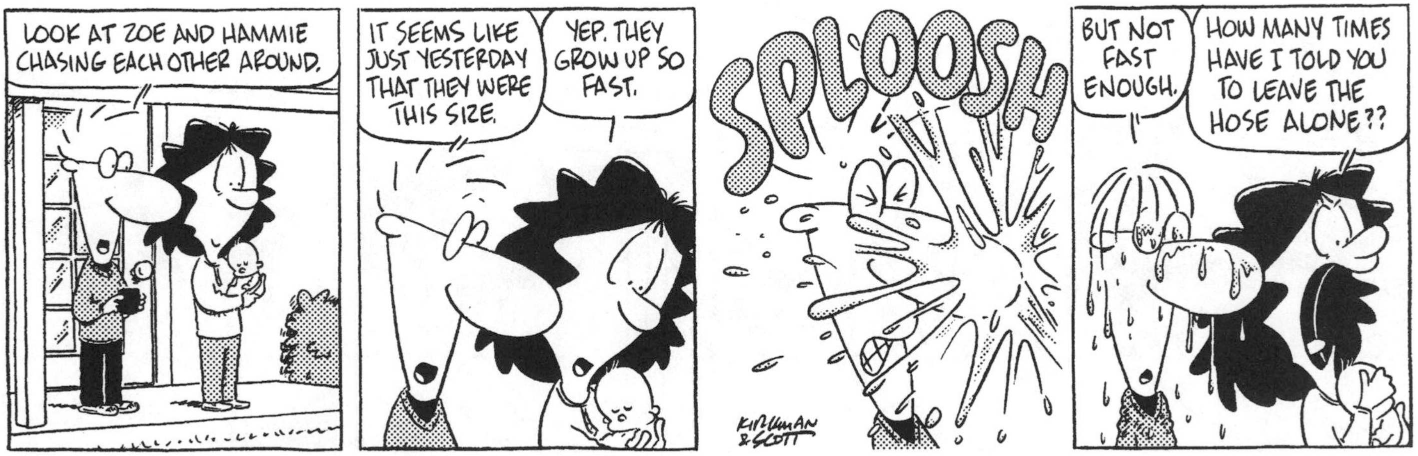
LOOK AT ZOE AND HAMMIE CHASING EACH OTHER AROUND.
IT SEEMS LIKE JUST YESTERDAY THAT THEY WERE THIS SIZE.
YEP. THEY GROW UP SO FAST.
SPLOOSH
KIRKMAN & SCOTT
BUT NOT FAST ENOUGH.
HOW MANY TIMES HAVE I TOLD YOU TO LEAVE THE HOSE ALONE??

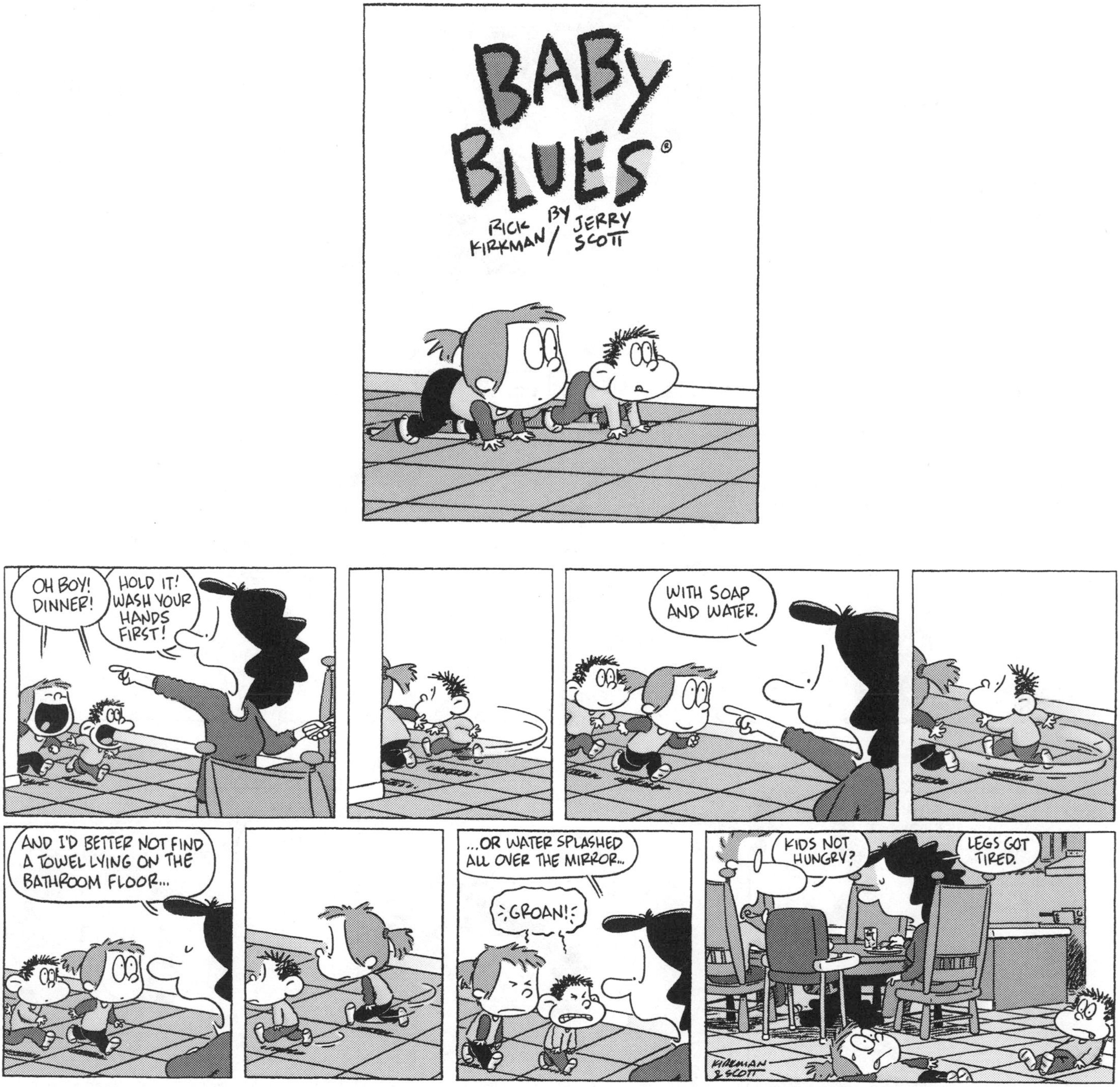
BABY BLUES®
BY RICK KIRKMAN / JERRY SCOTT
OH BOY! DINNER!
HOLD IT! WASH YOUR HANDS FIRST!
WITH SOAP AND WATER.
AND I'D BETTER NOT FIND A TOWEL LYING ON THE BATHROOM FLOOR...
...OR WATER SPLASHED ALL OVER THE MIRROR...
GROAN!
KIDS NOT HUNGRY?
LEGS GOT TIRED.
KIRKMAN & SCOTT

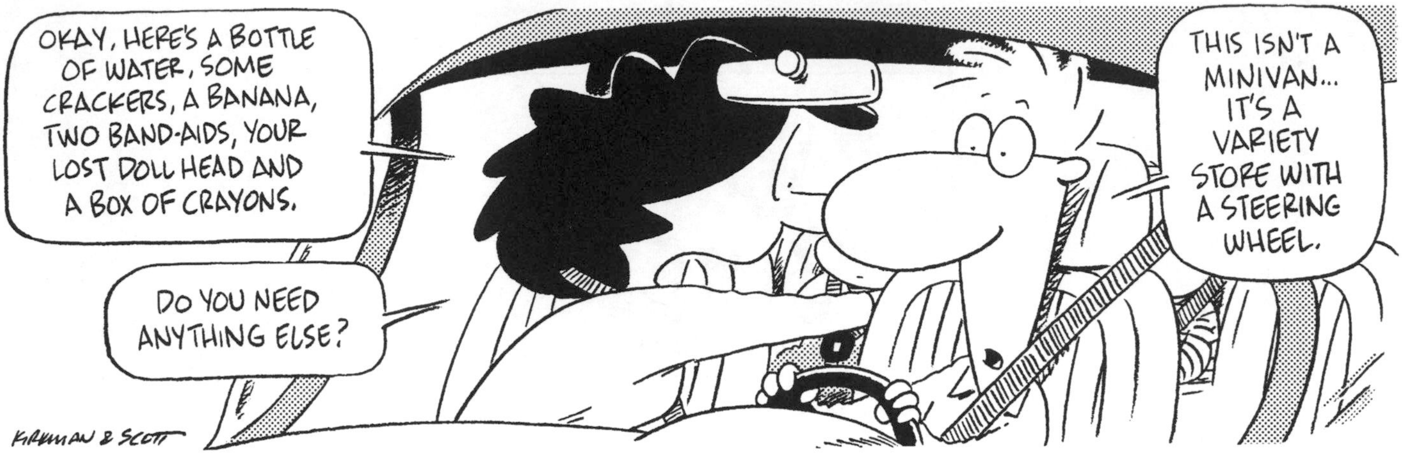
OKAY, HERE'S A BOTTLE OF WATER, SOME CRACKERS, A BANANA, TWO BAND-AIDS, YOUR LOST DOLL HEAD AND A BOX OF CRAYONS.
DO YOU NEED ANYTHING ELSE?
THIS ISN'T A MINIVAN... IT'S A VARIETY STORE WITH A STEERING WHEEL.
KIRKMAN & SCOTT

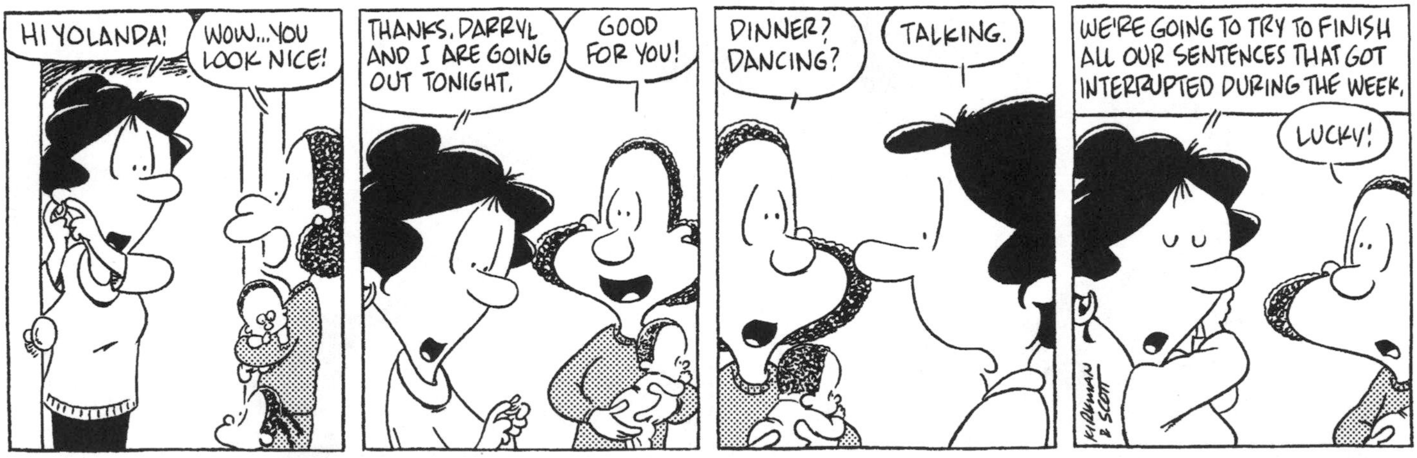
HI YOLANDA!
WOW...YOU LOOK NICE!
THANKS. DARRYL AND I ARE GOING OUT TONIGHT.
GOOD FOR YOU!
DINNER? DANCING?
TALKING.
WE'RE GOING TO TRY TO FINISH ALL OUR SENTENCES THAT GOT INTERRUPTED DURING THE WEEK.
LUCKY!
KIRKMAN & SCOTT

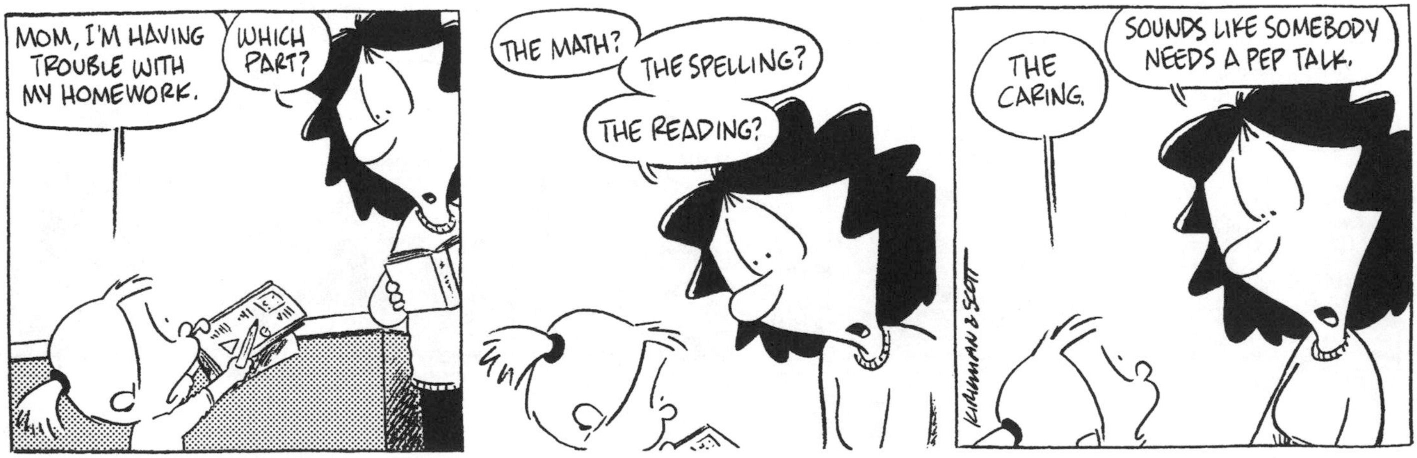
MOM, I'M HAVING TROUBLE WITH MY HOMEWORK.
WHICH PART?
THE MATH?
THE SPELLING?
THE READING?
THE CARING.
SOUNDS LIKE SOMEBODY NEEDS A PEP TALK.
KIRKMAN & SCOTT

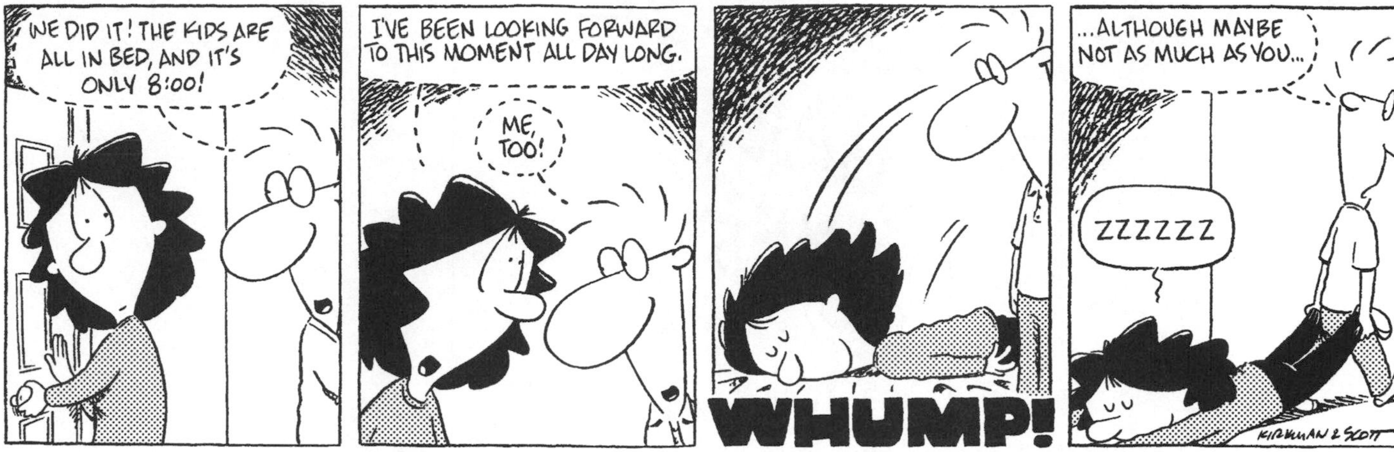
WE DID IT! THE KIDS ARE ALL IN BED, AND IT'S ONLY 8:00!
I'VE BEEN LOOKING FORWARD TO THIS MOMENT ALL DAY LONG.
ME, TOO!
WHUMP!
...ALTHOUGH MAYBE NOT AS MUCH AS YOU...
ZZZZZZ
KIRKMAN & SCOTT

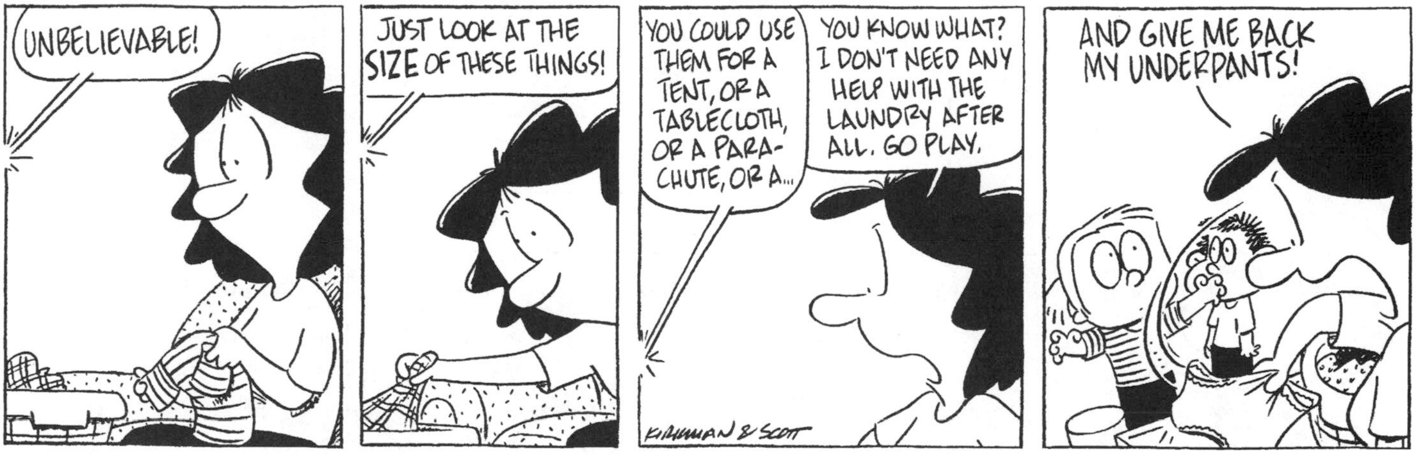
UNBELIEVABLE!
JUST LOOK AT THE SIZE OF THESE THINGS!
YOU COULD USE THEM FOR A TENT, OR A TABLECLOTH, OR A PARA-CHUTE, OR A...
YOU KNOW WHAT? I DON'T NEED ANY HELP WITH THE LAUNDRY AFTER ALL. GO PLAY.
KIRKMAN & SCOTT
AND GIVE ME BACK MY UNDERPANTS!

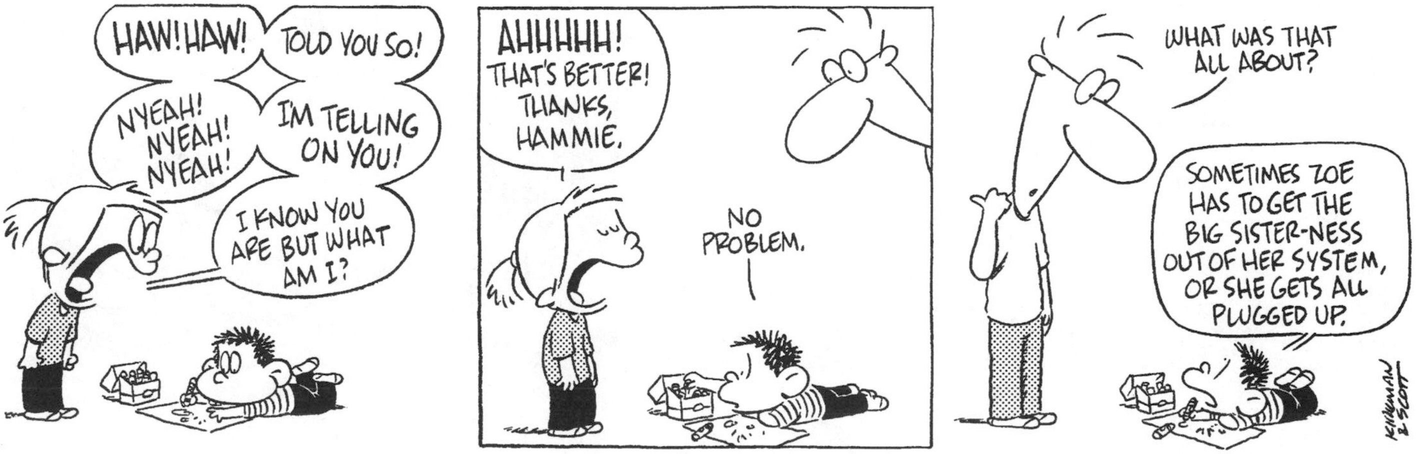
HAW! HAW!
TOLD YOU SO!
NYEAH! NYEAH! NYEAH!
I'M TELLING ON YOU!
I KNOW YOU ARE BUT WHAT AM I?
AHHHHH! THAT'S BETTER! THANKS, HAMMIE.
NO PROBLEM.
WHAT WAS THAT ALL ABOUT?
SOMETIMES ZOE HAS TO GET THE BIG SISTER-NESS OUT OF HER SYSTEM, OR SHE GETS ALL PLUGGED UP.
KIRKMAN & SCOTT

BABY BLUES®
BY
RICK KIRKMAN / JERRY SCOTT

HEY! LOOK AT THIS!
WHAT?
I THINK I MAY HAVE LOST A COUPLE OF POUNDS!
HOW??
I DON'T KNOW...
...BUT LOOK HOW LOOSE THIS WAIST-BAND IS!
THIS IS INCREDIBLE! I MEAN, I HAVEN'T EVEN BEEN TRYING!!
BUT HEY, DON'T BE TOO JEALOUS, SWEETIE. I PROBABLY JUST HAVE A HIGHER METABOLISM RATE THAN YOU DO.
WELL, I THINK I'LL GO HAVE A BIG BOWL OF ICE CREAM BEFORE I WASTE AWAY COMPLETELY!
ARE YOU GOING TO TELL DADDY THAT HE'S WEARING YOUR MATERNITY JEANS, OR SHOULD I?
OH, I WILL...
...EVENTUALLY.

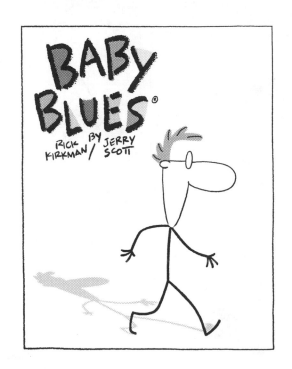

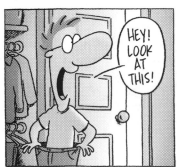

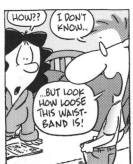

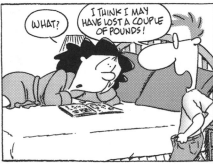

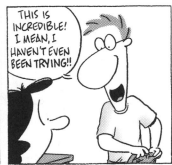

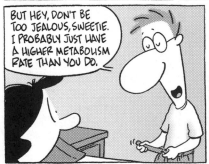

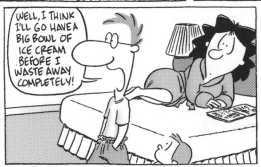

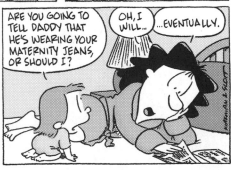

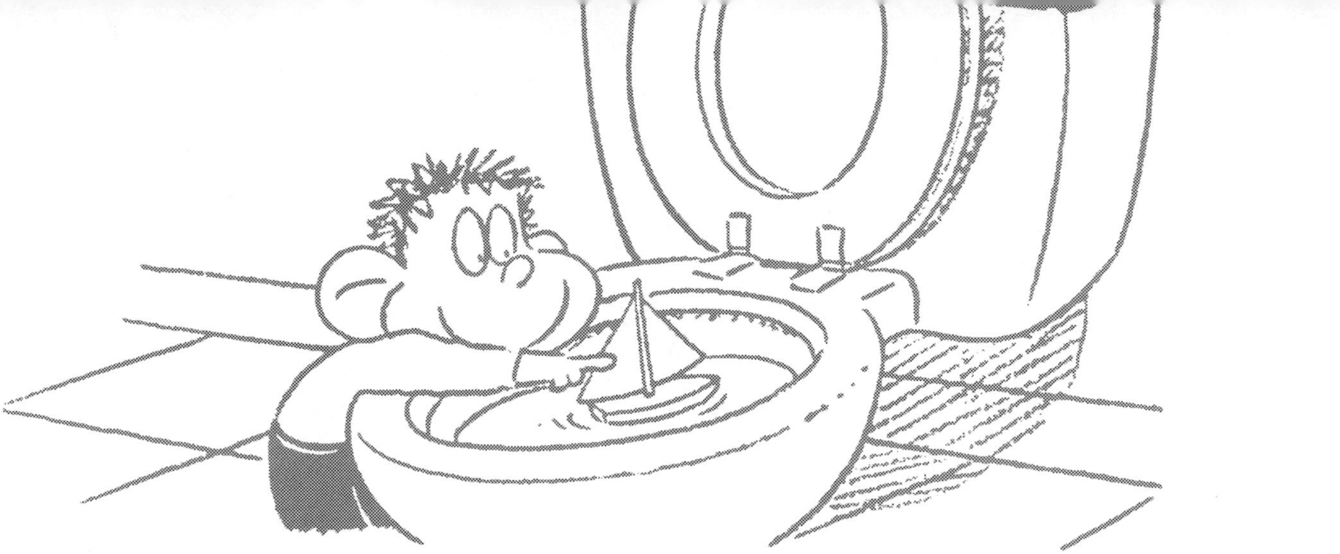

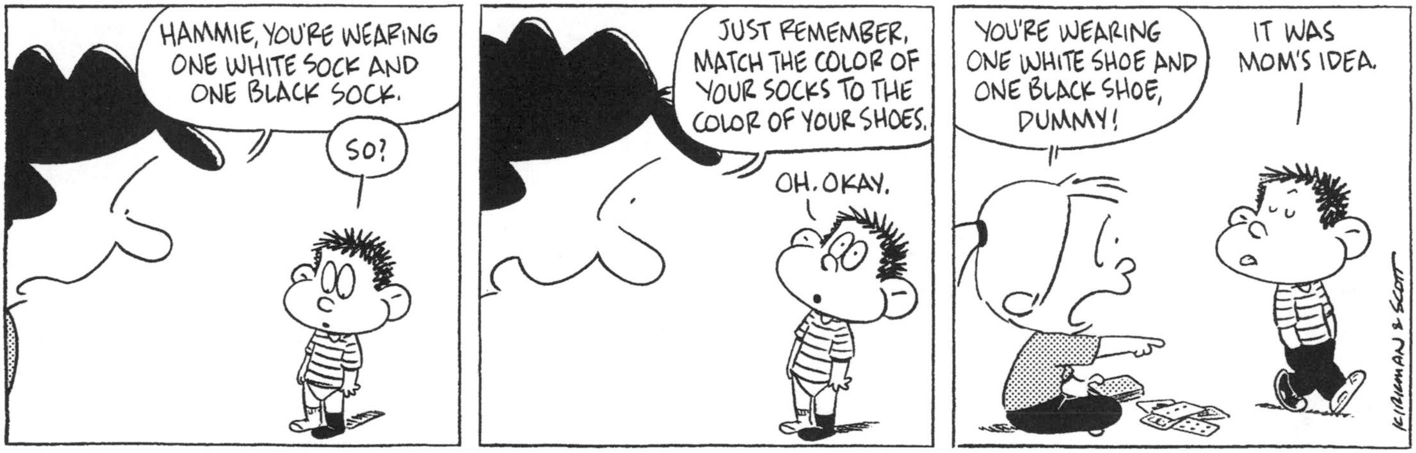
HAMMIE, YOU'RE WEARING ONE WHITE SOCK AND ONE BLACK SOCK.
SO?
JUST REMEMBER, MATCH THE COLOR OF YOUR SOCKS TO THE COLOR OF YOUR SHOES.
OH. OKAY.
YOU'RE WEARING ONE WHITE SHOE AND ONE BLACK SHOE, DUMMY!
IT WAS MOM'S IDEA.
KIRKMAN & SCOTT

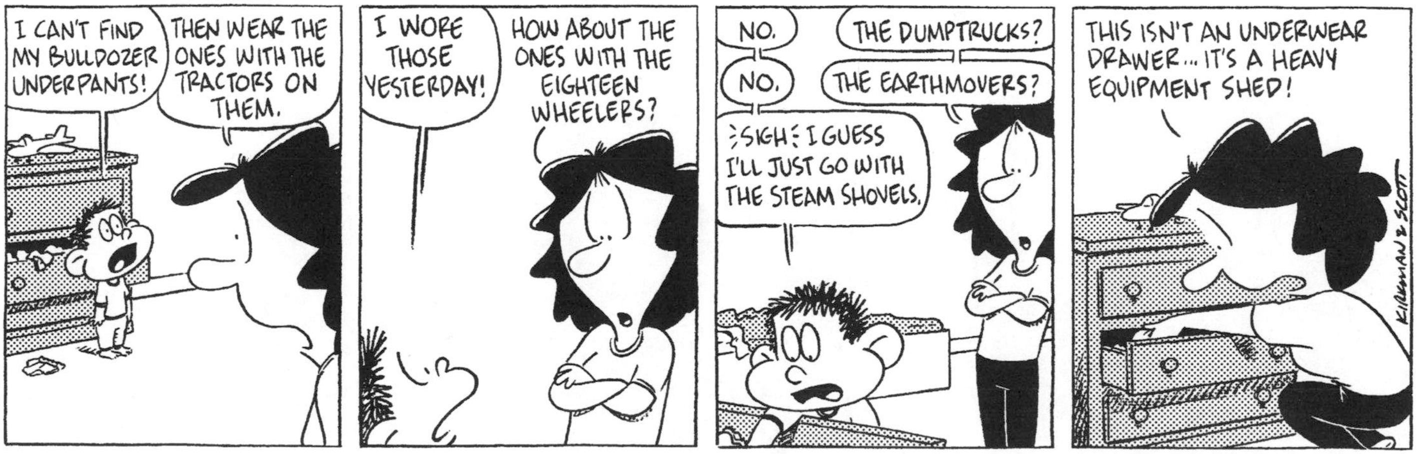
I CAN'T FIND MY BULLDOZER UNDERPANTS!
THEN WEAR THE ONES WITH THE TRACTORS ON THEM.
I WORE THOSE YESTERDAY!
HOW ABOUT THE ONES WITH THE EIGHTEEN WHEELERS?
NO.
THE DUMPTRUCKS?
NO.
THE EARTHMOVERS?
SIGH I GUESS I'LL JUST GO WITH THE STEAM SHOVELS.
THIS ISN'T AN UNDERWEAR DRAWER... IT'S A HEAVY EQUIPMENT SHED!
KIRKMAN & SCOTT

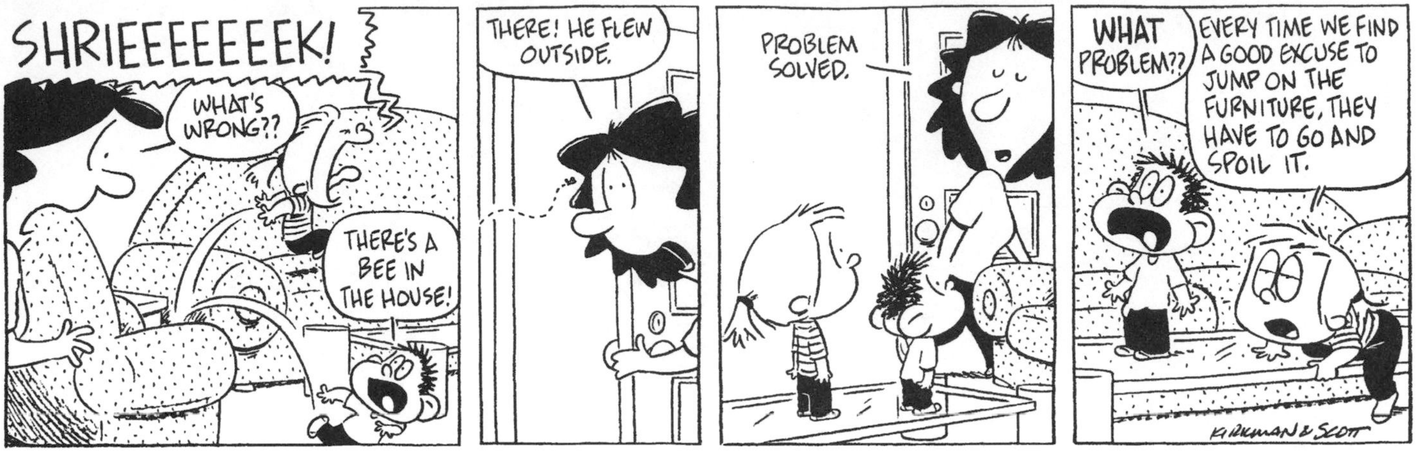
SHRIEEEEEEEEK!
WHAT'S WRONG??
THERE'S A BEE IN THE HOUSE!
THERE! HE FLEW OUTSIDE.
PROBLEM SOLVED.
WHAT PROBLEM??
EVERY TIME WE FIND A GOOD EXCUSE TO JUMP ON THE FURNITURE, THEY HAVE TO GO AND SPOIL IT.
KIRKMAN & SCOTT

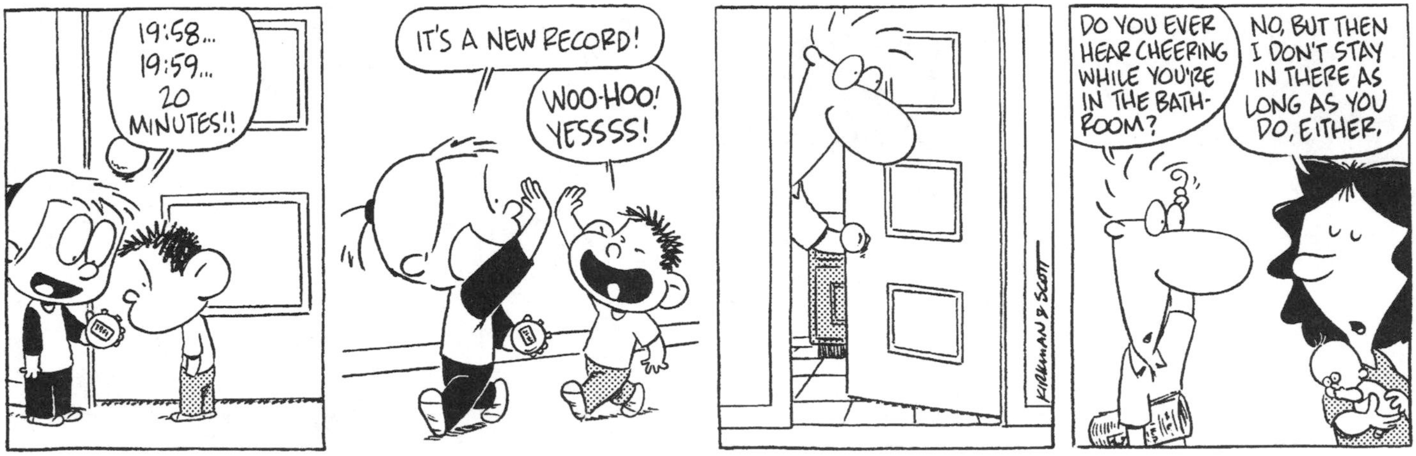
19:58... 19:59... 20 MINUTES!!
IT'S A NEW RECORD!
WOO-HOO! YESSSS!
KIRKMAN & SCOTT
DO YOU EVER HEAR CHEERING WHILE YOU'RE IN THE BATH-ROOM?
NO, BUT THEN I DON'T STAY IN THERE AS LONG AS YOU DO, EITHER.

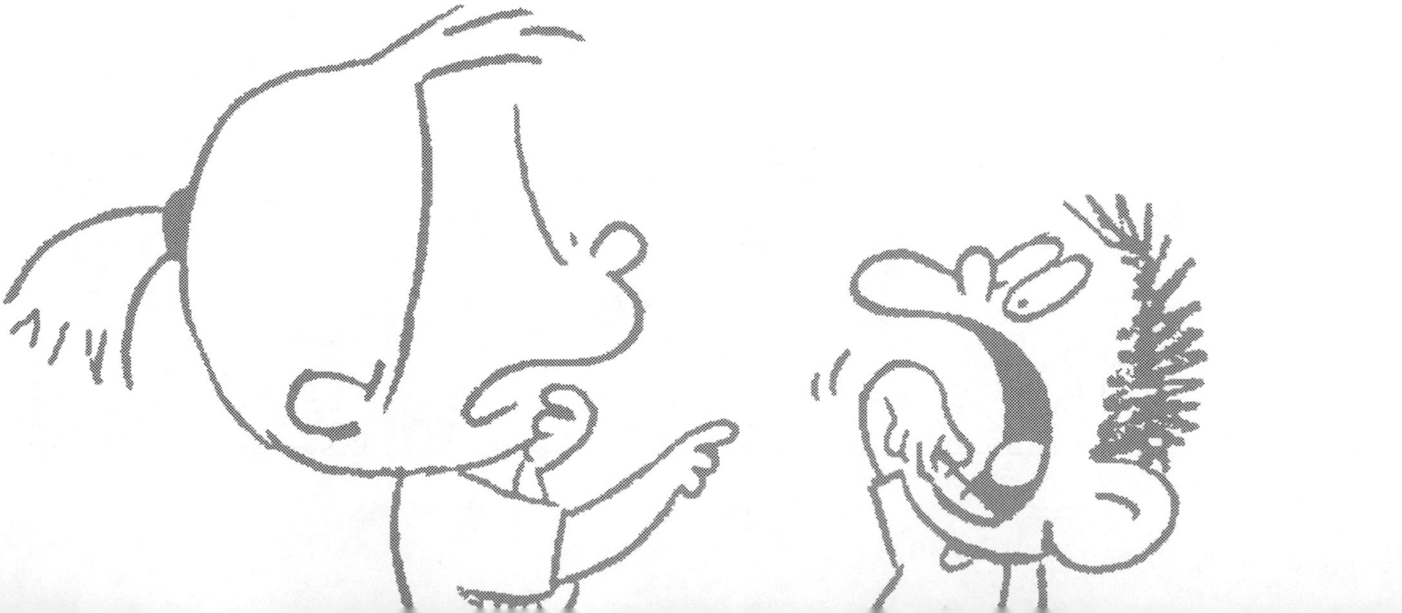

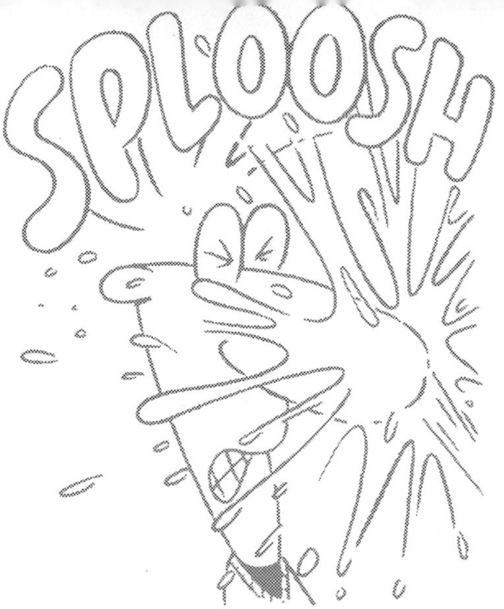
SPLOOSH

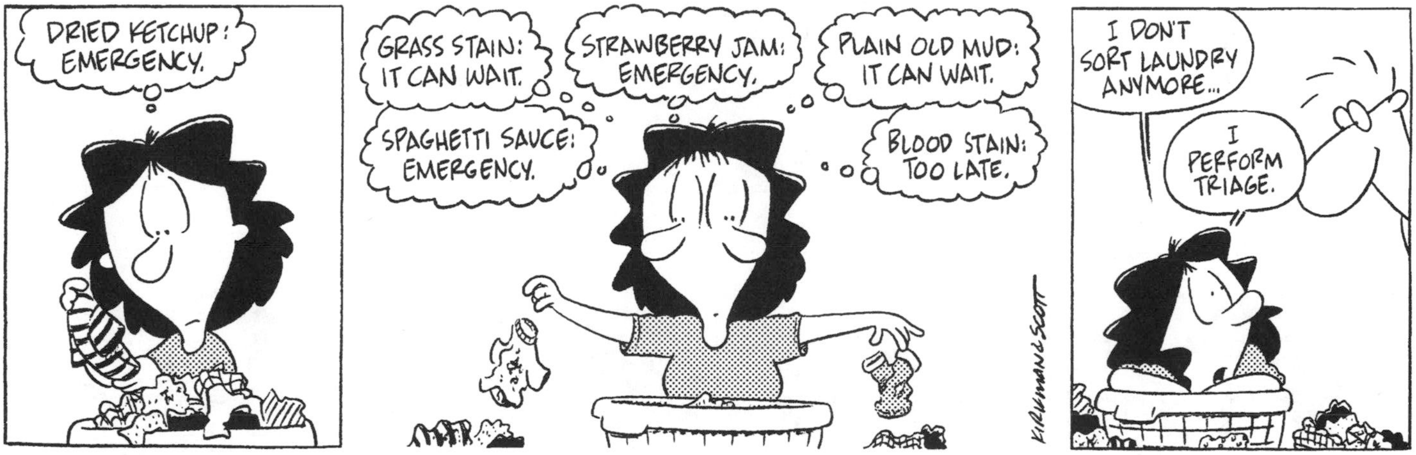
DRIED KETCHUP: EMERGENCY.
GRASS STAIN: IT CAN WAIT.
STRAWBERRY JAM: EMERGENCY.
PLAIN OLD MUD: IT CAN WAIT.
SPAGHETTI SAUCE: EMERGENCY.
BLOOD STAIN: TOO LATE.
I DON'T SORT LAUNDRY ANYMORE...
I PERFORM TRIAGE.

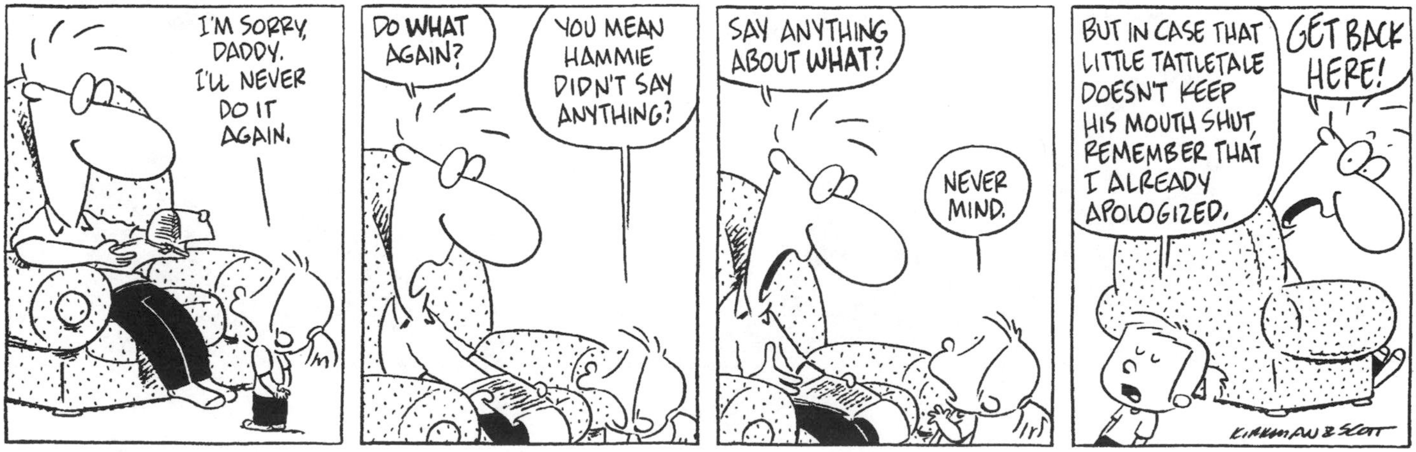
I'M SORRY, DADDY. I'LL NEVER DO IT AGAIN.
DO WHAT AGAIN?
YOU MEAN HAMMIE DIDN'T SAY ANYTHING?
SAY ANYTHING ABOUT WHAT?
NEVER MIND.
BUT IN CASE THAT LITTLE TATTLETALE DOESN'T KEEP HIS MOUTH SHUT, REMEMBER THAT I ALREADY APOLOGIZED.
GET BACK HERE!

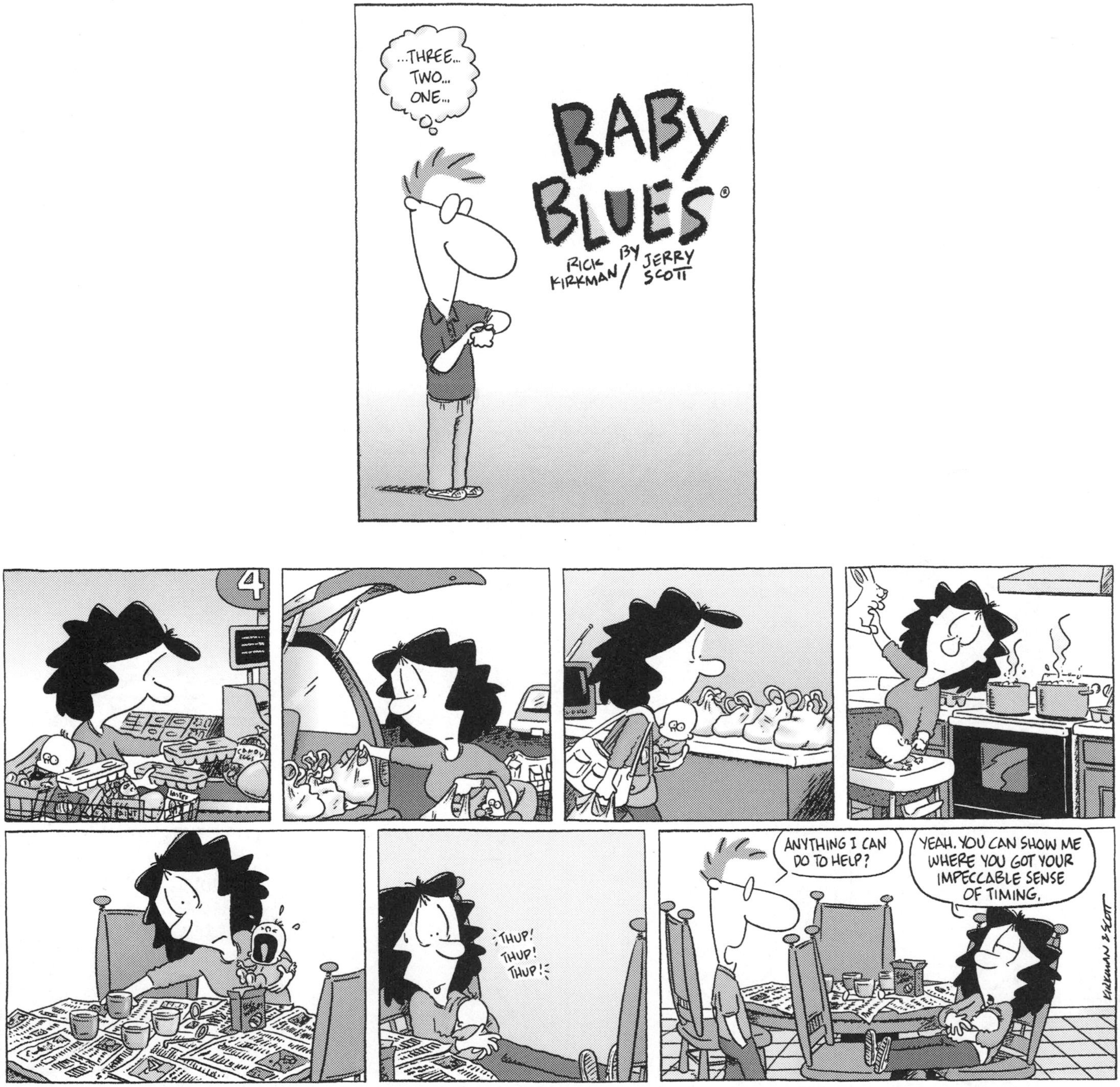
...THREE... TWO... ONE...
BABY BLUES®
BY RICK KIRKMAN / JERRY SCOTT
THUP! THUP! THUP!
ANYTHING I CAN DO TO HELP?
YEAH. YOU CAN SHOW ME WHERE YOU GOT YOUR IMPECCABLE SENSE OF TIMING.
KIRKMAN & SCOTT

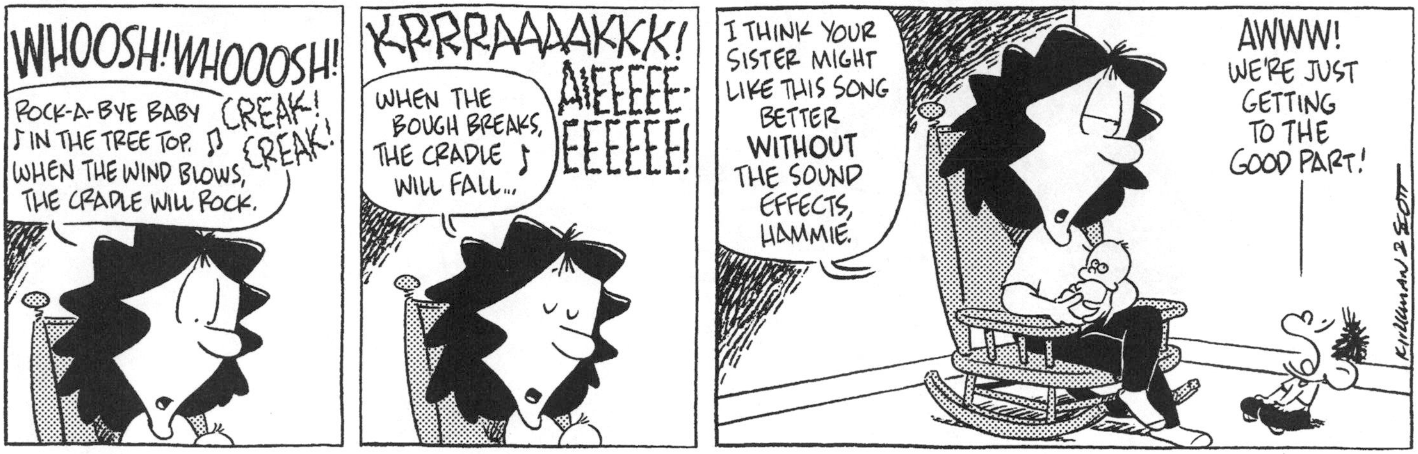
WHOOSH! WHOOOSH!
ROCK-A-BYE BABY ♪ IN THE TREE TOP. ♫ WHEN THE WIND BLOWS, THE CRADLE WILL ROCK.
CREAK! CREAK!
KRRRAAAAKKK!
WHEN THE BOUGH BREAKS, THE CRADLE ♪ WILL FALL...
AIEEEEE-EEEEEE!
I THINK YOUR SISTER MIGHT LIKE THIS SONG BETTER WITHOUT THE SOUND EFFECTS, HAMMIE.
AWWW! WE'RE JUST GETTING TO THE GOOD PART!

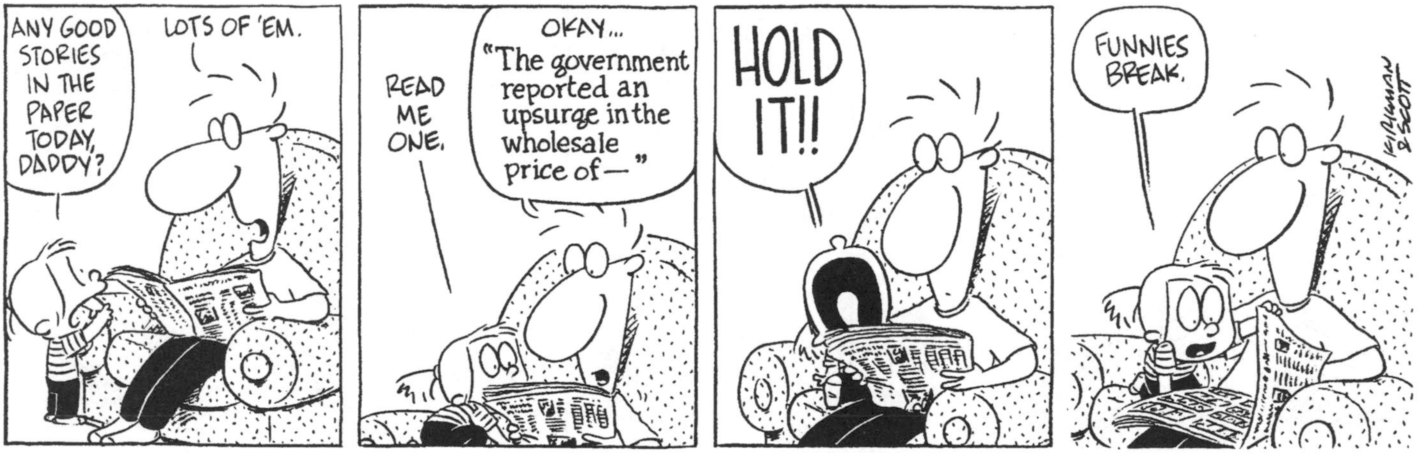
ANY GOOD STORIES IN THE PAPER TODAY, DADDY?
LOTS OF 'EM.
READ ME ONE.
OKAY... "The government reported an upsurge in the wholesale price of—"
HOLD IT!!
FUNNIES BREAK.

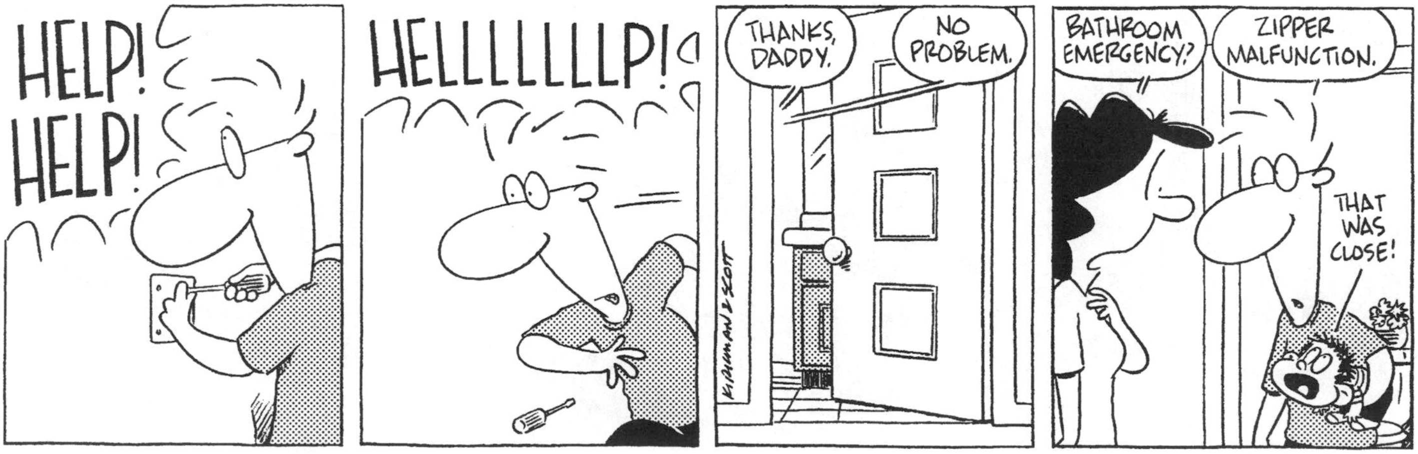
HELP! HELP!
HELLLLLLLP!
THANKS, DADDY.
NO PROBLEM.
BATHROOM EMERGENCY?
ZIPPER MALFUNCTION.
THAT WAS CLOSE!

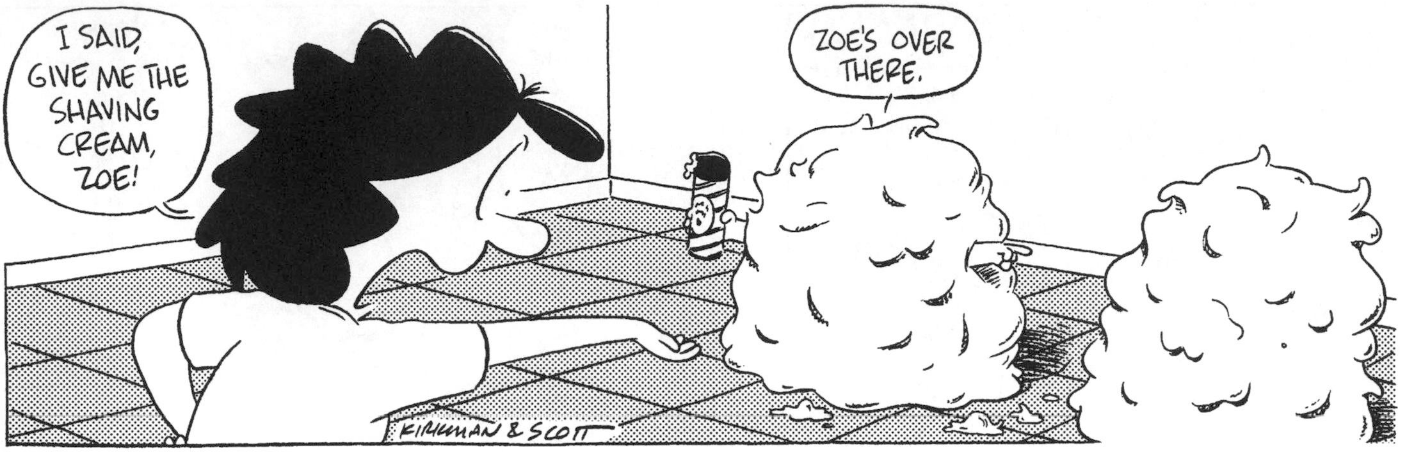
I SAID, GIVE ME THE SHAVING CREAM, ZOE!
ZOE'S OVER THERE.
KIRKMAN & SCOTT

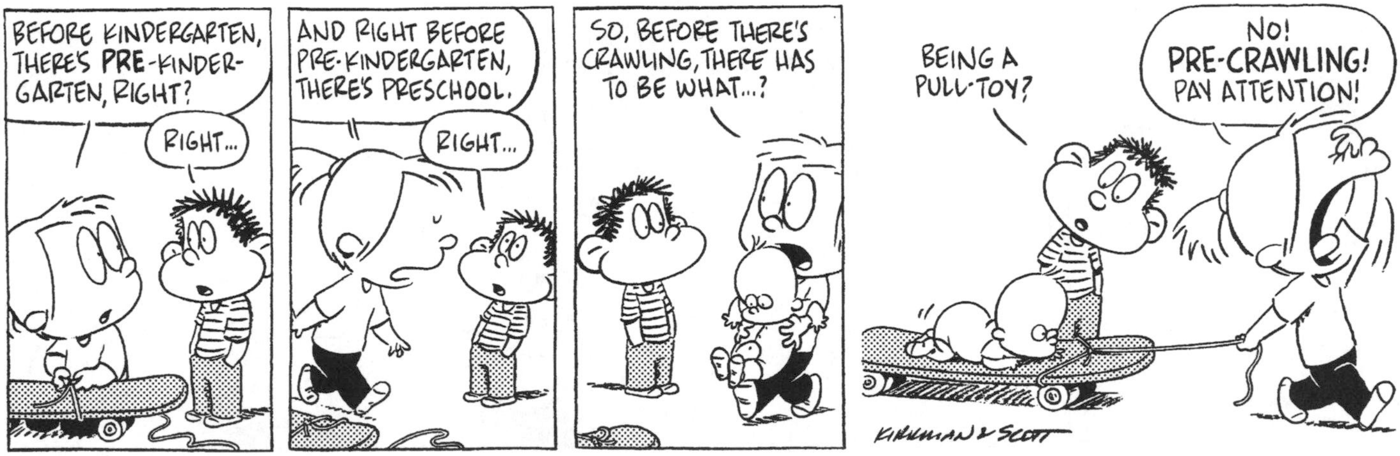
BEFORE KINDERGARTEN, THERE'S **PRE**-KINDER-GARTEN, RIGHT?
RIGHT...
AND RIGHT BEFORE PRE-KINDERGARTEN, THERE'S PRESCHOOL.
RIGHT...
SO, BEFORE THERE'S CRAWLING, THERE HAS TO BE WHAT...?
BEING A PULL-TOY?
NO! **PRE-CRAWLING!** PAY ATTENTION!
KIRKMAN & SCOTT

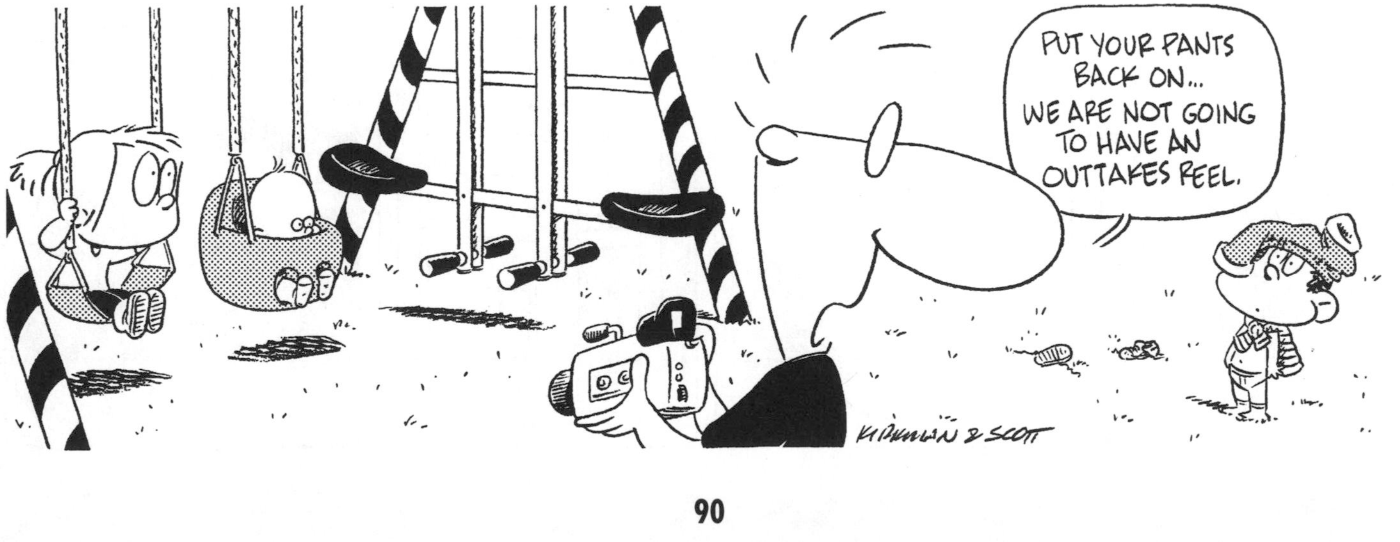
PUT YOUR PANTS BACK ON... WE ARE NOT GOING TO HAVE AN OUTTAKES REEL.
KIRKMAN & SCOTT

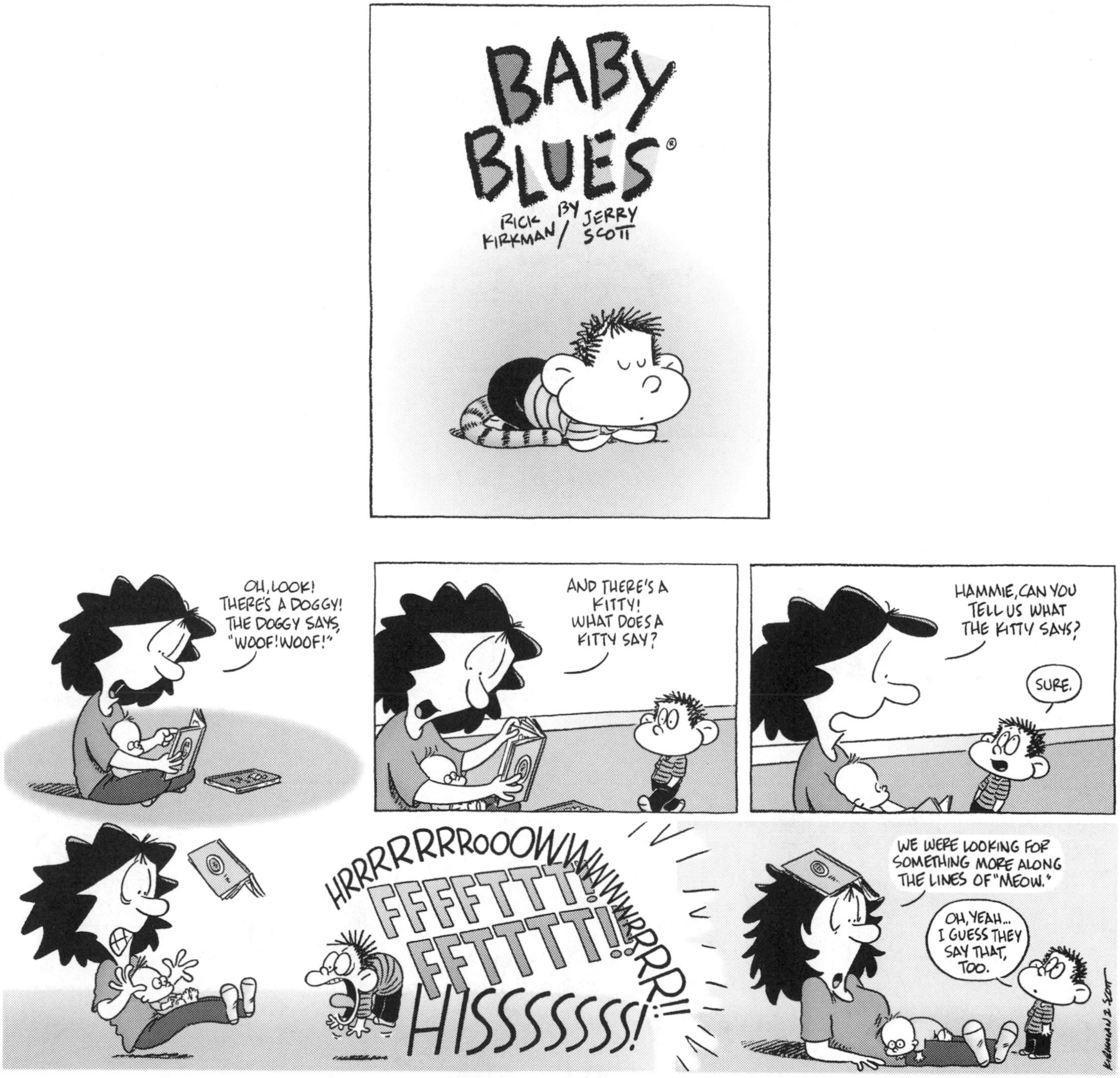
BABY BLUES®
BY RICK KIRKMAN / JERRY SCOTT
OH, LOOK! THERE'S A DOGGY! THE DOGGY SAYS, "WOOF! WOOF!"
AND THERE'S A KITTY! WHAT DOES A KITTY SAY?
HAMMIE, CAN YOU TELL US WHAT THE KITTY SAYS?
SURE.
HRRRRRRROOOWWWWWRRRR!!
FFFFTTT! FFTTTTT!!
HISSSSSSSS!
WE WERE LOOKING FOR SOMETHING MORE ALONG THE LINES OF "MEOW."
OH, YEAH... I GUESS THEY SAY THAT, TOO.

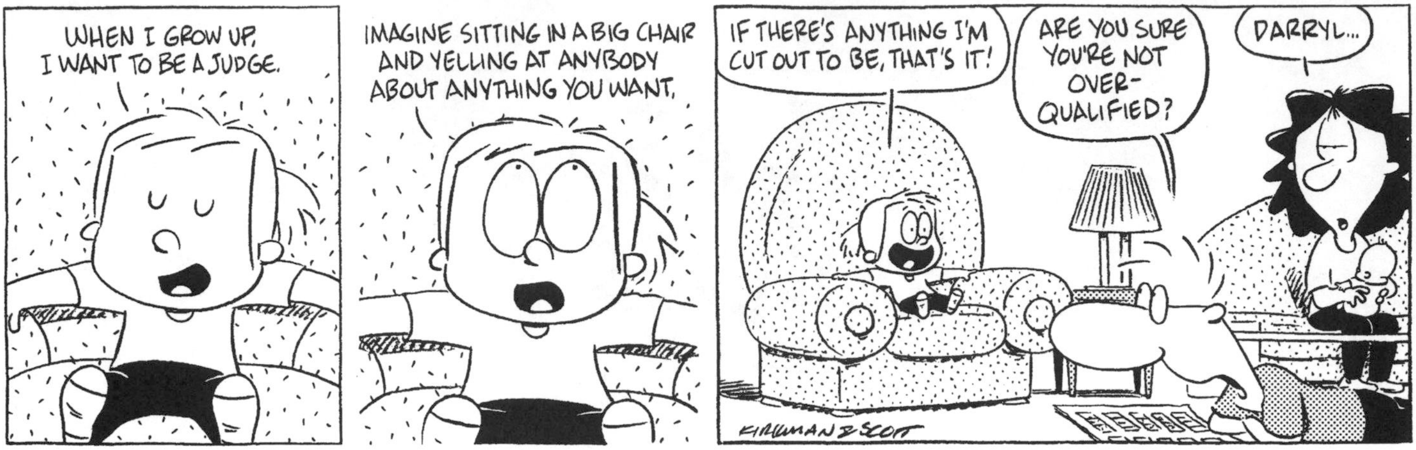
WHEN I GROW UP, I WANT TO BE A JUDGE.
IMAGINE SITTING IN A BIG CHAIR AND YELLING AT ANYBODY ABOUT ANYTHING YOU WANT.
IF THERE'S ANYTHING I'M CUT OUT TO BE, THAT'S IT!
ARE YOU SURE YOU'RE NOT OVER-QUALIFIED?
DARRYL...
KIRKMAN & SCOTT

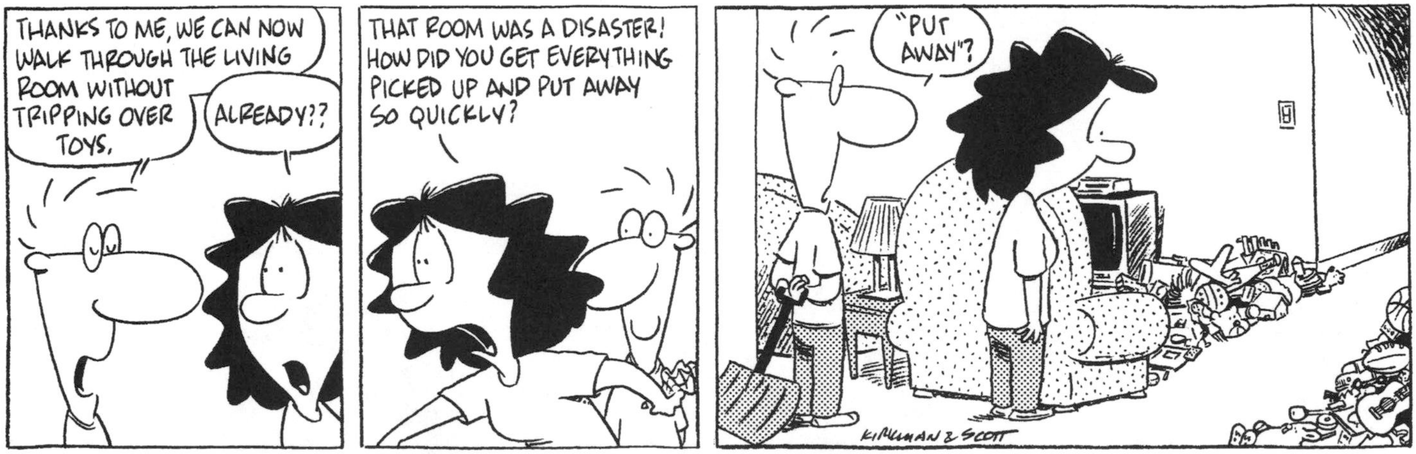
THANKS TO ME, WE CAN NOW WALK THROUGH THE LIVING ROOM WITHOUT TRIPPING OVER TOYS.
ALREADY??
THAT ROOM WAS A DISASTER! HOW DID YOU GET EVERYTHING PICKED UP AND PUT AWAY SO QUICKLY?
"PUT AWAY"?
KIRKMAN & SCOTT

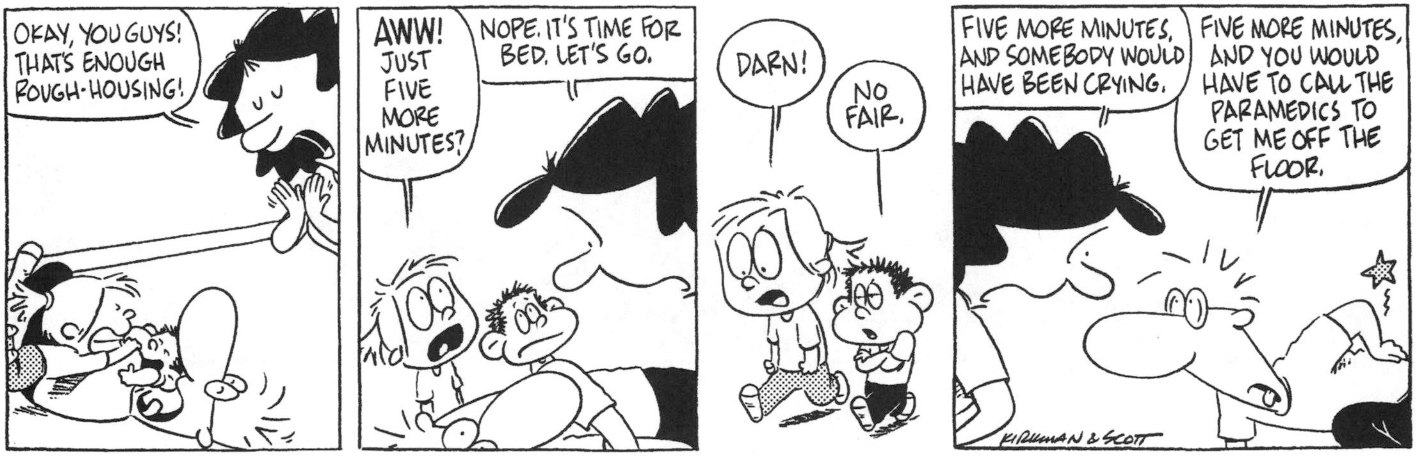
OKAY, YOU GUYS! THAT'S ENOUGH ROUGH-HOUSING!
AWW! JUST FIVE MORE MINUTES?
NOPE. IT'S TIME FOR BED. LET'S GO.
DARN!
NO FAIR.
FIVE MORE MINUTES, AND SOMEBODY WOULD HAVE BEEN CRYING.
FIVE MORE MINUTES, AND YOU WOULD HAVE TO CALL THE PARAMEDICS TO GET ME OFF THE FLOOR.
KIRKMAN & SCOTT

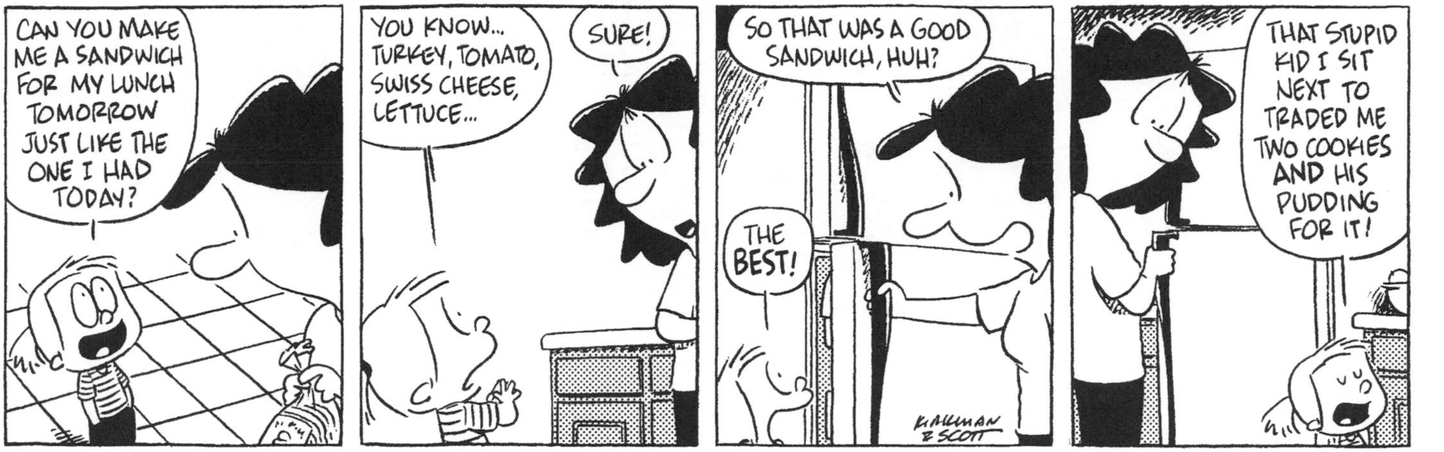
CAN YOU MAKE ME A SANDWICH FOR MY LUNCH TOMORROW JUST LIKE THE ONE I HAD TODAY?
YOU KNOW... TURKEY, TOMATO, SWISS CHEESE, LETTUCE...
SURE!
SO THAT WAS A GOOD SANDWICH, HUH?
THE BEST!
THAT STUPID KID I SIT NEXT TO TRADED ME TWO COOKIES AND HIS PUDDING FOR IT!
KIRKMAN & SCOTT

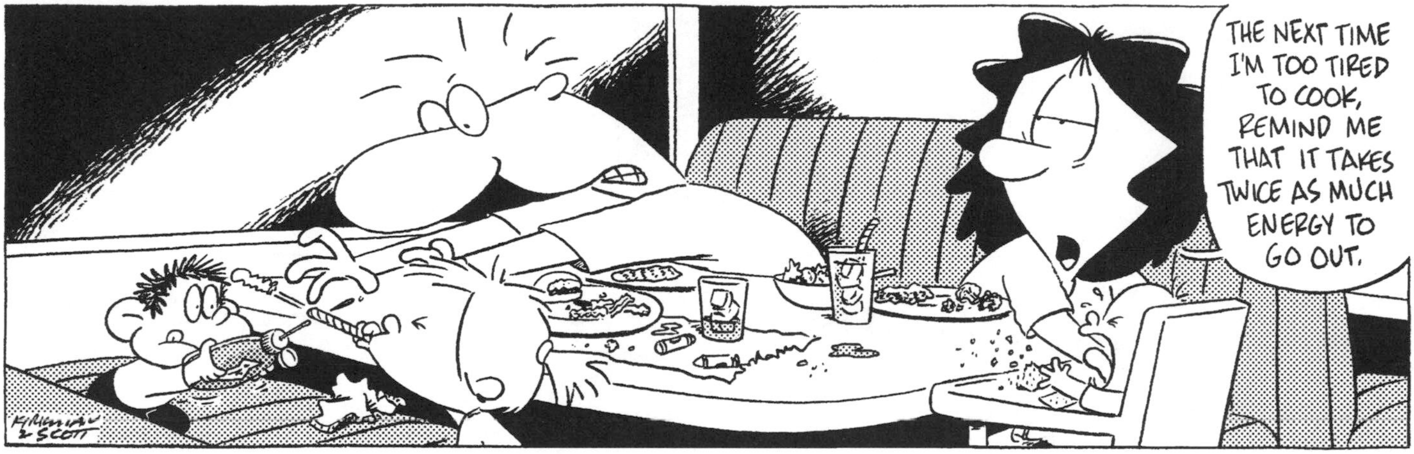
THE NEXT TIME I'M TOO TIRED TO COOK, REMIND ME THAT IT TAKES TWICE AS MUCH ENERGY TO GO OUT.
KIRKMAN & SCOTT

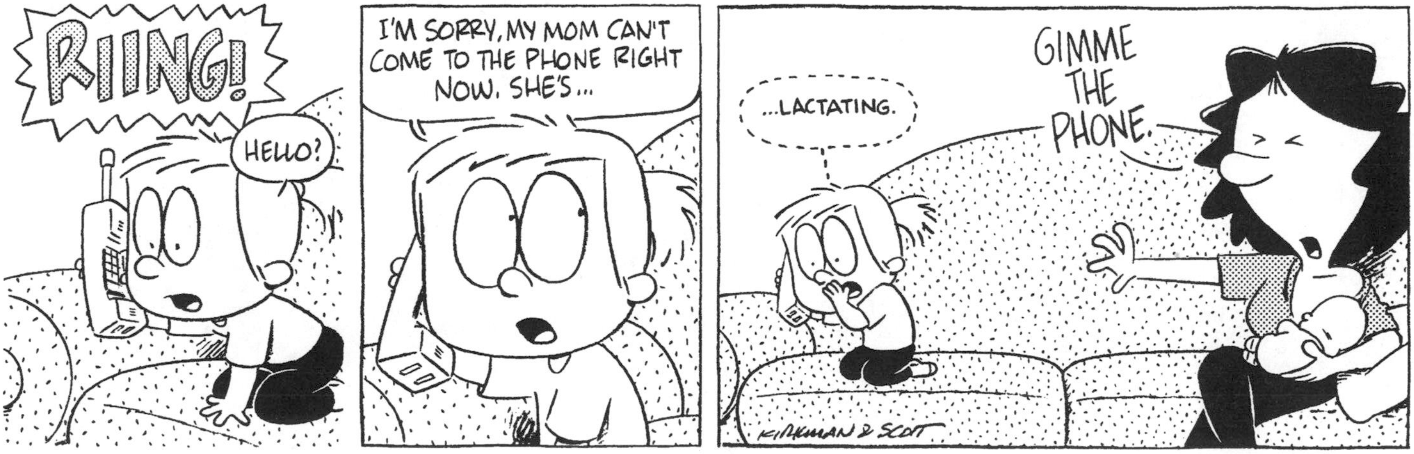
RIING!
HELLO?
I'M SORRY, MY MOM CAN'T COME TO THE PHONE RIGHT NOW. SHE'S...
...LACTATING.
GIMME THE PHONE.
KIRKMAN & SCOTT

BABY BLUES®
BY RICK KIRKMAN / JERRY SCOTT
KIRKMAN & SCOTT
WELL...?
I'VE SEEN WORSE.
HAMMIE SAYS IT'S NOT THAT MUDDY, MOM.
OKAY, YOU CAN PLAY IN THE YARD, BUT TRY NOT TO GET YOUR SHOES DIRTY.

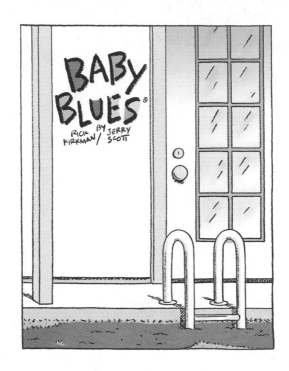

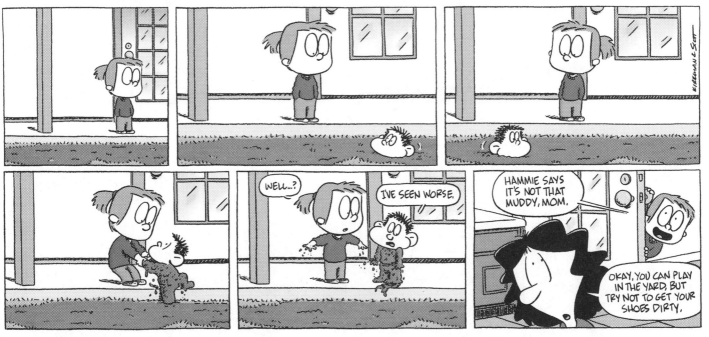

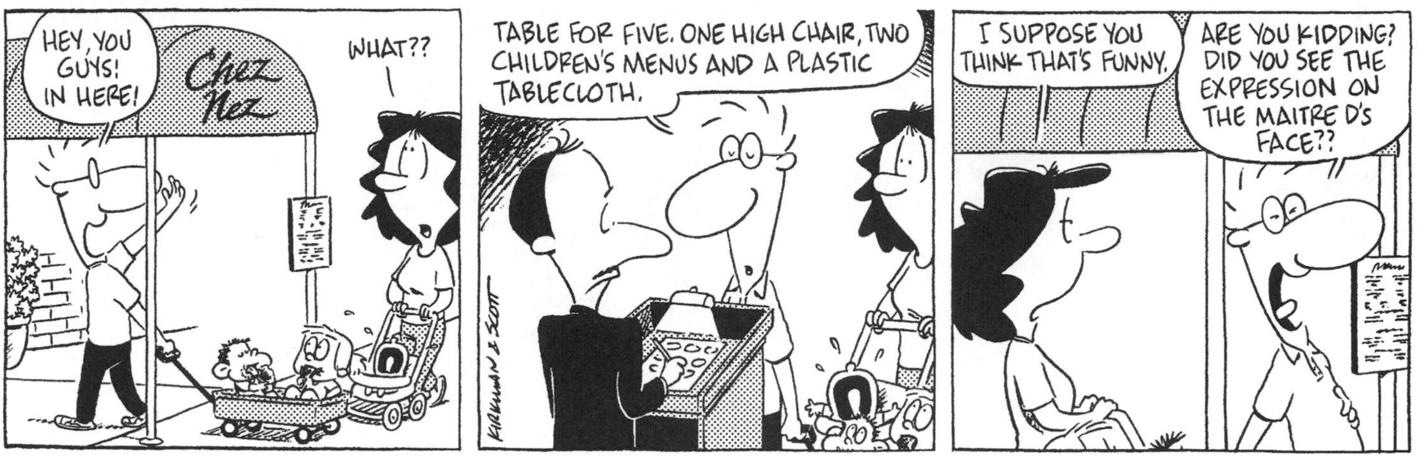
HEY, YOU GUYS! IN HERE!
Chez Nez
WHAT??
TABLE FOR FIVE. ONE HIGH CHAIR, TWO CHILDREN'S MENUS AND A PLASTIC TABLECLOTH.
KIRKMAN & SCOTT
I SUPPOSE YOU THINK THAT'S FUNNY.
ARE YOU KIDDING? DID YOU SEE THE EXPRESSION ON THE MAITRE D'S FACE??

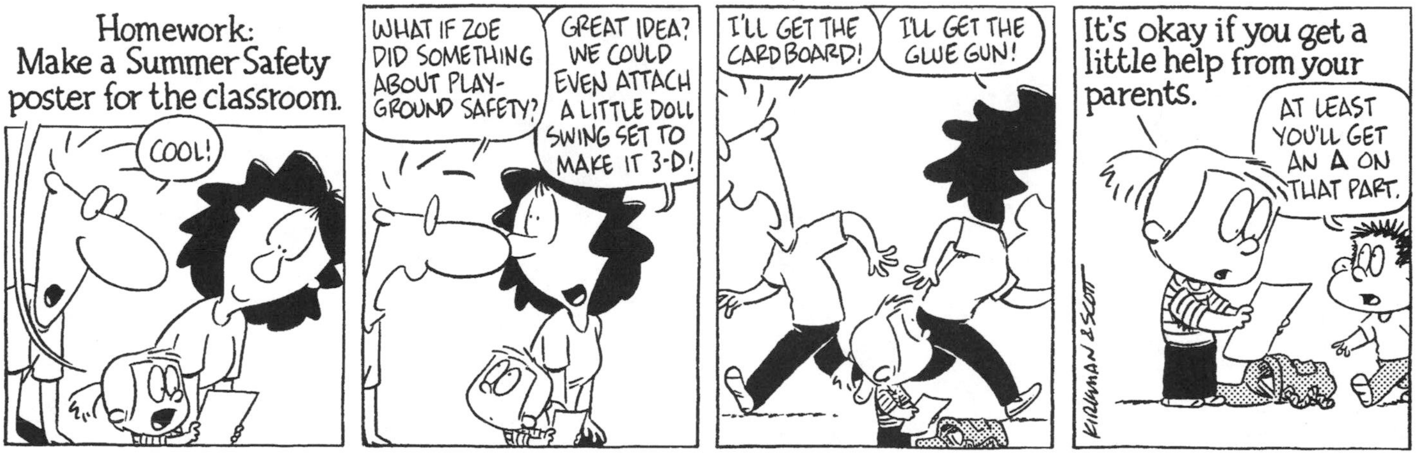
Homework: Make a Summer Safety poster for the classroom.
COOL!
WHAT IF ZOE DID SOMETHING ABOUT PLAY-GROUND SAFETY?
GREAT IDEA? WE COULD EVEN ATTACH A LITTLE DOLL SWING SET TO MAKE IT 3-D!
I'LL GET THE CARDBOARD!
I'LL GET THE GLUE GUN!
It's okay if you get a little help from your parents.
AT LEAST YOU'LL GET AN A ON THAT PART.
KIRKMAN & SCOTT

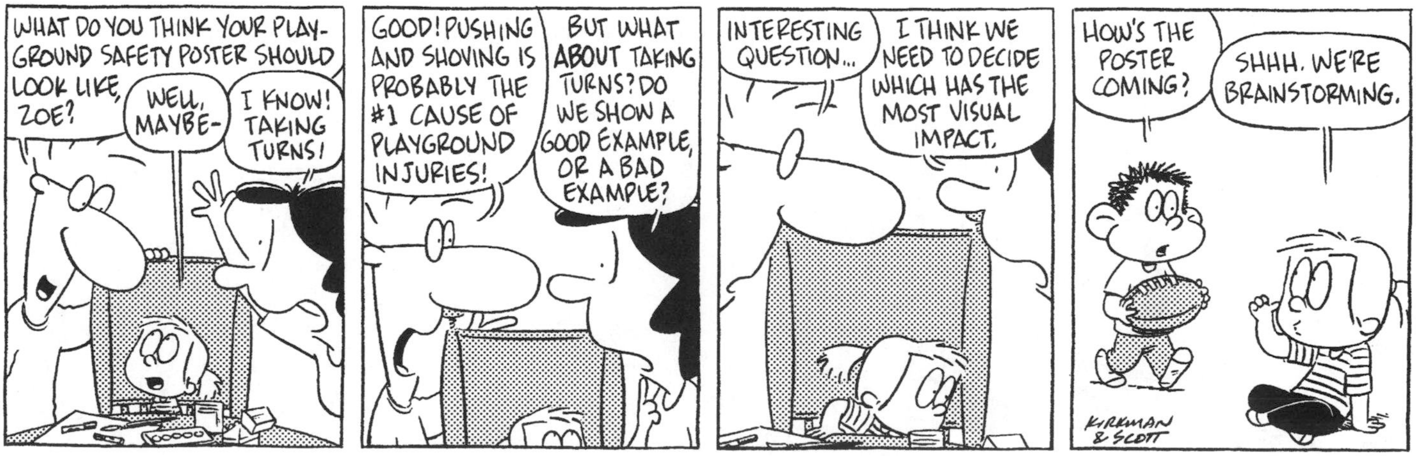
WHAT DO YOU THINK YOUR PLAY-GROUND SAFETY POSTER SHOULD LOOK LIKE, ZOE?
WELL, MAYBE-
I KNOW! TAKING TURNS!
GOOD! PUSHING AND SHOVING IS PROBABLY THE #1 CAUSE OF PLAYGROUND INJURIES!
BUT WHAT ABOUT TAKING TURNS? DO WE SHOW A GOOD EXAMPLE, OR A BAD EXAMPLE?
INTERESTING QUESTION...
I THINK WE NEED TO DECIDE WHICH HAS THE MOST VISUAL IMPACT.
HOW'S THE POSTER COMING?
SHHH. WE'RE BRAINSTORMING.
KIRKMAN & SCOTT

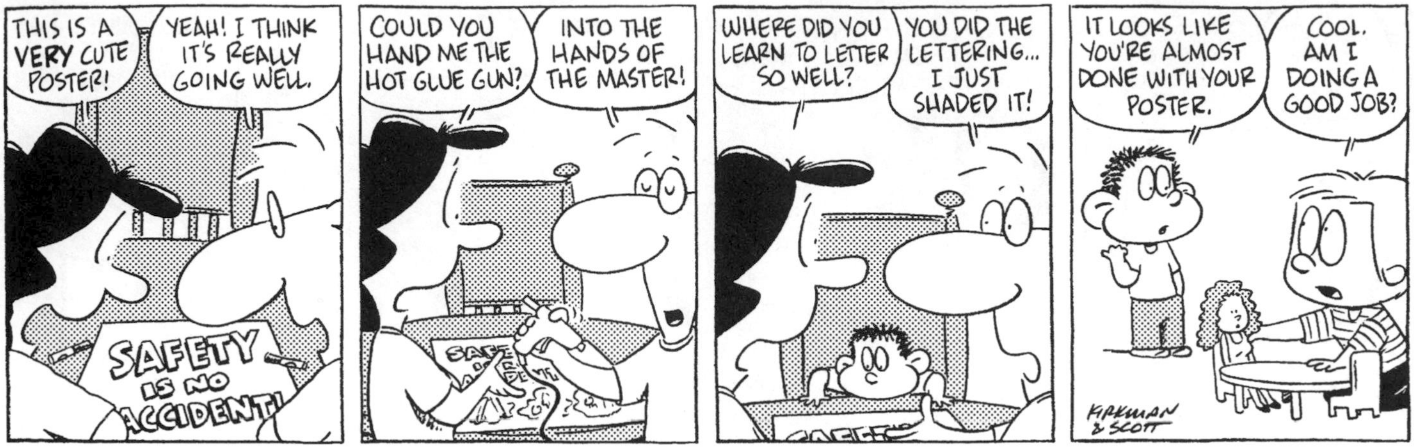
THIS IS A VERY CUTE POSTER!
YEAH! I THINK IT'S REALLY GOING WELL.
SAFETY IS NO ACCIDENT!
COULD YOU HAND ME THE HOT GLUE GUN?
INTO THE HANDS OF THE MASTER!
WHERE DID YOU LEARN TO LETTER SO WELL?
YOU DID THE LETTERING... I JUST SHADED IT!
IT LOOKS LIKE YOU'RE ALMOST DONE WITH YOUR POSTER.
COOL. AM I DOING A GOOD JOB?
KIRKMAN & SCOTT

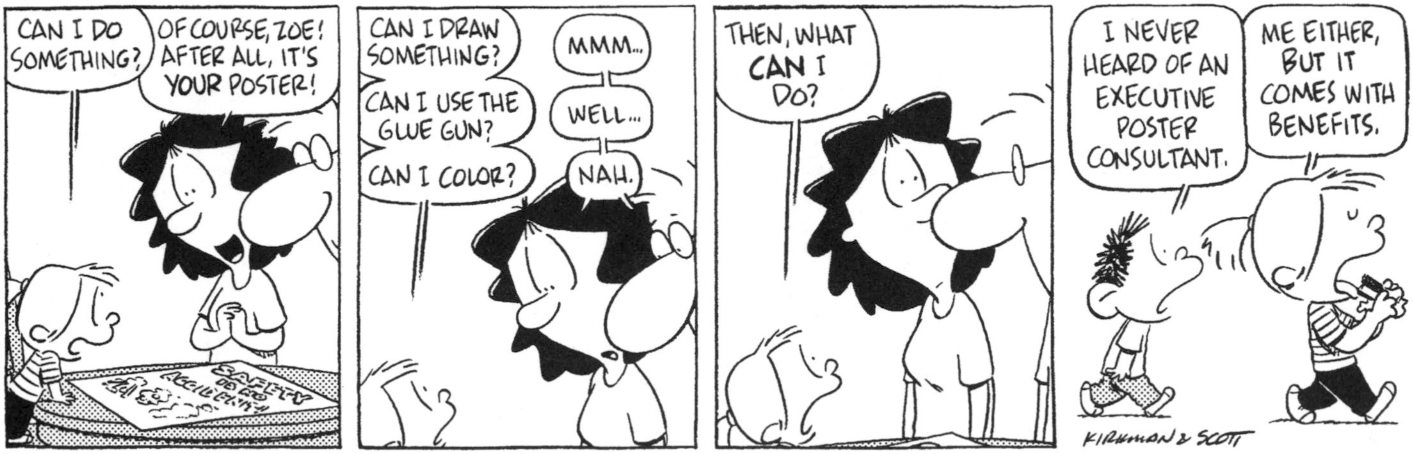
CAN I DO SOMETHING?
OF COURSE, ZOE! AFTER ALL, IT'S YOUR POSTER!
CAN I DRAW SOMETHING?
MMM...
CAN I USE THE GLUE GUN?
WELL...
CAN I COLOR?
NAH.
THEN, WHAT CAN I DO?
I NEVER HEARD OF AN EXECUTIVE POSTER CONSULTANT.
ME EITHER, BUT IT COMES WITH BENEFITS.
KIRKMAN & SCOTT

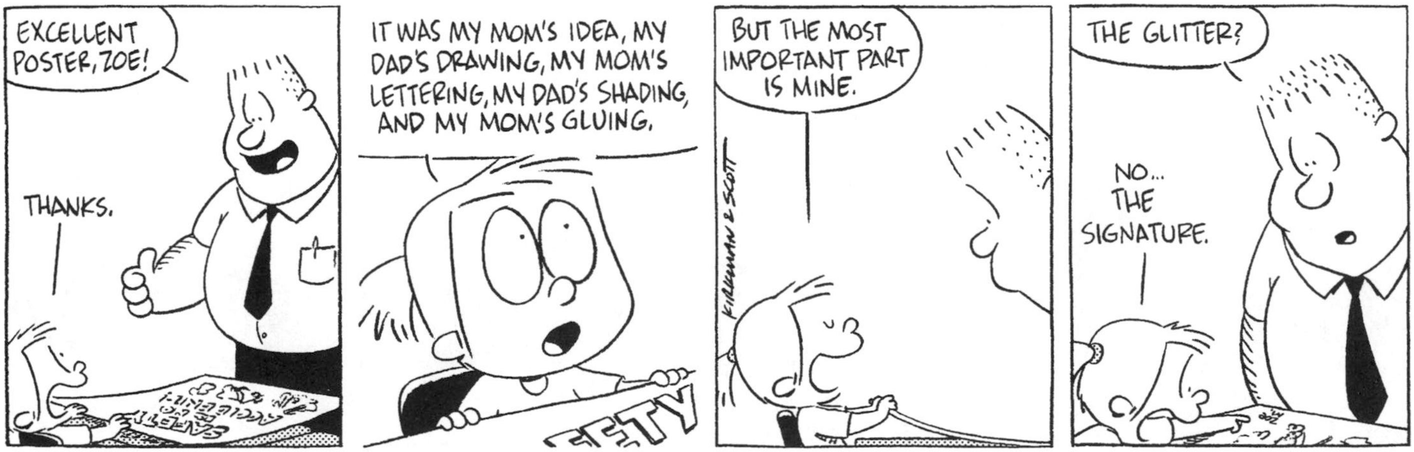
EXCELLENT POSTER, ZOE!
THANKS.
IT WAS MY MOM'S IDEA, MY DAD'S DRAWING, MY MOM'S LETTERING, MY DAD'S SHADING, AND MY MOM'S GLUING.
KIRKMAN & SCOTT
BUT THE MOST IMPORTANT PART IS MINE.
THE GLITTER?
NO... THE SIGNATURE.

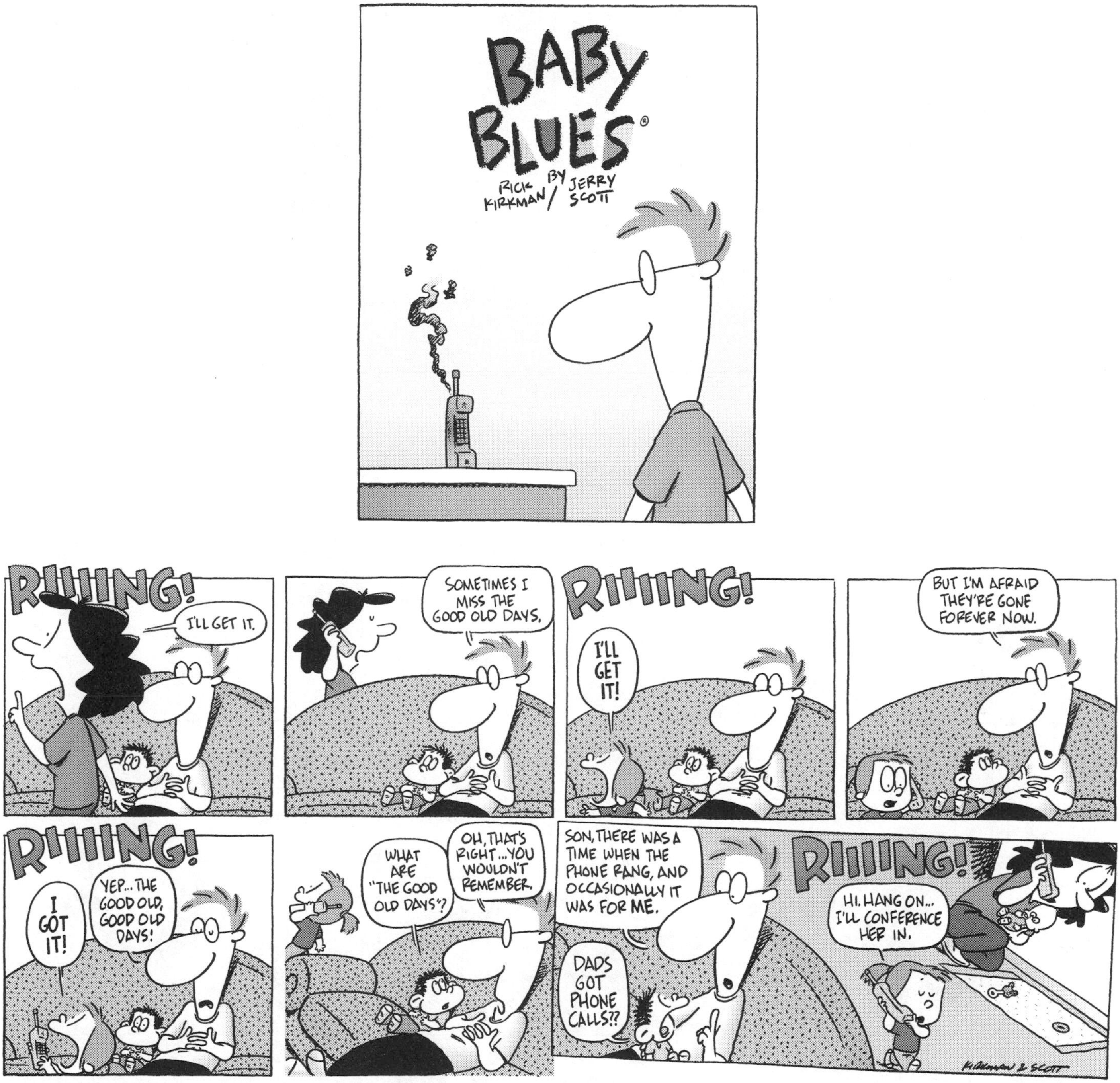
BABY BLUES®
BY RICK KIRKMAN / JERRY SCOTT
RIIIING!
I'LL GET IT.
SOMETIMES I MISS THE GOOD OLD DAYS.
RIIIING!
I'LL GET IT!
BUT I'M AFRAID THEY'RE GONE FOREVER NOW.
RIIIING!
I GOT IT!
YEP... THE GOOD OLD, GOOD OLD DAYS!
WHAT ARE "THE GOOD OLD DAYS"?
OH, THAT'S RIGHT... YOU WOULDN'T REMEMBER.
SON, THERE WAS A TIME WHEN THE PHONE RANG, AND OCCASIONALLY IT WAS FOR ME.
DADS GOT PHONE CALLS??
RIIIING!
HI. HANG ON... I'LL CONFERENCE HER IN.
KIRKMAN & SCOTT

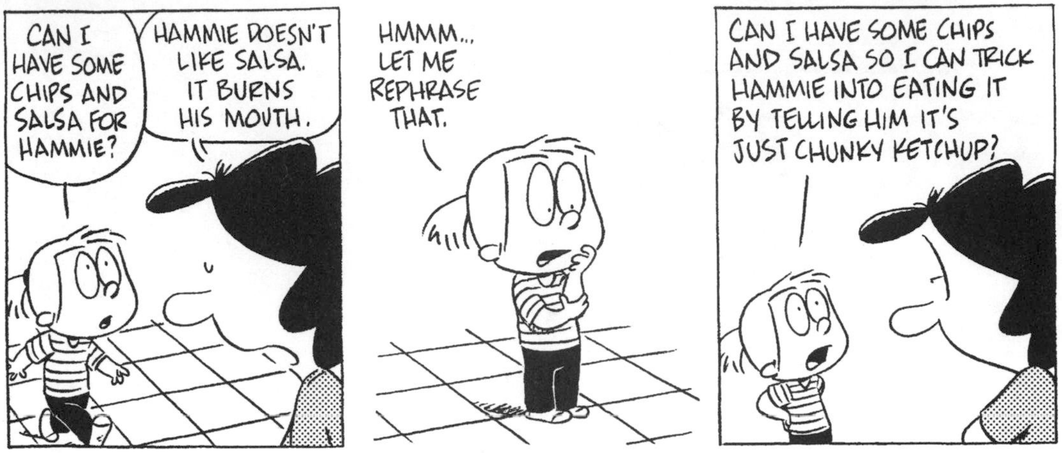
CAN I HAVE SOME CHIPS AND SALSA FOR HAMMIE?
HAMMIE DOESN'T LIKE SALSA. IT BURNS HIS MOUTH.
HMMM... LET ME REPHRASE THAT.
CAN I HAVE SOME CHIPS AND SALSA SO I CAN TRICK HAMMIE INTO EATING IT BY TELLING HIM IT'S JUST CHUNKY KETCHUP?
I NEVER GET WHAT I WANT WHEN I REPHRASE THINGS.
KIRKMAN & SCOTT

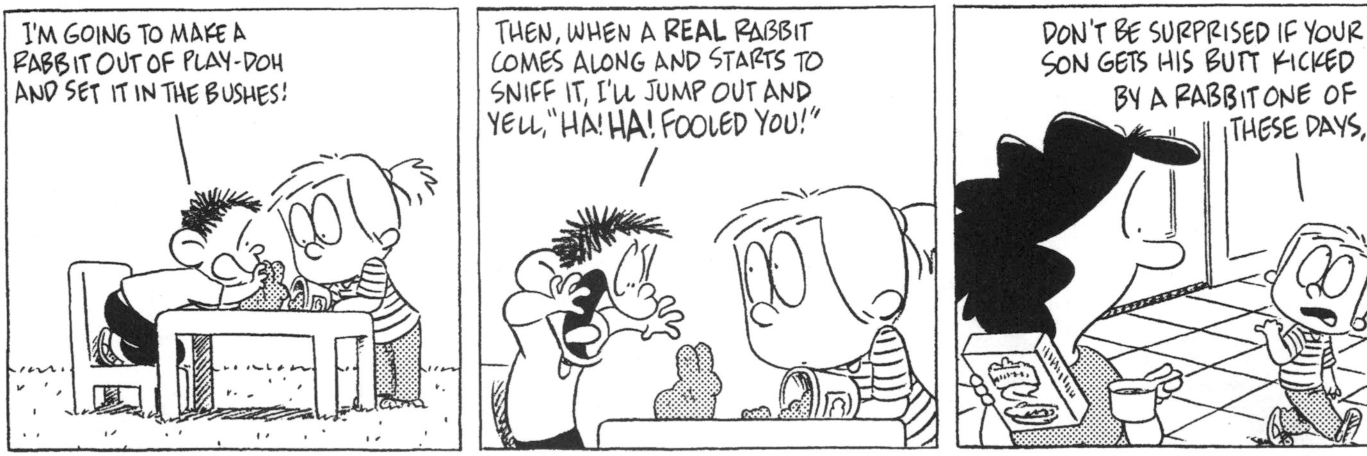
I'M GOING TO MAKE A RABBIT OUT OF PLAY-DOH AND SET IT IN THE BUSHES!
THEN, WHEN A REAL RABBIT COMES ALONG AND STARTS TO SNIFF IT, I'LL JUMP OUT AND YELL, "HA! HA! FOOLED YOU!"
DON'T BE SURPRISED IF YOUR SON GETS HIS BUTT KICKED BY A RABBIT ONE OF THESE DAYS.
KIRKMAN & SCOTT

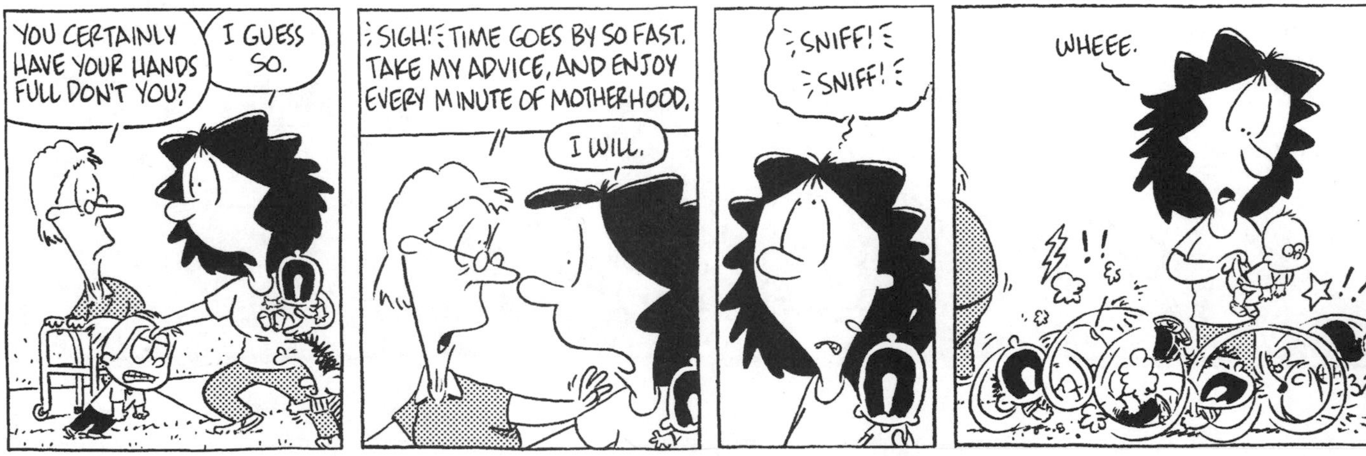
YOU CERTAINLY HAVE YOUR HANDS FULL DON'T YOU?
I GUESS SO.
SIGH! TIME GOES BY SO FAST. TAKE MY ADVICE, AND ENJOY EVERY MINUTE OF MOTHERHOOD.
I WILL.
SNIFF!
SNIFF!
WHEEE.
KIRKMAN & SCOTT

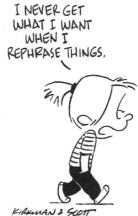

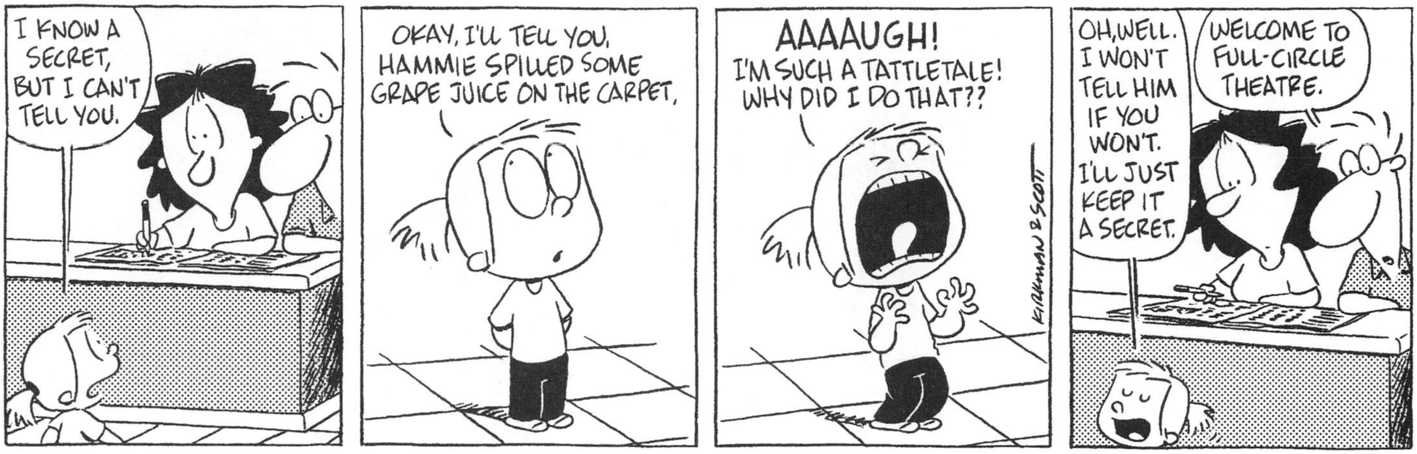
I KNOW A SECRET, BUT I CAN'T TELL YOU.
OKAY, I'LL TELL YOU. HAMMIE SPILLED SOME GRAPE JUICE ON THE CARPET.
AAAAUGH!
I'M SUCH A TATTLETALE! WHY DID I DO THAT??
KIRKMAN & SCOTT
OH, WELL. I WON'T TELL HIM IF YOU WON'T. I'LL JUST KEEP IT A SECRET.
WELCOME TO FULL-CIRCLE THEATRE.

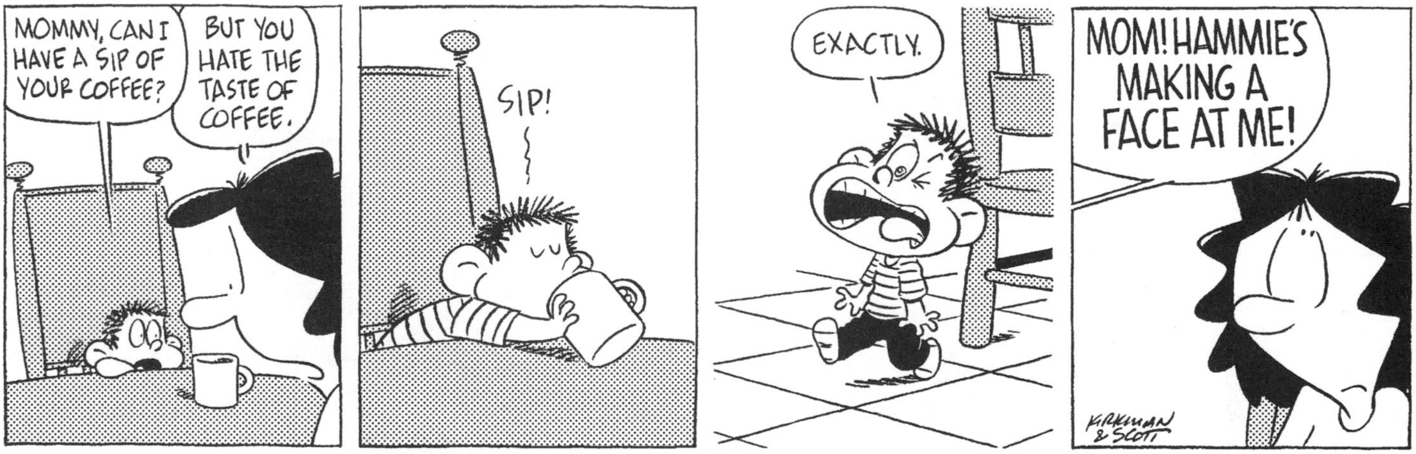
MOMMY, CAN I HAVE A SIP OF YOUR COFFEE?
BUT YOU HATE THE TASTE OF COFFEE.
SIP!
EXACTLY.
MOM! HAMMIE'S MAKING A FACE AT ME!
KIRKMAN & SCOTT

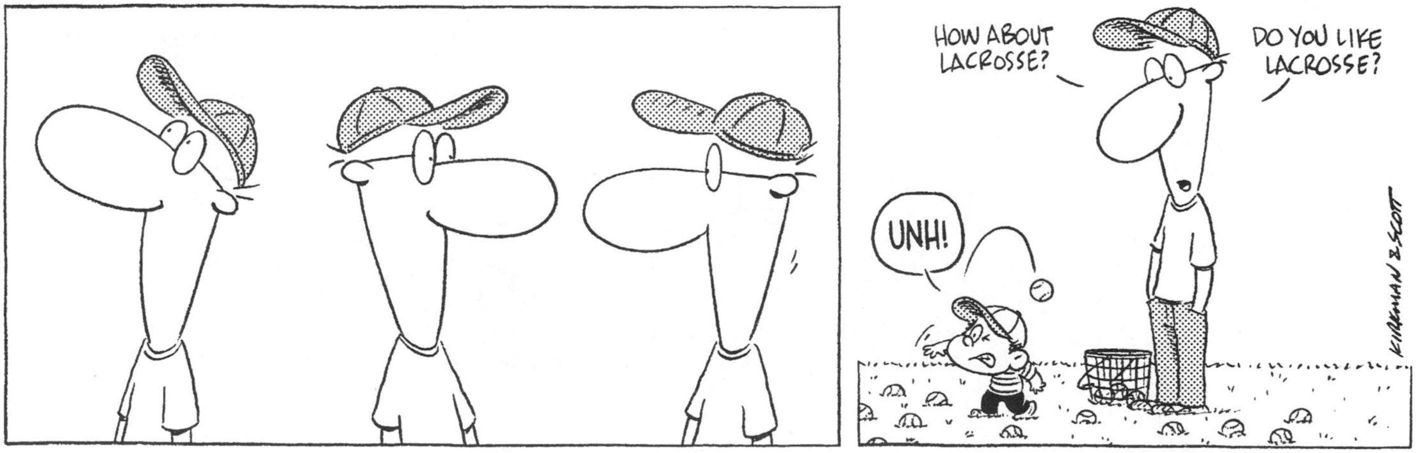
HOW ABOUT LACROSSE?
DO YOU LIKE LACROSSE?
UNH!
KIRKMAN & SCOTT

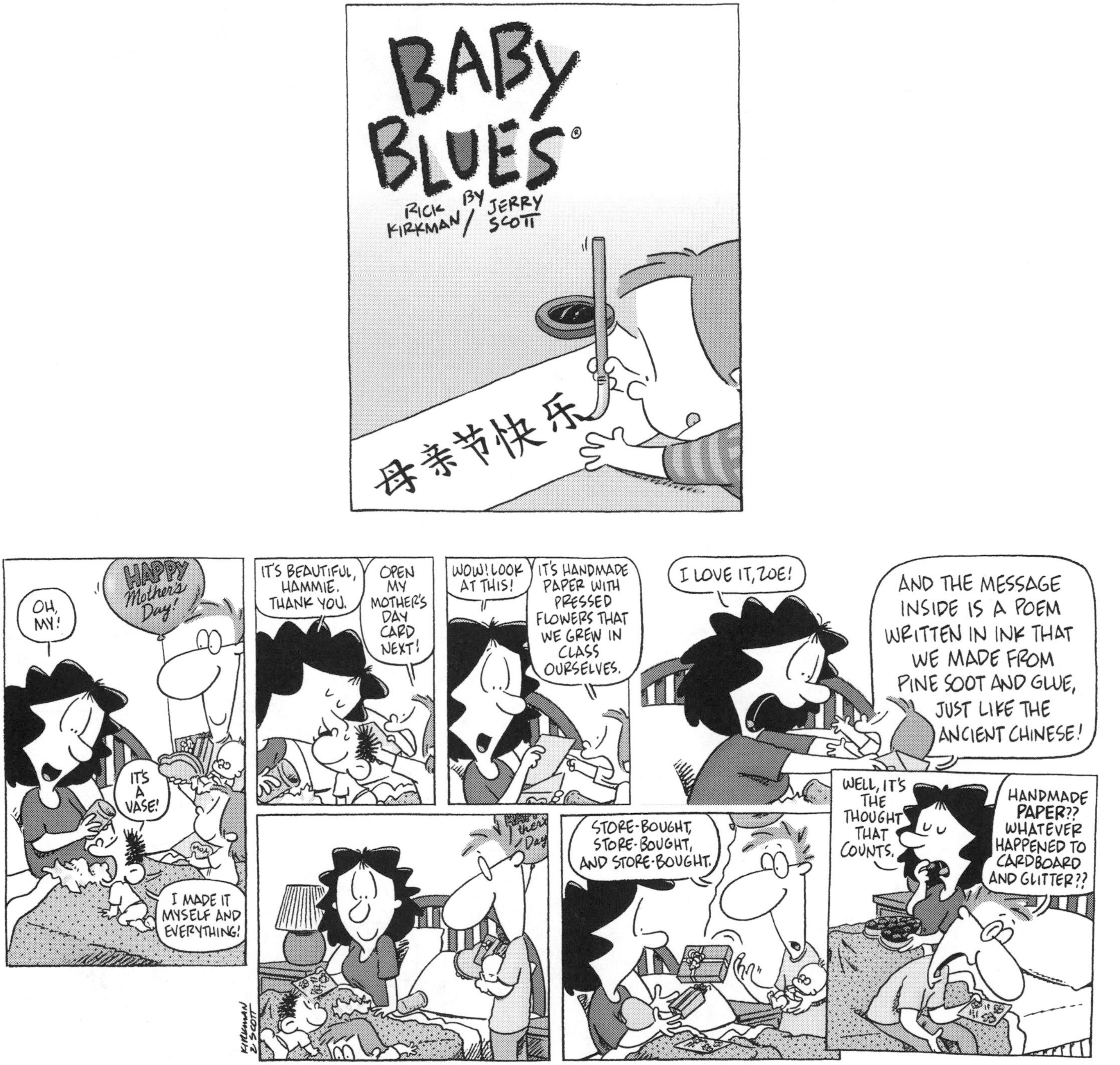
BABY BLUES®
BY RICK KIRKMAN / JERRY SCOTT
母亲节快乐
HAPPY Mother's Day!
OH, MY!
IT'S A VASE!
I MADE IT MYSELF AND EVERYTHING!
IT'S BEAUTIFUL, HAMMIE. THANK YOU.
OPEN MY MOTHER'S DAY CARD NEXT!
WOW! LOOK AT THIS!
IT'S HANDMADE PAPER WITH PRESSED FLOWERS THAT WE GREW IN CLASS OURSELVES.
I LOVE IT, ZOE!
AND THE MESSAGE INSIDE IS A POEM WRITTEN IN INK THAT WE MADE FROM PINE SOOT AND GLUE, JUST LIKE THE ANCIENT CHINESE!
STORE-BOUGHT, STORE-BOUGHT, AND STORE-BOUGHT.
WELL, IT'S THE THOUGHT THAT COUNTS.
HANDMADE PAPER?? WHATEVER HAPPENED TO CARDBOARD AND GLITTER??

KIRKMAN & SCOTT
WHAK!
OW!
OH DEAR!
HAMMIE, ARE YOU OKAY?
OKAY?? I'M GREAT!
A DRAWER HITS YOU IN THE EYE, AND YOU'RE "GREAT"?
I MUST BE GROWING... IT USED TO HIT ME WAY UP HERE!

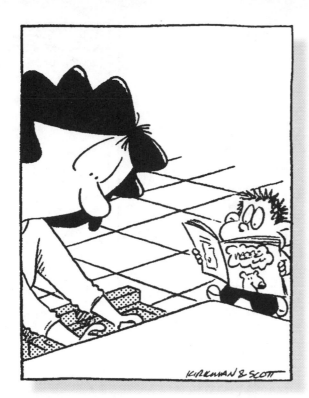

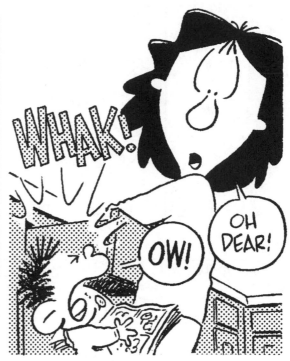

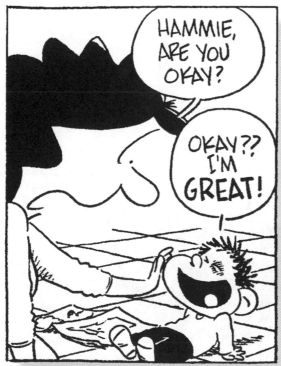

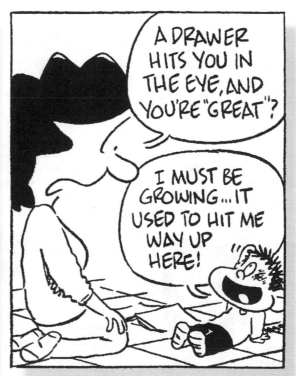

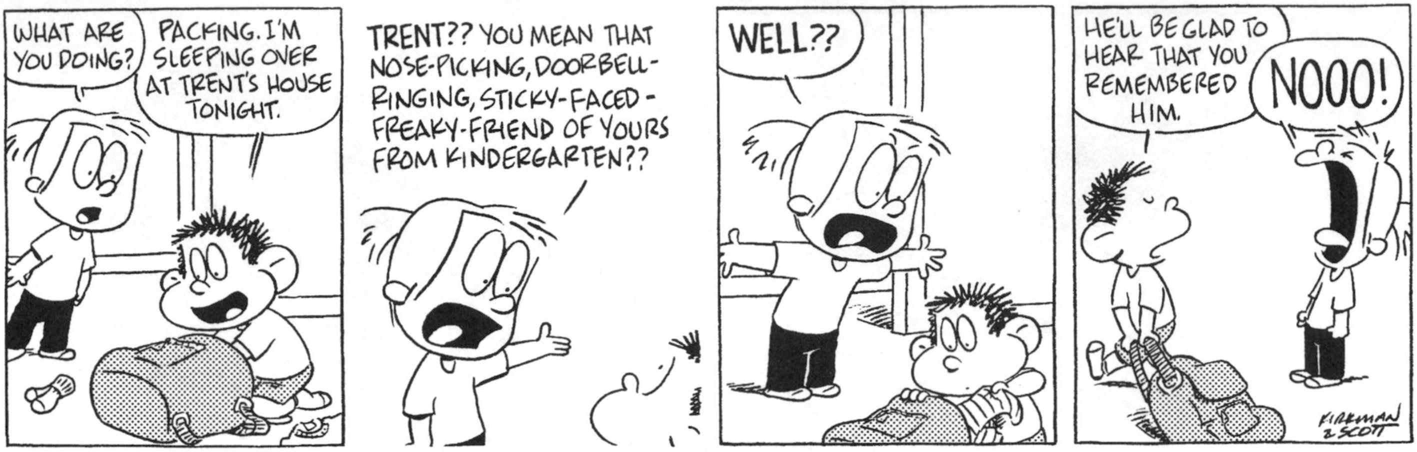
WHAT ARE YOU DOING?
PACKING. I'M SLEEPING OVER AT TRENT'S HOUSE TONIGHT.
TRENT?? YOU MEAN THAT NOSE-PICKING, DOORBELL-RINGING, STICKY-FACED-FREAKY-FRIEND OF YOURS FROM KINDERGARTEN??
WELL??
HE'LL BE GLAD TO HEAR THAT YOU REMEMBERED HIM.
NOOO!
KIRKMAN & SCOTT

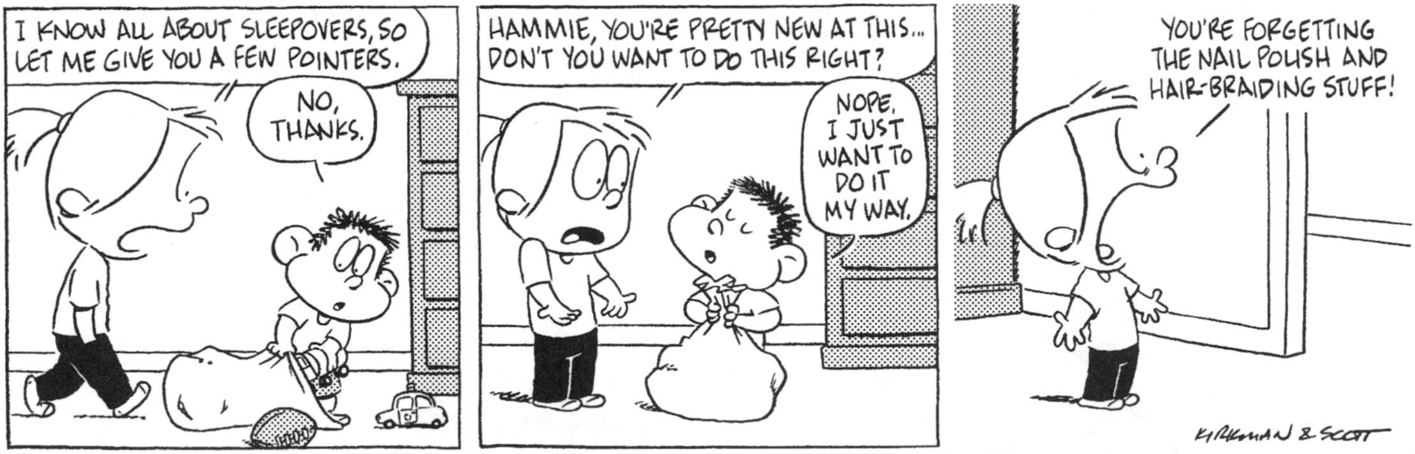
I KNOW ALL ABOUT SLEEPOVERS, SO LET ME GIVE YOU A FEW POINTERS.
NO, THANKS.
HAMMIE, YOU'RE PRETTY NEW AT THIS... DON'T YOU WANT TO DO THIS RIGHT?
NOPE. I JUST WANT TO DO IT MY WAY.
YOU'RE FORGETTING THE NAIL POLISH AND HAIR-BRAIDING STUFF!
KIRKMAN & SCOTT

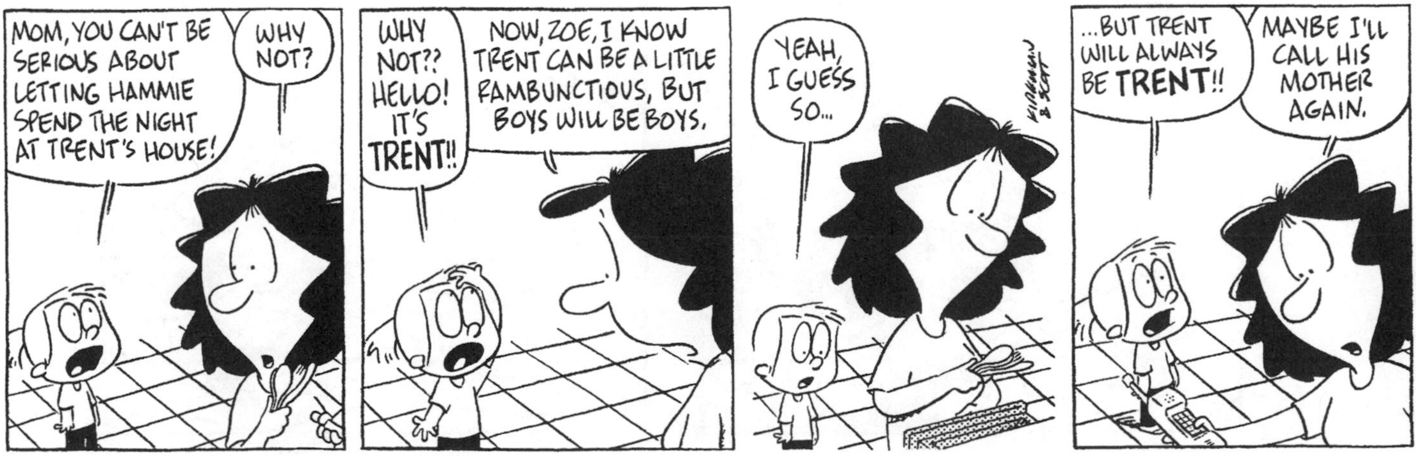
MOM, YOU CAN'T BE SERIOUS ABOUT LETTING HAMMIE SPEND THE NIGHT AT TRENT'S HOUSE!
WHY NOT?
WHY NOT?? HELLO! IT'S TRENT!!
NOW, ZOE, I KNOW TRENT CAN BE A LITTLE RAMBUNCTIOUS, BUT BOYS WILL BE BOYS.
YEAH, I GUESS SO...
KIRKMAN & SCOTT
...BUT TRENT WILL ALWAYS BE TRENT!!
MAYBE I'LL CALL HIS MOTHER AGAIN.

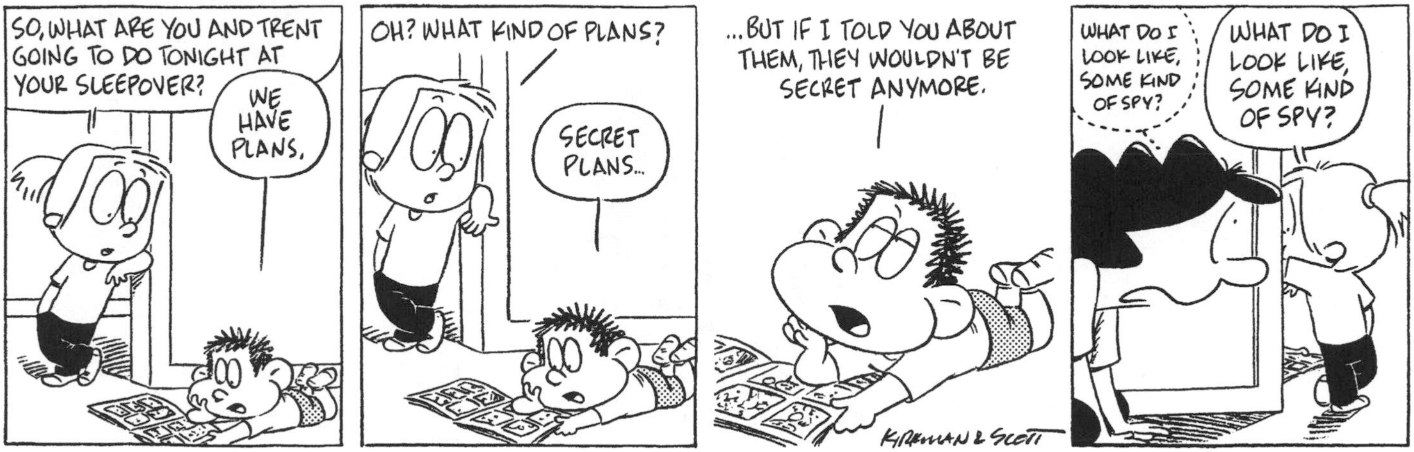
SO, WHAT ARE YOU AND TRENT GOING TO DO TONIGHT AT YOUR SLEEPOVER?
WE HAVE PLANS.
OH? WHAT KIND OF PLANS?
SECRET PLANS...
...BUT IF I TOLD YOU ABOUT THEM, THEY WOULDN'T BE SECRET ANYMORE.
KIRKMAN & SCOTT
WHAT DO I LOOK LIKE, SOME KIND OF SPY?
WHAT DO I LOOK LIKE, SOME KIND OF SPY?

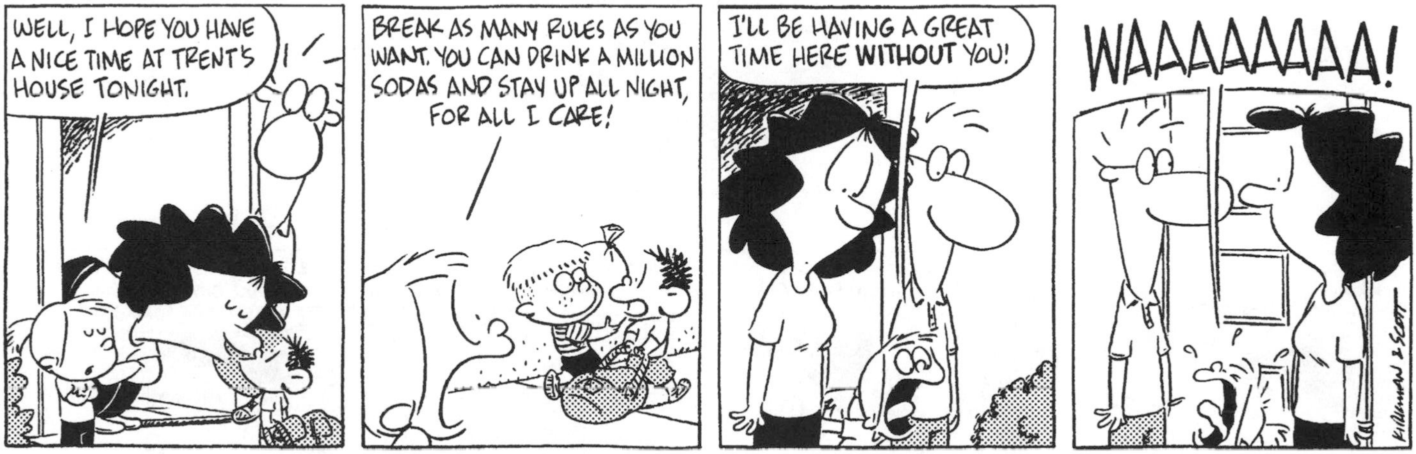
WELL, I HOPE YOU HAVE A NICE TIME AT TRENT'S HOUSE TONIGHT.
BREAK AS MANY RULES AS YOU WANT. YOU CAN DRINK A MILLION SODAS AND STAY UP ALL NIGHT, FOR ALL I CARE!
I'LL BE HAVING A GREAT TIME HERE **WITHOUT** YOU!
WAAAAAAAA!
KIRKMAN & SCOTT

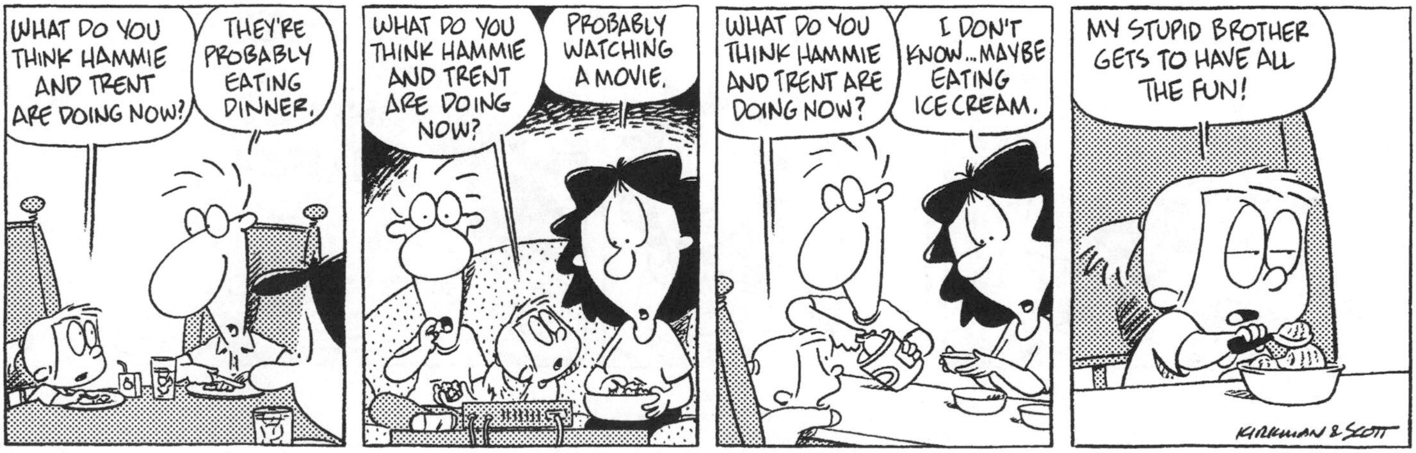
WHAT DO YOU THINK HAMMIE AND TRENT ARE DOING NOW?
THEY'RE PROBABLY EATING DINNER.
WHAT DO YOU THINK HAMMIE AND TRENT ARE DOING NOW?
PROBABLY WATCHING A MOVIE.
WHAT DO YOU THINK HAMMIE AND TRENT ARE DOING NOW?
I DON'T KNOW...MAYBE EATING ICE CREAM.
MY STUPID BROTHER GETS TO HAVE ALL THE FUN!
KIRKMAN & SCOTT

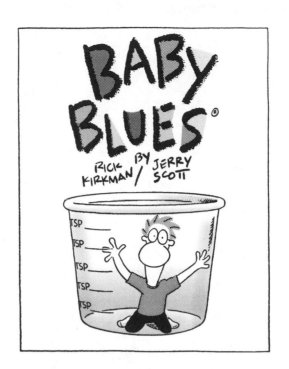

BABY BLUES®
BY RICK KIRKMAN / JERRY SCOTT
TSP
TSP
TSP
TSP
TSP

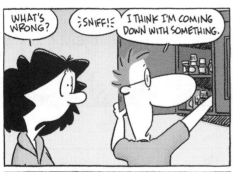

WHAT'S WRONG?
SNIFF!
I THINK I'M COMING DOWN WITH SOMETHING.
DID YOU TAKE ANYTHING?
I WOULD, BUT ALL WE HAVE IS THE KIDS' STUFF.
SO I EITHER HAVE TO DRIVE TO THE DRUGSTORE, OR FIGURE OUT THE ADULT DOSAGE OF THIS CHILDREN'S FORMULA.
YOU DON'T WANT TO DRIVE ALL THE WAY DOWN THERE. LET ME HAVE A LOOK.
WHAT DO YOU WEIGH...ABOUT 170?
GIVE OR TAKE.
SO YOU'RE ABOUT 14 TIMES WREN'S SIZE, WHICH MEANS YOU WOULD HAVE TO TAKE ABOUT...
...THIS MUCH.
I'LL GET MY CAR KEYS.
KIRKMAN & SCOTT

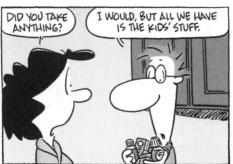

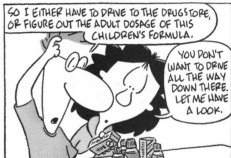

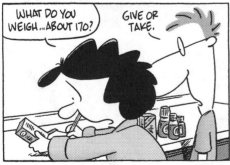

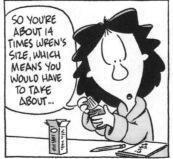

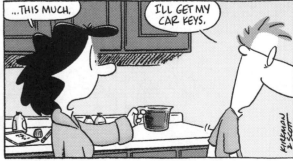

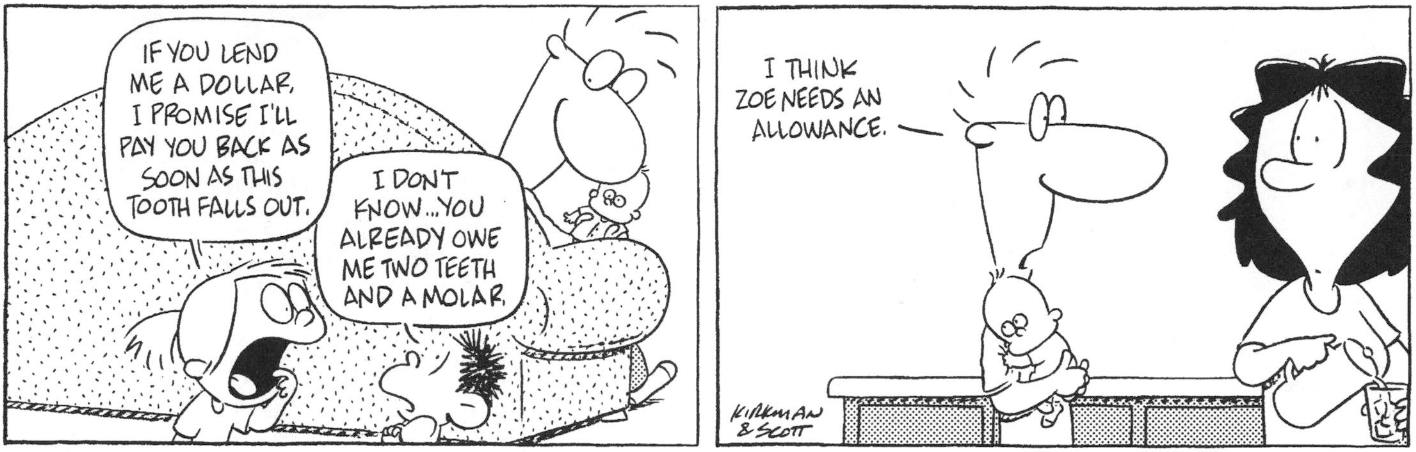
IF YOU LEND ME A DOLLAR, I PROMISE I'LL PAY YOU BACK AS SOON AS THIS TOOTH FALLS OUT.
I DON'T KNOW...YOU ALREADY OWE ME TWO TEETH AND A MOLAR.
I THINK ZOE NEEDS AN ALLOWANCE.
KIRKMAN & SCOTT

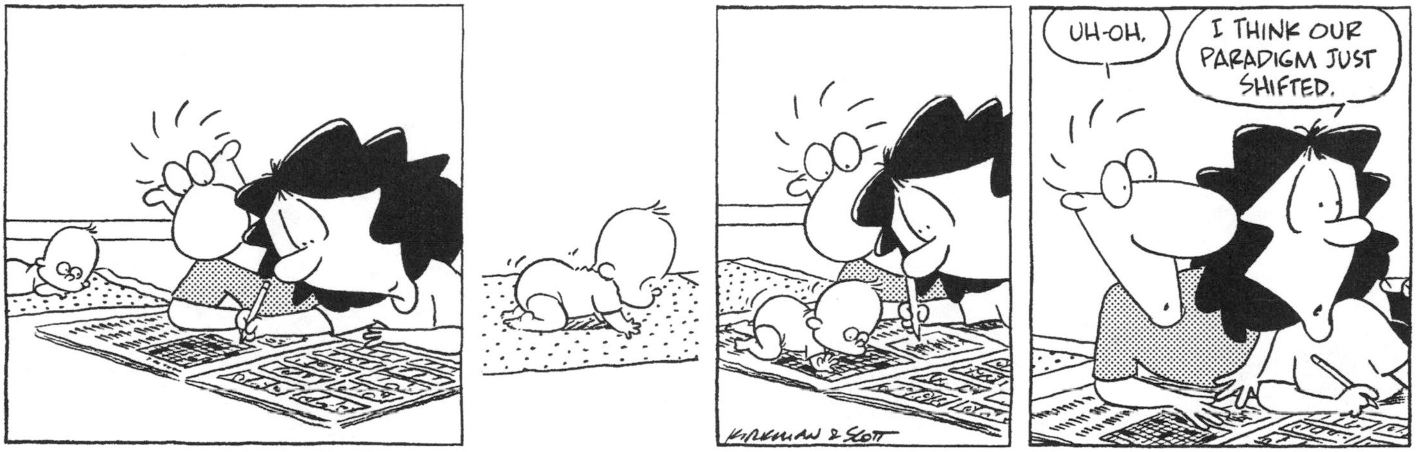
UH-OH.
I THINK OUR PARADIGM JUST SHIFTED.
KIRKMAN & SCOTT

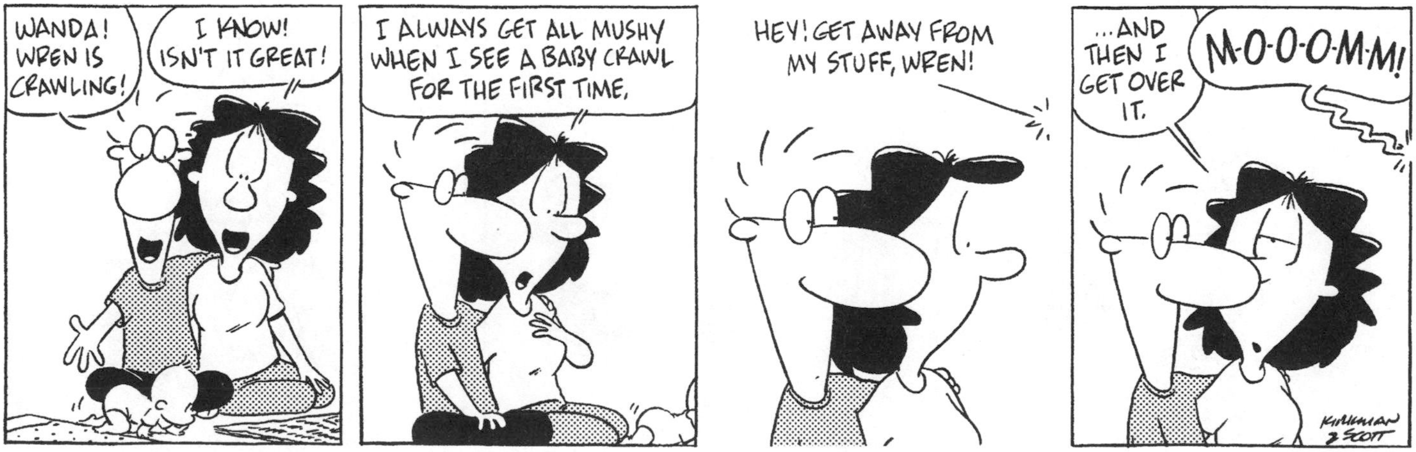
WANDA! WREN IS CRAWLING!
I KNOW! ISN'T IT GREAT!
I ALWAYS GET ALL MUSHY WHEN I SEE A BABY CRAWL FOR THE FIRST TIME.
HEY! GET AWAY FROM MY STUFF, WREN!
...AND THEN I GET OVER IT.
M-O-O-O-M-M!
KIRKMAN & SCOTT

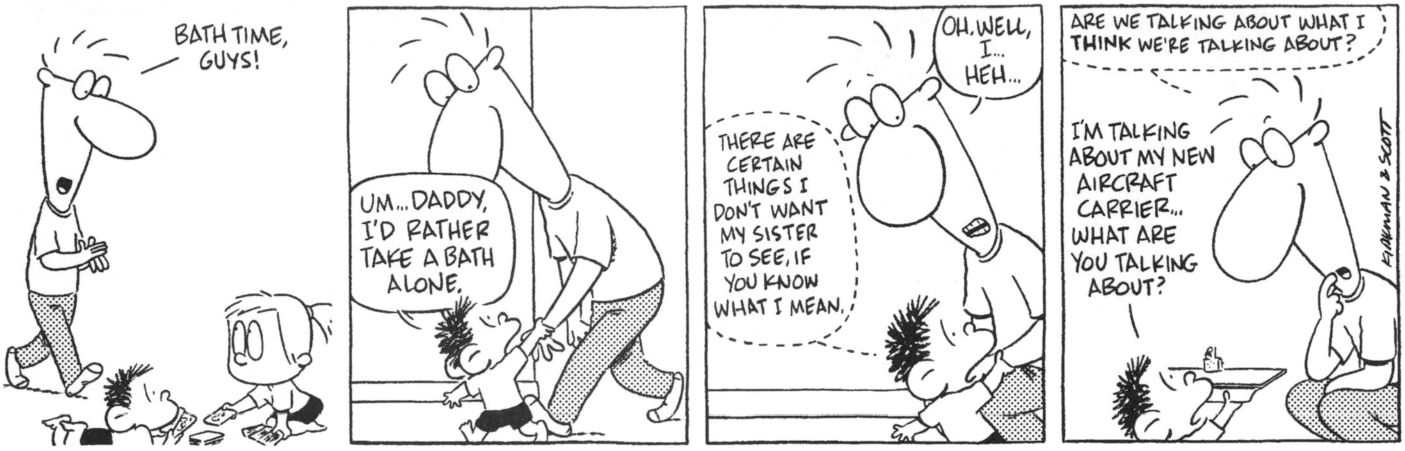
BATH TIME, GUYS!
UM... DADDY, I'D RATHER TAKE A BATH ALONE.
THERE ARE CERTAIN THINGS I DON'T WANT MY SISTER TO SEE, IF YOU KNOW WHAT I MEAN.
OH. WELL, I... HEH...
ARE WE TALKING ABOUT WHAT I THINK WE'RE TALKING ABOUT?
I'M TALKING ABOUT MY NEW AIRCRAFT CARRIER... WHAT ARE YOU TALKING ABOUT?
KIRKMAN & SCOTT

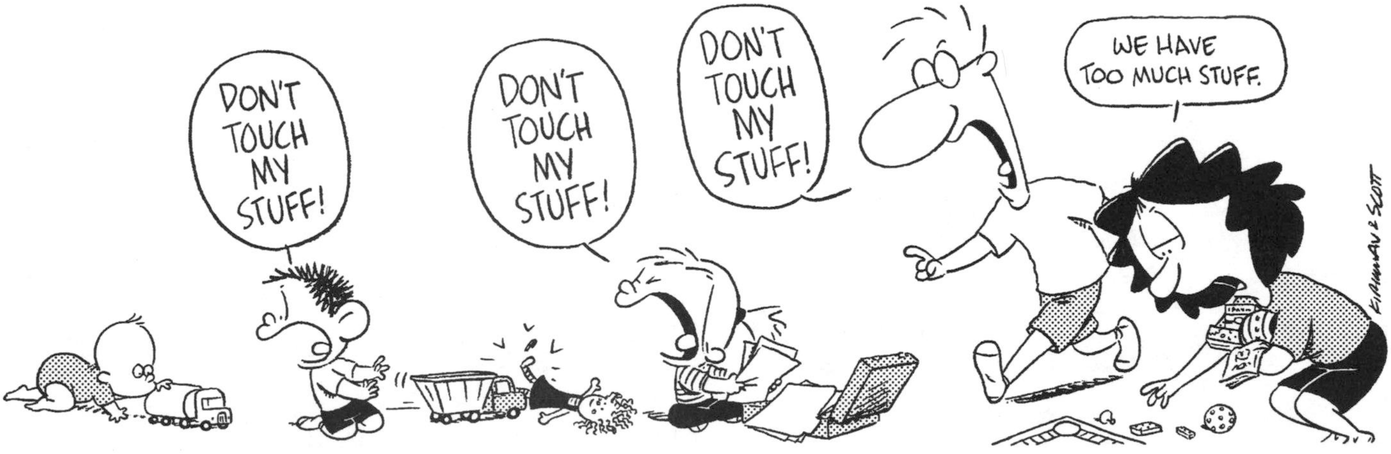
DON'T TOUCH MY STUFF!
DON'T TOUCH MY STUFF!
DON'T TOUCH MY STUFF!
WE HAVE TOO MUCH STUFF.
KIRKMAN & SCOTT

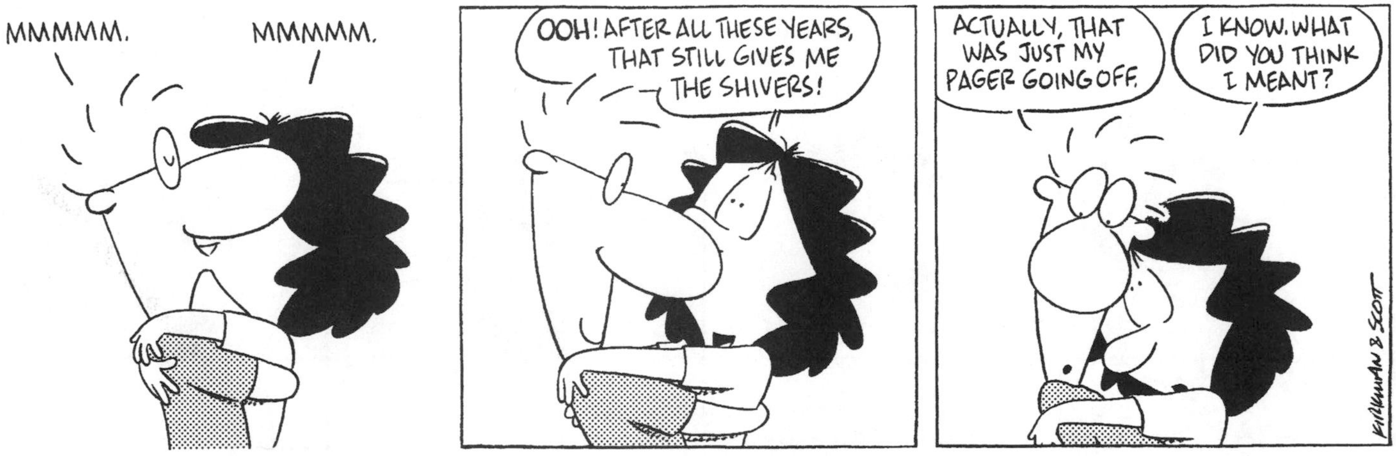
MMMMM.
MMMMM.
OOH! AFTER ALL THESE YEARS, THAT STILL GIVES ME THE SHIVERS!
ACTUALLY, THAT WAS JUST MY PAGER GOING OFF.
I KNOW. WHAT DID YOU THINK I MEANT?
KIRKMAN & SCOTT

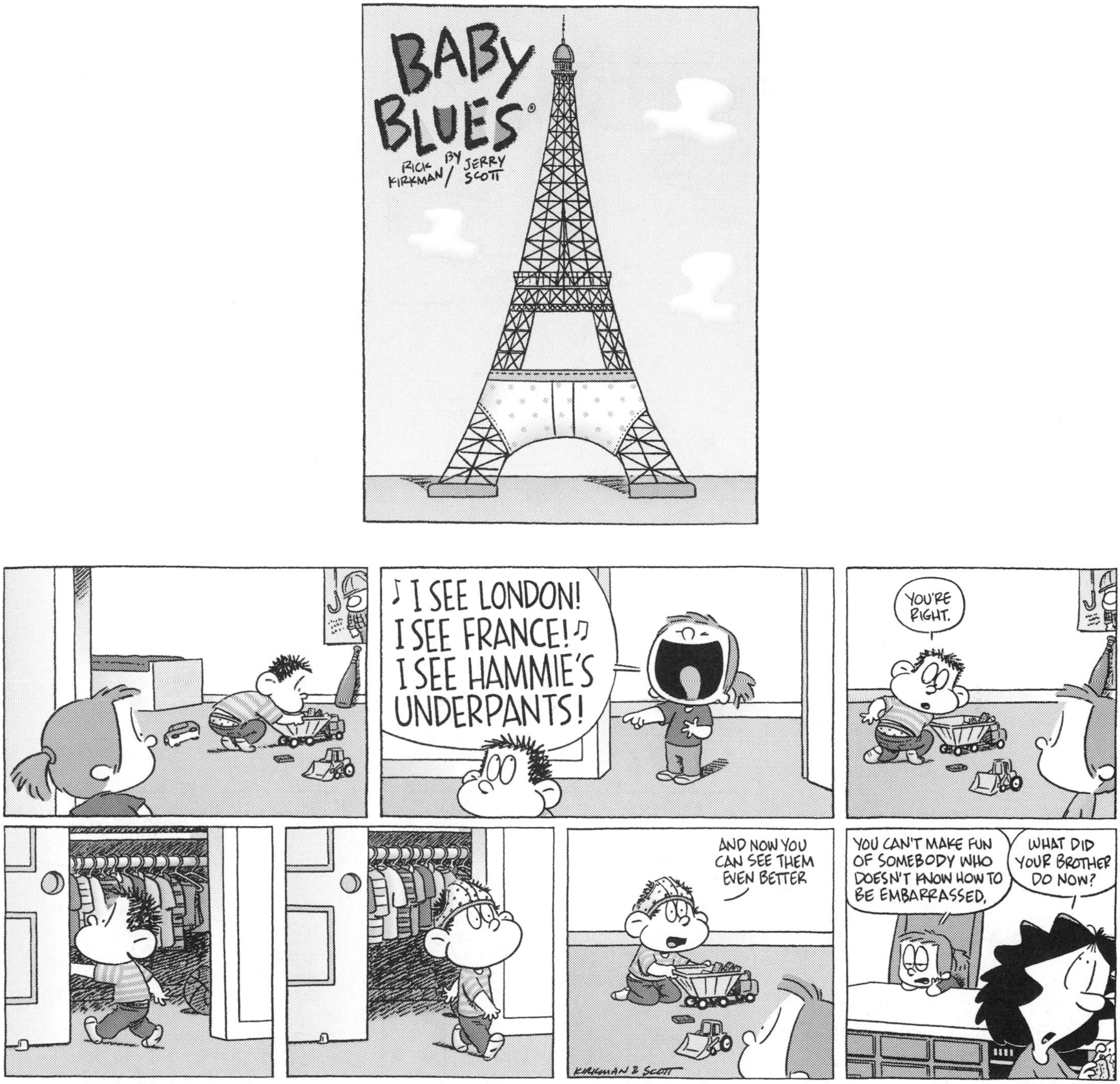
BABY BLUES®
BY RICK KIRKMAN / JERRY SCOTT
♪ I SEE LONDON! I SEE FRANCE! ♫ I SEE HAMMIE'S UNDERPANTS!
YOU'RE RIGHT.
AND NOW YOU CAN SEE THEM EVEN BETTER
YOU CAN'T MAKE FUN OF SOMEBODY WHO DOESN'T KNOW HOW TO BE EMBARRASSED.
WHAT DID YOUR BROTHER DO NOW?
KIRKMAN & SCOTT

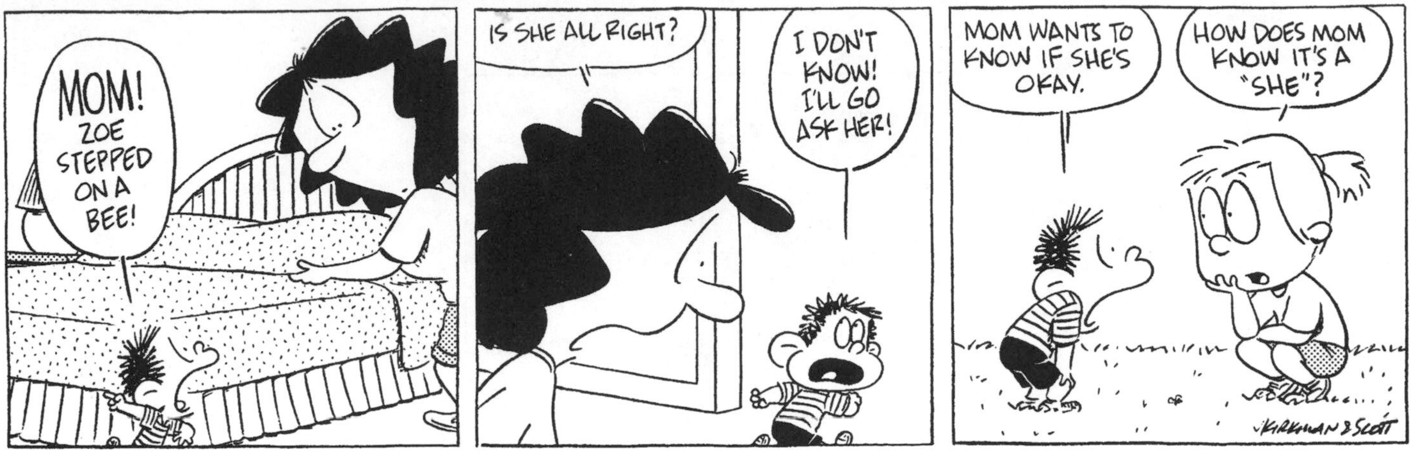
MOM! ZOE STEPPED ON A BEE!
IS SHE ALL RIGHT?
I DON'T KNOW! I'LL GO ASK HER!
MOM WANTS TO KNOW IF SHE'S OKAY.
HOW DOES MOM KNOW IT'S A "SHE"?
KIRKMAN & SCOTT

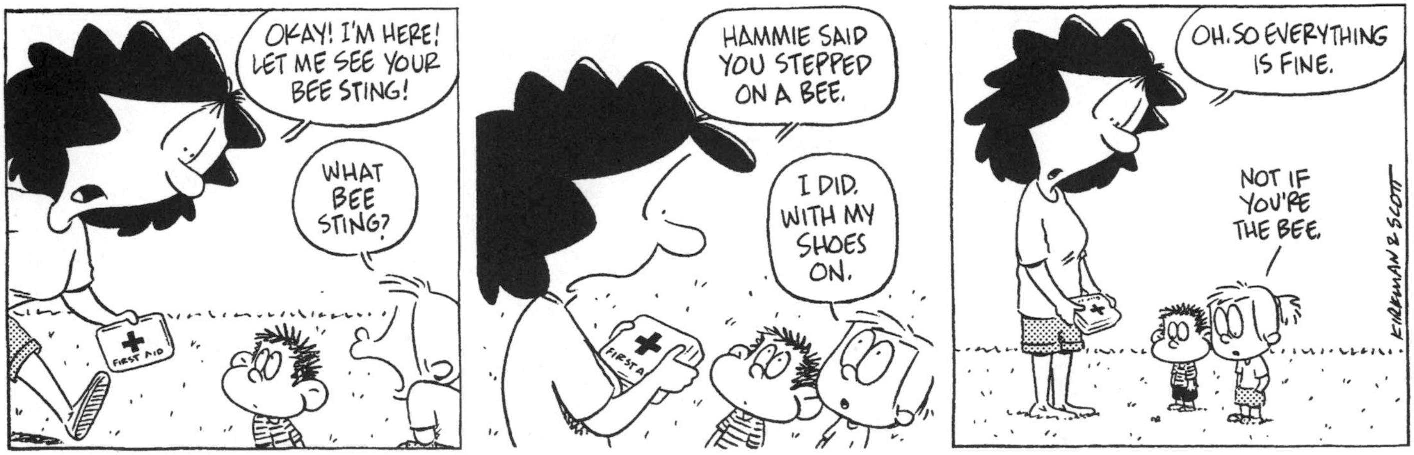
OKAY! I'M HERE! LET ME SEE YOUR BEE STING!
WHAT BEE STING?
FIRST AID
HAMMIE SAID YOU STEPPED ON A BEE.
I DID. WITH MY SHOES ON.
OH. SO EVERYTHING IS FINE.
NOT IF YOU'RE THE BEE.
KIRKMAN & SCOTT

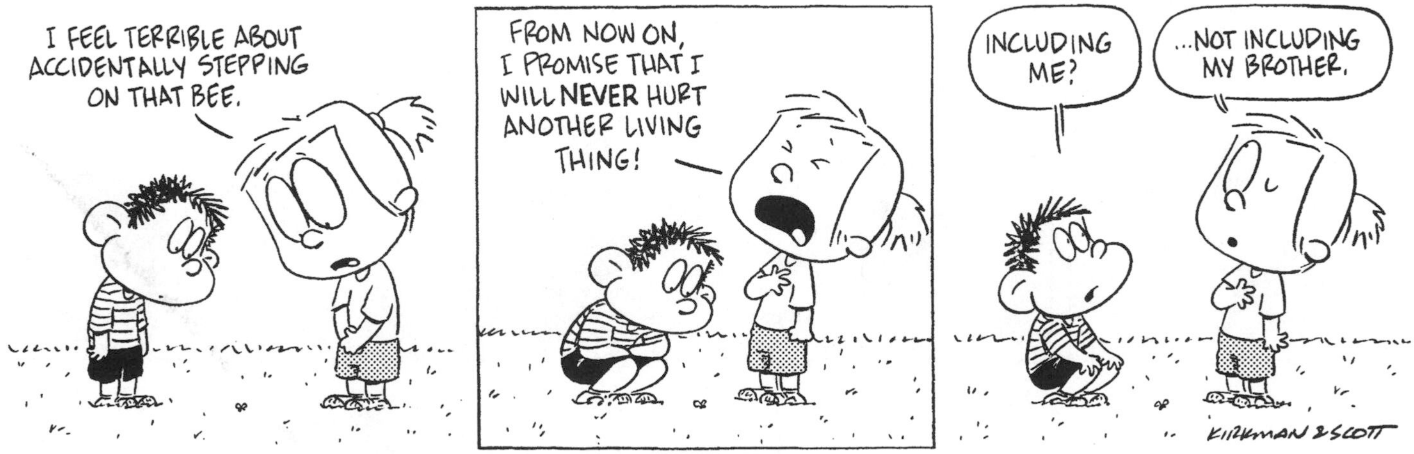
I FEEL TERRIBLE ABOUT ACCIDENTALLY STEPPING ON THAT BEE.
FROM NOW ON, I PROMISE THAT I WILL **NEVER** HURT ANOTHER LIVING THING!
INCLUDING ME?
...NOT INCLUDING MY BROTHER.
KIRKMAN & SCOTT

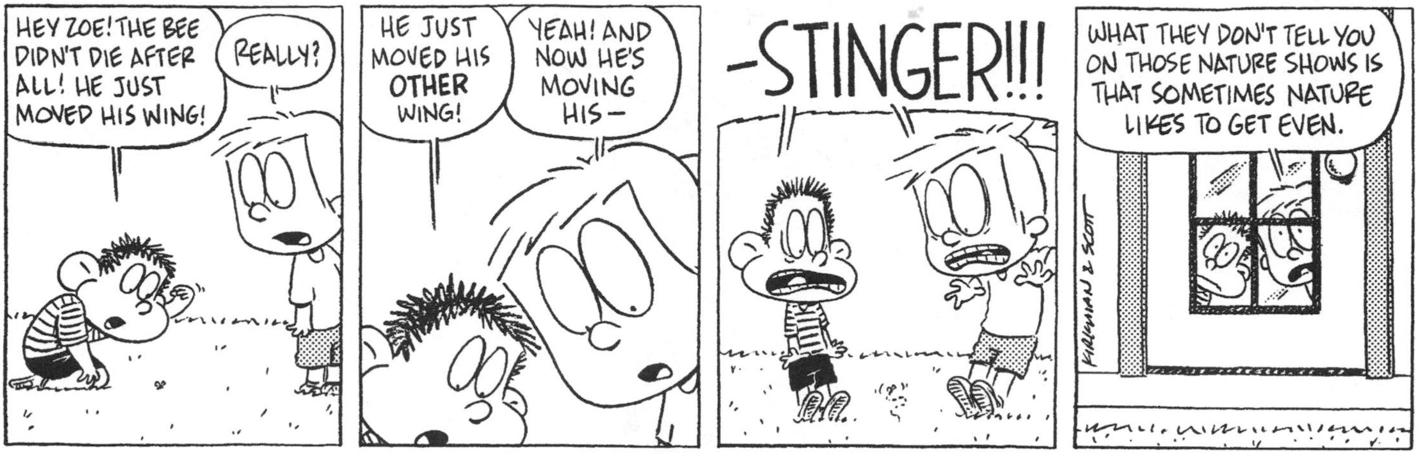
HEY ZOE! THE BEE DIDN'T DIE AFTER ALL! HE JUST MOVED HIS WING!
REALLY?
HE JUST MOVED HIS OTHER WING!
YEAH! AND NOW HE'S MOVING HIS —
-STINGER!!!
WHAT THEY DON'T TELL YOU ON THOSE NATURE SHOWS IS THAT SOMETIMES NATURE LIKES TO GET EVEN.
KIRKMAN & SCOTT

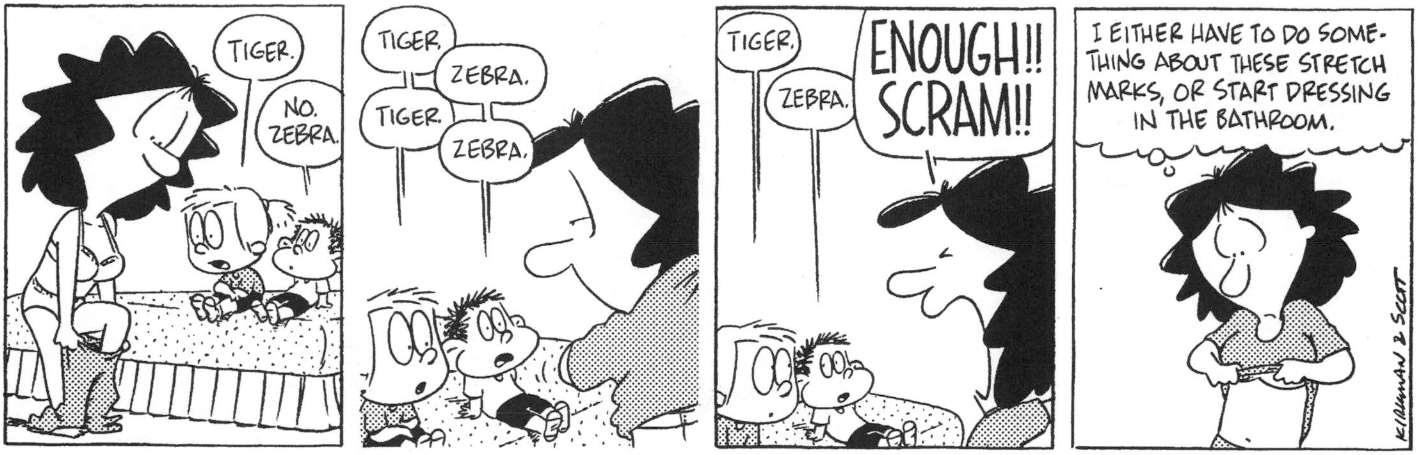
TIGER.
NO. ZEBRA.
TIGER.
ZEBRA.
TIGER.
ZEBRA.
TIGER.
ZEBRA.
ENOUGH!! SCRAM!!
I EITHER HAVE TO DO SOME-THING ABOUT THESE STRETCH MARKS, OR START DRESSING IN THE BATHROOM.
KIRKMAN & SCOTT

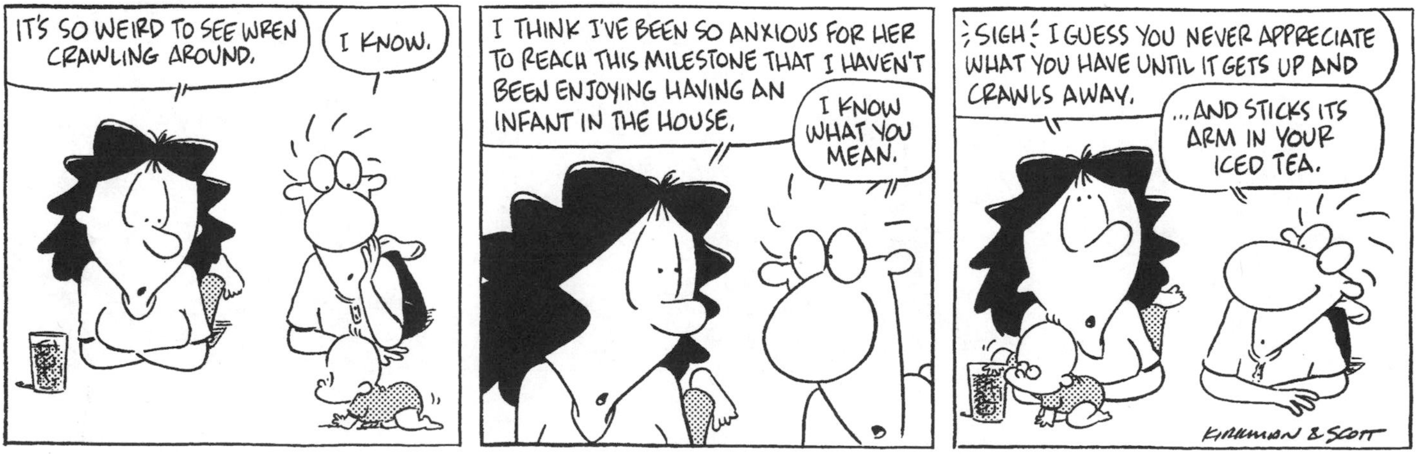
IT'S SO WEIRD TO SEE WREN CRAWLING AROUND.
I KNOW.
I THINK I'VE BEEN SO ANXIOUS FOR HER TO REACH THIS MILESTONE THAT I HAVEN'T BEEN ENJOYING HAVING AN INFANT IN THE HOUSE.
I KNOW WHAT YOU MEAN.
:SIGH: I GUESS YOU NEVER APPRECIATE WHAT YOU HAVE UNTIL IT GETS UP AND CRAWLS AWAY.
...AND STICKS ITS ARM IN YOUR ICED TEA.
KIRKMAN & SCOTT

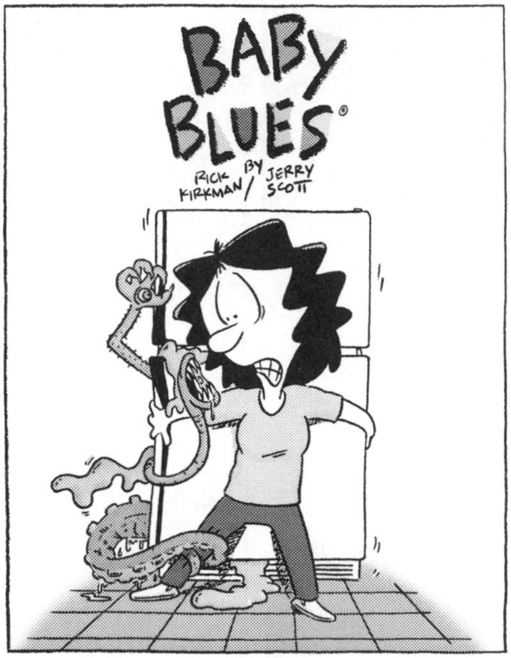
BABY BLUES®
BY RICK KIRKMAN / JERRY SCOTT

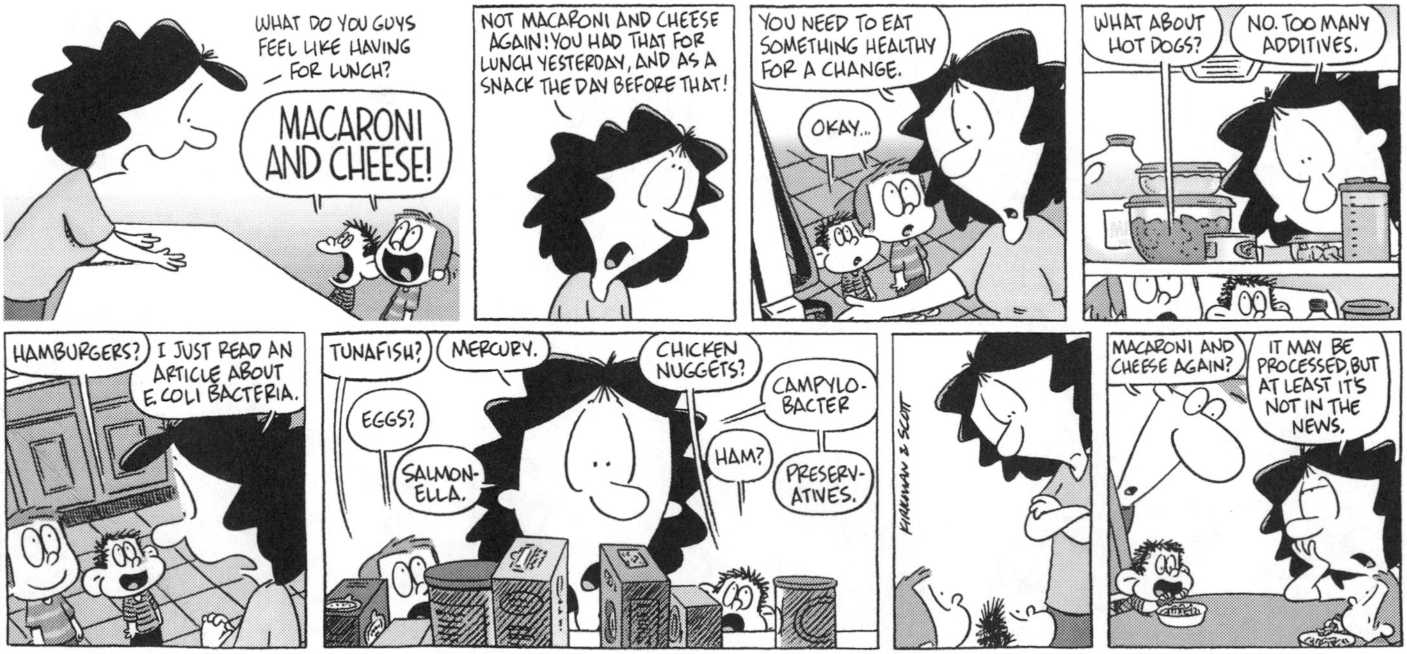
WHAT DO YOU GUYS FEEL LIKE HAVING FOR LUNCH?
MACARONI AND CHEESE!
NOT MACARONI AND CHEESE AGAIN! YOU HAD THAT FOR LUNCH YESTERDAY, AND AS A SNACK THE DAY BEFORE THAT!
YOU NEED TO EAT SOMETHING HEALTHY FOR A CHANGE.
OKAY...
WHAT ABOUT HOT DOGS?
NO. TOO MANY ADDITIVES.
HAMBURGERS?
I JUST READ AN ARTICLE ABOUT E. COLI BACTERIA.
TUNAFISH?
MERCURY.
EGGS?
SALMON-ELLA.
CHICKEN NUGGETS?
CAMPYLO-BACTER
HAM?
PRESERV-ATIVES.
KIRKMAN & SCOTT
MACARONI AND CHEESE AGAIN?
IT MAY BE PROCESSED, BUT AT LEAST IT'S NOT IN THE NEWS.

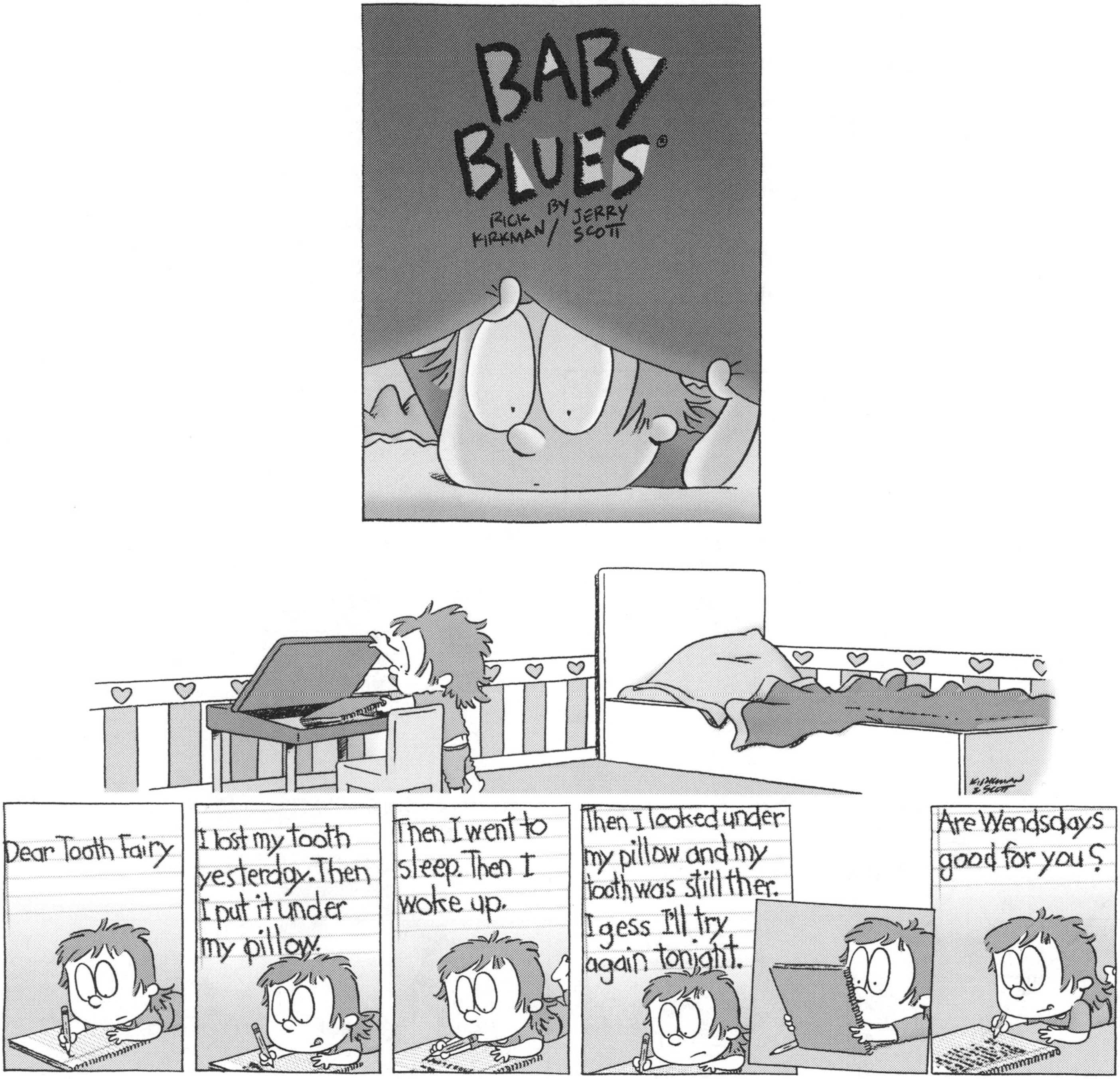
BABY BLUES®
BY RICK KIRKMAN / JERRY SCOTT
Dear Tooth Fairy
I lost my tooth yesterday. Then I put it under my pillow.
Then I went to sleep. Then I woke up.
Then I looked under my pillow and my tooth was still ther. I gess I'll try again tonight.
Are Wendsdays good for you?
KIRKMAN & SCOTT

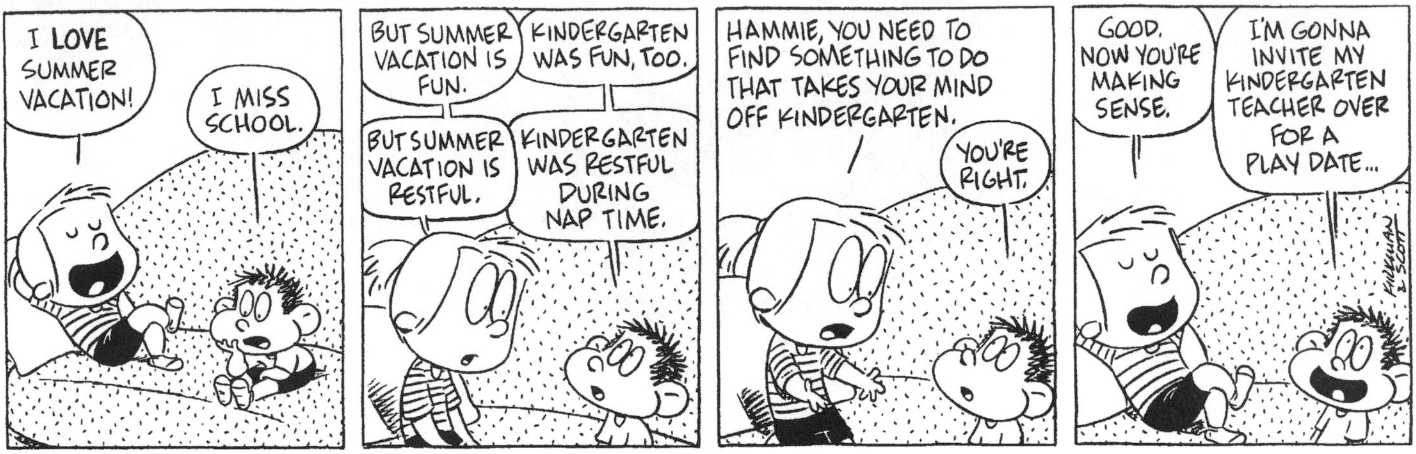
I LOVE SUMMER VACATION!
I MISS SCHOOL.
BUT SUMMER VACATION IS FUN.
KINDERGARTEN WAS FUN, TOO.
BUT SUMMER VACATION IS RESTFUL.
KINDERGARTEN WAS RESTFUL DURING NAP TIME.
HAMMIE, YOU NEED TO FIND SOMETHING TO DO THAT TAKES YOUR MIND OFF KINDERGARTEN.
YOU'RE RIGHT.
GOOD. NOW YOU'RE MAKING SENSE.
I'M GONNA INVITE MY KINDERGARTEN TEACHER OVER FOR A PLAY DATE...
KIRKMAN & SCOTT

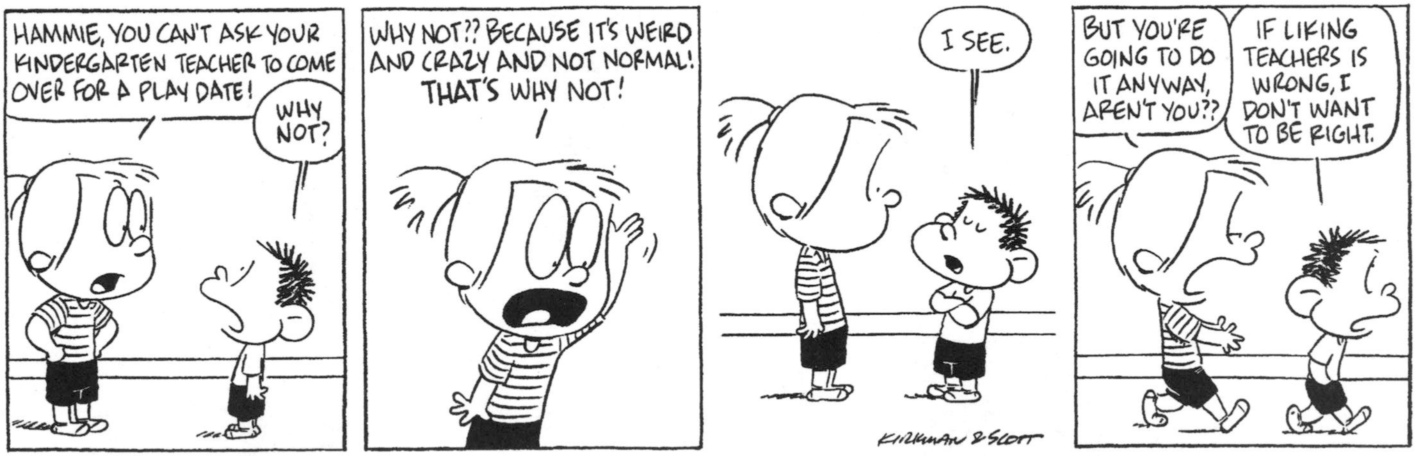
HAMMIE, YOU CAN'T ASK YOUR KINDERGARTEN TEACHER TO COME OVER FOR A PLAY DATE!
WHY NOT?
WHY NOT?? BECAUSE IT'S WEIRD AND CRAZY AND NOT NORMAL! THAT'S WHY NOT!
I SEE.
BUT YOU'RE GOING TO DO IT ANYWAY, AREN'T YOU??
IF LIKING TEACHERS IS WRONG, I DON'T WANT TO BE RIGHT.
KIRKMAN & SCOTT

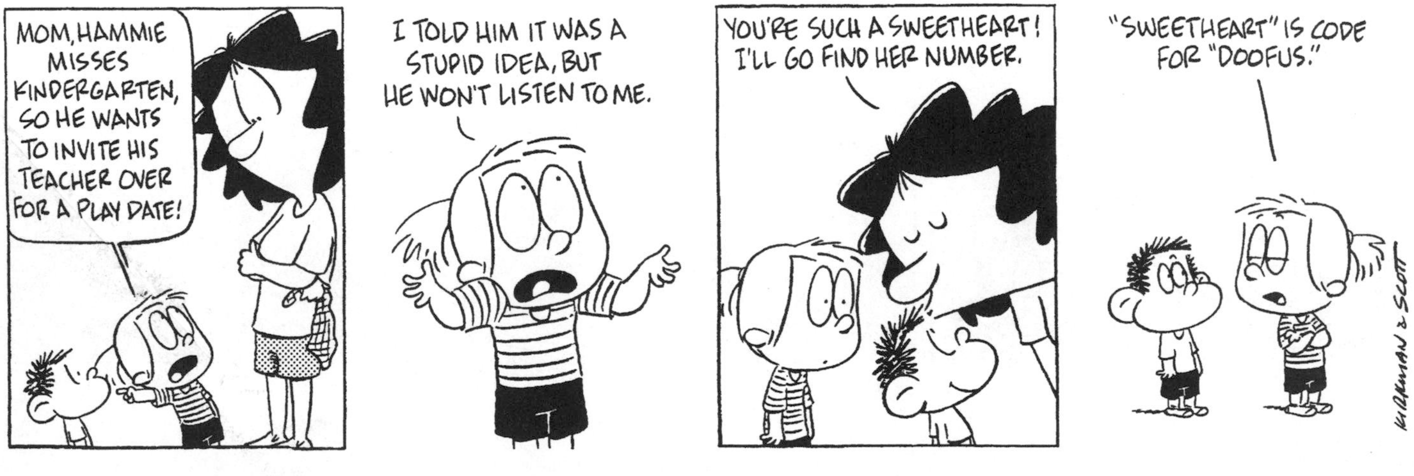
MOM, HAMMIE MISSES KINDERGARTEN, SO HE WANTS TO INVITE HIS TEACHER OVER FOR A PLAY DATE!
I TOLD HIM IT WAS A STUPID IDEA, BUT HE WON'T LISTEN TO ME.
YOU'RE SUCH A SWEETHEART! I'LL GO FIND HER NUMBER.
"SWEETHEART" IS CODE FOR "DOOFUS."
KIRKMAN & SCOTT

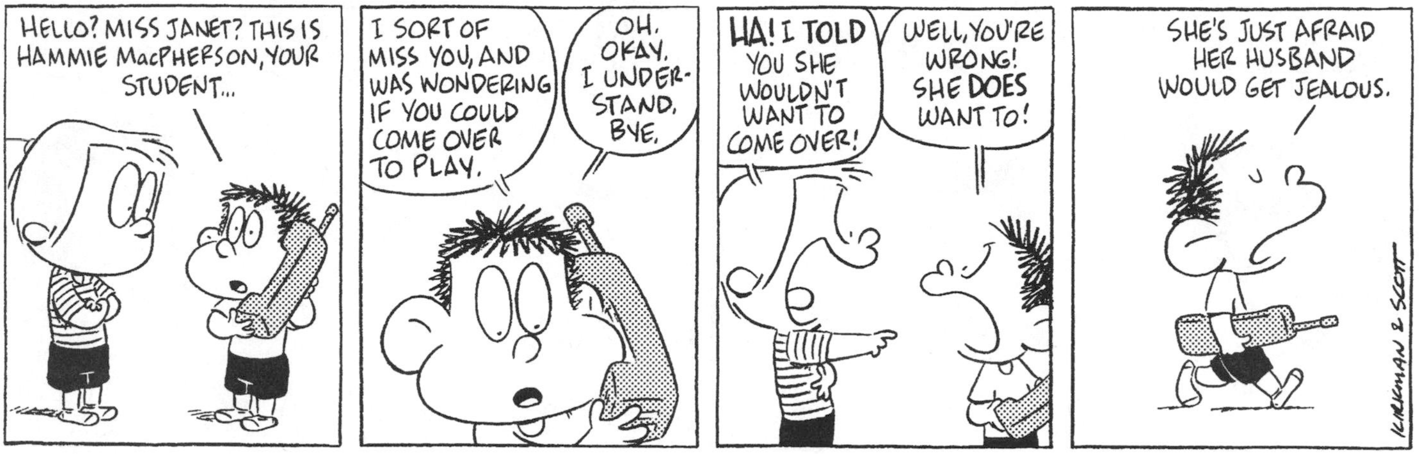
HELLO? MISS JANET? THIS IS HAMMIE MacPHERSON, YOUR STUDENT...
I SORT OF MISS YOU, AND WAS WONDERING IF YOU COULD COME OVER TO PLAY.
OH. OKAY. I UNDERSTAND. BYE.
HA! I TOLD YOU SHE WOULDN'T WANT TO COME OVER!
WELL, YOU'RE WRONG! SHE DOES WANT TO!
SHE'S JUST AFRAID HER HUSBAND WOULD GET JEALOUS.
KIRKMAN & SCOTT

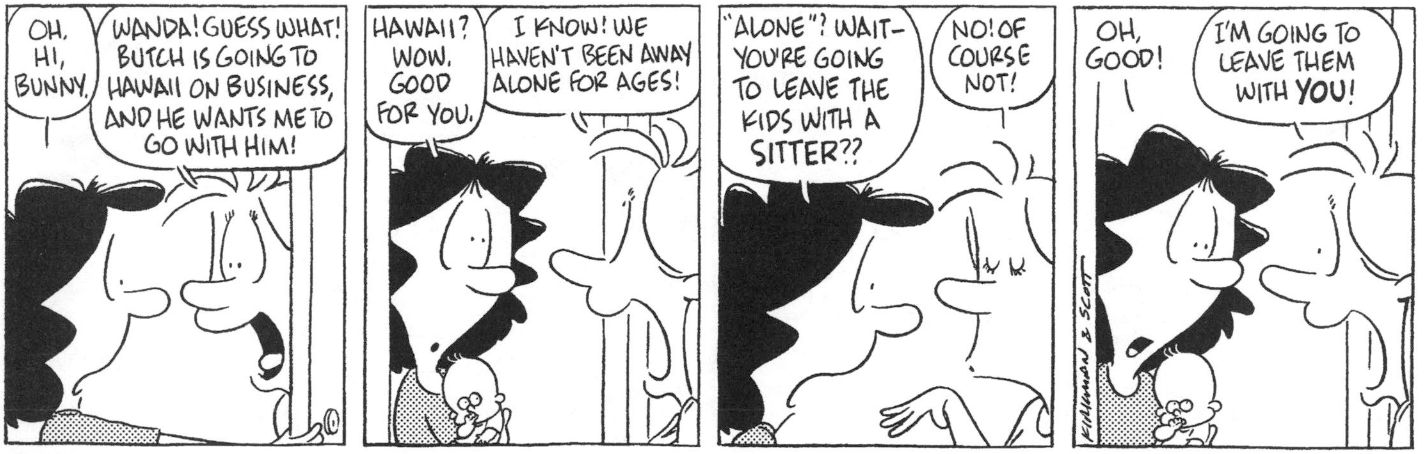
OH. HI, BUNNY.
WANDA! GUESS WHAT! BUTCH IS GOING TO HAWAII ON BUSINESS, AND HE WANTS ME TO GO WITH HIM!
HAWAII? WOW. GOOD FOR YOU.
I KNOW! WE HAVEN'T BEEN AWAY ALONE FOR AGES!
"ALONE"? WAIT- YOU'RE GOING TO LEAVE THE KIDS WITH A SITTER??
NO! OF COURSE NOT!
OH, GOOD!
I'M GOING TO LEAVE THEM WITH YOU!
KIRKMAN & SCOTT

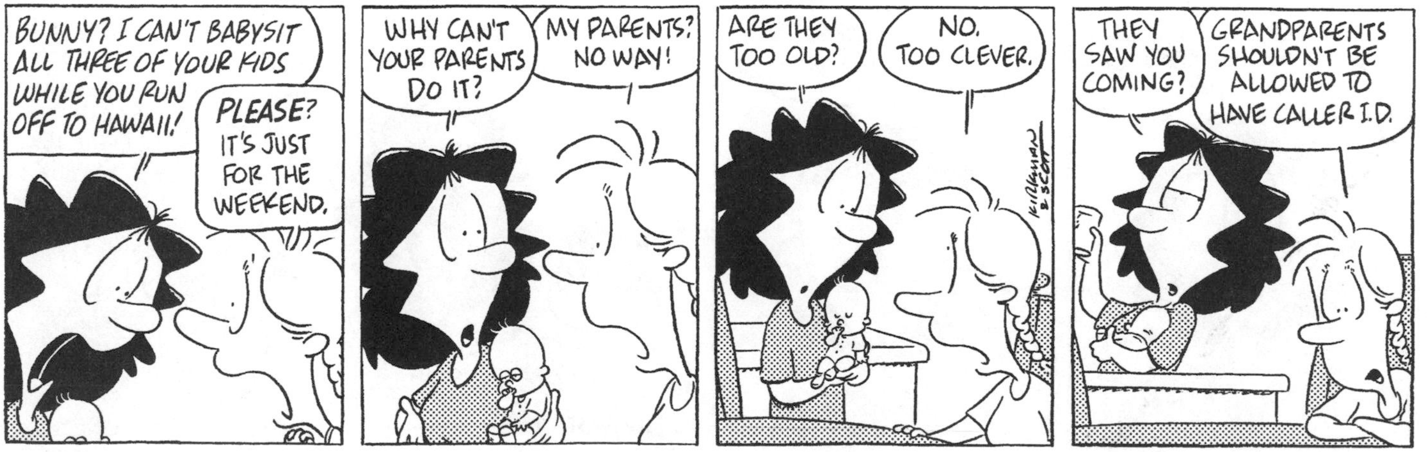
BUNNY? I CAN'T BABYSIT ALL THREE OF YOUR KIDS WHILE YOU RUN OFF TO HAWAII!
PLEASE? IT'S JUST FOR THE WEEKEND.
WHY CAN'T YOUR PARENTS DO IT?
MY PARENTS? NO WAY!
ARE THEY TOO OLD?
NO. TOO CLEVER.
THEY SAW YOU COMING?
GRANDPARENTS SHOULDN'T BE ALLOWED TO HAVE CALLER I.D.
KIRKMAN & SCOTT

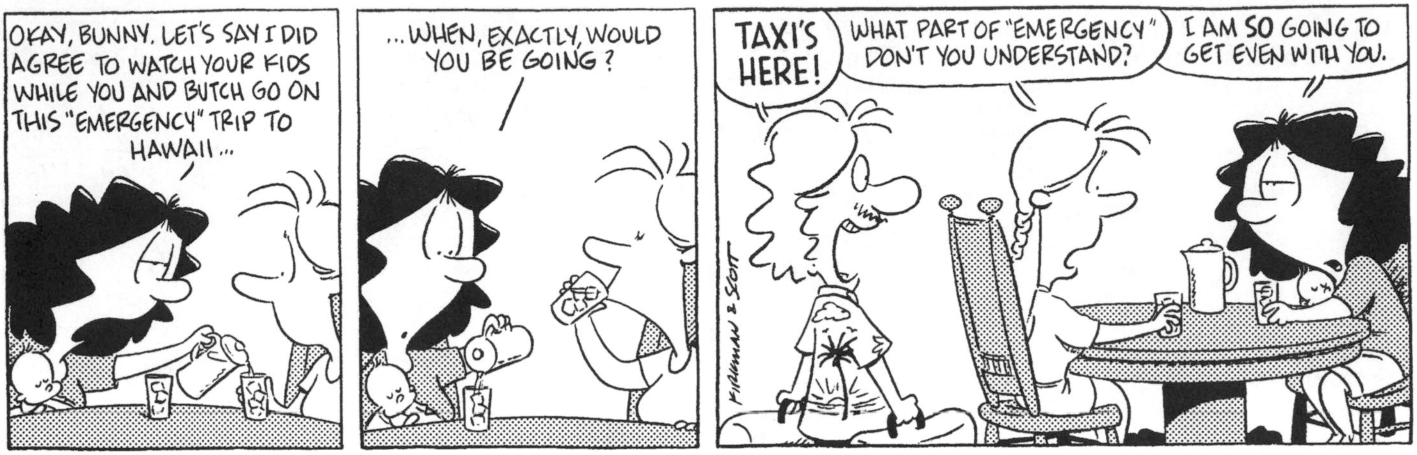
OKAY, BUNNY. LET'S SAY I DID AGREE TO WATCH YOUR KIDS WHILE YOU AND BUTCH GO ON THIS "EMERGENCY" TRIP TO HAWAII ...
... WHEN, EXACTLY, WOULD YOU BE GOING ?
TAXI'S HERE!
WHAT PART OF "EMERGENCY" DON'T YOU UNDERSTAND?
I AM SO GOING TO GET EVEN WITH YOU.

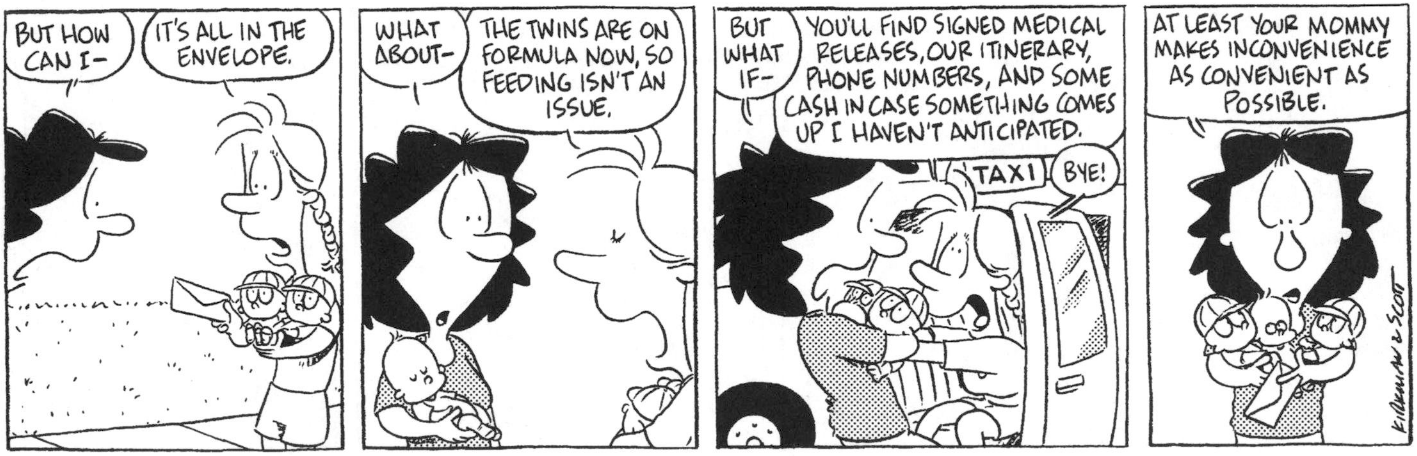
BUT HOW CAN I-
IT'S ALL IN THE ENVELOPE.
WHAT ABOUT-
THE TWINS ARE ON FORMULA NOW, SO FEEDING ISN'T AN ISSUE.
BUT WHAT IF-
YOU'LL FIND SIGNED MEDICAL RELEASES, OUR ITINERARY, PHONE NUMBERS, AND SOME CASH IN CASE SOMETHING COMES UP I HAVEN'T ANTICIPATED.
TAXI
BYE!
AT LEAST YOUR MOMMY MAKES INCONVENIENCE AS CONVENIENT AS POSSIBLE.

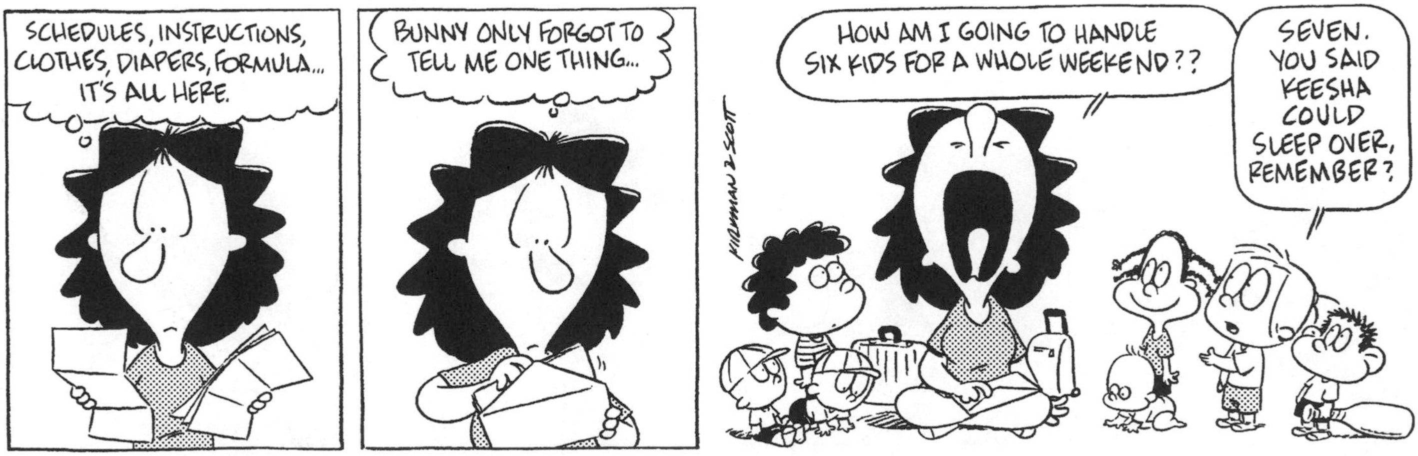
SCHEDULES, INSTRUCTIONS, CLOTHES, DIAPERS, FORMULA... IT'S ALL HERE.
BUNNY ONLY FORGOT TO TELL ME ONE THING...
HOW AM I GOING TO HANDLE SIX KIDS FOR A WHOLE WEEKEND??
SEVEN. YOU SAID KEESHA COULD SLEEP OVER, REMEMBER?

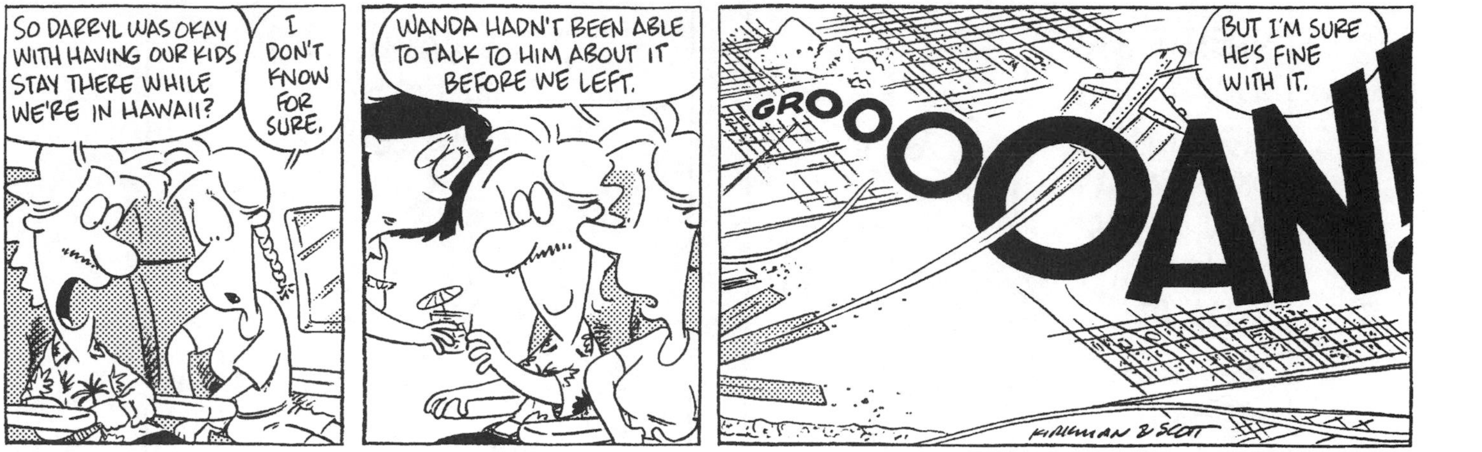
SO DARRYL WAS OKAY WITH HAVING OUR KIDS STAY THERE WHILE WE'RE IN HAWAII?
I DON'T KNOW FOR SURE.
WANDA HADN'T BEEN ABLE TO TALK TO HIM ABOUT IT BEFORE WE LEFT.
BUT I'M SURE HE'S FINE WITH IT.
GROOOOAN!
KIRKMAN & SCOTT

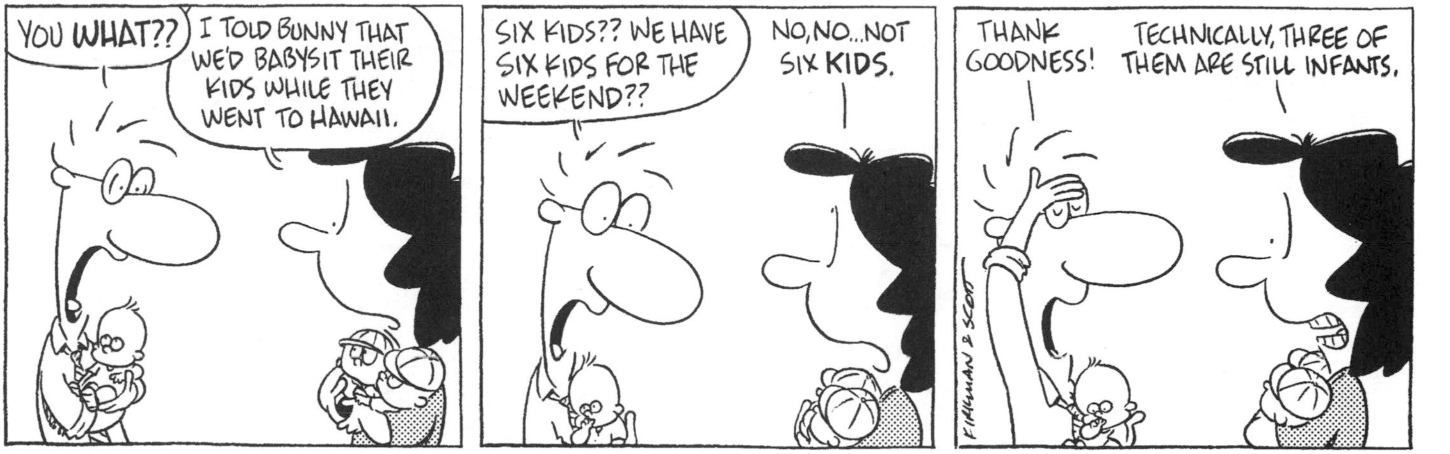
YOU WHAT??
I TOLD BUNNY THAT WE'D BABYSIT THEIR KIDS WHILE THEY WENT TO HAWAII.
SIX KIDS?? WE HAVE SIX KIDS FOR THE WEEKEND??
NO, NO... NOT SIX KIDS.
THANK GOODNESS!
TECHNICALLY, THREE OF THEM ARE STILL INFANTS.
KIRKMAN & SCOTT

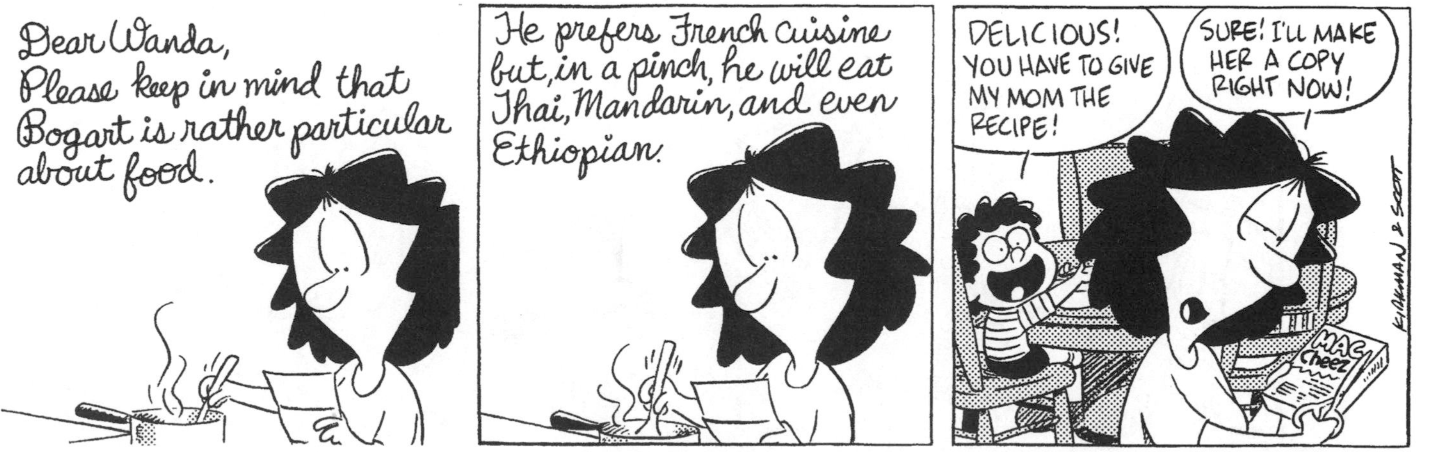
Dear Wanda,
Please keep in mind that Bogart is rather particular about food.
He prefers French cuisine but, in a pinch, he will eat Thai, Mandarin, and even Ethiopian.
DELICIOUS! YOU HAVE TO GIVE MY MOM THE RECIPE!
SURE! I'LL MAKE HER A COPY RIGHT NOW!
MAC Cheez
KIRKMAN & SCOTT

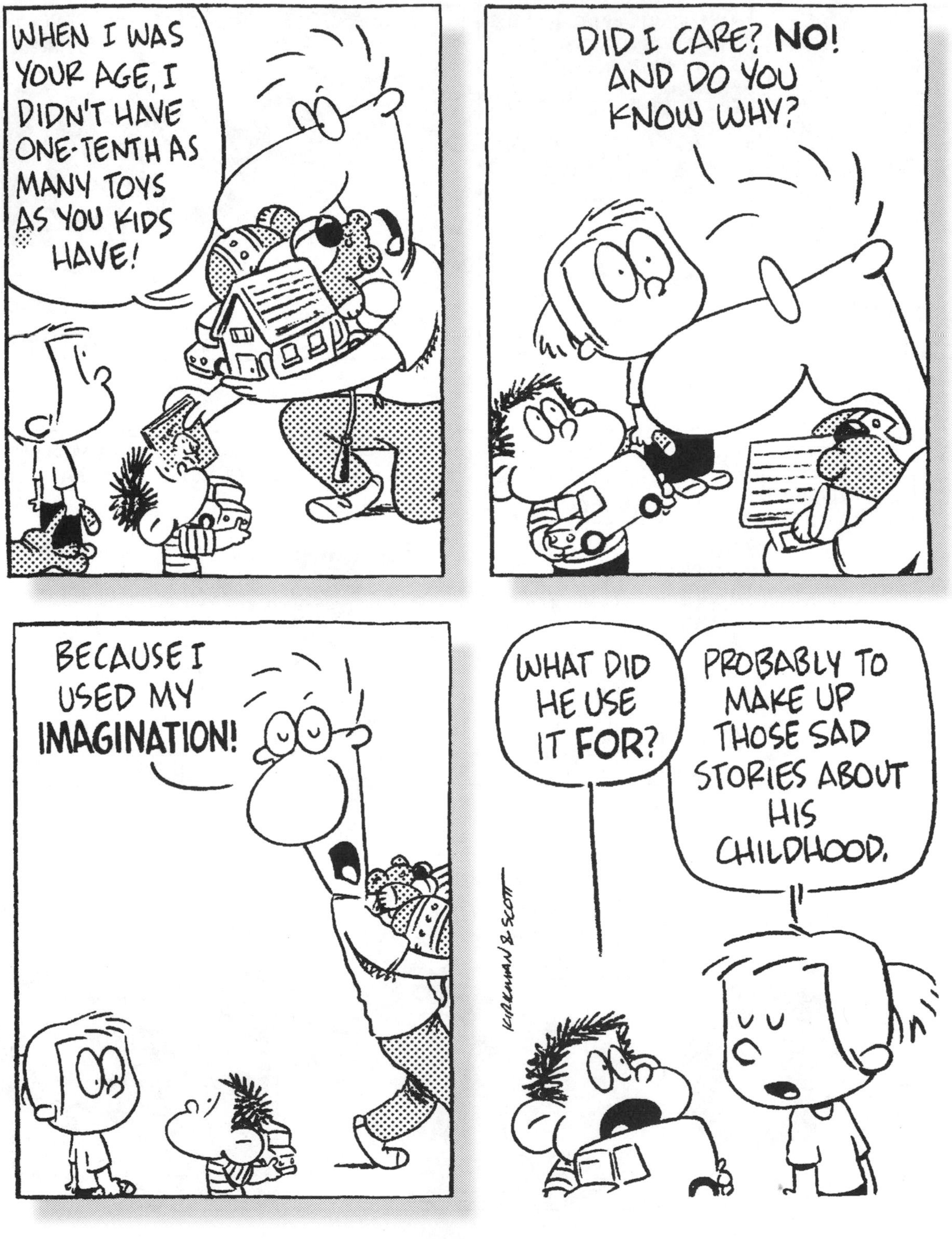
WHEN I WAS YOUR AGE, I DIDN'T HAVE ONE-TENTH AS MANY TOYS AS YOU KIDS HAVE!
DID I CARE? NO! AND DO YOU KNOW WHY?
BECAUSE I USED MY IMAGINATION!
WHAT DID HE USE IT FOR?
PROBABLY TO MAKE UP THOSE SAD STORIES ABOUT HIS CHILDHOOD.
KIRKMAN & SCOTT

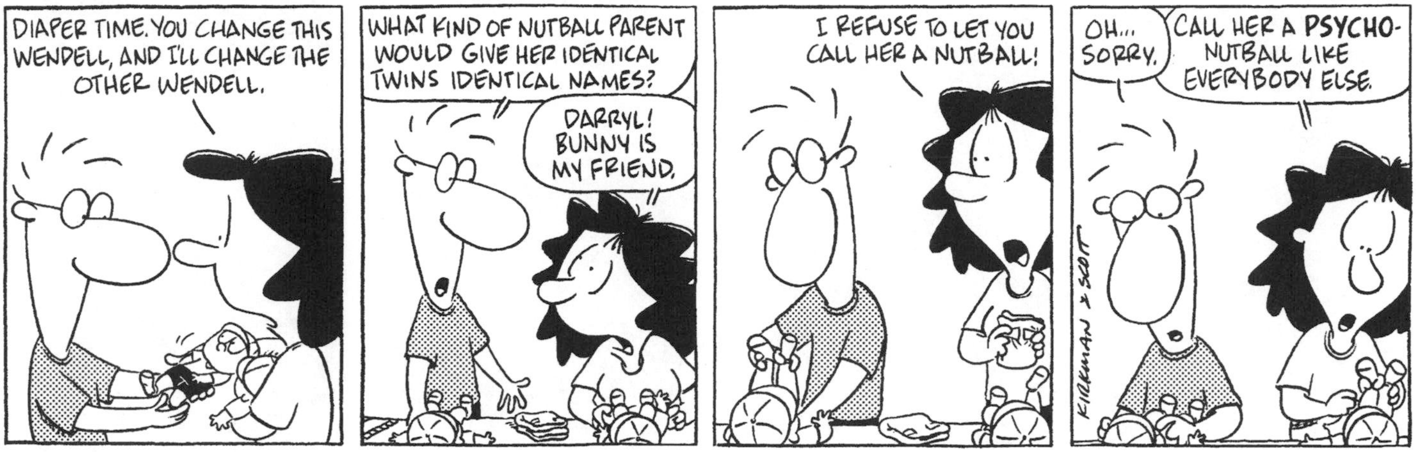
DIAPER TIME. YOU CHANGE THIS WENDELL, AND I'LL CHANGE THE OTHER WENDELL.
WHAT KIND OF NUTBALL PARENT WOULD GIVE HER IDENTICAL TWINS IDENTICAL NAMES?
DARRYL! BUNNY IS MY FRIEND.
I REFUSE TO LET YOU CALL HER A NUTBALL!
OH... SORRY.
CALL HER A **PSYCHO**-NUTBALL LIKE EVERYBODY ELSE.
KIRKMAN & SCOTT

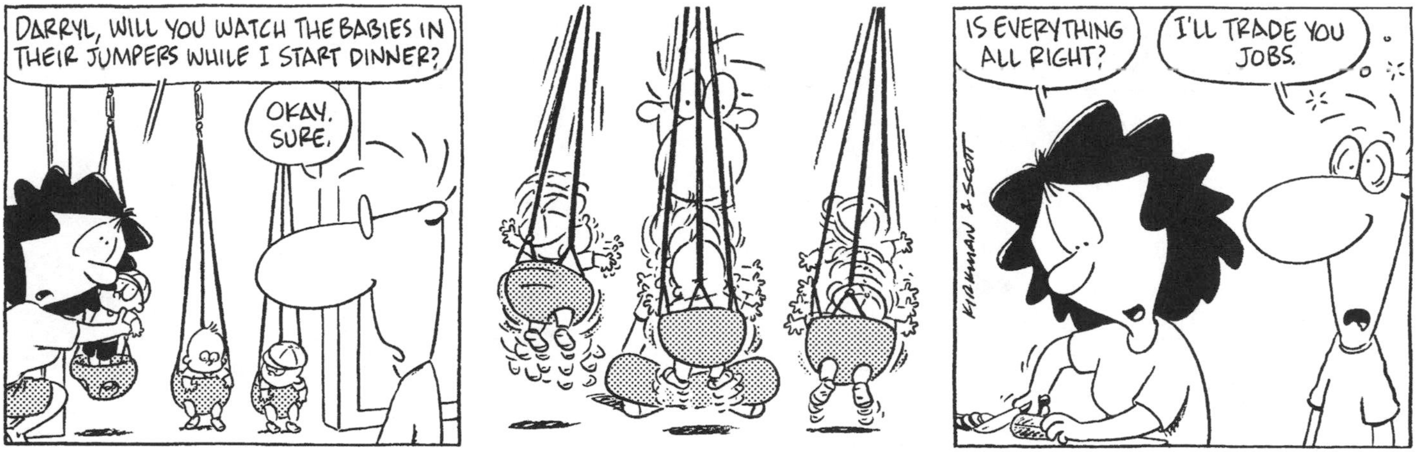
DARRYL, WILL YOU WATCH THE BABIES IN THEIR JUMPERS WHILE I START DINNER?
OKAY. SURE.
KIRKMAN & SCOTT
IS EVERYTHING ALL RIGHT?
I'LL TRADE YOU JOBS.

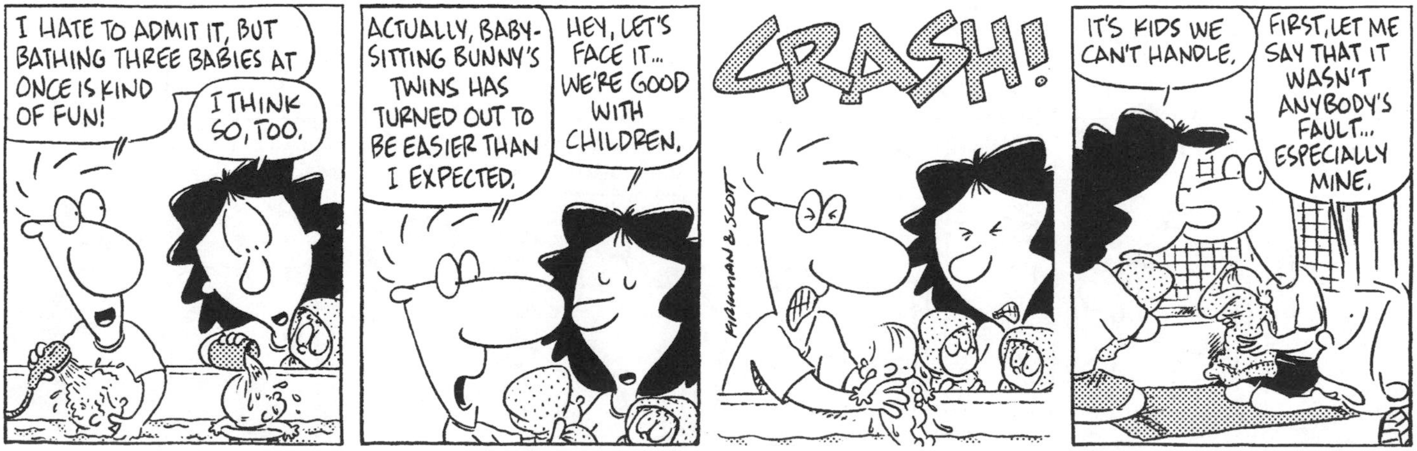
I HATE TO ADMIT IT, BUT BATHING THREE BABIES AT ONCE IS KIND OF FUN!
I THINK SO, TOO.
ACTUALLY, BABY-SITTING BUNNY'S TWINS HAS TURNED OUT TO BE EASIER THAN I EXPECTED.
HEY, LET'S FACE IT... WE'RE GOOD WITH CHILDREN.
CRASH!
KIRKMAN & SCOTT
IT'S KIDS WE CAN'T HANDLE.
FIRST, LET ME SAY THAT IT WASN'T ANYBODY'S FAULT... ESPECIALLY MINE.

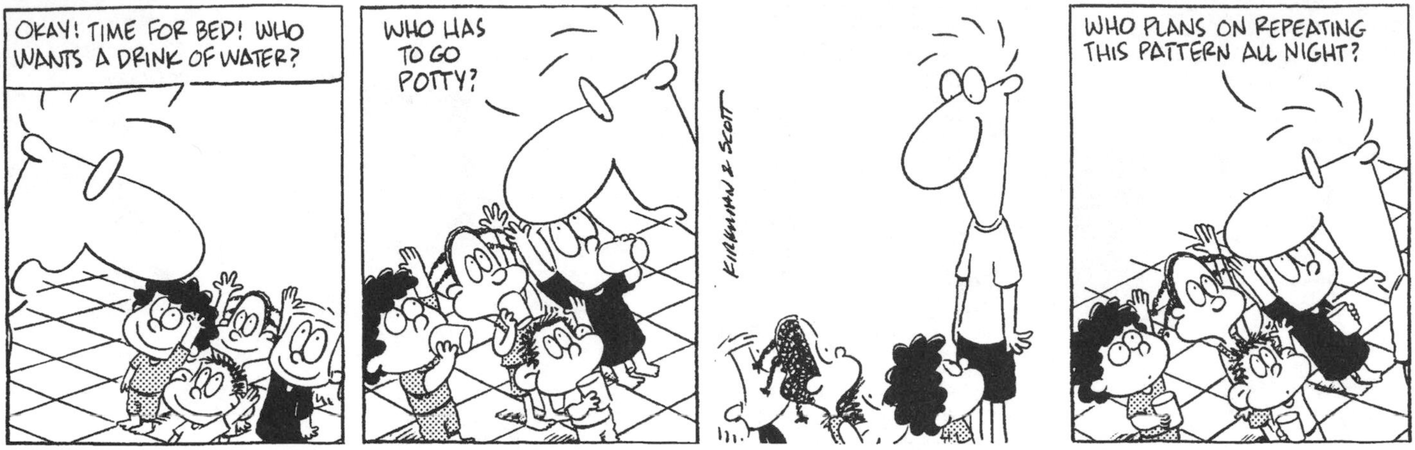
OKAY! TIME FOR BED! WHO WANTS A DRINK OF WATER?
WHO HAS TO GO POTTY?
KIRKMAN & SCOTT
WHO PLANS ON REPEATING THIS PATTERN ALL NIGHT?

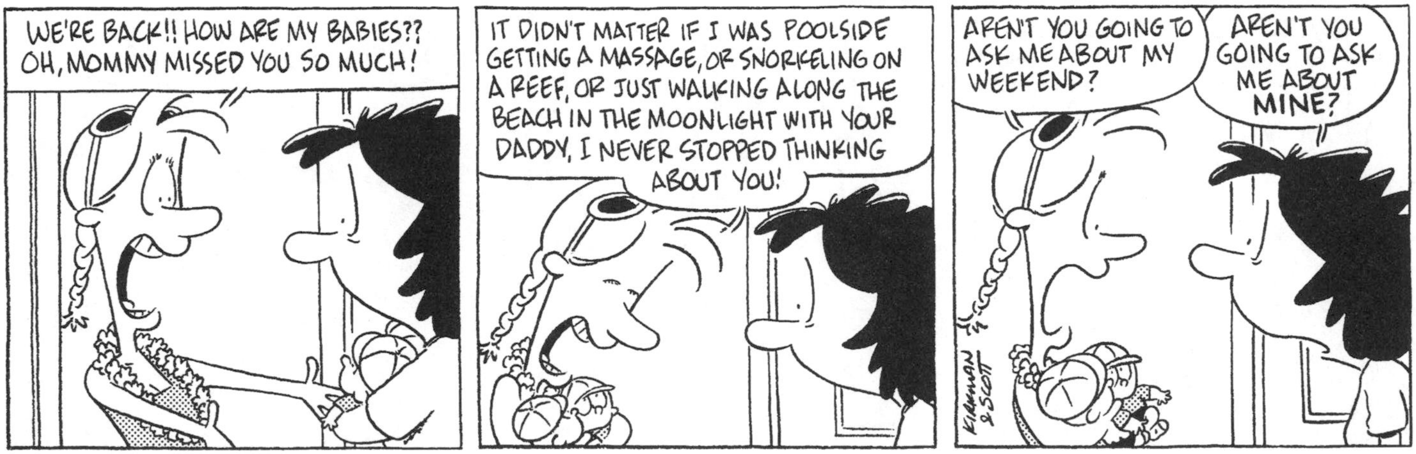
WE'RE BACK!! HOW ARE MY BABIES?? OH, MOMMY MISSED YOU SO MUCH!
IT DIDN'T MATTER IF I WAS POOLSIDE GETTING A MASSAGE, OR SNORKELING ON A REEF, OR JUST WALKING ALONG THE BEACH IN THE MOONLIGHT WITH YOUR DADDY, I NEVER STOPPED THINKING ABOUT YOU!
AREN'T YOU GOING TO ASK ME ABOUT MY WEEKEND?
AREN'T YOU GOING TO ASK ME ABOUT MINE?
KIRKMAN & SCOTT

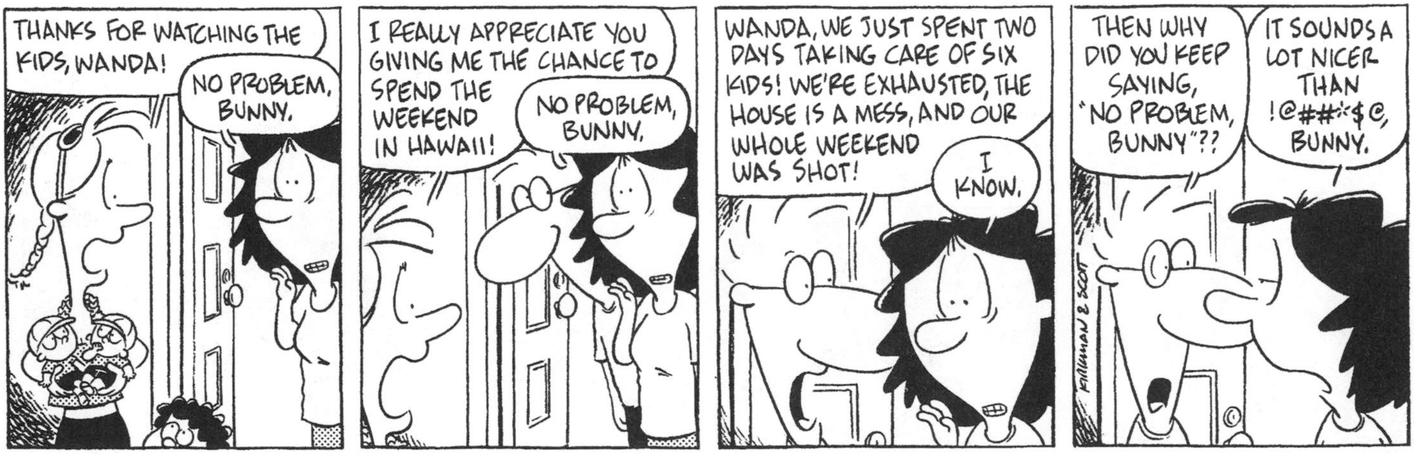
THANKS FOR WATCHING THE KIDS, WANDA!
NO PROBLEM, BUNNY.
I REALLY APPRECIATE YOU GIVING ME THE CHANCE TO SPEND THE WEEKEND IN HAWAII!
NO PROBLEM, BUNNY.
WANDA, WE JUST SPENT TWO DAYS TAKING CARE OF SIX KIDS! WE'RE EXHAUSTED, THE HOUSE IS A MESS, AND OUR WHOLE WEEKEND WAS SHOT!
I KNOW.
KIRKMAN & SCOTT
THEN WHY DID YOU KEEP SAYING, "NO PROBLEM, BUNNY"??
IT SOUNDS A LOT NICER THAN !@##*$@, BUNNY.

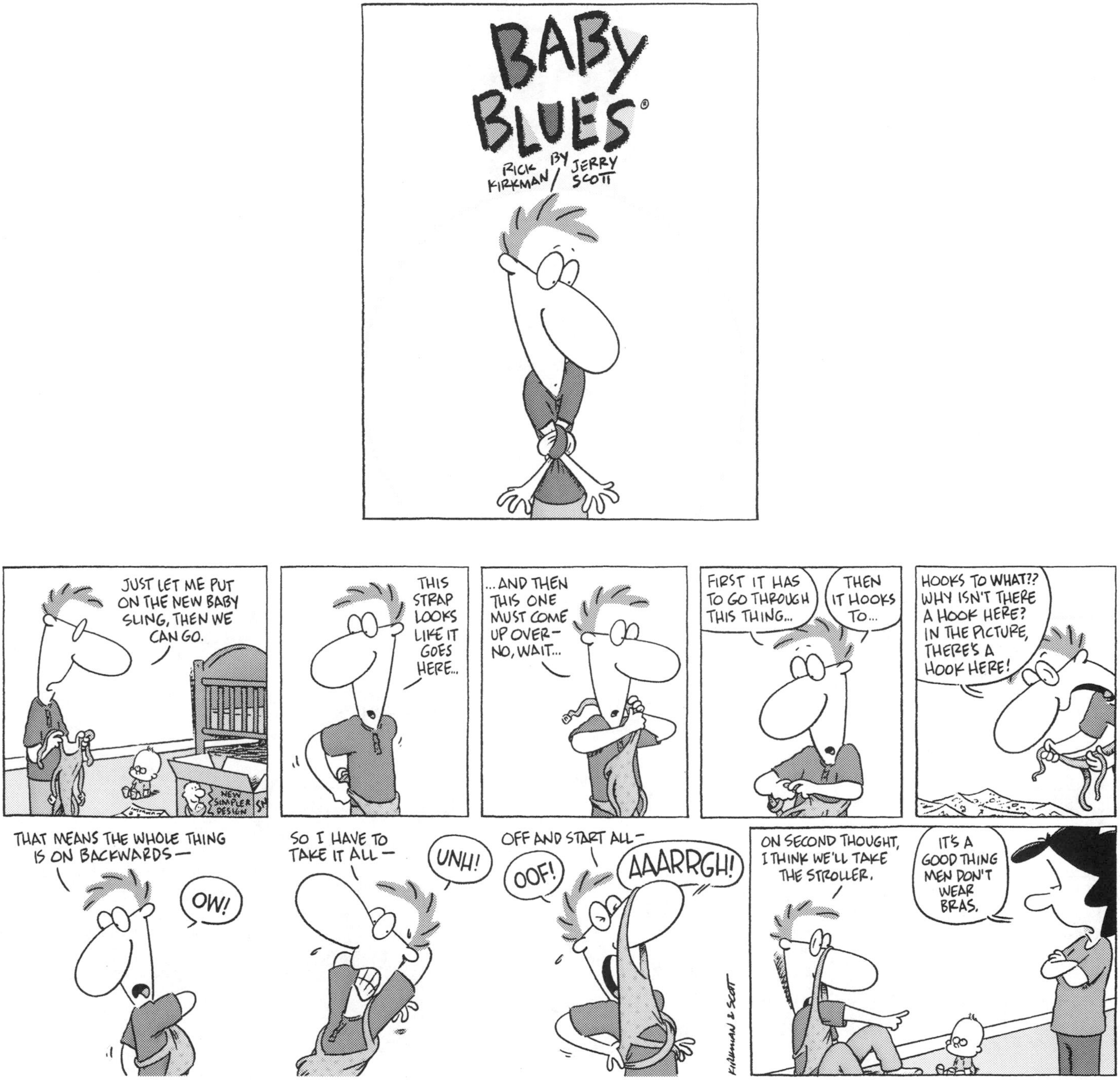
BABY BLUES®
BY RICK KIRKMAN / JERRY SCOTT
JUST LET ME PUT ON THE NEW BABY SLING, THEN WE CAN GO.
NEW SIMPLER DESIGN
THIS STRAP LOOKS LIKE IT GOES HERE...
...AND THEN THIS ONE MUST COME UP OVER— NO, WAIT...
FIRST IT HAS TO GO THROUGH THIS THING...
THEN IT HOOKS TO...
HOOKS TO WHAT?? WHY ISN'T THERE A HOOK HERE? IN THE PICTURE, THERE'S A HOOK HERE!
THAT MEANS THE WHOLE THING IS ON BACKWARDS—
OW!
SO I HAVE TO TAKE IT ALL—
UNH!
OFF AND START ALL—
OOF!
AAARRGH!
KIRKMAN & SCOTT
ON SECOND THOUGHT, I THINK WE'LL TAKE THE STROLLER.
IT'S A GOOD THING MEN DON'T WEAR BRAS.

BABY BLUES®
BY RICK KIRKMAN / JERRY SCOTT
HAMMIE!
WHAT??
WHERE ARE YOU?
IN MY ROOM!
WE HAVE TO— HEY, WHAT'S THAT THING?
IT'S A BIKE SIREN. CHECK IT OUT!
RRRRRRRRRRRRRRRRRRRRRRRRRRRRRRRRRRRRR
HAR! HAR! HAR! THAT'S GREAT!
AND LOOK WHAT ELSE I FOUND! TAP SHOES!
I REMEMBER WHEN MOM BOUGHT THOSE AT A GARAGE SALE! LET ME TRY ONE!
TAP! TAP! TAPPITY-TAP! TAP! TAP! TAPPITY-TAP-TAP!
HEY—DIDN'T YOU COME IN HERE TO TELL ME SOME-THING?
OH, YEAH... I FORGOT.
TAPPITY! TAPPITY-TAP! TAP! TAP! TAPPITY-TAP-TAP!
IT'S FATHER'S DAY, SO WE'RE SUPPOSED TO LET DADDY SLEEP LATE!
KIRKMAN & SCOTT

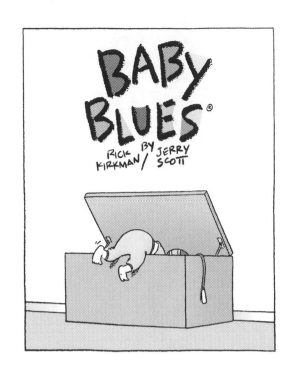

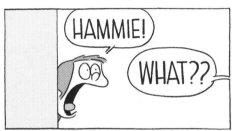

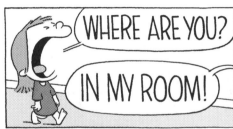

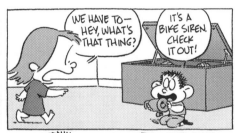

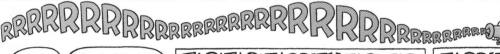

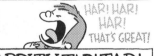

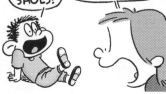

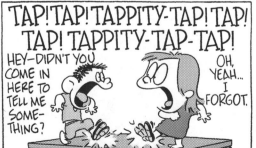

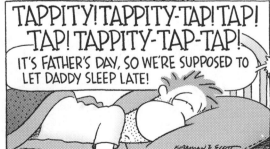

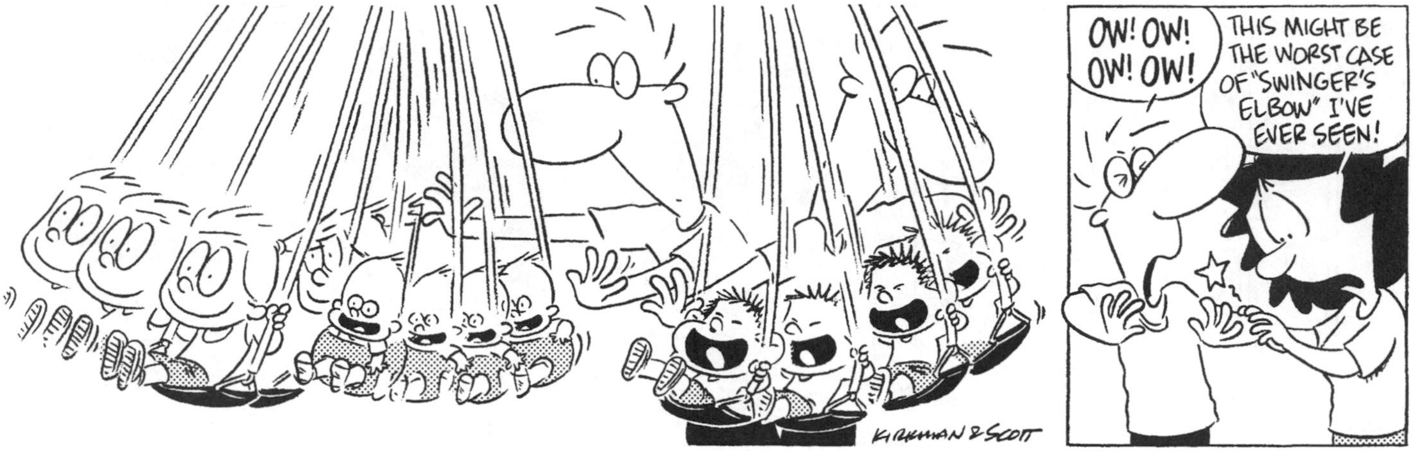
OW! OW! OW! OW!
THIS MIGHT BE THE WORST CASE OF "SWINGER'S ELBOW" I'VE EVER SEEN!
KIRKMAN & SCOTT

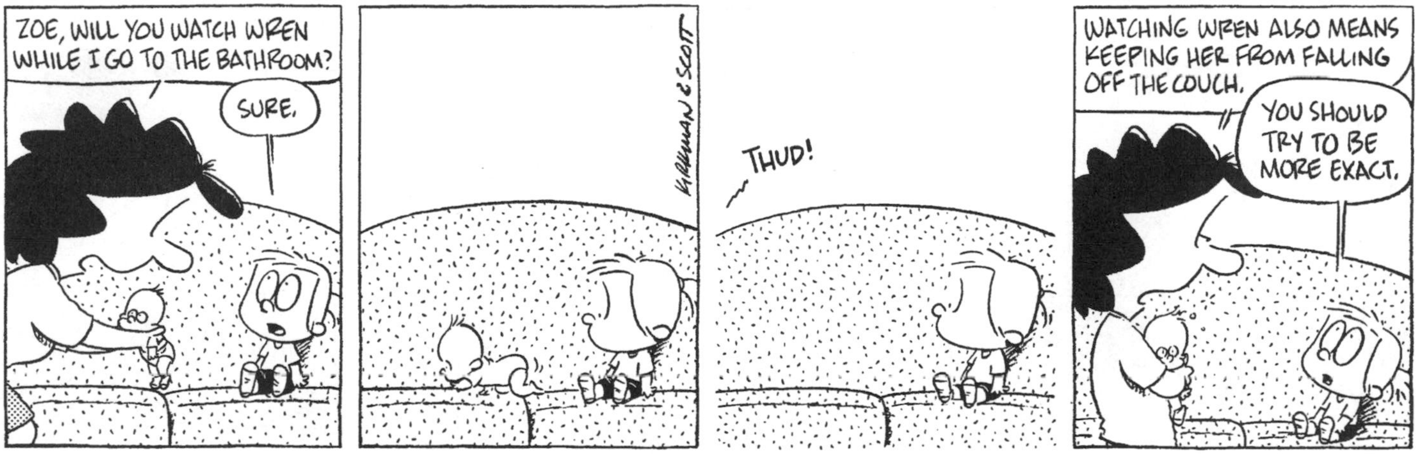
ZOE, WILL YOU WATCH WREN WHILE I GO TO THE BATHROOM?
SURE.
KIRKMAN & SCOTT
THUD!
WATCHING WREN ALSO MEANS KEEPING HER FROM FALLING OFF THE COUCH.
YOU SHOULD TRY TO BE MORE EXACT.

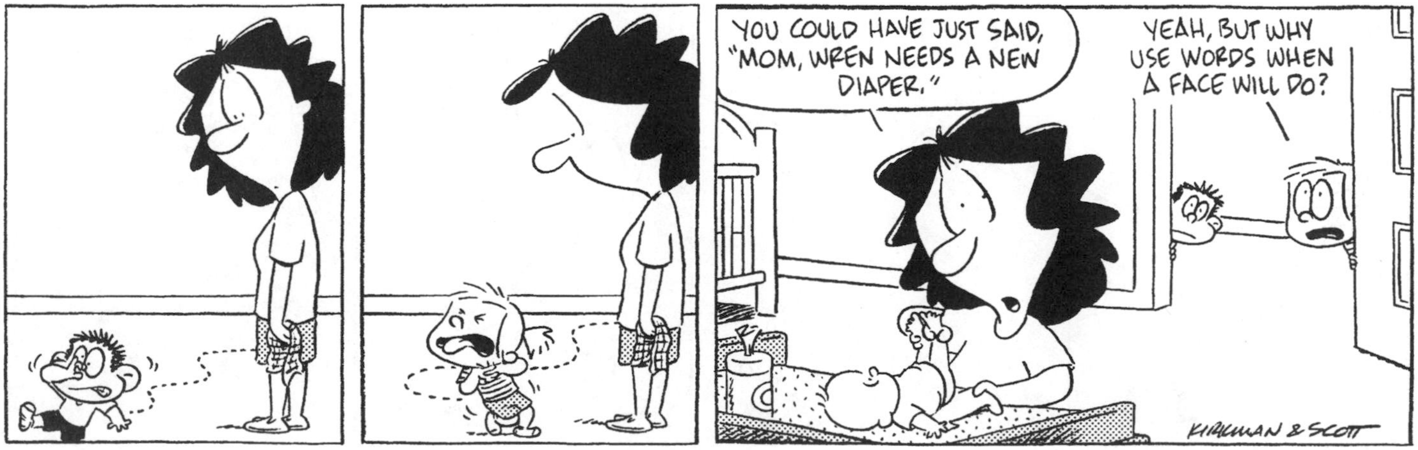
YOU COULD HAVE JUST SAID, "MOM, WREN NEEDS A NEW DIAPER."
YEAH, BUT WHY USE WORDS WHEN A FACE WILL DO?
KIRKMAN & SCOTT

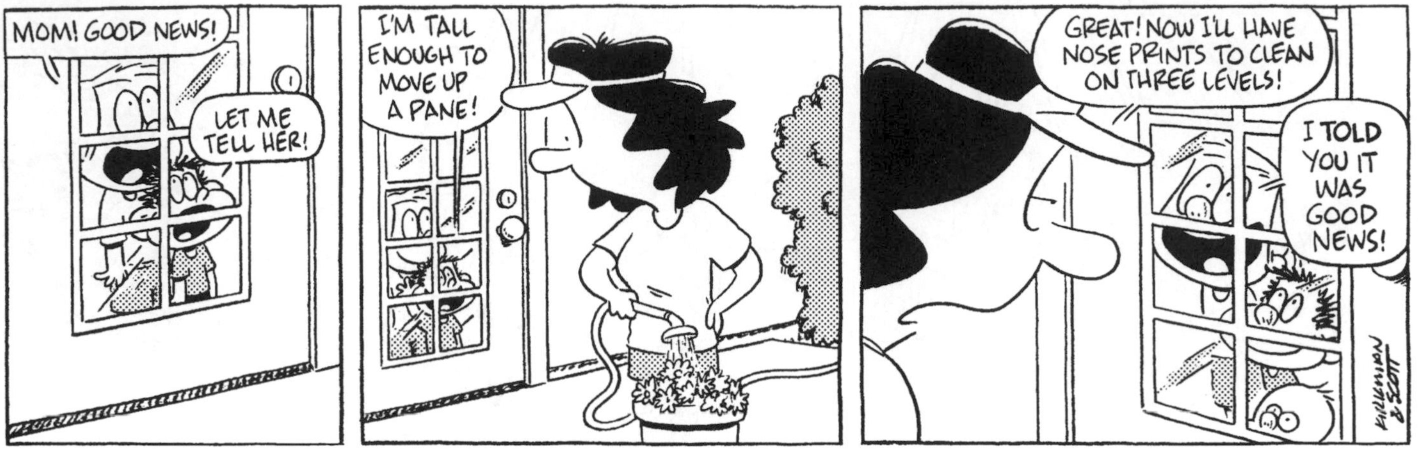
MOM! GOOD NEWS!
LET ME TELL HER!
I'M TALL ENOUGH TO MOVE UP A PANE!
GREAT! NOW I'LL HAVE NOSE PRINTS TO CLEAN ON THREE LEVELS!
I TOLD YOU IT WAS GOOD NEWS!
KIRKMAN & SCOTT

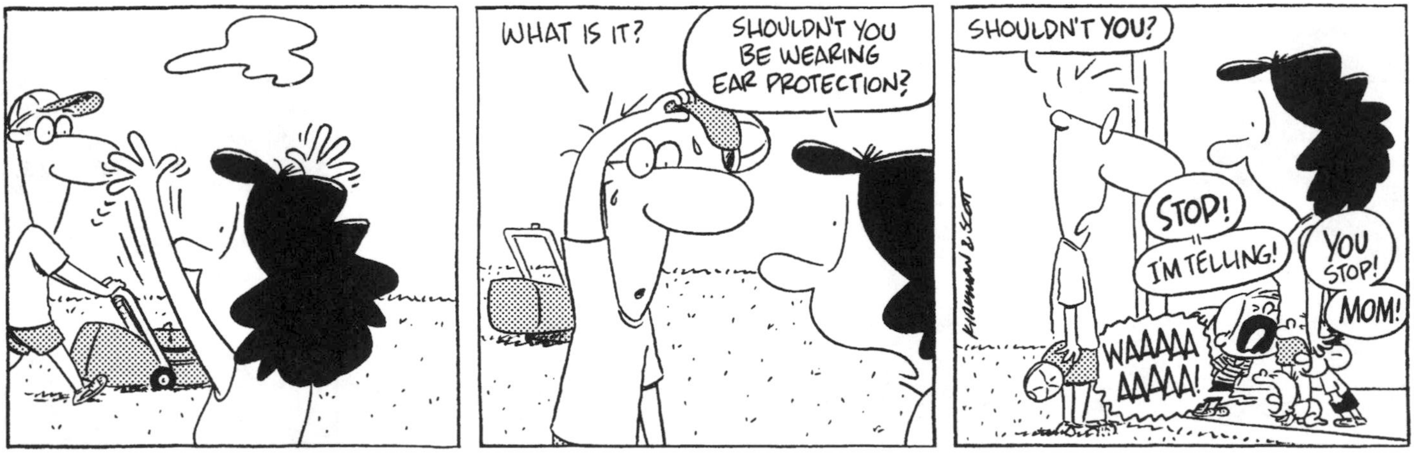
WHAT IS IT?
SHOULDN'T YOU BE WEARING EAR PROTECTION?
SHOULDN'T YOU?
KIRKMAN & SCOTT
STOP!
I'M TELLING!
YOU STOP!
MOM!
WAAAAA AAAAA!

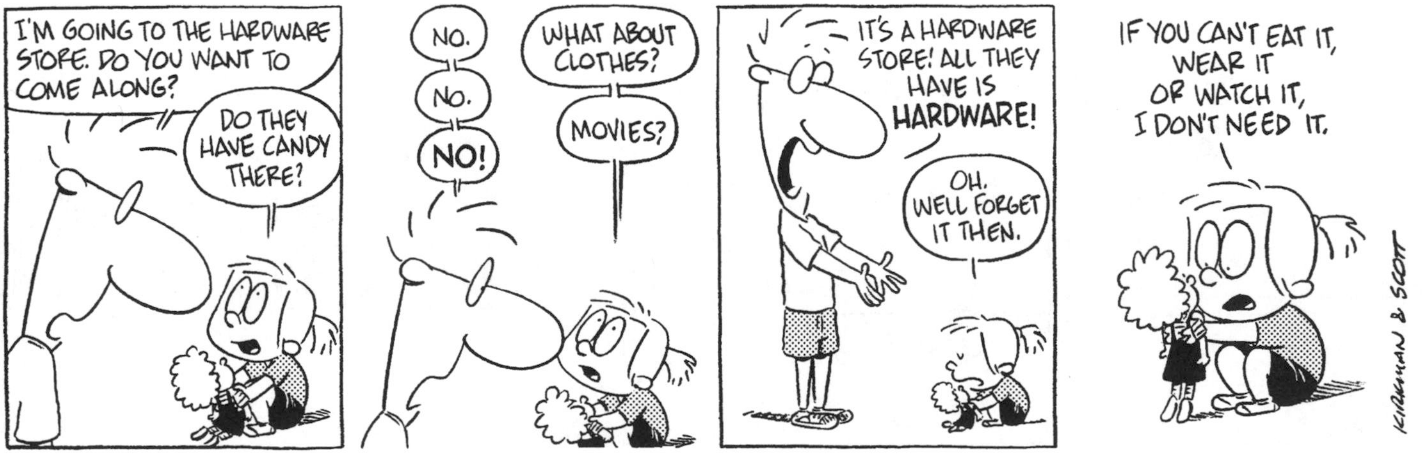
I'M GOING TO THE HARDWARE STORE. DO YOU WANT TO COME ALONG?
DO THEY HAVE CANDY THERE?
NO.
NO.
NO!
WHAT ABOUT CLOTHES?
MOVIES?
IT'S A HARDWARE STORE! ALL THEY HAVE IS HARDWARE!
OH. WELL FORGET IT THEN.
IF YOU CAN'T EAT IT, WEAR IT OR WATCH IT, I DON'T NEED IT.
KIRKMAN & SCOTT

BABY BLUES®
BY RICK KIRKMAN / JERRY SCOTT

COME ON. MOM WANTS US TO SET THE TABLE.
REALLY?
WHOOO!
AAAAGGHH!!
YOU'D THINK SHE'D KNOW BETTER BY NOW.
YOU'D THINK.
KIRKMAN & SCOTT

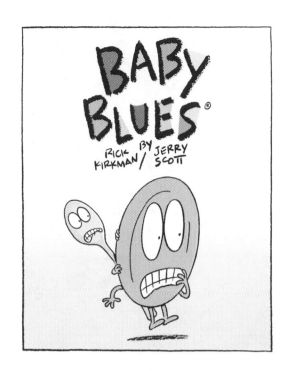

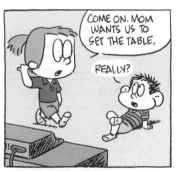

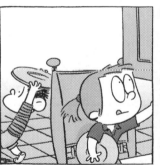

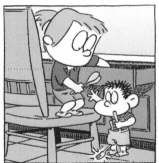

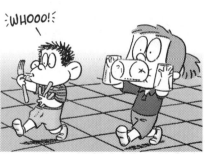

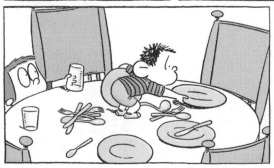

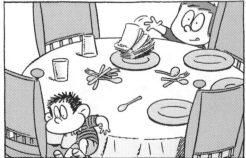

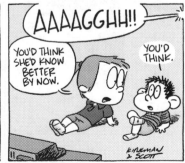

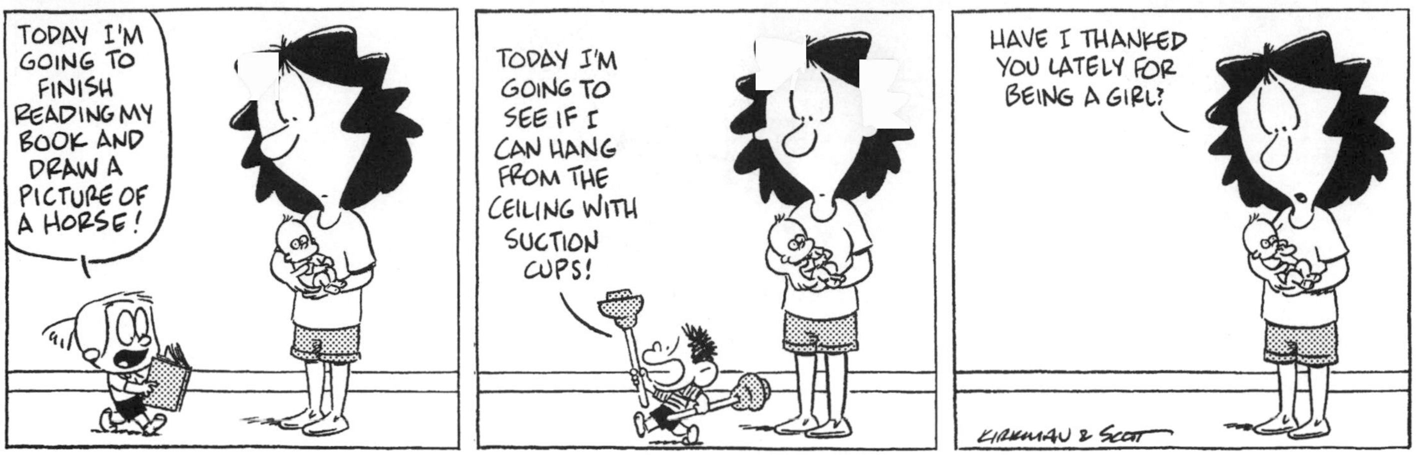
TODAY I'M GOING TO FINISH READING MY BOOK AND DRAW A PICTURE OF A HORSE!
TODAY I'M GOING TO SEE IF I CAN HANG FROM THE CEILING WITH SUCTION CUPS!
HAVE I THANKED YOU LATELY FOR BEING A GIRL?
KIRKMAN & SCOTT

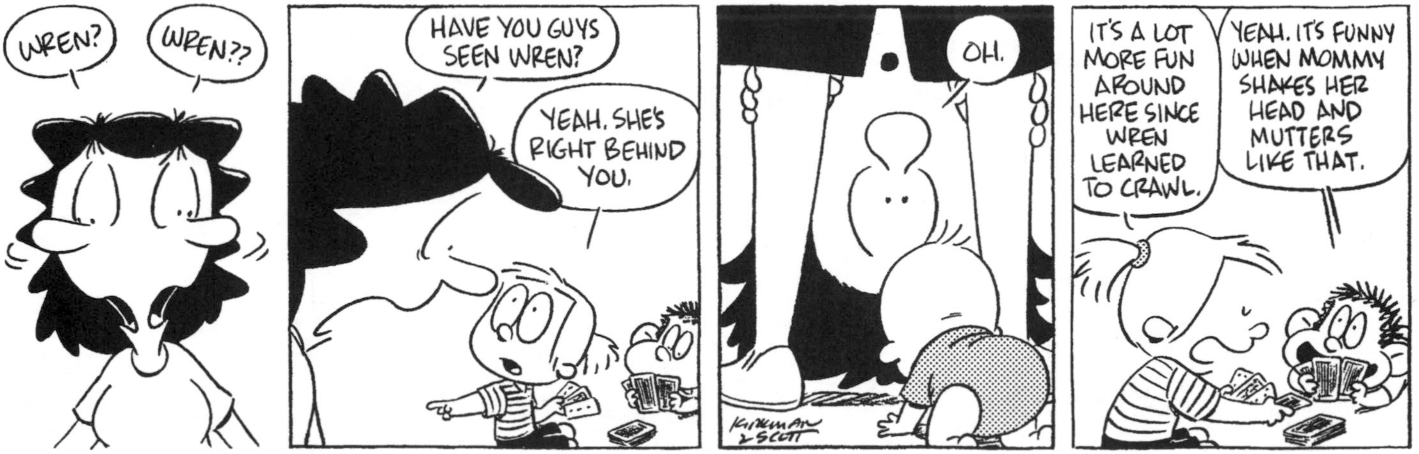
WREN?
WREN??
HAVE YOU GUYS SEEN WREN?
YEAH. SHE'S RIGHT BEHIND YOU.
OH.
KIRKMAN & SCOTT
IT'S A LOT MORE FUN AROUND HERE SINCE WREN LEARNED TO CRAWL.
YEAH. IT'S FUNNY WHEN MOMMY SHAKES HER HEAD AND MUTTERS LIKE THAT.

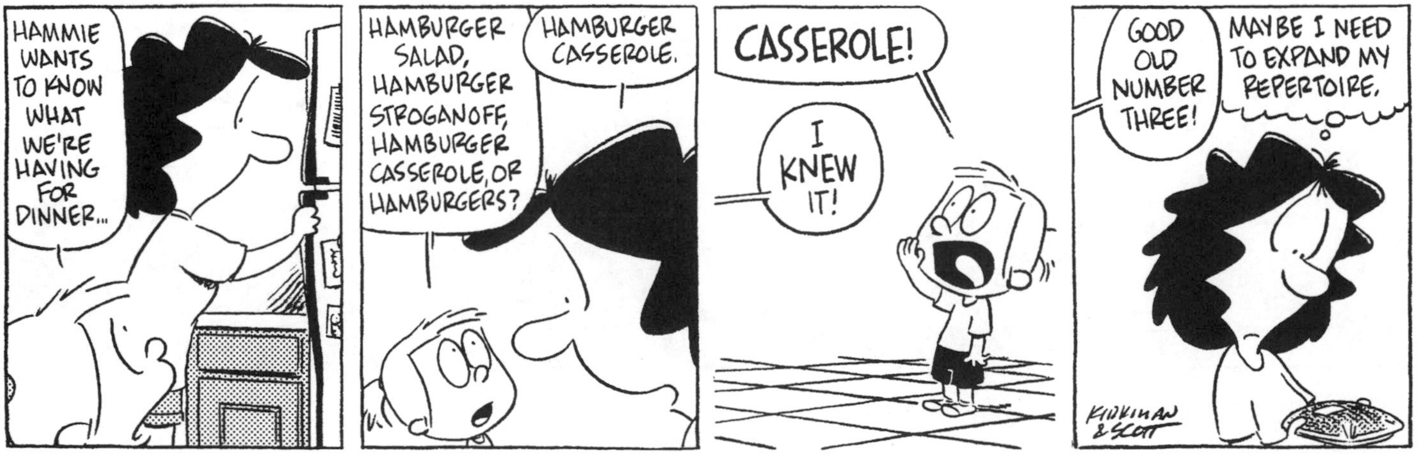
HAMMIE WANTS TO KNOW WHAT WE'RE HAVING FOR DINNER...
HAMBURGER SALAD, HAMBURGER STROGANOFF, HAMBURGER CASSEROLE, OR HAMBURGERS?
HAMBURGER CASSEROLE.
CASSEROLE!
I KNEW IT!
GOOD OLD NUMBER THREE!
MAYBE I NEED TO EXPAND MY REPERTOIRE.
KIRKMAN & SCOTT

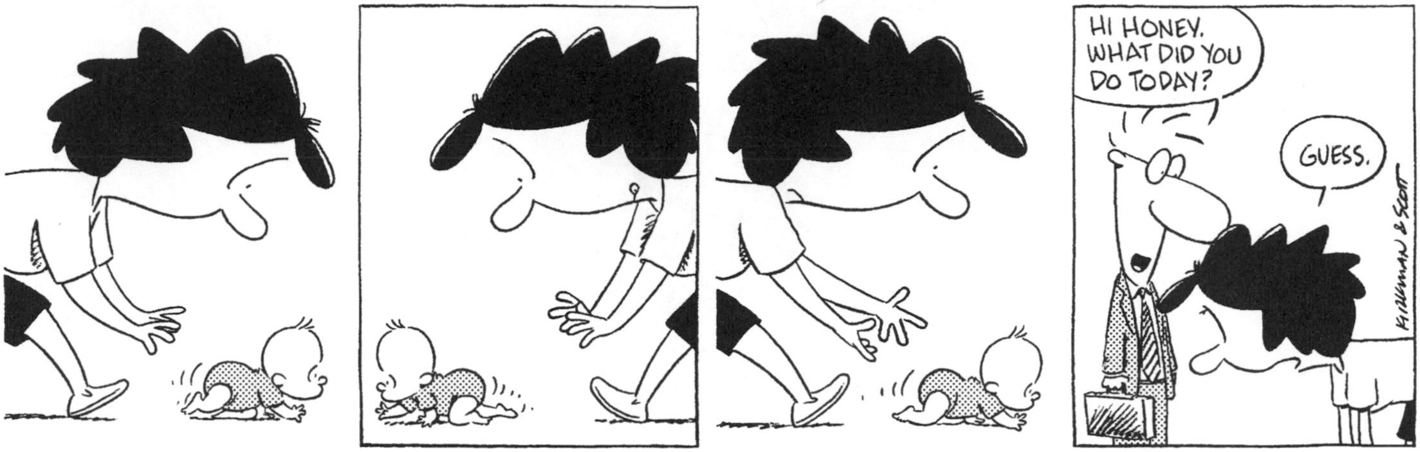
HI HONEY. WHAT DID YOU DO TODAY?
GUESS.
KIRKMAN & SCOTT

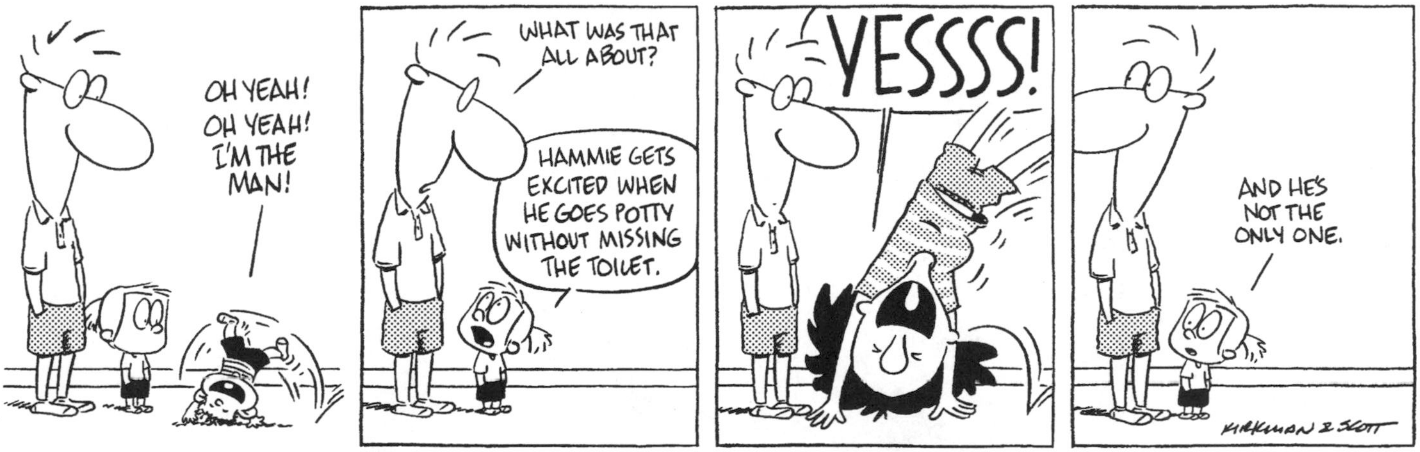
OH YEAH! OH YEAH! I'M THE MAN!
WHAT WAS THAT ALL ABOUT?
HAMMIE GETS EXCITED WHEN HE GOES POTTY WITHOUT MISSING THE TOILET.
YESSSS!
AND HE'S NOT THE ONLY ONE.
KIRKMAN & SCOTT

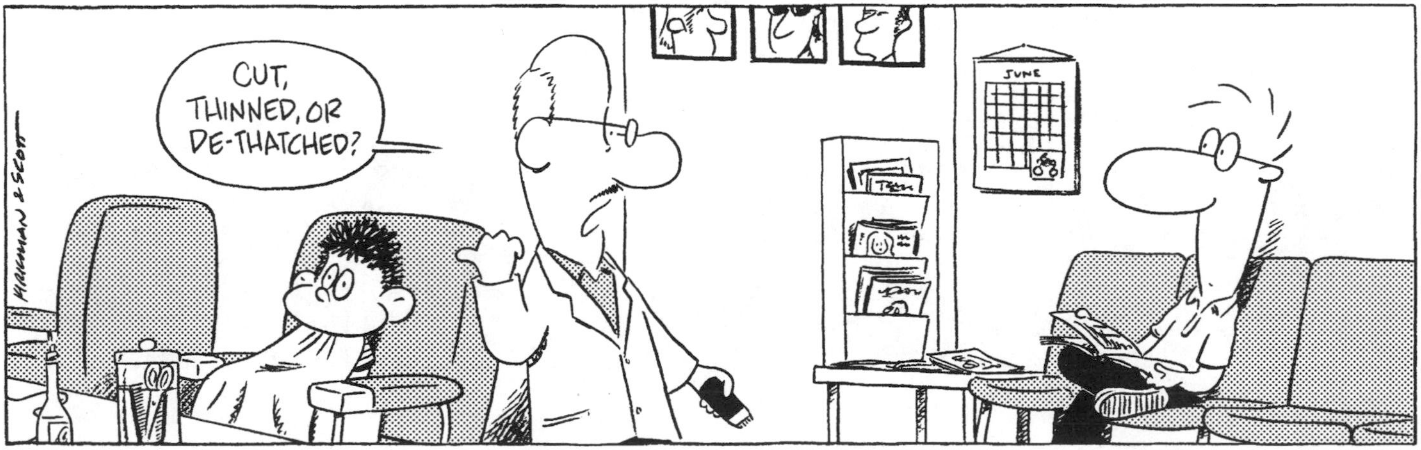
KIRKMAN & SCOTT
CUT, THINNED, OR DE-THATCHED?
JUNE

BABY BLUES®

BLAH BLAH BLAH

OW! OW! OW! OW!

HOW IN THE WORLD DID YOU GET KETCHUP IN YOUR EYE?

WELL, WHEN I WAS SQUIRTING IT OUT OF THE BOTTLE I DIDN'T HAVE IT POINTED IN THE RIGHT DIRECTION...

SO IT SQUIRTED YOU IN THE EYE?

NO. I ACCIDENTALLY SQUIRTED SOME ON MY HAND,

OH. THEN YOU RUBBED YOUR EYE WITH YOUR HAND.

NO. THEN I WIPED MY HAND ON MY NAPKIN.

AND YOU WIPED YOUR EYE WITH YOUR NAPKIN...

NO. I THREW THE NAPKIN AWAY, THEN I PICKED UP THE KETCHUP BOTTLE, THEN I SQUEEZED IT, AND THEN I ACCIDENTALLY SQUIRTED MYSELF IN THE EYE.

TOO MUCH DIALOGUE AND NOT ENOUGH PLOT.

BOYS...

TYPICAL ZOE STORY.

AND NOW I'LL TALK ABOUT MY FEELINGS DURING THIS UNFORTUNATE EVENT.

KIRKMAN & SCOTT

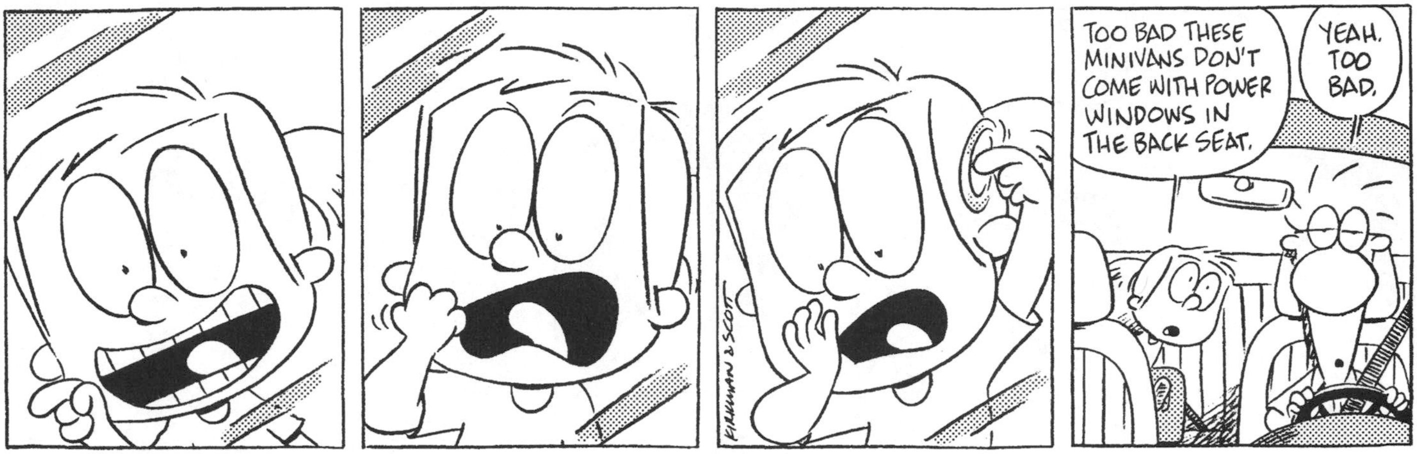

TOO BAD THESE MINIVANS DON'T COME WITH POWER WINDOWS IN THE BACK SEAT.
YEAH. TOO BAD.

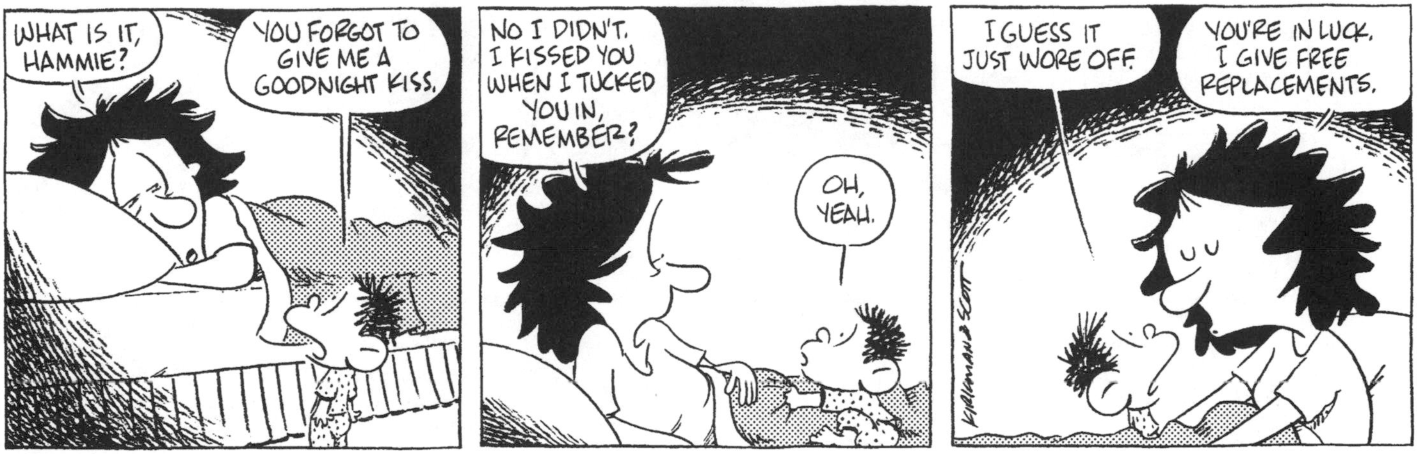

WHAT IS IT, HAMMIE?
YOU FORGOT TO GIVE ME A GOODNIGHT KISS.
NO I DIDN'T. I KISSED YOU WHEN I TUCKED YOU IN, REMEMBER?
OH, YEAH.
I GUESS IT JUST WORE OFF.
YOU'RE IN LUCK. I GIVE FREE REPLACEMENTS.

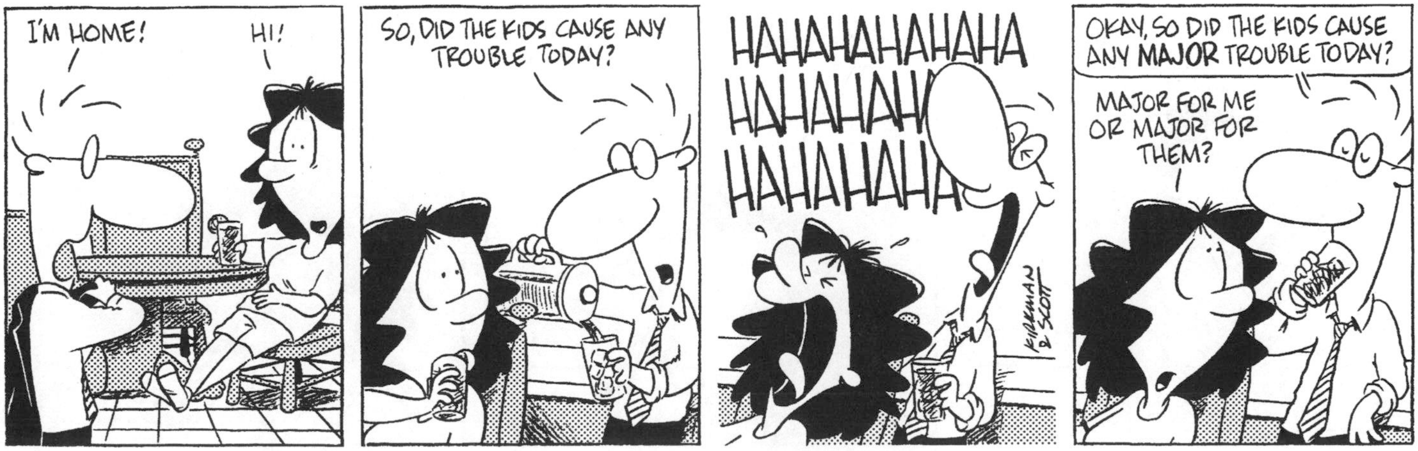

I'M HOME!
HI!
SO, DID THE KIDS CAUSE ANY TROUBLE TODAY?
HAHAHAHAHAHAHA HAHAHAHAH HAHAHAHA
OKAY, SO DID THE KIDS CAUSE ANY MAJOR TROUBLE TODAY?
MAJOR FOR ME OR MAJOR FOR THEM?

MORNING. HI!

YOU'RE UP EARLY.

YEAH. I FELT LIKE HAVING A FEW MINUTES ALONE BEFORE THE SOUNDTRACK STARTS.

SOUNDTR-??

GOOD MORNING EVERYBODY! BOY! I HAD THE WEIRDEST DREAM LAST NIGHT! I CAN'T WAIT TO TELL YOU ALL ABOUT IT. WHAT'S FOR BREAKFAST? I HOPE IT'S PANCAKES. PANCAKES IS A FUNNY WORD. TRY SAYING IT OVER AND OVER A HUNDRED TIMES. WEIRD, HUH? SAME THING WITH SYRUP. TRY IT... SYRUP... SYRUP... SYRUP... SYRUP... SYRUP... SYRUP... SYR... SYRUP... SYRUP... SYRUP... SYRUP...

OH.

WHY DID YOU NAME ME HAMMIE?

BECAUSE IT WAS YOUR GREAT-GREAT-GRANDFATHER'S NAME. THEY CALLED HIM "HAM."

AND HE WAS A REAL PERSON?

OF COURSE HE WAS A REAL PERSON!

I TOLD YOU I WASN'T NAMED AFTER A SANDWICH!

OKAY, BUT HOW DO YOU KNOW HE WASN'T?

ZOE!

WHERE DO YOU WANT TO GO THIS SUMMER?

NOWHERE.

NOWHERE??

TRAVELING IS A PAIN... GAS PRICES ARE OUTRAGEOUS... LET'S JUST STAY HERE AND ENJOY A NICE VACATION AT HOME!

YOU KNOW, THAT ACTUALLY SOUNDS PRETTY G—

THE TOUGH PART IS GOING TO BE CONVINCING THE KIDS TO STAY AWAY FOR TWO WEEKS.